MW00803948

Ragnar's Action Encyclopedia of Practical Knowledge and Proven Techniques

Warning

Some of the activities discussed in this book are dangerous and should not be attempted by those who are not trained in the correct procedures. Other items may be regulated by federal, state, or municipal agencies. It is up to the reader to research appropriate ordinances and ensure that he is in compliance with all applicable laws. Failure to do so could result in heavy fines or imprisonment. Neither the author nor publisher accepts any responsibility for the use or misuse of information contained in this book. It is presented for *academic study only*.

VOLUME 1

Ragnar's Action Encyclopedia of Practical Knowledge and Proven Techniques

RAGNAR BENSON

REVISED EDITION

Paladin Press • Boulder, Colorado

Also by Ragnar Benson:

Acquiring New ID
Do-It-Yourself Medicine
Eating Cheap
Guerrilla Gunsmithing
Live Off the Land in the City and the Country
Mantrapping
Modern Survival Retreat
Modern Weapons Caching
Most Dangerous Game
Ragnar's Guide to the Underground Economy
Ragnar's Action Encyclopedia, Vol. 2
Ragnar's Guide to Interviews, Investigations, and Interrogations
Ragnar's Tall Tales
Ragnar's Ten Best Traps
Ragnar's Urban Survival
Starting a New Life in Rural America
Survival Nurse
Survival Poaching
Survival Retreat
Survivalist's Medicine Chest
Switchblade

*Ragnar's Action Encyclopedia of Practical Knowledge
and Proven Techniques, Vol. 1*
by Ragnar Benson

Copyright © 1995 by Ragnar Benson

ISBN 10: 0-87364-801-3
ISBN 13: 978-0-87364-801-1

Printed in the United States of America

Published by Paladin Press, a division of
Paladin Enterprises, Inc.
Gunbarrel Tech Center
7077 Winchester Circle
Boulder, Colorado 80301 USA
+1.303.443.7250

Direct inquiries and/or orders to the above address.

PALADIN, PALADIN PRESS, and the "horse head" design
are trademarks belonging to Paladin Enterprises and
registered in United States Patent and Trademark Office.

Visit our Web site at www.paladin-press.com

Contents

Preface

Perhaps it is unnecessary to point out that these are indeed perilous times. One need only look out across the globe to see events in Haiti, the former Yugoslavia, the former Soviet republics, South Africa, Rwanda, Italy, Cuba, and even Canada to name a few of the more obvious examples. Astute observers, able to read between the lines, note with terror that the balkanization that is overtaking the world may also be striking at the heart of our own country. Events in California, Texas, and Washington, D.C., provide frightening examples of this.

Today it is common for one economic class to be played off against another. Different religious, racial, and other minority interests have become, in their own eyes, "entitled" to the blood sweat of other groups. Previously legitimate, reputable businesses are suddenly declared illegal with disastrous results. One can only wonder how far this dangerous practice will go and when or how it will end.

Historically, internal problems of a society have resulted when governments, in their official capacity, plunder less numerous or politically aware groups in favor of others. With the passing of the republic in the United States, this has become a pervasive problem. Law and order have deteriorated as our society has crumbled. In many cases, officials have oppressed law-abiding citizens by using illogical technicalities to put these folks on the wrong side of the law.

All of this brings to mind the time in 1983 when visiting what was then Communist East Berlin—complete with dividing wall; nasty, quick-shooting guards; and severe travel restrictions—I watched in astonishment as a small, stuffed-to-the-gills, covered Japanese pickup truck pulled up and parked near the corner of Unter den Linden and Muellerstrasse, right downtown. Just as if they had rehearsed the whole thing, people immediately started lining up along the curb; a block-long line formed before I even knew what was going on.

Two farmers were selling bunches of carrots on the black market. As quickly as they could, two entrepreneurs jumped out of the truck and began exchanging clusters of about 20 nice, plump carrots for 20-ostmark notes. Since the enterprise of raising and selling directly to the people was obviously illegal, these two entrepreneurs dispersed their wares and collected their money in an almost frenzied fashion. It was obvious why and how the pair had an incredibly expensive, imported pickup out of which to do business: they were supplying a need for which the average man on the street was willing to pay handsomely.

Laws prohibiting the sale of carrots are agreeably ridiculous. Yet think about the proliferation of rules, regulations, and outright laws in our own society that prohibit everything from owning purely defensive devices, such as Mace or aerosol pepper spray, to buying iron castings not made in government-approved facilities to hanging bird houses on one's property to possessing or driving unapproved cars and trucks. Those not properly documented by Big Brother cannot install electrical wiring, give haircuts, fix plumbing, prepare food for sale, or repair television sets. We cannot look after the neighbor's children, formulate or apply simple pesticides, install gas pipes, or construct a home without government approval.

The East Germans changed their system. They can now raise and sell carrots. But these changes did not occur without a great deal of trauma. The resultant trauma in America may be more intense. Animals raised in zoos don't long for freedom; those captured from the wild fly into a rage when their freedoms are taken.

We may yet change our current system, but as with all other severely restrictive societies worldwide, change may not come easily. Free citizens may very well require information in a number of different areas.

What follows is a concise compilation of information detailing how one might survive in an extremely hostile environment. It has been gathered by men who have made this type of data their life's work. Just think of it as the average guy's 21st-century CIA and KGB operations manuals rolled into one easy-to-read, much-condensed volume.

For men of action—what few of us remain in today's mollycoddled, pabulum-based society—there are a great number of areas in which a basic working knowledge is vital. These include firearms, martial arts, knives, heavy weapons, action careers, survival hunting and gathering, lock picking, and electronic surveillance—to name just a few. We don't have to be experts in all these undertakings, but, in today's world, some familiarity is required.

This is, after all, supposedly the age of information. Information properly applied is both power and freedom. Most all of the information that men of action require is currently out there, waiting to be absorbed. Yet in many cases, the good information is obscured by the assumption (usually erroneous) writers make that a reader will wish to make a life's work out of becoming proficient in that given field. Becoming a First Dan black belt in karate, for instance, takes a minimum of three years of dedicated practice.

Well-rounded men of action generally need to know something about all these skills, rather than becoming an expert in just one. By so doing, they can avoid danger and know where to seek further information when circumstances dictate.

This volume is all about these skills. It is a compilation of action talents as recorded by the finest practitioners in the world. Those requiring information beyond the basics contained herein should consult the bibliography at the end of each chapter, visit their local library, or do pertinent research on the Internet.

CHAPTER

Improvised Firearms

1

Our own U.S. government has seemingly done more work on improvised firearms than any other entity, public or private. It is therefore appropriate to go to them for literature on the subject.

During World War II, a great many simple, essentially improvised firearms were designed, manufactured, purchased, and distributed by Uncle Sugar in Europe, especially Yugoslavia, and the Philippines. In addition, Office of Strategic Services (OSS) personnel were given a great deal of training in assembling improvised firearms. Huge numbers of printed instructions on firearms improvisation were also distributed to partisans and other resistance groups.

Partly as a result of this vast experience, several mostly philosophical considerations permeate any discussion on homebuilt firearms. These involve the following facts:

1. Improvised firearms should always be viewed as temporary expedients with which you could obtain a real, workable military-type firearm and ammunition.

2. All firearms regulations notwithstanding, there will be huge numbers of small arms and ammunition in circulation in any totalitarian society. One can easily test this hypothesis by noting the number of violent crimes in Washington, D.C., and New York, in spite of the number of heavily armed police.

   As a result, it becomes less and less of a chore to find someone from whom a real firearm can be borrowed. Historically, it is also true that as the standard of living plummets in police states, low-level security officials place more of their weapons for sale in the black market.

3. One usually assumes that ammunition of some sort will be available for improvised firearms. Improvised weapons most frequently are constructed for available ammo and not the other way around.

1

The first improvised weapon I personally made was a type commonly known as a "zip gun." The manufacture and design were sufficiently common that when I used mine in a state park around hundreds of visitors, virtually everyone there correctly identified it.

My device, made out of a piece of car radio antenna, rubber bands, a standard door cross bolt and a piece of oak chair leg survived 227 rounds of .22 gallery Shorts before shattering. I'm certain it was 227 rounds because I shot out of a 250-round box and simply counted those few rounds remaining.

In spite of numerous attempts to shoot sunning mud turtles at 40 feet, I was never successful. Past 3 or 4 feet it is impossible to hit even the inside of a barn (from the inside) with a crude smooth bore "zipper." They don't hold well, and the trigger is crude, truly defining inaccuracy. I have no firsthand experience with the destructive powers of tumbling zip gun bullets but assume reasonable lethality at short range.

My next homebuilt was a 12-gauge slip pipe gun discharged by ramming a 12-inch-long piece of 3/4 water pipe back into a 1-inch breech piece. Accuracy is not a big issue with improvised shotguns, but range and killing power are. Sans a snug chamber and choked barrel of any sort, patterns were widely dispersed and erratic. The shot lacked penetration, due in part to poor chamber sealing and rough-barrel shot deformation.

But returning again to the issue at hand, one usually puts together improvised firearms so that a real one can be obtained. Even at my tender age, I had a 12-gauge single shot and a .22-caliber pistol. It was easier for me to purchase guns than to make them.

I homebuilt a gun or two just to see if it could be done. In that regard, my record of 227 shots fired was meaningless. Generally, reloading clumsy homebuilts is sufficiently slow that a second shot is impractical. Eventually, I did construct a double-barrel zip gun. But it, too, was functionally worthless, and besides it blew on the 12th round, destroying the breech. But to fulfill their purpose, homebuilt weapons need to discharge only one lethal round.

Under these constraints, one should plan only the simplest barrel and breech block mechanism. Ronald B. Brown in his excellent book *Homemade Guns and Homemade Ammo* details plans to build a 12-gauge shotgun using heavy-duty 3/4-inch pipe, a threaded end cap, and a piece of 2 x 8 board. Brown uses a firing pin that rides in a pipe end cap. After each shot, the cap is screwed off and the empty round replaced.

The trigger is a long, thin bolt holding back an external U-shaped hammer made from steel bracket material. When pulled, the trigger releases the spring-powered bracket to swing up, striking the firing pin. This striker is something of a departure since most home builders use various sizes of door bolt mechanisms for both breech block and firing mechanisms. This design has a bit of charm since the trigger is slightly more conventional than door bolt types.

Reloading this weapon is accomplished by screwing the end plug off, punching out the old and inserting the new. This is not a speedy process: fully 45 seconds are required.

Two grades or strengths of pipe can be purchased from most large plumbing supply shops. Standard water pipe grade is called Schedule 40. Farmers customarily run tractor hydraulic systems of 5,000 psi with this pipe. Extra-strong water pipe, which sometimes must be special-ordered along with appropriate fittings, is called Schedule 80 pipe. Double extra-strong pipe or Schedule 160 is available in some sizes from steel fabrication shops. In all cases, pipe measurements are not precise in terms that gunsmiths use, and, of course, water pipe is never rifled.

Even given the inherent problems of loose chambers and barrels allowing gas leakage, pipe is often easier and better to work with than scrounged firearms barrels that might not have suitable chambers. Many home builders, however, try first to find an old firearms barrel on which to base their creations.

Smith & Wesson .38, .38 Special, and .357 Magnum rounds will all work nicely in 1/4-inch pipe, provided you have a 23/64-inch drill with which to "clean out" a chamber for the round. Use Schedule 40 pipe, available in 1/4-inch diameter, and cut the chamber in 1 1/4 inches. These are relatively low-pressure pistol rounds; Schedule 40 pipe is quite heavy. Makers may be surprised to discover how many rounds a gun of this type would endure. If possible, consider constructing a rifle with a 16- or 18-inch barrel. Accuracy will be marginally better and penetration surprisingly good, provided you can make do with this sometimes cumbersome length.

An extremely practical firearm can be made using 3/8-inch Schedule 40 pipe, firing .44 Mag and .44 Special, .45 auto rim, .45 Colt, and .410 shotgun ammo. Again, these are not common military cartridges, but the fact that it is both a hard ball and shot shell-type weapon recommends it. As with the .38 family of ammo, these are relatively low-pressure rounds throwing a huge projectile eminently useful at short ranges.

Among improvised firearms it generally would be useful to know how to make either a long-barrel or pistol-length 9mm. Because 9mms (except .380) are rimless rounds, an additional expedient must be deployed before they can be used in simple homebuilts. Otherwise, the rounds will fall into the barrel unless you are very careful about chamber reaming.

Use common 3/8-inch snap rings—available from most automotive supply houses—to headspace the cartridge. Place the ring on the cartridge in the extractor groove. When replacing the cartridge, change snap rings as well.

Use a length of 1/4-inch Schedule 40 pipe for a 9mm barrel. Using a 13/32 bit, drill down into the pipe on the breech end 3/4 inch. Be extremely cautious that this chamber is centered on the bore and that it does not go too deep.

The breechblock can be a threaded-pipe-type end cap or a coupling and plug drilled to accept a firing pin. Dies can be purchased to cut threads for these breechblocks, but generally you are better served by allowing a plumbing shop or machine shop to do the work. Cost is extremely minimal, and you do not create undue suspicions since most plumbing supply people assume that the pipe is of little value unthreaded.

Home builders either construct a hammer out of heavy strapping or use an appropriate-size door bolt. Either way, novice builders are usually surprised to discover how many rubber bands or retention springs it takes to reliably detonate a round.

Triggers can be longer, small-diameter bolts with serrations filed in them as a sear notch to hold the hammer, or the hammer can simply be held back with your thumb. Real working triggers are always tough for home builders, but people often seem to

come up with some extremely simple, clever, workable patterns.

People should not give up just because they live where restrictive laws have caused crime to become rampant. Under conditions of extreme duress, similar to those in New York City today, it may be possible to construct a workable homebuilt firearm with nothing but empty cartridge cases for ammo. Remember, it takes only one or two shots to come up with a real firearm. Expedient reloading proceeds as follows.

Carefully punch the spent primer from the empty case. Using a stout pin, pick the little anvil out of the back of the primer. Pick out all the used priming mixture from the little stamped-steel cup. Using a small nail, pop the dent back out of the cup.

Recharge the primer with a mixture of the type made for dynamite primers or use the tip (only) of strike-anywhere matches. Using a sharp razor blade and a drop or two of distilled water on a glass sheet, sever the match tips, cut them into pieces, and make a paste. Before it dries, carefully place this paste back into the straightened primer cup.

Rather than attempting to replace the primer anvil in the tiny primer, drop the anvil into the case primer pocket first before replacing the recharged primer. This works well but rusts barrels so quickly that most users claim a mouse piddled there.

Generally, home builders seem to prefer to manufacture sugar chlorate powder rather than old-fashioned black powder as a propellant. Use equal volumes of potassium chlorate and regular granulated household sugar.

Very gently, without adding *any* water, melt the sugar as though you were starting a batch of fudge. When the sugar is melted, remove it from the fire and continue to stir vigorously. When the sugar cools to 135 degrees (or the point at which you can comfortably place your fingers in the melted sugar), dump in an equal volume of potassium chlorate. Continue to stir vigorously till everything is thoroughly mixed. If the sugar was initially too cold during the melting process, it won't accept all the potassium chlorate. If the sugar is too hot when it is being blended, a nice cheery fire will result. Either way, the situation is not what you want.

Start with small batches till the process is more familiar. Sugar is easy to find and cheap, but spoiling one's potassium chlorate can be a bit pricey.

Because barrels on homebuilts are not tight, excessive pressures are rare. Fill up the case and cram in the bullet. Use pieces of bolt or lead chunks whittled to size as projectiles when nothing else is around.

Those who do not wish to play around with sugar chlorate powder can simply substitute ground match heads as the propellant powder. Use common match heads, *not* strike-anywhere match head tips. Figure about eight match heads for a 9mm load and 33 for a 12-gauge shotgun. Too many match heads do not cause excess pressure; they simply melt the case. Little destruction happens other than a failure to throw the projectile with workable velocity.

When I was living in East Africa, I sometimes encountered natives using extremely simple muzzle-loading rifles made from water pipe stocked with raw split wood fired by a cigarette-like slow match. At times, this match was simply inserted by hand into the pipe breech.

Projectiles were cut bolts, nails, and other scraps and bits of steel—in short, whatever the gun owner happened across. The powder was a mixture of fine fire ash and gasoline. Range and penetration were poor if mixing was more than 15 minutes old. Evidently they became expert at keeping in mind the original intent of their weapons.

I asked one group of weapon owners why they didn't just go all the way back to their spears as per their grandfathers. The men assured me that this was a good weapon as long as their powder was fresh and they got in close. Even the occasional Cape buffalo fell to one of these devices, they assured me. Most Africans I have hunted with are not good hunters. How they ever got in close enough, holding a smoking match, and then why the buff didn't just tromp them rather than somberly run off to die with a chunk of 5/8-inch bolt in its belly, escape me.

J. David Truby and John Minnery point out in their classic book, *Improvised Modified Firearms,* that many homemade firearms are made from other devices. These include toy pistols, starter pistols, flare guns, fuze lighters, and cigarette lighters. Even an ax has been used as the basis for a firearm.

In a dire emergency, one could use the trigger mechanism from a cap pistol to fire a 9mm round through a steel replacement barrel. The mechanism might have to be beefed up with stronger springs, but generally grips, trigger, and cradle for the barrel

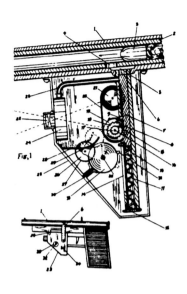

Patent sketch for a camera inside a gun. (Illustrations taken from *Improvised Modified Firearms* by J. David Truby and John Minnery and courtesy of U.S. Patent Office.)

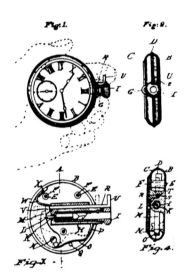

Leonard Woods' patent for a gun inside a pocketwatch.

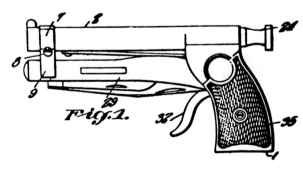

Patent sketch of representative knife-firearm combination designed in 1924.

are all there. Some excellent models (for homebuilts) have been built with little more than electrician's tape, steel tube, and rubber bands on a toy pistol frame.

Some prisoners in a Michigan penitentiary assembled a homebuilt that used a wood screw as a projectile. They also produced a reasonably effective silencer good for several rounds. How or where these cons got ammo for their device taxes one's imagination. Probably the same place they get marijuana and other illicit drugs.

Though they probably did not intend them as practical weapons, individual machinists and gunsmiths have made numerous firearms from common items. You can find firearms in clasp knives, pipes (smoking type), umbrellas, whip handles, and, of course, walking sticks and canes.

Those who are sufficiently motivated can use nothing more than simple machinist's files to produce excellent copies of regular firearms. Khyber Pass gunsmiths are notorious for their clever adherence to exact detail. Excellent revolver, submachine guns, machine guns, and even grenade launchers are all made by these clever folks in northern Pakistan. Prosperity induced by the Afghan War has apparently led to increased use of modern lathes, milling machines, and power drill presses, but their weapons are still made one at a time using another original as a pattern.

The Vietcong turned out excellent weapons in the early days of the Vietnam War, as did the Israelis during their war of independence in 1947-48.

Brazing is often used to assemble frames, slides, and more complex smaller parts rather than millings or stampings. Many barrels are smoothbore or make use of salvaged gun barrels. Steel used in some such weapons may be of very low grade. Experts who have used these copies tend to view them as excellent, well-made, nonshootable models rather than real firearms that they reassembled.

In places where labor is very cheap—such as China, Thailand, and Taiwan—good functional replicas of virtually every weapon are commonly manufactured. Production is undertaken in extremely primitive village workshops. Weapons produced may find their way into insurgens't camps, gangsters' hands, or, more commonly, simply be hung on the wall as nonfunctional decorations.

The Japanese police complain incessantly about the ease with which Thais own firearms and the frequency with which some of these weapons find their way back into "nefarious" hands in Japan.

From very simple to very complex, it is not difficult to produce a good, serviceable weapon in a home workshop. First, home builders must realize that many others have built such devices, then they must become sufficiently motivated to put the necessary time and effort into the project. Patience is, of course, golden. At times this includes costly, time-consuming trial and error. But as cons in our nation's joints have demonstrated, firearms and ammunition can be produced even in very restrictive environments.

BIBLIOGRAPHY

Brown, Ronald B. *Homemade Guns and Homemade Ammo*. Port Townsend, WA: Loompanics, Unlimited, 1986.

Truby, J. David and John Minnery. *Improvised Modified Firearms*. Boulder, CO: Paladin Press, 1992.

U.S. Technical Manual TM 31-210. Washington, D.C.: U.S. Government Printing Office.

CHAPTER

Silencers

2

Back when I was a lad in the 1930s and 1940s, the subject of silencers—their construction, theory, and use—was pretty much in limbo. Other than a mere handful of hunters who used them, nobody paid any attention to silencers.

My first contact with them occurred as a result of hunting with genuine, certified, card-carrying hillbillies from Harlan County, Kentucky. These were truly wonderful, salt-of-the-earth people who made their living largely in the woods. They caught wild bees; fished; dug roots (mostly ginseng); hunted squirrels, deer, fox, coon, and possum; and ran profitable trap lines in winter when most of us were not profitably employed.

When squirrel hunting, they used standard-velocity .22 Shorts of a type I doubt are even manufactured today. Nine times out of 10 they nailed the critters in the head out of 50- to 60-foot trees.

Wearing complete cammie outfits, they liked to creep from one big hickory tree to another in an attempt to catch the critters feeding. Some of these feed trees were right out in the middle of open farm fields. But they attracted squirrels during the nut season, often by the dozen.

Today, common street wisdom suggests that no firearm can be completely silent. These "wise" people never saw hillbillies shoot squirrels. With silencers mounted on heavy, long-barreled rifles, the loudest noise was the sound of the bullet splitting the squirrel's head 50 feet up in the tree. Neither humans nor other squirrels realized from the noise what was going on.

Slipping around like smoke and shadows, these people were able to bring home a dozen or more squirrels virtually every time they went out during the season. Usually, the only reason they stopped hunting was because they tired of packing around the meat. I often walked 10 miles with these people on an "easy" morning's hunt.

Principally, the silencers they used were old Maxim types, made in the 1920s and 1930s. Generally, they kept them in good condition. Pulling maintenance on silencers is far more work than people could even suppose had they gained most of their information at the movies. These hunters were masters at it. As baffles wore out, they either made simple stamps to turn out new ones or ordered factory-made replacements from the Parker-Hale firm in England.

By having these baffles sent over as motorcycle mufflers and other parts, they were also able to import sufficient new silencers to replace those that wore out or went to work for one of the multitude of children they sired.

Other than realizing that the ammunition they used had to be subsonic (under 1,190 fps), these people gave absolutely no thought to the theory of operation.

In this day and age, the situation is dramatically different. It has been at least five or more years since I have encountered a single man of action who did not know how silencers worked. This includes the general theory of operation, construction, mounting problems, and several new, promising design concepts.

Yet movie and TV propaganda still affects the thinking of even those quite knowledgeable about silencers. Most people, for instance, continue to believe that noise attenuation with large rounds is far greater than is true in the real world and that the size of the average silencer is dramatically smaller than what the laws of physics and science require.

In other words, those tiny little 3/4-inch cans 4 inches long shown on TV would never silence a .22 Short, much less a 9mm from a short-barreled automatic.

In all probability, outlawing silencers occurred at a bad time in the United States. They were made illegal before population density and the fear of guns exploded. Silencers are commonly used in England, France, and Germany by groundskeepers who do not wish to rile close neighbors with unruly, threatening sounds and those who wish to target shoot without disturbing the neighbors. In the United Kingdom, .410 bore shotguns are commonly silenced, confounding contemporary wisdom that suggests shotguns cannot be quieted down.

Actually, most guns are not really totally silenced in spite of new technology employing sound-attenuating plastics and squeeze-bore devices that slow bullets and squirt discharge gases into sealed chambers. The noise of discharge is usually altered into a longish, deep, pneumatic "thump" not easily recognized as a firearm discharge. This is a practical, achievable goal for all silencers. If listeners are not certain what they heard and if the noise does not alarm them, then many of the criteria for these devices have been met.

Because unlicensed silencers are completely illegal in the United States and because enforcement people with dramatically expanded powers are increasingly skilled in their entrapment techniques, many thoughtful gun nuts are looking at alternatives. Some of these cheap, easy, and legal devices accomplish missions identical to those of real silencers.

Custom reloading is one good alternative. The area on the mountain where I live is becoming increasingly built up. Each year I find I must defend my cherry trees for democracy against hordes of marauding robins.

I do not wish to give the feds cause to harass me or arouse my neighbors—and I doubly do not wish to allow worthless, freeloading robins the luxury of my cherries—so I defend my cherries with .22 CB caps made by CCI in Lewiston, Idaho. This round is identical in function to the old, old BB cap made during the 1920s, '30s, and '40s in the United States. It has a larger, longer, heavier projectile, producing quieter discharge and better accuracy. The CBs also feed through conventional mechanisms and avoid the fumble and fooling characteristic of antique BBs.

I have had similar success suppressing large-bore rifles and pistols by intentionally reloading for quiet. Reloaders, no matter which round is chosen, can easily up the weight of their bullets while jumping as many as seven or eight speed grades to slower, reduced powder charges. Results can be quite quiet. These rounds work best in longer-barreled rifles, but then all silenced rounds do.

Three come immediately to mind. First is a standard 9mm loaded with five grains of H-110 behind 160-grain bullets.

The second is the 9mm Bergmann-Bayard, also known as a 9mm Steyr, an excellent round easily capable of quietly taking deer. At this writing, Spanish-made, bolt-action, 9mm Bergmann carbines are being imported that are absolutely ideal for men of action with some clandestine and quiet—yet heavy—shooting to do. Load with 160-grain 9mm bullets and 9 grains of Reloader #7. These rounds easily bring big deer to grass if they are hit in the head.

Several domestic commercial rifles are now available that fire .45 ACP rounds. Loaded with 275-grain bullets and 4 grains of Reloader #7, they pack a nice, quiet punch. A friend thought he might catch the bullets in a first baseman's mitt at 200 yards, but after seeing the round in action on a very large, very nasty feral dog, he quickly changed his mind.

The third option is for men of action needing quiet firearms that, at present, break no one's laws and are simpler and easier than owning a silencer: a subcaliber device. Although I featured them in a book a few years back, subcaliber devices remain one of the best-kept secrets in the industry.

These are little steel-and-aluminum inserts that allow you to shoot .22 LRs, for instance, in .30 caliber rifles. Some models fire .32 ACP in .30-caliber rifles and everything from 30-30 to .223 to 9mm in shotguns. Most of these inserts are made for 12-gauge break-action singles and doubles, but few 20-gauge models exist.

(Usually, shotgun inserts are quite noisy and not worth considering for purposes of this chapter. In some cases they make a wonderful, deadly, clandestine weapon in places that permit only shotguns, but this chapter is about quiet.)

The models for .22 caliber are not as quiet as one would hope and suffer from being incredibly tough to reload. One must fiddle with a number of BB-size parts, definitely "ungood" out in the bush or when one's hands are cold.

The absolute queen of these devices is the .32 ACP firer. In actual tests, this insert was completely inaudible at 100 yards in the woods when fired in a .308 with 20-inch barrel, in a gentle 6- or 8-knot wind.

Two types (mechanical) of inserts are made. One makes use of the host firearm's existing barrel and therefore must fire a smaller round of basically the same caliber. A .32 ACP is close enough to .30 caliber to work well in a .308, 30-06, or .300 Winchester Magnum. A second type carries with it its own integral barrel. A .223 fired from a 12 gauge makes use of its own stubby 6-inch barrel. Barrels on 9mm devices are 4 1/2 inches long.

It is surprising how accurate these inserts can be. I have fired 15 to 20 9mm rounds in a row at a clod of dirt out about 200 yards in a plowed field. The rounds always came close enough that had the clod been my head I would have been very worried.

Penetration and power of these little rounds fired from a long rifle barrel are surprising. Out to 150 yards, my .308 with .32 ACP adapter shoots in the same hole using a scope as with its regular ammo. I don't have a .32 ACP pistol with which I can hit a phone book at 150 yards to compare, but .32 ACPs whistled right through a telephone directory the size of one for Cleveland.

Those who do feel a genuine need for a silencer probably require one for a handgun. Many perfectly adequate, homemade models are available. One can be constructed of household scrap found in virtually any American home. Unfortunately, these models tend to be short-lived, but bear in mind that regular, machined, metal types require huge amounts of disassembly and cleaning. I well recall my hillbilly friends sitting by the hour, using old toothbrushes to polish their silencers, which were disassembled into scores of pieces.

One semipermanent model takes advantage of newer silencer technology that produces better results with modern, high-impact plastics, which themselves tend to absorb noise. Start with a 9-inch piece of heavy-duty plastic water pipe of sufficient diameter to slip over the barrel of your weapon. If this happens to be a heavy, high-powered rifle, considerably more than 9 inches of tube is required.

Drill dozens of 1/4-inch holes in the plastic pipe and then, using a hose clamp, securely fasten it to the gun barrel. Place a dowel through the center of the perforated liner into the gun bore. If the dowel is about the same diameter as the bore, a better job will result. Use this dowel to line up a solid hard rubber or wooden disk of a diameter about 1 inch bigger than that of the plastic pipe.

The hole through the wooden disk should be larger than the bore diameter of the firearm. To some extent, firing through the disk will open it a bit, but correct alignment now is best.

Wrap a tight layer of copper scouring pad material around the plastic tube to the diameter of the rubber or wooden disk. In most cases, four or five pads will be required. This layer must be evenly solid so that no thin spot is evident over the holes in the tube.

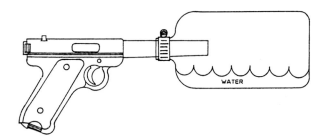

One of the earliest improvised silencer designs was the 2-liter plastic bottle, usually filled with stuffers or liquid. BATF regulations require that you register this unit like any other silencer, of course. (Illustration from *The Hayduke Silencer Book* by George Hayduke and courtesy of William Seymour.)

Finish by generously wrapping an even layer of duct tape around the scouring pad material from the disk at front to hose clamp at rear. This silencer performs well with subsonic ammo until 100 to 150 rounds have passed through. After this point, it begins to carbon. To a limited extent, these silencers can be cleaned in detergent and water, but they only cost about $2.39, so there's not much expense to starting over.

Mufflers from small gasoline engines work fairly well as silencers, provided you can find a model with correct diameter to facilitate clamping to the barrel. Internal tolerances (bore diameter) must not be so great that the blast simply carries on through the device. To a certain extent gases at discharge must be trapped. German engineers at the end of World War II even played with pinch-bore silencers that essentially swaged a soft lead slug down inside a silencer barrel, forcing gases into sound-deadening material.

Small engine mufflers usually have steel baffles that must be drilled out, allowing the bullet to pass straight through. Keep this hole as small as possible. Getting this hole drilled through in perfect alignment with the barrel is tougher than one might initially suppose. The cost of these mufflers is about $10, when they can be found. Dealers do not usually carry them because they seldom wear out on small engines. These devices are effective and fairly easy to construct and make work, but—as with most expedient silencers—they are tough to clean.

Those who need pistol silencers that are cheap, easy to make, and effective over short ranges are advised to try plastic soft-drink containers. These

devices really work and can be assembled almost anywhere in a matter of seconds.

Use a 2-liter plastic bottle taped or clamped to the pistol's muzzle. Fill the bottle with Styrofoam packing peanuts to which about 2 tablespoons of boric acid have been added. Shoot right through the bottle, peanuts and all. Accuracy is OK at average pistol ranges of 7 to 10 feet. Durability, of course, leaves something to be desired. Expect about 10 silenced shots from a .22 and two or three from a 9mm.

The best actual field use of a silencer I have experienced occurred while deer hunting with the hillbillies. Two of us circled a very large brush-covered, knob-like dome. My partner below carried a 25-20 with an ancient original Maxim silencer of the type somewhat popular before 1934. I had a .308 with a subcaliber device.

While heading south into the wind, I jumped two nice fat deer at close range. They ran ahead out of sight for 100 yards and then circled back, running with the wind toward my partner below. We both stalked through very quietly, stopping and standing often. Shots in those conditions with the weapons we carried were, by necessity, very, very short. We were separated by 80 yards, but we could not see each other in the scrub.

After a bit, I heard a kind of thumping noise—sort of like a pumpkin hitting the pavement from the fourth floor. Another short wait and then a single, low whistle came. I silently worked downhill to find my companion gutting out a nice, fat, forked horn. We were only 50 yards from a house.

As he later told it, in an attempt to circle and get my wind, the deer ran straight into him. He heard it coming and stood still as steel till it was about 25 paces away. When the deer stopped, he shot it right between the eyes, slightly high. The hunter ran up, jumped on the deer, and cut its throat as it began to regain consciousness.

The first big chore for those who require a genuine quasi-regulation silencer is to have the gun barrel threaded. This is a bigger job than one would first suppose because threading must be done on a lathe so that it is straight and true. Some friction couplings are available to which the silencer can be screwed. These devices are held on the barrel by friction but tend to shoot loose and are tough to get on straight. Threaded barrels are an immediate

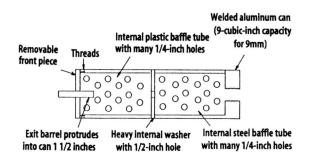

Rhodesian silencer. (Illustration by Ragnar Benson.)

Labels in illustration:
Removable front piece — Threads — Internal plastic baffle tube with many 1/4-inch holes — Welded aluminum can (9-cubic-inch capacity for 9mm) — Exit barrel protrudes into can 1 1/2 inches — Heavy internal washer with 1/2-inch hole — Internal steel baffle tube with many 1/4-inch holes

warning to casual observers: when threading is done, clever caps or covers must be made with which to hide the threads.

Some silencer builders take great pride in threading the inside of their pistol barrels so that nothing shows to alert casual observers. The best silencers I have seen are threaded flat and tight right to the outside of the gun barrel. This allows screwing the muzzle into the can so that the can remains straight and true and the muzzle extends into the can about 3/4 inch.

Muzzle blast will expand forward as well as backward onto the back wall of the can and then be thrown forward in the otherwise tight container.

Cans for 9mm pistol on a 6-inch barrel must contain a minimum of 9 cubic inches of space. You can achieve this with either length or diameter. Construct the can out of aluminum, securely heli-arcing everything together. Plan for pressures that are fairly severe.

Turn the inside threads on the front of the can so that a specially designed muzzle piece can be screwed into it. The owner's machine shop must make a muzzle piece of the same diameter and thread containing a short bullet-exit barrel. This stub barrel should be 1/2 inch in diameter for 9mm and extend back into the can 1 1/2 inches. This is important information not commonly understood in the United States.

Gases from the shot roll back inside the can from muzzle to can's rear wall. They are then bounced forward into the front of the can against the plug with the stub barrel extending rearward. Only a slight amount of gas exits through the 1/2-inch hole till long after the round is gone.

Complete the can by inserting two steel inner liners inside it. These liners must be perforated with hundreds of 1/4-inch holes. Slide one piece that reaches back from the muzzle about 4 inches (assuming a 9-inch-long can), drop a solid washer with half-inch hole over this liner, and install the second liner, which is about 5 inches long. Clamp this down by screwing in the front piece. On discharge, gases are further diffused and bounced by the inside tubes and flat washer.

Models I saw in Rhodesia also had foam rubber salvaged from old auto interiors wrapped securely around the outside of the metal tube. Noise levels were further reduced, and glare was also cut.

This is an extremely simple, effective unit, but it is only available to one having access to a sophisticated machinist. Performance levels with heavy subsonic rounds are as good as one could hope for. Maintenance with no stainless steel wool packing or complex baffles is excellent. They are easily disassembled and brushed out. We often got a tablespoon of crud out of these devices after a day or two of use. Cost of these units would be at least $100, not including the hassle and expense of having the barrel threaded.

Silencers of one type or another are not very difficult to build. Anyone can build them from scrap or can use reduced loads or subcaliber devices.

BIBLIOGRAPHY

Benson, Ragnar. *Hard-Core Poaching*. Boulder, CO: Paladin Press, 1987.

Flores, J. *How to Make Disposable Silencers, Vol. & II*. Miami, FL: J. Flores Publications, 1984.

Hayduke, George. *The Hayduke Silencer Book*. Boulder, CO: Paladin Press, 1989.

Truby, J. David and John Minnery. *Improvised Modified Firearms*. Boulder, CO: Paladin Press, 1992.

CHAPTER

Assault Shotguns

3

Long ago before the term was fully defined, Mike Sparks was a foulmouthed, punk kid. We farm kids played with other poor kids, but we were not supposed to associate with ill-mannered punks. In seventh grade, for instance, Sparks borrowed my gym socks and ran around in them without shoes till they were completely full of holes. But that is not how Mr. Sparks achieved notoriety.

Jerry Hunter bought a brand-new single-shot, break-action Iver Johnson .410 shotgun, and Mike Sparks was green with envy. As a result, he tried to belittle Hunter's new purchase.

"That's just a puny little toy gun," Sparks said, "not a real shotgun like my big 20 gauge." He went on and on till everyone was sicker than usual of Mr. Sparks.

Jerry Hunter was one of those big kids in seventh grade who either grew up early or was held back a grade somewhere along the line. We didn't

really know which. He often brought some of his many family guns to school for us kids to see. Neither teachers nor administrators paid much attention in those days.

"Your .410 is a wimpy little gun," Sparks continued, "so small that if you gave me a count of 10 I could even outrun a charge of shot from it." And so a deal was struck. Probably 35 of us, including several girls, went out to the big field south of school after school was out to see how fast Sparks could really run.

Admittedly, Jerry counted a bit fast, but even if he hadn't, results would have been much the same. It was so funny that we doubled up on the ground laughing even while Sparks was screaming. It was the large quantity of blood that finally sobered us up.

A full load of number 4 caught Sparks in the posterior and on down his legs. He fell like a pole-axed steer. Over and over he rolled, screaming, "I'm shot, I'm shot!"

We couldn't even take off his pants to look because of the girls. Next day, the whole gang of us really caught it from our home-room teachers, boys' phys-ed teacher, and, of course, the principal. It was from that time that I knew a shotgun was a pretty good tool—not a great tool, or it would have blown Jerry's ass right off, but a pretty good tool.

Shotguns have several advantages that make them especially desirable in the United States at this writing. An incredible number of excellent models are currently available that can be the basis of easily done, legal customization by men of action. Unlike handguns, they are relatively quick and easy to learn to use. They can deliver a tremendous amount of firepower, and shotguns are usually the last firearms to be outlawed by despotic authorities. Using properly tailored loads, shotguns can be used safely where rifles and pistols cannot. But this same lack of range and penetration precludes their effective use against prepared, trained personnel using body armor or ballistic shields.

In actual field trials, men trained with custom, modified shotguns have outperformed similarly trained men using submachine guns at close ranges. Unlike submachine guns, shotguns can be easily modified using existing, often very inexpensive aftermarket parts and accessories. Some new shotguns come so well equipped that any further customization is unnecessary.

Even the U.S. government has gotten into the game by doing extensive testing and evaluation of assault shotguns. In many cases various agencies have made recommendations leading to the accouterments and models now commonly available.

The Benelli Super 90 M-1, 12-gauge, for instance, now comes complete with 9-shot magazine extension, pistol grip, and combat sights. Theoretically, this weapon could be pressed into service right off the rack. Importation, which at this writing is not restricted, is handled by Heckler & Koch.

Franchi models come similarly equipped with extra-capacity magazines and pistol grips, but over-the-counter status is in question because of the demise of the single U.S. importer.

Of the basic U.S. shotgun actions, probably the finest pump, experts claim, is the Ithaca Model 37. This action is really an improvement of a Remington Model 17 invented by John Browning himself. Unfortunately, Ithaca went T.U. (toes up) in 1986, ending almost 50 years of dominance in the field.

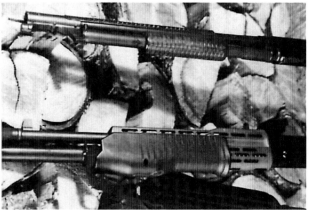

Two generations of combat shotguns: (top) the venerable old Springfield Model 12 12-gauge military guard shotgun was one of the first combat shotguns; and (bottom) the SPAW-12 modern, state-of-the-art 9-shot shotgun. (Photos by Ragnar Benson.)

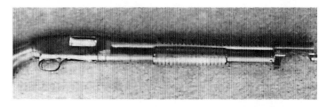

This Springfield Model 12 was made in the old Springfield Armory.

Remington purchased tools, dies, and patterns for the 37 and reissued this gun as the Model 87. Although both the original 37s and later 87s are remarkable for their rugged simplicity, there were few accessories available for these guns. No magazine extensions, pistol grips, or forearm grips, for instance, could be had.

Hunters traditionally have been pleased with the 37's light weight, as well as the fact that loading and ejecting is accomplished through the same bottom port in the receiver. Dirt, snow, and mud had to fall uphill to get into that gun's action.

Model 37s proved the old adage that anybody can make something complex, but it takes a genius to make it simple. Perhaps because this was an old model "hunters' gun," few people thought of it as an assault shotgun.

But all this has changed under Remington's tutelage. There is now a Model 87 military and police 12 gauge with 20-inch barrel, cylinder choke, and 8-shot magazine capacity! Choate makes aftermarket composition stocks and foregrips for this model.

Mossberg, much to the chagrin of those who recall its days as supplier to Sears, has captured a significant share of the assault shotgun market with its Model 500 series. Model 500s were designed to take advantage of modern industrial manufacturing techniques and materials. These are inexpensive yet very durable guns.

During the mid-1980s, the U.S. Army set up standards and field trials leading to the adoption of a new shotgun. Only Mossberg 500s and related 590s passed the tests. They were the only models capable of firing 3,000 consecutive rounds without parts breakage. There were only two slight malfunctions during the test.

Additionally, Mossberg has come out with numerous models, including a number of stock variations, interchangeable barrels, extended magazines, and foregrips for its Model 500s. Those looking for a good shotgun system can have virtually anything they need from Mossberg right off the rack. This could include extremely short, cut-down, 12-inch-barreled guns. Extra barrels are so inexpensive it is relatively easy to make up a pump shotgun pistol with an extra barrel that one keeps stashed away.

Depending on your predisposition, Remington Model 870s may be better or worse systems on which to build an assault shotgun. Unlike on older pump Ithacas, the trigger on an 870 simply cannot be held back and rounds run through it as fast as you can pump. Also, 870s have trigger disconnects, meaning that they are marginally safer but that skilled shooters cannot lay down fire as they can with Ithaca pumps.

Some users feel that the lack of a trigger disconnector is overly dangerous. Partly because of Remington's greater market clout, 870s have always sold in greater numbers.

Early on, Remington offered a wider range of barrels, magazine extensions, folding stocks, and finishes than its competition. Several government agencies adopted 870s, including our army in Vietnam. Aftermarket suppliers were quick to provide folding stocks and other accouterments because so many 870s were out there.

One problem with 870s that led, in part, to testing and adopting Mossberg shotguns by some government agencies involved the fact that rounds in 870s tend to pop out of the magazine tube, jamming the action. Because of solid ammunition carriers used in this design, the weapons must be disassembled to clear jams. Some users have even cut slots in the lower carrier so that knife blades can be inserted to shove offending rounds forward out of the way.

Recently, Remington has offered numerous combat Model 870s that feature a great many items usually supplied by aftermarket people. If you want an inexpensive, reliable shotgun, easily doubling as a hunting gun by the addition of an inexpensive second barrel for which virtually any accessory is available, the Remington 870 is the easy, obvious choice.

In test after test, skilled users with pump-action weapons have been able to lay down more controlled fire more quickly than those with semiauto guns. Some pump gun aficionados can outshoot full autos if speed is the only criterion.

Nevertheless, there is a tendency among some men of action to look first to semiautos as the basis for their customized assault shotguns. But dangers lurk. Chuck Taylor writes in no uncertain terms that Remington 1100s are sufficiently unreliable that he cannot recommend them to serious users.

Perhaps because of the 1100's poor press, Remington brought out its Model 11-87 in 1987. This model partly corrected problems with gas operating systems of the 1100. Users claim quite a bit of improvement, especially using longer barrels, but that shorter-barreled versions of the 11-87 can still be cantankerous with some ammunition. Off-the-shelf versions of the 11-87 can be had with rugged composition stocks, extended magazines, and parkerized finishes.

Winchester makes an automatic shotgun system called a 1400. These are reasonably well-made guns but include several internal parts of plastic. This may not be a serious problem. Model 1400s seemingly never achieved sufficient popularity to constitute a valid test of their ruggedness. Not only are we somewhat in the dark regarding ruggedness, but have to take whatever Winchester 1400 is offered right off the rack. Aftermarket supplies of folding stocks, magazine extensions, forearm grips, and even sling swivels are mighty thin.

Even now, 20 years after dropping popular Model 12s from its line, people think of this model when they think of Winchester. Model 12s are far too valuable to cut down and install folding stocks on, but 1300s have proved to be very rugged and in some ways (especially price) superior to older models. Numerous aftermarket supplies are available to custom designers or builders.

In all cases, whatever configuration you come up with, great care must be paid to ammo selection. Number 4 buckshot is generally a recommended standard for self-defense but is not always a wise choice in any one shotgun. This load, even with buffers and plastic collar wads, is effective only at relatively short ranges: most experts claim 60 yards max with consistent results. At very short ranges it may overpenetrate, endangering innocent bystanders. There is a delicate balance between using number 2 or 4 birdshot, number 4 buck, or 00 buckshot. To make matters more confusing, not all buckshot will pattern well in all guns, and some of it may not even cycle reliably. Most, however, will at least feed and fire through most pump guns. You must test extensively for both function and pattern idiosyncrasies of shot size.

When customizing a shotgun, keep in mind that unless you are willing to do a great deal of *sometimes* expensive paperwork, a finished assault shotgun must have a barrel 18 inches or longer and be no fewer than 27 inches overall. Maximum velocity occurs in shotguns with about 24-inch barrels. Loss of velocity dropping to 18 inches may be very slight, given modern plastic wads, but shorter barrels preclude longer extension magazines unless you are willing to risk blasting off the end of an extension tube.

Before it went broke, Hi-Standard produced a factory-issue bullpup-type shotgun called a Model 10A. It was a wonderful concept, but it was a bit hard to learn to shoot, as well as well as being discouragingly unreliable. Had reliability problems

been solved and Hi-Standard been able to survive till black shotguns hit their stride, the company probably would have had a real winner.

Originally, Hi-Standard's Model 10s were envisioned as weapons carried by law enforcement personnel under one's shoulder on a carry hook, covered by a loose overcoat. Tremendous amounts of hidden firepower were available to users under these circumstances—if they could endure the noise and spattering from burning pieces of powder and wad.

At this writing, still-secret reports from Ram-Line and Choate suggest that a real bullpup stock similar to ones made for the Ruger Mini-14 may be under development for use on popular automatic models.

Certainly, a bullpup stock built around a popular Remington 11-87 or Winchester 1400 auto would sell well. But though these aftermarket devices are rumored, they are not actually available.

As of this writing, people who want good, functional assault shotguns can either purchase their favorite model with many or most features they desire or choose from many custom aftermarket supplies. These include foregrips, magazine extensions, composition stocks, pistol grips, and very clever folding stocks.

Since Vietnam, a number of strictly military shotguns have come on the scene. These include SPA-12s, Strikers, and Streetsweepers. SPA-12s are heavy, rugged, hybrid pump-semiautos that will ingest virtually any ammo. Both Strikers and Streetsweepers are 12-shot revolver-type guns. Of the two, Strikers are the best made, although both are patterned after models developed in South Africa. All genuinely raise the hackles of antigunners. Further production was recently outlawed by Treasury Department directive.

A few military and law enforcement people see the need for a box-fed, full-automatic shotgun. Most people familiar with full-auto fire see little practical value to such a hard-to-control device. Concepts of this type seem to cycle in and out of popularity on a regular basis. Since no full-auto shotgun system has ever been adopted by any major world military power or police organization, one might realistically conclude that the idea is a nonstarter.

While working in Cuba in the late 1950s, I became acquainted with a man who owned a 20-gauge Ithaca Auto-Burglar pistol, as well as a seeming endless supply of ammunition. We spent many an evening blasting away at sea gulls from a new jetty under construction near us. Cuban law forbade private ownership of pistols and rifles but said little about shotguns—even shotgun pistols.

Shooting that monster was instructional in several regards. Unless held firmly, it had a strong tendency to smack one in the forehead on discharge. We quickly learned to hold it at absolute arm's length and then to duck after experiencing a couple of especially nasty clunks. Also, the piece threw a very wide pattern, allowing one to make what seemed to be some spectacular wing shots—provided we fired quickly at relatively short ranges. Penetration was evidently poor since we seldom knocked a gull completely out of the air with one shot.

In this country, shotgun pistols have traditionally been popular. Many Old West gunfighters, sheriffs, and marshals used them, if not as their primary weapon at least as a backup.

For a number of years, ownership of shotgun pistols was questionable under the National Firearms Act. At present, pistols with smooth bores theoretically require only a $5 transfer tax.

The paperwork to transfer is sometimes about the same as that for full-auto weapon transfer or for cutting down a full-sized shotgun. The problem is that you never seem to know for sure going in and can get into lots of trouble finding out. Yet a number of short shotgun pistols are going on the market. It is best to check cautiously with the maker and other civilians who have done similar deals before purchasing the weapon.

As an alternative, a number of weapons have hit the market that will accept standard ball ammo as well as custom-loaded shot shells or regular, off-the-shelf .410 rounds. These are legal handguns, available under the same rules and regulations as any other handgun.

American Derringer Corporation makes a nice 2-shot, over/under, .45 long Colt model that will handle .410 rounds nicely. Rifled barrels spoil pattern and range a bit, but modern plastic wads mitigate this problem to an extent. At close range, .410 loads will tear about as big a hole as anything going.

Another recently popular .45 long Colt called the Thunder Five is a 5-shot revolver that uses .410 shot shells. Even with its stubby 2-inch barrels, it is reportedly quite effective at short distances.

Our assumption must be that shotguns have definite limitations as offensive weapons. They are, however, reasonably inexpensive, easy to purchase, and have a definite sporting purpose that can be redirected at moment's notice. You must pick and choose wisely when a new purchase is made. Customizing must also be done judiciously so that the system that results will suit your particular needs.

Shotguns do not replace other weapons. They are part of an integrated system.

BIBLIOGRAPHY

Long, Duncan. *Super Shotguns—How to Make Your Shotgun into a Do-Everything Weapon.* Boulder, CO: Paladin Press, 1992.

Taylor, Chuck. *The Combat Shotgun and Submachine Gun.* Boulder, CO: Paladin Press, 1985.

CHAPTER

Submachine Guns

4

A friend living in the heavy mountains west of Denver invited me over to fire some of his automatic weapons. With his Class III license and remote mountain location, we neither bothered the neighbors nor violated any laws.

He had some paper targets set in front of a cut bank about 100 yards away, but to make things really interesting we set out three plastic gallon jugs full of water. At first we set them out near the paper targets. As the afternoon wore on and our fingers grew stiff and numb from loading clips, we moved them forward to the 50-yard line.

As I recall, we blasted away fully 5,000 rounds, hitting the jugs once or twice at most. It was good fun, but, had the jugs been bad buys, they would have escaped for the most part unscathed.

One of the weapons was a Ruger 10/22, professionally modified to fire full auto. We seldom got off a full 50-round magazine without a jam, but it was still enjoyable to shoot. Little .22 bullets

ricocheted and splashed in the mud around the jugs, creating a nice display.

Another weapon we ran a bushel basket of ammo through was a 9mm MAC-10. It functioned OK if you were content not to actually hit the target—even on semiauto. At the time, it was popular for law enforcement people to complain about being shot at with full-auto MAC-10s. Had I a choice about which weapon in the whole world was firing at me, a MAC-10 would be my first selection.

During that session, we discovered that the old Eastern Bloc theory of small arms fire by which everyone discharges their weapons in the direction of the target, but only specially designated snipers actually *aim at* the target, left something to be desired. Israeli commandos use similar tactics to force the enemy to stay down because of the noise, as they boldly overrun enemy's position. But one would think accurate, well-aimed fire from skilled marksmen would usually carry the day.

Our third weapon was a .45 Colt 1911 pistol professionally modified for full-auto fire. Its owner got the idea while living in Cuba, where such

Although some submachine guns can be as large as rifles and weigh just as much, new weapons are quite small and nearly as easy to handle as pistols. Shown are the larger KK-94 (top), the TEC-9 (center right), and the SGW 9mm Carbine (bottom). (Photos from *Assault Pistols, Rifles and Submachine Guns* by Duncan Long.)

weapons were commonly encountered as replacements for real submachine guns (SMGs). It had a 50-round extended magazine and a foregrip, making it possible to fire. Function was good if you did not include the necessity of hitting a target now and then. Weaknesses of the system included the problem of loading long, straight-line magazines and that, after 2,500 rounds, the piece was close to being a junker. Full-auto fire is very hard on that model pistol.

No matter what else you can say about SMGs, which, by definition, fire pistol ammo, they are a great deal of fun to shoot. We had dirt, mud, rock chips, and water flying all over the place. As long as they can afford the ammo, most people find SMGs to be one of the most enjoyable weapons to fire.

The basic concept for SMGs started in Italy during World War I. Americans, to a degree, contributed to interest in small, easily deployed, rapidly firing weapons by developing and bringing out the Peterson device. This is a subcaliber insert, used in 1903 bolt-action Springfields firing a short, .30-caliber, pistol-type cartridge. Only six or eight examples of these devices survived at war's end.

As always, technology starts complex, gradually becoming simpler, cheaper and better. John Thompson brought out a beautiful, handcrafted, full-automatic, carbine-type weapon called a Thompson submachine gun in 1919. It was solid, heavy, and reliable but consisted of hundreds of intricate parts.

In 1921 he tried again with a somewhat simpler, less costly, more reliable model. His 1928 model was still complex and expensive but found acceptance in our army, navy, and various police departments. Estimates are that if legally made today, 1928 Thompsons would have to sell for about $2,500 each. But, of course, no one would continue to produce such intricate, hard-to-manufacture weapons today.

My theory is that gangsters picked up on Thompsons because they were fun to shoot and because on full auto with 50- or 100-round magazines, they were fairly easy to learn to shoot reasonably well. Thompsons could be fired semiauto. With locked breeches, long barrels, and heavy weight, accuracy was surprising, somewhat like Heckler & Koch M5s today. Another often overlooked reason why gangsters used Thompsons was because they could afford both gun and ammo with which to practice. Common citizens could do neither.

During the Spanish Civil War, leading up to World War II, considerable work was done designing SMGs assembled with stamped-steel receivers, barrels made on automatic screw machines, folding stocks, and more reliable magazines. Eventually SMGs became very small, handy, light, and cheap. Some were issued with integral silencers, useful for commandos and other special-purpose personnel.

As a result of this cheapening and simplification, SMGs have become extremely inexpensive and relatively easy to construct in a home workshop, should people wish to do so without BATF approval. The most difficult part of modern SMGs is the magazine. Magazines are very tough to make in a home workshop, but most can be purchased inexpensively from surplus and sporting goods outlets.

Given the fact that SMGs are more fun than practical, it is wise for a man of action to ask himself if he is willing to risk having BATF shoot him and his wife and children over something that is basically recreational. Based on recent events, one can easily and validly conclude that members of the BATF are leading the charge into a police state. In most cases, it is probably best to avoid the issue and to find something else to play with. Nevertheless, if one believes the risks are less than the rewards, SMGs are relatively easy to build.

One idea that has faded as the popularity of M1 carbines decreases, and the price for ammo for them increases, is to purchase surplus parts necessary to convert a standard semiauto version to the select-fire M2 version of the carbine. These parts are not as commonly available as they were a few years ago, but they are still out there. Ownership of these parts is prima facie evidence of guilt in the eyes of the BATF.

Probably the easiest submachine gun to build from scratch at this writing is a 9mm Sten gun. All the parts, except the receivers, are commonly available in complete packages from several different suppliers. All you need do is purchase the parts from one supplier and standard steel tubing from another dealer or steel supply house, weld the parts together, and assemble them as required. Study current military weapons reference books to see how simple this is. Stens are so simple that they were made around the world during World War II for as little as $7 each.

Since these volumes are widely circulated among government agencies, it would be foolish to place exact names and addresses where Sten gun parts kits could be purchased. Nevertheless, keep asking around among friends and at gun shows and stay alert to advertisements in gun magazines. Sooner or later an excellent source will surface.

A receiver for a Sten gun is little more than 1-inch steel tubing with several simple slots cut in it. Common pipe will work, but it is more difficult to cut trigger and bolt handle slots in it. Pipe is also much heavier than steel tubing. Steel tubing, in the case of a Sten, can be quite light—only sufficiently thick to weld. Required slots are easily cut with a hacksaw and finished with files.

Great numbers of people sell machinist blueprints of popular-model SMGs. Some of these include wraparound templates for Stens. After gluing the template on the tube, even a klutz could produce a receiver. Using these much more sophisticated machinist drawings, a skilled machinist could either make, or have made, anything from a Thompson to a Schmeisser.

Military Armament Corporation (MAC) SMGs are relatively easy to put together in a home workshop. All parts, including barrel, bolt, and trigger mechanism, are currently available in kit form. Receivers are made out of flat steel sheet. You can either purchase complete prepunched flat receivers that must be bent into a U shape or properly formed receivers that must be drilled. Either way, this is not a tough project, although most people prefer to bend a prepunched flat receiver.

Another option for those wishing to own a working SMG is to modify existing SMG-like weapons. These can be automatic pistols to which foregrips and extended magazines are added or more popular look-alikes.

Great numbers of MAC-10 semiauto guns are floating around that are fairly easy to convert to full auto. You might as well alter the triggers because they are of very little practical value as semiauto pistols. They have gone up in price, but legal, commercially available semiauto Uzis are also available. Shrewd purchasers can find original Uzi parts needed to convert these guns back to full auto. Failing that, you can simply cut the barrel down, machine the breech, and file the trigger.

Although not technically SMGs, both AK-47s

Perhaps in an effort to capture the "assault pistol" market, Israel Military Industries created a pistol version of the Uzi, which is generally encountered only in semiauto form. (Photo courtesy of Action Arms.)

and SKS carbines are easily converted to full auto by changing parts or refining ones currently in your gun. In either case, it's like castrating the tomcat. Once it's done, it's done. The operation cannot be reversed. If one is caught with these weapons or parts, consequences are severe.

My earnest suggestion is not to believe what you see in the movies regarding the effectiveness of SMGs. Find a friend who has a legal model, purchase 500 rounds of ammunition, and fire them through his weapon. My bet is that few readers will take the next step and actually put together a working full-auto SMG, no matter how easy the job.

BIBLIOGRAPHY

Long. Duncan Long. *Assault Pistols, Rifles and Submachine Guns.* Boulder, CO: Paladin Press, 1986.

Taylor, Chuck. *The Combat Shotgun and Submachine Gun.* Boulder, CO: Paladin Press, 1984.

Switchblade Knives

5

Readers may question inclusion of switchblade knives in a book with heavy weapons that initially seem to be far more lethal. Are switchblades as deadly as claymores, assault shotguns, or a batch of high explosives?

The real answer is that they may be. It all depends on the circumstances. Rifles are not the same as pistols, and mines are not the same as night vision devices. Switchblades are a surprisingly silent, deadly tool when used by skilled practitioners. As is true with all implements used by men of action, skill provides the final advantage.

I am not alone in my belief that a properly deployed switchblade is an extremely lethal weapon. Since *Switchblade: The Ace of Blades* came out, dozens of readers have taken the time to write, agreeing with me that automatic knives are both practical and lethal. The problem with switchblades is that most men in our culture have had extremely limited contact with them. When they have used

them, they tend to be elcheapo models from south of the border. It is the same as if one got his knowledge about pistol accuracy and function from zip guns built with car antennas and door bolts.

Inner-city hoods who grew up in the 1950s recall switchblades with some nostalgia. They were a kind of symbol of manhood back then. Not much utilitarian function, just symbolic. This is probably one reason the U.S. media jumped on the bandwagon in opposition to switchblades.

During the 1950s, shrill propaganda-type articles with little factual basis ran in endless succession, claiming switchblades were responsible for countless children's deaths. If switchblades were banned, inner-city gangs would collapse and cease to function, and crime would suddenly atrophy and die, the critics claimed.

Politicians, being the thieves and criminals they really are, are disinclined to allow such a bandwagon to move very far without a leader. Estes Kefauver, the coonskin-capped senator from Tennessee, saw his chance and seized it. In 1957 he

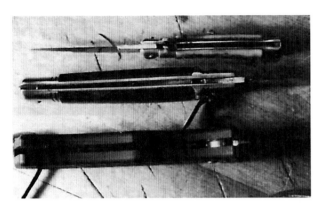

Swithcblades have a variety of uses for the man of action. (Photo by Ragnar Benson.)

introduced a bill to prohibit interstate commerce in switchblades. But because Senator Kefauver's star was waning and he was increasingly seen as something of a nut, the U.S. Senate told him, as only U.S. senators can, to take his bill and stuff it!

Next session, the same prohibitionists took a different approach to getting their antiswitchblade bill passed. Representative Mack from Illinois, where gang warfare no doubt ran rampant, introduced the measure in the House of Representatives. It passed against the recommendation of the Department of Justice. On July 31, 1958, the U.S. Senate also confirmed the bill.

In retrospect, it seems obvious that switchblade knives became illegal because they had no constituency. No punks were willing to travel to Washington, D.C., in support of these knives, and who would have listened to them anyway? Honest, hard-working farmers, mechanics, and loggers were not available to say that "switches" were practical, useful knives that are a great asset in emergencies and that politicians should not outlaw them. Some U.S. knife companies made and profitably sold modest numbers of switchblades, but probably validly reasoned that people who could no longer own switches would simply purchase some other kind of knife from the companies' large selections. They basically stood in silence as another freedom was lost.

Switchblades slipped into oblivion, and no one who mattered really cared. In 1968–70, bills to greatly strengthen and expand switchblade law were introduced in the U.S. House of Representatives. In a rare display of honesty and wisdom, House members agreed that the 1958 bill had done no good and voted the additional measure down.

Unfortunately, today, even collectors and people who could be greatly assisted by them in their work seldom see and virtually never actually use switches. It's about like outlawing long-handled screwdrivers because someone might poke an eye out.

I cannot remember exactly when we first started using switches on the farm. It seems as though one of us kids (probably not me) saw them in action and immediately recognized their utility. Switchblades are especially useful while making hay, when a one-handed knife is *really* handy. In one instance, I saved the fingers on my right hand, which were stuck in a combine belt, by instantly opening my knife and cutting the belt. Without that switch, I would now be writing with my left hand.

In addition to federal law making transportation of any self-opening knife between states illegal, ownership of switchblades is also regulated by various states. Ownership in the various states ranges from absolutely forbidden to absolutely permitted. Federal and state prosecution through the years has been light and spotty. A handful of dealers have been prosecuted for movement of switches across state lines, and some importers have been similarly nabbed in what seems like arbitrary enforcement proceedings. As a rule, any prosecution for switches is undertaken in conjunction with multiple offenses such as the possession of switchblades with drug, illegal firearms, resisting arrest, or transportation of stolen goods charges. Most federal cases are initiated by the U.S. Customs Service.

Generalizing, one can say that switches are not prima facie illegal, for which prosecution will certainly follow, and that—legal or illegal—they are an extremely practical tool.

They are also one of the most dangerous weapons you are ever likely to encounter. Victims of a well-done switchblade attack are completely unaware that their assailant even has a weapon till it is much too late. Switches are very easy to hide and as silent as poison.

Switches have, in the past, been issued to U.S. paratroopers, Special Forces, and special-assignment soldiers, including SEALs and Marine Corps reconnaissance teams. They are even rumored to have been issued by our CIA. German military pilots and paratroopers are commonly issued switches, generally of excellent quality.

It hasn't been fully tested in court, but most switchblade makers automatically assume that all military and police personnel are exempt under the law. A fairly brisk business has developed selling switches to military and police personnel regardless of the intended end use. The fact that these various professional agencies have opted to use fast, safe, convenient, and often discreet one-handed knives speaks well for the design's basic utility.

Some especially skilled readers could probably build acceptable, reliable switches, but times are changing. This is no longer necessary. Oregon's Supreme Court has ruled that ownership, including manufacture, of switches is guaranteed by that state's constitution. Several custom and limited-production switch makers have set up shop there. Most significantly, these makers have done two things that make ownership of a good, high-quality switch reasonably easy, provided one has the necessary cash.

First, they sell completed, ready-to-go knives to virtually any military or police personnel. Simply send a photocopy of an official military ID along with a check and back comes a beautiful, immediately functional switch. These days, almost everyone can find someone in the armed forces who will do the deal for them. Even Coast Guard personnel can order these knives.

Second, modern makers have perfected some absolutely genius-class designs that can be legally shipped to anyone. They come without springs installed but can be easily activated using either common, locally purchased springs or ones sent by the maker under separate cover.

As a result virtually anyone can own a good-quality springer. Local laws do not apply till the activating spring is actually installed. Federal law is not broken, because the original writers of the law made a great to do about the fact that common folding knives are not covered—only "gangster-type switchblades." Perhaps the only real downside of all of this is the fact that all these knives are expensive, being custom built a few at a time. No knives or parts can be imported from places where labor is cheap. Yet switchblade sales in the United States, even in the "bad old days," were never very large. Apparently, what we now see is a pent-up demand slowly built during the time when switches were illegal.

Custom makers such as Butch Vallotton (621 Fawn Ridge Drive, Oakland, OR 97462) make knives of their own design in small batches. They do not use large, cost-cutting automated equipment, useful if they were turning out knives by the tens of thousands. Models are pricey to extremely pricey, ranging from about $50 to $800 in some cases. To further complicate matters, most people—even if they can't afford it—genuinely feel that a Vallotton knife at $800 is well worth the price in practical day-to-day utility. It's unfortunate when one must admit that "yes, the knife is very expensive; I can't afford it, but it's worth every penny."

At the other end of the country, Ralph Harris (Box 597, Grovetown, GA 30813) is also making some nice utility switches that are generally priced a bit lower than Vallotton's. Harris knives are also shipped in two parcels with easily installed separate springs. They are also of high quality but perhaps are more suited to camping, fishing, and hunting.

In Germany, springers are commonly available in most sporting goods and knife shops, in spite of the fact that official paranoia regarding firearms is quite high. One particularly heavy, well-made model with a wide blade, generous handle, and stout spring is designed specifically for farmers. German knife store clerks claim this is a popular model in spite of its almost $70 price tag.

"Farmers need this model for daily chores," they say. This model must actually have great value for farmers to spend such a princely sum on something that casual observers would say is little more than a clasp knife. Demand there among those definitely inoffensive rural people who know about switches is probably as great as it is currently in the entire United States.

The Edge Company (Box 826, Brattleboro, VT 05301) has been the U.S. leader in getting popularly priced switches into people's hands. From time to time, it offers completed kits, butterfly knives, disassembled switches, and fully assembled copies of old stilettos somehow delivered right to one's doorstep.

Some of its models, such as the front-opening NATO at about $14.95, are certifiable junk. Others, including side-openers, farmers' knives, hunters' models, and catch/release knives running from $19.95 to $139, are really very good. Generally, those offered as military or general-purpose knives are better than the older classic model Italian stilettos some of us knew as kids.

Not all Edge Company models are available all the time. Edge seems to cycle in and out of the picture as a switchblade supplier.

Switches require a good deal more maintenance than standard knives. Owners must use gun cleaner to swab out between the bolsters and a drop of light oil on the blade swivel and switch about twice a year.

Switches do a great deal more for their owners. In that regard, price is not always the best criterion. Switches in general will always be more expensive than regular knives, and, thus, people will usually get what they pay for. Men of action are well advised to purchase the best switch they can afford and then see firsthand for themselves if this type of knife is as good as many believe it is.

In closing this somewhat obscure subject, I recall the quote from Art Krom, a genuine duck-tailed greaser who now drives a truck for a living, but still wears a black horsehide jacket. Art has cut several people in his life and recommends that "you keep your switch hidden in your hand while deciding if you are going to use it. When you do [use it], snap it open and strike instantly. Usually the guy will get his arm up, and you give him a bad cut on the arm or shoulder. Then you can decide if you want to cut him more. Done right, switches are always very surprising," he claims.

BIBLIOGRAPHY

Benson, Ragnar. *Switchblade: The Ace of Blades*. Boulder, CO: Paladin Press, 1989.

CHAPTER

Bulletproof Vests

6

As with most gun nuts, my interest in and contact with ballistic vests has cycled in and out since they were first developed in 1972. Before that time, true, light, concealable vests that would actually turn or catch a pistol round were mostly a pipe dream. My first real field experience occurred in the early 1980s.

Several of us, including some close business associates, wore them during a kind of award ceremony in the South Philippines at a time when we were reliably informed that the Muslim National Liberation Front would attempt to embarrass the Ferdinand Marcos regime by mounting an attack. It was at a time when virtually no outsider ventured to the island of Mindanao in the Philippines.

The vests, made of modern Kevlar fiber, were extremely hot, heavy, and cumbersome. We sweated profusely. Risks in this case were virtually not worth the burden. However, their use allowed us to appear openly in the public, giving great support for work being done there. It was perhaps one of the first uses by private citizens for which I would like to thank Clinton Davis, president of Second Chance. We are still appreciative that he bent the rules regarding sales to business executives.

It wasn't till after probably five different sales to various business executives that I deciphered the welter of often confusing standards, models, and configurations in which ballistic vests are offered. Liability concerns, custom of the trade, and plain, old writing skill problems obscure what should be a clear, easy understanding of performance levels one can expect from various grades of ballistic vests.

It is often said that "no gun made can shoot through a bale of cotton." The same is not true for "bulletproof" vests. Even bulky, heavy vests with extra titanium plates can be defeated by some firearms. On the other hand, these vests will always stop all rounds from some weapons. Like most physical realities, heavier, denser vests (that are more uncomfortable to wear) stop larger, harder, faster rounds.

The National Institute of Standards and Technology (the former National Bureau of Standards) and the National Institute of Law Enforcement and Criminal Justice have established standards for modern body armor. Their standards include identification of threat levels. These threat levels are often seen as contradictory and overlapping. The range of vest protection is Threat I through IV, with two "A" designations, IIA and IIIA. In both cases, A signifies a level less than the full number.

Briefly the threat levels run as follows:

- Threat Level Four (IV) will catch a .30-06 armor-piercing round, or anything smaller, fired at 2,850 fps from 100 meters. More like packs than vests, these units are designed for military and SWAT units. Many layers of Kevlar material overlapped by ballistic plates provide strength and density.

  Ballistic plates are usually fabricated from titanium and are placed only at the front of the vest. Weight per unit, assuming only frontal protection, is about 28 pounds! The angle at which a round strikes a vest greatly influences penetration. Surprisingly enough, angled rounds tend to penetrate greater distances, causing more damage.

  Even at this relatively heavy weight, these are remarkable units. Although defined by a .30-06 armor-piercing round, they will also catch 7.62x39 armor-piercing rounds, .375 H&H hunting rounds, and .300 Win Mag rounds, all at 100 meters. This performance is absolutely astounding by World War II or Korean-era standards.

- Threat Level Three (III) body armor will reliably turn a 7.62 NATO round with full-metal jacket fired at 2,750 fps from 100 meters. These models must also have titanium plates covering the Kevlar, but this is the last threat level requiring ballistic plates. Any given vest in this "traditional" category can be either Threat III or IV, depending on how many additional plates are installed in the unit pockets.

  Some manufacturers offer hard plates made of special, high-impact ceramic material rather than laminated titanium alloy. But ceramics may fracture like glass when hit. Should a second round find basically the same spot, it may

actually penetrate. Rough handling of the type common in military situations may also damage ceramic ballistic plates.

Threat III and IV units are called tactical vests because of their weight and the fact that ballistic plates are deployed.

- Threat Level Three A (IIIA in the trade) is the highest threat level ballistic soft vest that is made entirely of Kevlar and is concealable under normal street clothes. These are maximum security vests made for everyday use—if one is a guard or a cop. Level IIIA vests stop .44 mag lead bullets fired at 1,400 fps and high-velocity FMJ 9mm (1,400 fps) rounds fired point blank. This level provides protection from all common handguns but virtually no rifles.

  Even .22 rimfire magnum rounds can be made to penetrate most Kevlar soft vests by coating them with spray-on Teflon or firing them at close range from rifles. No ballistic vest is absolutely secure at any given range. Steps can always be taken to defeat them.

  Threat IIIA is currently the most popular vest. As technology improves and they become lighter, more of this model will undoubtedly be deployed.

- Threat Level Two (II) vests catch high-velocity .357s and medium-velocity (1,175 fps) 9mm bullets. Many police users prefer this vest because of its lighter weight. Threat Level II vests weigh about 3.5 pounds as compared to IIIA vests weighing in at about 5 pounds. To some extent, weight depends on the size required to cover one's frame and the degree of wraparound side protection chosen.

Two additional lesser threat level ballistic vests are also sold: Threat Level One (I) and Two A (IIA). Their protection is comparatively limited today, though originally they were far superior to absolutely anything else. They are much lighter and cheaper than heavier vests but are now virtually obsolete. Any vest will protect from shotguns except at extremely close ranges. Even a load of 00 buckshot at 40 feet will be turned by a Threat I vest. Threat I vests turn lead round-nose bullets from .38 Specials. Threat IIA vests are designed to handle low-velocity .357s (1,250 fps) and low-velocity 9mms (1,090 fps).

The trend at this writing is to go to even higher threat levels due to increased use of 9mm pistols in

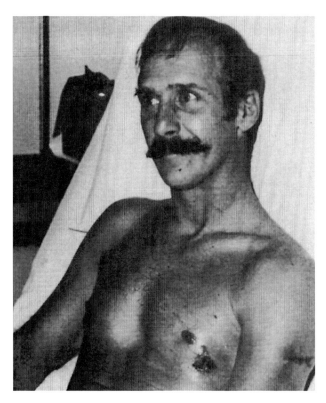

Blunt trauma created by bullets is not too great a problem, provided that the protection level of the vest is adequate. Officer Steve Gazdik was shot twice in the chest with a .357 Magnum fired from 1 inch and 4 inches; his Second Chance vest stopped both bullets. A third shot grazed his left arm. (Photos from *Modern Ballistic Armor* by Duncan Long. This one is courtesy of Second Chance Body Armor, Inc.)

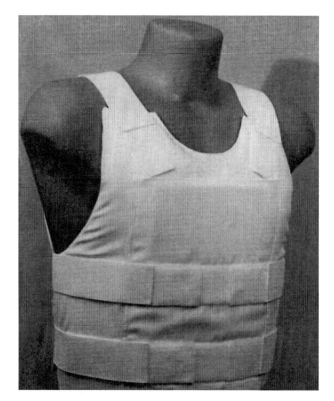

Many manufacturers have done a good job of offering a wide variety of styles and sizes of ballistic vests for both men and women. Many models are also adjustable through the use of Velcro connectors and straps that hold the vest tightly in place. (Photo courtesy of Second Chance Body Armor, Inc.)

the United States. Penetration by 9mm rounds is better than most revolver rounds. Initially, Threat I vests were considered adequate, but as people upgraded their firepower, vest users found they had to ratchet up their protection.

Reportedly, European offices have used heavier ballistic vests for a number of years due to the more common use of 9mm bullets and their increased penetration. All suppliers of vests caution that if an assailant sees that an officer is wearing a ballistic vest, he will try for a head shot. Recently, there have been a number of attacks on officers in California characterized by head and neck wounds, many of which were fatal. Apparently, the word on the street is to now shoot for the head if one is serious about taking out a police officer.

Rounds fired from pistols are notoriously inaccurate, especially when discharged under stress by people who believe marksmanship is part of

manhood. Although vests protect the center of mass nicely, a round can still be caught in the femoral artery in the thigh or the brachial artery in the the arm, causing rapid death. One can never predict random occurrences. In one case, a vest protected an officer from being gored by an angry bull. But, in general, one is wise to assure only limited protection against knife threats and attacks with various pointed objects such as ice picks and screwdrivers.

All modern vests are constructed using at least some amount of Kevlar fabric, which is freakishly remarkable for its high strength. DuPont discovered and began marketing the fabric in 1972. It is high tech at its finest.

Kevlar is five times stronger than an equal weight of steel. Used not only in ballistic vests, it is found increasingly in radial tires, rubber gloves, condoms, gaskets, tape, and in many aircraft, automotive, and aerospace applications. When used

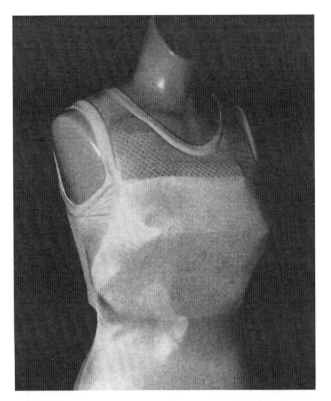

Lightweight and form fitting, this vest gives a high level of protection without calling attention to itself. (Photo courtesy of Second Chance Body Armor, Inc.)

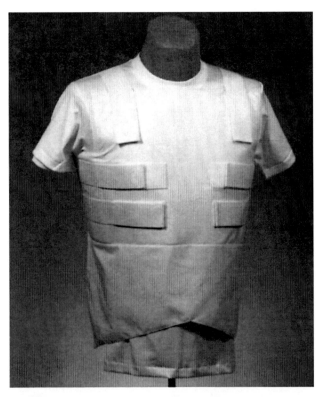

Silent Partner's "Traditional" vest, like those of many other manufacturers, uses adjustable straps with Velcro connectors to hold the vest tightly in place. (Photo courtesy of Silent Partner.)

in vests, it is tightly layered from eight to 25 times, depending on threat level. About 45 million pounds of Kevlar are sold worldwide annually.

When soft body armor made of Kevlar is hit by a bullet, fibers in the dense weave distribute the impact, thereby dispersing energy to other fibers in the weave. Bullets are flattened and disfigured by the dense material.

A boyhood buddy was a helicopter pilot on duty in Vietnam when Kevlar first came on the market. I came to believe that he could really benefit from this technology and spent lots of time and money trying to "track" it down. Initially, both manufacturers of Kevlar and fabricators of vests were difficult to discover. I spent hundreds of dollars calling around trying to find just one square yard of material to send to Vietnam for my friend to sit on. At last I found a manufacturer in Spokane, Washington, who had hundreds of Kevlar remnants left from some sort of manufacturing process.

Wild rumors regarding the material's abilities floated about like Kansas wheat chaff in a summer dust devil. We were initially led to believe that Kevlar was made from microscopic sapphire fibers and that a light triple layer would stop a .50-caliber round at 500 yards, but that a blunt trauma wound would likely be fatal. Rumors still circulate regarding blunt trauma and Kevlar. As the story goes, being hit solidly on a vest by a round from a large-bore firearm, such as a .44 mag, could cause victims to die of internal shock from squashed innards. Yet incident after incident has proven that human bodies protected by Kevlar will be bruised a bit by stopped rounds, but no one has yet been killed or seriously hurt by blunt trauma. Hundreds of ballistic vest "saves" are used to make that evaluation. Theoretically, a hard blow over the heart could kill, but so far this has not happened to anyone wearing a ballistic vest.

Kevlar vests do have a couple of weaknesses. First, vests soaked in a pouring rain or dunked in a puddle will lose 40 percent of their bullet-stopping power; however, normal body sweat is not sufficient to cause this. Gentle, slow, complete drying restores

This ordinary-looking nylon jacket contains ballistic panels that make it into a practical ballistic vest. It comes in a variety of colors. (Photo courtesy of Second Chance Body Armor, Inc.)

the vest to its full stopping capability. Second, over time (about five years), ultraviolet light will deteriorate and ruin Kevlar. Many vests purchased for police department use some years ago are now being replaced because of this deterioration.

Cost of maximum-coverage vests with good side panels ranges from about $400 for Threat Level II to about $550 for a Threat Level IIIA. At times, it is difficult for ordinary nonmilitary, nonpolice people with otherwise excellent references and personal history to buy ballistic vests. However, based on my experience purchasing them for business people, those who are persistent can be successful.

Manufacturers to try include the following:

American Body Armor
135 North New York Ave.
Halestie, NY 11743

Armour of America
P.O. Box 1405
Beverly Hills, CA 90213

Blauer Mfg. Co., Inc.
20 Aberdeen Street
Boston, MA 02215

Davis Company
3942 Trust Way
Hayward, CA 94545

DuPont Company/Textile Fibers
Department/Kevlar
Center Road Bldg.
Wilmington, DE 19818

Point Blank Body Armor
55 St. Mary's Pl.
Freeport, NY 11525

Protective Materials Co.
Folly Mill Road
Seabrook, NY 03874

Rhino Armor
18430 Ward Street
Fountain Valley, CA

Safariland Ballistics
1941 S. Walker Ave.
Monrovia, CA 91016

Second Chance Body Armor, Inc.
Box 578
Central Lake, MI 49622

Silent Partner, Inc.
612-618 Third Street
Gretna, LA 70053

What is the future for ballistic vests? One does not have to be much of a prophet to predict lighter and stronger! Based on past history, one can only wonder when the point of diminishing returns will be reached, but even with today's technology, bulk and weight of basic Kevlar fabric have again been significantly cut. DuPont's new Kevlar is approximately half the bulk, and unit for unit is 15 percent stronger than older Kevlar, which admittedly was in a class all by itself.

Users of new model vests can now upgrade to Level IIIA protection with no obvious increase in bulk or detectability.

Whenever people use ballistic vests, it should not be a substitute for doing their homework. People can still be hurt or killed quite easily while wearing them. Ballistic vests are, however, remarkable in terms of the level of protection they afford. Certainly, they are far superior to the magic bracelets worn by Sudanese as they charged British Field Marshal Kitchener's positions at Omdurman or the kapok-filled sacks issued to Russian soldiers in Afghanistan for psychological reasons.

BIBLIOGRAPHY

Long, Duncan. *Modern Ballistic Armor.* Boulder, CO: Paladin Press, 1986.

CHAPTER

Night Vision Devices

7

I had never paid an inordinate amount of attention to night vision devices (NVDs). Like light switches, they were just around to use without my giving them much thought. My family has had them around off and on since the early 1980s when they first became available on the civilian market. In that regard, I was simply the product of a generation that takes miracles for granted.

My real awakening to the incredible technology that NVDs concentrate occurred recently when my 81-year-old immigrant mother tied on a pair of goggles and went for a walk. Even in her very arthritic condition, in the black of blackest night, she was easily able to navigate mountainous terrain around our home. Had the batteries on the device expired, she would have had to sit down and call for help, it was so dark.

Here was an old lady who had already seen it all in her lifetime. But she walked round and round for perhaps an hour muttering to herself: "Are these ever something." It occurred to me then that we

have at hand a new wonder, on a par with the invention of dynamite, cartridge firearms, or even smokeless powder, with which to contend. It is very difficult at this time to perceive where the ability to see at night will eventually take us. It's like Eskimos of the North Slope who live 300 miles from the nearest tree. Without seeing the tree, it's hard to believe.

Modern passive NVDs almost defy description. They are absolutely, completely remarkable and, unfortunately, worth every last penny you might have to pay for them in today's admittedly pricey market. They are the man of action's last "get out of jail" card, a great equalizer that is absolutely necessary in his arsenal. I have come around to seeing no alternative but for men of action to have at least a passive night vision scope in their possession—in spite of the fact that many models can run $6,000 or more.

Night vision actually started with research done at Radio Corporation of America in the mid- to late-1930s, when television image tubes were developed

The Dark Invader Night Vision System is a high-performance, second-generation night vision device that can be connected to most weapons to provide a 70,000X-light-gain, high-resolution image. (Photo courtesy of B.E. Meyers & Co., Inc.)

that could be used to convert infrared (heat) images to a TV display.

Work continued with more enthusiasm after the outbreak of World War II and the involvement of the United States in 1941. By 1944, technicians at the U.S. Army Engineering Board at Fort Belvoir, Virginia, were able to fashion a crude arrangement consisting of an electronic telescope linked with an infrared, sealed-beam light source. Using some Rube Goldberg techniques, they attached the entire mess to an M1 .30-caliber carbine. Common, lead-acid batteries used to power the contraption were carried in a small backpack.

The maximum range of the device was only 100 feet, if winds were favorable. Yet it was the first U.S. device to allow one to see in total darkness. The greatest immediate challenge was linking it to a rifle and making the device portable. Wires, heavy fixtures, sockets, and fragile glass were hung about in a precarious manner. Theoreticians didn't even try to mount these units on a Garand because the package was too heavy to hold.

Prototype models sent to various subcontractors under a "secret" classification were improved, simplified, and hardened to the rigors of field use.

Bell & Howell did extensive testing and discovered that about 90 percent of the devices would not survive a shock and function test. A great deal of additional work was done modifying and improving the tubes on which these devices depended. Mounts were made for M1 carbines that allowed better, more secure, and faster coupling. Carbines modified for

special infrared use were called T-3s. The completed package was still very ungainly.

These new field-ready devices were called M2 Sniper Scopes, something of a misnomer since they were far too limited for actual sniping. Eventually, sufficient numbers of these units were sent out to influence action on Okinawa and the Philippines. Users reported greenish, ghostly images and that the invisible light produced maddening shadows, but they were still able to produce about 30 percent of the total Japanese casualties inflicted by small-arms fire during the first seven days of the Okinawa Campaign. Only roughly 200 of the 2,000 devices produced were ever actually pressed into action against the Japanese.

Japanese technicians and commanders knew that infrared sniper scopes existed and were being deployed against them, but they were basically helpless to do anything about them. Highly trained infiltrators who had previously been successful were mysteriously shot down in front of U.S. lines by the score.

American use of night vision infrared technology was limited in the European theater. German scientists had been working energetically on portable infrared units since early 1943. A few units were deployed, affixed to MP-43 assault rifles, but generally German tacticians viewed infrared technology as useful only on tanks or trucks, allowing operation at night.

In anticipation of Allied use of infrared sights, Germany produced a cheap, little paper tube device

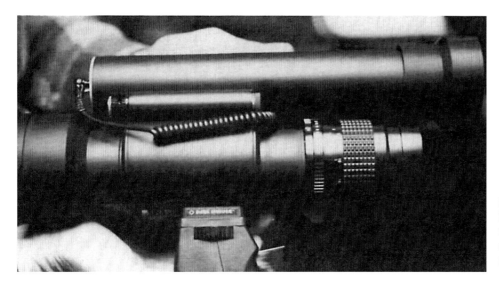

Night vision device with an infared auxillary setup being used as a hand-held observation device. (Photo by Ragnar Benson.)

that could be used to detect infrared light, even allowing users to pinpoint its source. In this regard, the Germans were slightly ahead of their time. When infrared night vision passed from the scene, it was, in part, because enemy detection devices could quickly and easily locate users. Fire could then be directed onto the infrared light owner who foolishly exposed his position.

Some—but not much—work continued on night vision after the war. Most was directed at active-type units that projected a beam visible only to users of the secret viewing scope. Korea was initially fought with existing supplies of World War II arms, including tanks, small arms, and night vision.

A crash program was started, resulting in the last and presumably best infrared NVD, called the M3. It was a 20,000-volt model with portable, rechargeable battery pack. M3s were much more rugged than any predecessor and were useful out to about 200 meters. This same type of basic unit was used extensively by the Israeli army.

By this time, any warring soldier using infrared night vision always looked through the scope first for other infrared light before turning his unit on! Unlike GIs in the South Pacific, grunts in Korea did not like their infrared devices. "Too bulky, short-lived, limited, and subject to hostile fire," they claimed.

M3 units were initially pressed into service in Vietnam in the early 1960s. Their range in the jungle and high grass with fresh batteries was estimated to be about 400 feet. Tropical foliage, grass, and trees

tended to restrict effective use. Our troops were well aware that Russian-supplied infrared equipment could turn them into instant targets.

Demand for something better was always there, and in 1955 technology had again taken a quantum leap. Technicians at the Army Warfare Vision Unit began work on a totally passive system relying completely on existing light, rather than on any kind of projected artificial light to operate. By 1957, work was sufficiently advanced on a two-stage cascade image-intensifier tube to construct several prototypes. These early units were sufficiently encouraging that contracts for further engineering design were awarded to Bell & Howell in 1962.

Bell & Howell made enough progress so that first production contracts could be awarded in 1964. Ironically, Xerox was the best bidder, securing this first work on passive NVDs. Progress then was rapid. By 1967, several different companies were producing Starlight scopes for our forces in Vietnam. As is often true with quantum leaps in technology, results in the field were initially excellent.

Only the most senior combat personnel were first trusted with Starlight scopes. Strictest orders were given to shoot them through the tube, crush them under a truck, or destroy them with a termite grenade if their loss or capture seemed imminent.

It is with horribly bittersweet feelings that I recall the young Israeli captain who saw himself about to become a captive or casualty on the Golan Heights. Before the man was killed, he used his last

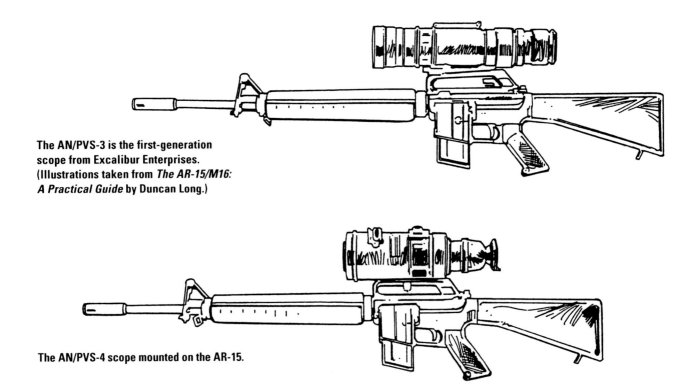

The AN/PVS-3 is the first-generation
scope from Excalibur Enterprises.
(Illustrations taken from *The AR-15/M16:
A Practical Guide* by Duncan Long.)

The AN/PVS-4 scope mounted on the AR-15.

two .45 rounds to blow his precious Starlight telescope to pieces. He gave his life to protect a device that now virtually anyone with the relatively low price of admission can own.

First-generation Starlight devices used three-stage light intensifiers. What little natural light is available strikes a bundle of millions of fiber-optic strands, bringing it into an electronic tube where the light strikes a photoemissive surface. Electrons are then discharged into a vacuum, where they are energized by 15,000 volts of electricity. They go on, eventually striking a screen similar to a TV tube. Image intensification of these early, first-generation models was about 40,000 times what one could see with the unaided eye.

These units emitted no light other than a very faint light deep within the tube itself. Early designers were aware that infrared or other passive devices might pick this light up. They designed a butterfly orifice held open by pressure against the user's eye socket. Range was about 200 yards. Magnification on rifle scopes was four power (4X). Weight was about 5 pounds, and the scopes went about 100 hours on a set of AA batteries. Limitations included the fact that some ambient light from some source, no matter how subdued, had

to be present. Users are often surprised that moonlight creates deep shadows. Fog, smoke, and dust can severely reduce effective range.

Intermittent, inadvertent bright light was the most severe problem: when a sudden pinpoint of light hit the scope, a bubble-like apparition appeared that, like a little balloon, slowly drifted off the scope. Really bright lights damaged early models, so automatic shutoffs were installed that protected the unit from this light. First-time purchasers must ask about this feature. A few models currently for sale don't have this essential safety switch.

Second-generation night vision generally operates on a much more efficient two-stage intensifier. These units may not "see" as much in very dark conditions but generally have better optics, thus allowing one to see just as far. Ballooning is not a problem on most second-generation equipment, and maintenance seems to be minimal compared to the first-generation units. Weight is less than 4 pounds.

First-generation U.S. military night vision scopes were designated AN/PVS-1 (Army-Navy/Portable Visible-Light Detection Series 1; first model fielded). An AN/PVS-2 and 2B came later. These were improved first-generation models. Users today seem to favor the AN/PVS-2B because of its internal strength, durability, and ability to intensify available light. Cost at about $1,500 is significantly less than that for second-generation night vision.

It is unclear whether an AN/PVS-3 model was ever built, but there is an AN/PVS-4, which is the current favorite among commercial second-generation users. Because of their high profile and price (about double that for first-generation U.S. equipment) some users prefer older models. The cost of an AN/PVS-4 unit is about $3,000.

The concept of using night vision binoculars is extremely appealing. Potential owners correctly reason that binoculars would be more universally useful than a simple rifle scope or goggles that do not magnify. This concept is excellent, but execution must wait for technology to catch up. Currently, Starlight binoculars exceed the financial capacity of even those with unlimited budgets. Technological problems in matching magnification and light intensification are just too costly to resolve at this time.

Tank drivers and pilots, among others, use a zero-magnification goggle labeled an NVG-500. These provide excellent general nonmagnified night vision for only $6,000 per pair!

NVG-500s are second-generation models with 60,000–80,000 light multiplication. They weigh about 4 pounds, are fairly comfortable to wear, and, most important, provide users with three-dimensional vision. One can walk the darkest trails with these devices. There is, however, a kind of strange psychological phenomenon caused by the eerie green light: grotesque shadows are compounded by fatigue after using the device for any length of time without prior conditioning. In a plane cockpit, control lights are often too bright and perhaps too close to be seen through these goggles.

Using the NVG-500 to drive down a mountain road is a bit risky. Oncoming vehicle lights are observable at great distances, but if you should encounter oncoming lights suddenly, the result could be disastrous. Any other drivers on the road will be discomfited by a vehicle driving without lights.

It is possible (but clumsy) to use night vision goggles with conventional scopes and binoculars, but not with conventional sights on rifles or pistols. Laser sights function to astronomical ranges with night vision goggles, but most users do not have

their lasers sighted into the great ranges possible with goggles.

At this time, a great number of different makes and models of Russian NVDs are flooding into this country. Generally, these models sell at bargain prices as compared to those of U.S. models. Yet proceed cautiously. Users report that some Russian models provide no greater light intensification than good-quality optical binoculars or scopes. General agreement exists that Russian equipment is not nearly as rugged as standard U.S. models, and repairs are apparently virtually impossible. Certain models of Soviet-made NVDs are being stopped by Customs because of radiation emissions. On the other hand, major distributors of U.S. military NVDs offer excellent in-house repair service.

Volumes could be written about the problems of sighting in newly mounted night vision scopes, which cannot be used other than in darkened conditions. Conventional spotting scopes won't work to register rounds, and past 25 yards it is sometimes even difficult to find one's target. Some experienced users have good luck shooting at a sheet of heavy steel, watching for the flash of the bullet striking. Plan to use lots of patience and ammunition before the job is done.

Early night vision scopes were tough to mount on rifles other than AR-15s. Later AN/PVS-4s are much easier, but ask first about mounting one to your specific rifle before plunking down a couple of grand.

I wish it were otherwise, but hunting with night vision is not as effective as one would hope. Hunters are used to observing game peripherally, which is impossible with night vision. You must swing either a scope or goggles continually from side to side in trying to locate game. Animals, on the other hand, naturally see well in the dark without night vision. They will quickly pick up the hunter in their peripheral vision as he moves about. Also, your vision into shadows at extended ranges is often marginal. A deer or coyote can be standing or watching without a hunter using night vision ever being aware of it.

In military situations, camouflage clothing is now used along with special infiltration tactics to allow a person to sneak up quite close to sentries who are using night vision. Essentially, this is a two-step process.

Using night vision themselves, infiltrators pinpoint opposing sentries. Wearing specially made green and gray infrared-absorbing camouflage, they move in very slowly through shadows till they are close to their target. Special camouflage helps, but sheer patience and knowledge of how night vision works are of more value.

The most successful battlefield deployment of night vision occurred in the Falkland Islands. British units landed at remote, uncontested places to minimize losses from coming in over the surf and from Argentine aircraft. Using night vision almost universally, the British were able to use dramatic forced marches to close on Argentine conscripts in unexpected places from unexpected directions at unexpected speed. British soldiers proved that wars will no longer be fought without night vision; the Argentine side demonstrated that troops with few or inferior NVDs do not stand a chance.

What's next for night vision technology? Most knowledgeable people do not expect another quantum leap. Prices may come down a bit, reliability may go up, and range may be extended. But even this is a question relative to current, reliable, well-built models. We are absolutely certain that infiltration tactics used so successfully by the Japanese and the Vietnamese early in their wars will never again be effective. For a time, NVDs may provide an edge to those wishing to defend themselves against intruders. Wise men of action must become familiar with night vision because there is no alternative. But this can be a problem because reliable units are so pricey.

BIBLIOGRAPHY

Benson, Ragnar. *Hard-Core Poaching*. Boulder, CO: Paladin Press, 1987.

Long, Duncan. *The AR-15/M16: A Practical Guide*. Boulder, CO: Paladin Press, 1985.

Senich, Peter R. *The Complete Book of U.S. Sniping*. Boulder, CO: Paladin Press, 1988.

CHAPTER

AR-15 Models and Development

8

Ask most American gun nuts which firearms design had the most influence on the history of weapons development and they will probably be stumped for an answer. We are just too close culturally and historically to the issue to evaluate it fairly. Some knowledgeable people might nominate the AK-47 because of the quantity manufactured and the number of armies that have used it.

Although the pieces of this puzzle are only now falling into place, it is not too early to project that the "honor" of being the most influential firearms design in history so far goes to our plain, old, garden-variety AR-15 rifle. No other single weapon in history has had such a profound influence on history and on the conduct of warfare.

Even semitrained soldiers using AR-15-type weapons can—according to experts—deliver at squad level as much accurate, directed fire as could a full company of their counterparts in World Wars I

and II. Those who have supposed that AKs were better weapons should keep in mind that the old Soviet Union was in the process of switching over to an AR-15-like weapon with high-tech, stamped parts and high-velocity .22 ammunition when it collapsed. And as Charles Caleb Colton said: "Imitation is the sincerest form of flattery."

AR-15 weapons systems have proven superior as a result of dramatic human ingenuity cross-pollinated with a profit-seeking, free enterprise system. One could validly argue that this happy circumstance will never be repeated in our society. Increasingly restrictive gun laws along with social policies hamstringing the startup of any new type of enterprise almost certainly preclude other new Sam Colts, John Brownings, or Gene Stoners from displaying their genius. People such as these would be seen as social misfits and likely subjected to immediate punitive action by the BATF.

Unlike previous weapons systems, AR-15s, once produced, are around for a long, long time. Some AR-15 owners can document having put

An early Armalite AR-10. (Illustrations taken from *AR-15/M16 Super Systems* by Duncan Long.)

100,000 rounds through their weapons since their purchase from Colt in 1963 when these weapons first came on the civilian market. Since patent rights on AR-15s have expired, numerous private and governmental makers around the world have created their own version of the weapon. Including parts and aftermarket suppliers, makers of AR-15s number in the hundreds.

Development of the AR series of weapons started in the United States in the early 1950s at the Armalite Division of Fairchild Engines and Airplane Corporation. This was a company expressly formed by U.S. investors with the intention of developing and marketing new firearm designs produced through ultramodern manufacturing techniques and materials. Products and concepts of this fortunate union of capital and technology will dominate the industry for the foreseeable future.

One of Armalite's first commercial weapons was the AR-10, a space-age weapon built on designs first tried out by Germany during World War II. Although never a roaring success, this weapon is familiar to collectors. The first AR-10s used .30-06 rounds. Later, they were switched over to .308 Winchester ammo. Colt bought, produced, and marketed firearms of this design, but other than a few insignificant sales, production was limited.

Armalite then tried an AR-12 that also used .308 rounds. AR-12s made extensive use of steel, rather than alloy stampings, very much like German MP-43s. But neither this nor an AR-14 (a sporting model AR-10) caught the public eye.

Like many of our nation's important weapons systems, AR-15s were developed by the fortuitous convergence of a three-man team. Eugene Stoner, a weapons engineer and entrepreneur visionary of the highest order, joined with L. James Sullivan, the team designer/draftsman, and Robert Fremont, who handled the often-overlooked but very important function of building prototypes.

Between 1956 and 1959, this team put into place most of the elements we see today, including design, manufacturing techniques, and exotic materials. Armalite was ready to submit the AR-10 and AR-15 to the U.S. Army for testing in 1959. As all too frequently happens with bureaucrats, no positive decision was made regarding adoption of a radical, new system. As a result, Armalite management became demoralized and discouraged and decided to sell rights to the AR-15 and AR-10 designs to others.

The management at Colt Firearms Corporation had had a long, successful history producing and—more important—marketing military weapons. To their credit, they saw AR-15s as potential winners in the arms market. All you need to do is market them correctly, top management reasoned. Colt bought all rights to the AR-15 and began marketing these rifles, mostly offshore. South Vietnam, for example, bought a number of the light, sturdy, low-recoil rifles for its diminutive soldiers.

Good reports from Vietnam encouraged the U.S. Air Force to purchase the weapon, and the name was changed from AR-15 to M16 at this time.

But rifle design was only one portion of the package purchased by Colt. Eugene Stoner developed 5.56mm cartridges for AR-15s in the early 1950s by using .222 Remington brass and .224 (.22 caliber) 55-grain bullets. Stoner reckoned that average battlefield casualties were caused at ranges of a few feet to 300 yards at most—not 700 yards as claimed by military people. He did, however, acknowledge that his new ammunition and weapons must be accurate and lethal out to 500 yards. Stoner also knew he needed a 55-grain round zipping along in excess of 3,000 fps to penetrate a Russian helmet at 500 yards. Little Remington .222s were not up to this performance level. Stoner upgraded to something very much like the .222 Remington magnum. (With resizing and trimming, handloaders can substitute brass.)

Stoner specified the newest, most effective Improved Military Rifle (IMR) extruded powder for his new rounds. This was the newest, latest, hottest technology in propellants, which was also ideally suited to an in-bolt, gas locking system. Later, under pressures of war procurement, ammunition makers switched from IMR to ball powder.

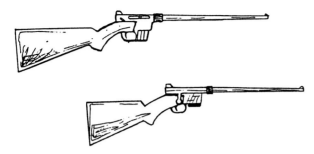

The AR-7 (top) and AR-5 (bottom).

The AR-15 "submachine gun" (1965).

Ball powders were generally remanufactured from reclaimed "salvage" powder. Some of this powder started to deteriorate, causing recyclers to increase the amount of inert calcium carbonate (CaCO3) in the powder mix from .50 to .70 percent. This additional calcium carbonate traveled unburned down the gas tube into the bolt assembly, fouling it badly. Rifles designed to fire 1,000 rounds between cleanings were getting fouled at 400.

During World War II, an average grunt at the front might have gone two weeks before firing 400 rounds through his M1 Garand. In Vietnam this was often a morning's ration. To make matters worse, few cleaning kits were issued to M16 users in the early days when ball powder rounds hit the front.

There were other problems with early military M16s, but they were not as pervasive. Twenty years ago, it was common knowledge among firearms designers that the next great hurdle was magazine design. Without better magazines, reliability, capacity, and utility of any weapons system could not really progress. In Israel, soldiers fighting in the desert used their magazines to open water bottles. Reliability suffered, so designers took the unusual step of putting a "bottle opener" on their Galil rifles.

But in the United States, it was, perhaps, the failure of AR-15 magazines that pushed design people into finally cracking that nut. Modern AR-15 magazines are so well built that users assume flawless functions just happened. It wasn't always that way.

Armalite, with its design people still in place and with its stated goal of using ultramodern materials and manufacturing techniques, did try at least one more weapon—this time, successfully. The company brought out a collapsible, bolt-action AR-5 rifle in .22 Hornet. This was an excellent survival rifle that found only limited acceptance in the U.S.

military because large stocks of older survival weapons of this basic type were still on hand. A second design was, in retrospect, a screaming success. This is the little, collapsible AR-7 semiauto .22 LR rifle. Perhaps because they saw James Bond use one to shoot a bad guy escaping a building in Istanbul and then bring down a helicopter, gun nuts bought it in the thousands.

But, alas, poor old Armalite management grew impatient again. They sold the rights to the AR-7 to Charter Arms Corporation, which continues to sell these little workhorse rifles today.

Armalite also came out with a nice two-shot automatic shotgun (the AR-17) with fiberglass barrel and light aluminum receiver. But, again, the company was ahead of its time. Hunters did not understand two-shot autos. AR-17s were only on the market for a few years.

Soon after the sale of AR-15 rights, Stoner left Armalite for Cadillac Gage Corporation in Detroit. Cadillac manufactured M1 carbines by the thousands for the military effort in Vietnam during the 1960s, as well as providing a place from which Stoner could bring out his "Weapons System 63." This was an interesting mix-and-match weapon by which users could assemble a submachine gun, carbine, regular rifle, sniper rifle, light machine gun, medium machine gun, or even a tank-mounted machine gun, depending on which component parts were put with which. The U.S. Navy and Marines undertook evaluation on the system, but no significant numbers were purchased by anyone except the Navy SEALs. By 1964, the 5.56mm caliber was considered optimal for military use.

Heckler & Koch did eventually adopt this mix-and-match concept to some extent. But, because of the extremely heavy receiver necessary for a long-lived machine gun, weight was excessive for an

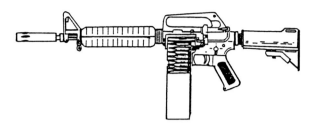

Commercial belt-fed Commando version.

individual shoulder weapon. The idea for a convertible multiple weapons system was pretty well dead by 1966 in the United States.

During this same period—the late 1950s and early 1960s—Colt once again demonstrated its superior product development and marketing skills. They came out with several well-known and still popular variations of the AR-15, as well as some others not as well known or fondly remembered.

Renamed the Colt Automatic Rifle, Colt brought out a CAR-15 with 10-inch barrel, described as a replacement for a submachine gun. The short barrel created problems with complete powder burn. A kind of combination flash hider/silencer was added to the weapon. This device worked OK but is seldom seen today because of adverse classification by the BATF.

In 1965 Colt came out with a 29-inch survival rifle. In 1966 it introduced another shorter version of the AR-15 called a Commando. This little powerhouse incorporated several new features demanded by our military. Most notable were a forward assist and a slower cyclic rate of automatic fire. Colt also brought out a simple 9mm blowback weapon based on AR-15 manufacturing techniques and materials. It was not greeted with great enthusiasm, principally because 5.56mm rounds were far more effective in submachine-gun-size weapons. Users wanted the greater penetration of the 5.56mm. There was even talk of 5.56mm pistols at this time.

By 1984 the evolutionary process was complete. We had the basic system of AR-15s we still see today. These include AR-15 sporting rifles, AR-15 target and medium-range sniping rifles, and CAR-15 carbines with short barrels, short heavy barrels, collapsible stocks, and various types of grips. Numerous hermaphrodites were developed, including a .22 LR look-alike model.

A few of the aftermarket accessories—such as stocks, handguards, and barrel—available for the AR-15. (Photos from *AR-15/M16 Super Systems* by Duncan Long.)

E&L Manufacturing's slip-on butt pad (left) comes with a rubber insert (right) that allows the length of pull to be varied to suit the tall shooter's build and clothing.

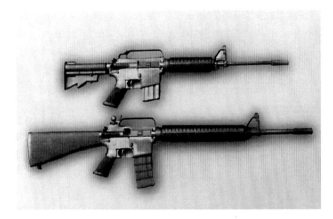

Two of the many stock configurations available in the marketplace. At top is Colt's plastic and metal telescoping stock; the lower example is Colt's new A2 stock.

Type 68 rifle from Taiwan.

The M16A2.

Colt made some heavy-barreled machine-gun-type AR-15s for SAW tests. Some featured belt-fed mechanisms, but experts concluded that simpler, more reliable magazine-fed systems were best. Few of these mostly prototype weapons exist today. Most have never been seen outside military evaluation and procurement circles.

Because of Colt's aggressive licensing arrangements worldwide and the expiration of patent rights in the late 1970s, a previously undreamed-of number of manufacturers, both domestic and foreign, got into the AR-15 business. These people made parts; whole systems; add-ons; and aftermarket stocks, clips, and pistol grips, as well as special-purpose barrels, bolt carriers, and other items. Labor problems in the 1980s caused Colt to discontinue domestic sales temporarily, thereby giving many new gun makers a tremendous boost.

Howa Machinery Company of Nagoya, Japan, is an example of a more regular manufacturer. But during the Vietnam War, the Japanese were prevented by their constitution from sending their model Howa AR-18s to the United States for military testing. Reportedly, Japanese AR-18s were excellent rifles that may have replaced Colt AR-15s.

Manufacturers in Singapore, the Philippines, and South Korea all turned out AR-15-type weapons. Those in Singapore and South Korea had different names and numbers but were essentially AR-15s. Some rifles were even imported back into the United States for sale in the civilian market. In the Philippines, they simply produced CAR-15s, perhaps because of the small size of most Filipinos. Daewoo in Korea made AR-18s; Chartered Industries of Singapore, Ltd., made the SAR-80, based on AR-18 designs and tooling that it bought

from Stirling of England, which had produced the AR-18/AR-180 under license from Stoner.

Canada replaced its Fabrique Nationale (FN) FALs with an M16A2-type weapon it named the C-8. FN won a bid to produce AR-15-type weapons for the U.S. military in 1989. FN established a manufacturing plant in Columbia, South Carolina, from which it filled orders from Europe, Asia, and the rest of the world.

Even Taiwan produced an AR-15-type rifle, the Model 68. Singaporean, Filipino, Korean, and Chinese makers have not sold large numbers of their weapons, in large part because of the extensive number of surplus shoulder weapons left in Vietnam by U.S. troops. These weapons have moved around the world, often at distressed or discounted prices.

What's ahead for AR-15 designs? Obviously, these rifles, which defy breakage and wear and tear, will be around for a long time. Certainly the AR-15's dominance in world military affairs will not significantly diminish till well after the year 2,000. Even then, expect manufacturing techniques of newer designs to remain much the same.

Significant improvement of new, larger-capacity magazines into flawlessly functioning units could evolve. Some of these magazines may hold cartridges in a helix. Others may stack ammo crosswise in piles, much like cord wood, over the receiver.

Caseless ammo is virtually perfected at this writing. All that remains is to solve the relatively minor problems of damage during rough handling, cook-offs, and reliable ignition.

Existing case-type rounds may be improved by the addition of a second projectile piggy-backed on the main round. This might allow a greater likelihood of a hit.

Powders may also be marginally improved, providing for more velocity at lower pressures.

AR-15s will probably be with us in great numbers through the 21st century. Some of their hundreds of thousands will continue to surface in little wars fought here and there. Remember that some owners have fired 100,000 rounds through their AR-15s, and the rifles are still functional. These weapons can be readily rebuilt if they do expire, meaning they will practically never go out of service.

This is not something we can say about Russian AKs, which have been replaced by AK-74 .22-caliber models. AKs always were much closer to disposable weapons. It may take years of use in ugly little wars before all the 7.62x39 AKs are gone, but gone they will be—while Armalite has carved a permanent niche in history.

BIBLIOGRAPHY

Long, Duncan. *The AR-15/M16 Practical Guide*. Boulder, CO: Paladin Press, 1985.

_____. *AR-15/M16 Sourcebook*. Boulder, CO: Paladin Press, 1992.

_____. *AR-15/M16 Super Systems*. Boulder, CO: Paladin Press, 1989.

CHAPTER

Personalizing the AR-15

9

No common weapons system in history has been as easy to customize as the AR-15. Even such simple systems as the bow and arrow have never had the number and variety of parts, supplies, and after-market accouterments available that AR-15 owners can find easily. Enthusiasts can build exactly what they feel they require, down to the most minute detail.

Thirty years is a long time, but if my memory is correct, my first AR-15 was one of the initial 3,000 Colts built to test the civilian market. I believe that its serial number was 1036 or some such low number, purchased at a time when the common refrain from supposedly combat-seasoned veterans was "I don't want to carry a rifle into combat that I wouldn't take bear hunting."

Shortly after receiving my civilian model Colt AR-15, I decided to take it bear hunting. Because it was important to me to actually try the rifle on a

bear, I offered $250 per bear to a local hound man as "bear bait."

We loaded up his five hounds and drove off very early one morning to a small town dump of the type found around every little burg in those pre-EPA days. It was about 40 miles into the mountains to our destination dump ground. As is true the first day of almost every bear season, it was cool, crisp, and incredibly invigorating. My guide kidded me about hunting bears with a "buggy whip," a direct reference to my rifle. But I felt so encouraged that hunting bears with an actual whip did not seem out of the question.

Frost covered the ground in impossible-to-predict little white patches. We pulled onto the slimy little road cut into a small 30-acre clearing. It was September 1. Residents could not raise tomatoes in this country, we agreed.

The grizzled, hound man pulled old Rose out of her kennel, snapped on a lead rope, and handed me the rope. Quickly, he grabbed Reb and Luke, hooking them up as well. They almost yanked him over in their excitement. Once on the ground, the hounds bayed and lunged in a most frightening manner. They were quickly joined by those still in the truck till it was absolute bedlam.

"Turn 'em loose! Turn 'em loose!" the old veteran hollered. "They got one goin'." Not wanting to be dragged bodily through the mounds of stinking garbage, I unsnapped Rose and let 'er rip.

Collectively, we ran back to the truck to turn Blue and Sam loose and grab our flashlights and guns. But it was already too late to try to keep up with the hounds. We could hear them baying as they topped the first ridge, but then it was as quiet as a graveyard.

I made a great show, as I always did with my AR-15, of snapping on the bayonet and slapping in a fresh 20-round magazine. For those unaccustomed to modern "Mattel-toy-like" AR-15 rifles, the effect is great.

We ran up on the first ridge. It was mostly quiet, except far in the distance an occasional tracking-type yelp could be heard. My guide decided it was still too dark to follow, so we lollygagged along till the canyon lit up a bit. My guide climbed up to the top of an especially steep following ridge and hollered down that he could hear Reb and Luke in the distance on tree. With great expectations, we pushed through cedar thickets and climbed a great hill before finally reaching a small clearing about half a mile distant. Two great, bushy Douglas firs were all that grew in the clearing.

Three hounds were taking turns running up to the smaller of the two firs, jumping up and letting out a mournful bay. We tied the dogs to adjoining saplings. They were still so excited that it appeared that they might tear out the little trees.

The bear was not in the tree the dogs thought it was. Instead, it was clutching and clawing furiously to thin the topmost branches of the adjoining, much larger Doug fir. It was 60 or more feet up and would have gone higher had there been sufficiently stout branches at that level. It appeared as though the bear would soon fall out of the tree without any help from us.

"Shoot him quick while I turn loose the dogs!" my old bear-hunting buddy hollered. I stepped up to the plate, pulled the cocking ears resolutely, snapped the selector to fire, and put a round in the middle of the critter's back. It did not appear to have much influence on it. "Shoot again, you gol'-darned fool!"

my guide indelicately admonished. I fired four quick rounds, all striking the bear in the upper back and shoulders.

Slowly, as if done in slow motion for the movies, the bear quit holding on and fell out of the tree. As it did, I put two more rounds in it. Because the dogs were loose, we could have easily lost one in a fight had the bear still been alive.

It hit the ground like 20 pounds of ham spattering the pavement from the twentieth floor. There was no movement from the 185-pound, 3-year-old even though Old Reb was mashing its testicles.

"Where is Rose and Old Blue?" the old guy asked as we rolled the dead bear. "All we got here is Reb, Luke, and Sam." We couldn't hear anything off in the distance.

My guide scurried off up another steep hill. "There, over west, about quarter of a mile," he hollered. "I think Rose is barkin' a tree!"

It was full light and coming on to the warm of the day before we got over to a truly huge pine, coincidentally with a huge bear sort of in it. Obviously, in its haste, the bear picked a tree too big to climb. It clung to a first limb up about 15 feet and could go no higher. Hugely rotund, this was obviously a berry-fat fall bear.

I took careful aim at the giant hairball head. At the shot, the bear simply went limp and wrapped around the limb. It looked like it wouldn't fall. I threw three or four more rounds into the body and down it finally came. Gutted three hours later, the bear still weighed 342 pounds!

In roughly three hours, I had killed two very nice black bears with my little aluminum Mattel toy, as my friends called it. I didn't use the bayonet, but like many AR-15 add-ons, it was mostly for show anyway.

Usually, the first serious decision new AR-15 system owners must make involves whether to keep the standard longer, straight stock or purchase and install a shorter, collapsible one. Telescoping stocks are available from numerous aftermarket suppliers, most of whom advertise regularly in *Shotgun News*. Shorty Stock Kits cost about $60 complete, ready to install. Initially, most were made of aluminum, but structural nylon is currently popular. Those who have used both prefer nylon. You can purchase Shorty Stock Kits from Quality Parts Company (Box 1479, Windham, ME 04062).

Choate's magazine connector on the left and Mag-Pac on the right. The Choate unit is a bit more compact, while the Mag-Pac can be removed without tools. The magazines on the left are staggered to keep the left magazine from blocking the ejection port cover. (Photos from *AR-15 Super Systems* by Duncan Long.)

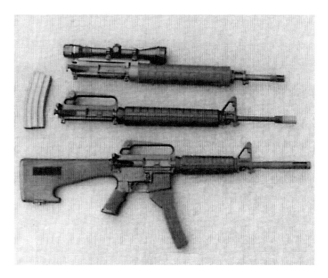

An example of the "family of rifles" potential of the AR-15 design. Shown here is the SGW CAR-9 kit (bottom), mounted on the lower AR-15 SGW receiver assembly with a Choate E2 stock. The center barrel is a lightweight A1 barrel with A2 stock for "everyday" use. At top is the Insight Systms Model 1 for super accuracy.

Remove the old stock by unscrewing the single top stock screw from the butt of the AR-15. This will release the rear detent pin, allowing you to withdraw the rear push pin. Buffer tubes can now be unscrewed—except on some military models, which also must be unpinned. Drift out this pin, if necessary. Slide the old stock off the buffer tube. All of this will appear much more obvious with both replacement stock and weapon in hand.

Another option simply involves replacing old-style 20-round magazines with 30s or 40s. If you have older-style magazines, it is mandatory to update. Numerous changes have been made in modern magazines, allowing for much more flawless operation. As an AR-15 user, you should also consider purchasing some of the new magazine-coupling devices allowing you to mate two huge-capacity magazines into one 60- or 80-round unit. Both magazines should face up when coupled and deployed. The older method of taping two magazines together with one facing down makes for something a bit more compact but hopelessly obsolete and risky in terms of functioning. Dirt always seems to find its way into the bottom magazine.

Under many circumstances, modern rugged scope sights are valuable on the AR-15 rifle, which will definitely shoot far enough with accuracy to justify adding a scope.

Contemporary owners need not stand on their heads spitting wooden nickels to get a scope mounted, as was true when AR-15s first appeared on the commercial market. Now almost everyone makes bases that clamp down into the weapon's carrying handle, and that will accept standard rings. These V-bed mounting plates come from Weaver, Tasco, or one of the many aftermarket suppliers, such as Quality Parts, SGW/Olympic Arms, or Nesard.

Owners who have used scopes extensively on AR-15 systems generally report a preference for lower-power, wide-angle models of the most rugged design possible. Colt, among others, has a military model that seems able to take the beating to which any scope or an AR-15 will be subjected. Variable seems OK, but lower power settings providing a wider field of view are more common. Laser sights that are effective only at night seem pretty gimmicky to most owners.

Depending on the intended use, an AR-15 can become a squad automatic weapon (SAW) or a type of submachine gun, depending on the barrel system used. Those wanting a SAW will probably install a 20-inch barrel of the heaviest types available. Submachine gun owners look for heavy barrels that

The Colt AR-15 A2 H-BAR can serve as the starting point for the creation of a do-it-yourself SAW. The rifle has a fully adjustable rear sight and a heavy barrel capable of absorbing extra heat. This model is equipped with a special cheek mount, A.R.M.S. scope mount, and rubber-armored, 8-9X variable-power Tasco scope. (Photo courtesy of Colt Firearms.)

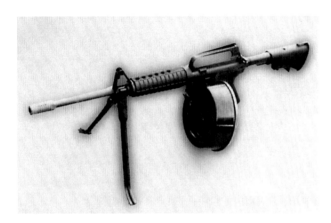

The lightweight carbine SAW offers a high rate of firepower in a short, light package. Such a weapon would be ideal for firing from a vehicle, during house-to-house combat, or while on patrol.

The hardest of the selective-fire parts to rework to the Colt configuration is the bolt carrier. Shown on top is a properly altered bolt carrier; military style is shown on the bottom.

are only 16 inches long, including the flash hider. Commonly, owners will set themselves up with entire barrel and upper receiver assemblies that, although expensive, allow one to have both a small machine pistol and a SAW.

These complete upper assemblies are purchased from SGW/Olympic Arms or from Quality Parts Company. No FFL or other paperwork is required once you have a basic AR-15 from which to start.

Long, tubular flash suppressors that come with heavy-barreled, Shorty upper assemblies are pinned or silver-soldered to the barrel. These are easily removed and replaced with smaller, shorter muzzle breaks, yielding a very compact, powerful package. Some custom installers use flash hiders from AK, MAC-10, or other similar weapons to create a potent little carbine that can be packed around inconspicuously in a standard briefcase.

These weapons are under the legal minimum of a barrel of less than 16 inches and much less than 26 inches total overall length. Since these guns are presently illegal anyway, many owners take the next step, converting their weapons to genuine SAWs or machine carbines.

Some survivalists feel there is value in owning a weapon that sounds like a full-auto machine gun. But you should ask yourself whether the sound will scare people off or concern the BATF enough that it brings in tanks and helicopters. Certainly, the sound of gunfire will not produce casualties.

Being a person who does not even hunt with a round in the chamber of my bolt-action rifle, I have little faith in full-auto fire—for whatever effect. Sniping is, in my opinion, where it is all at. But for those who insist on converting to a military-type AR-15/M16, it isn't much of an operation. Many tomcats have undergone worse.

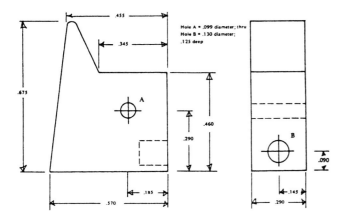

Hole A = .099 diameter; thru
Hole B = .130 diameter;
.125 deep

AR-15 sear. (Illustrations on this page taken from *The AR-15/M16: A Practical Guide* by Duncan Long.)

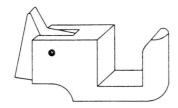

An assembled drop-in auto sear for the AR-15.

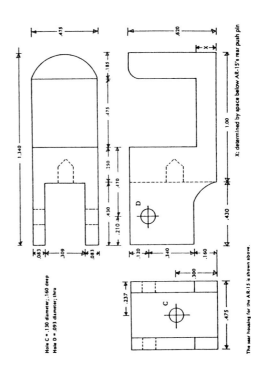

Hole C = .130 diameter; .160 deep
Hole D = .093 diameter; thru

The sear housing for the AR-15 is shown above.

Perhaps because BATF has gone to such lengths to develop trigger mechanisms that can't be turned into full auto, gun nuts have seriously taken up the challenge to find quick, easy methods of undoing BATF's handiwork. What follows is one method. It perhaps is not the best method, nor is it the only method, but it does convert a standard civilian AR-15 to full auto.

Keep in mind that the following is very illegal and should never be undertaken except in the most dire emergency. BATF agents have shot and killed numerous gun owners just on the suspicion that they possessed fully automatic weapons.

Ownership of the parts necessary for conversion is considered to be prima facie evidence of guilt even if you do not otherwise own an AR-15.

Those not wishing to drill incriminating, nonreversible, easily seen holes in their nonmilitary AR-15 receivers are relegated to using a "drop-in" auto sear to convert to full-auto fire. But first, semiauto parts must be replaced by their military counterpart. These include the bolt carrier, trigger, hammer, sear and selector. Some commercial rifles may already have some of these parts. Check carefully

before spending money on expensive, incriminating-by-purchase parts that may already be on hand.

Again, remember that although numerous parts houses can supply these items, having them all together is a serious felony. Increasingly, parts dealers require proper paperwork before purchase of even one or two of these needed items.

Drop-in sears should be tooled out of steel, although many commercial aluminum ones were made and sold during the late 1970s before they are declared illegal. Well-made, nicely fitted, and matched Colt rifles work best with drop-in sears. Yet any well-made, well-fitted rifle will do.

Carefully machine or have your machine shop do the work, as shown above. The single sear spring required should be made of about 10 turns of #18 music wire on a 1/10-inch mandrel, yielding a final compression spring about .125 inch in diameter, 1/2 inch long. These same springs can be purchased as stock items from automotive supply stores.

Some final file work is always required to make the device fit evenly and solidly into the space behind the safety selector. Any wobble will cause erratic functioning.

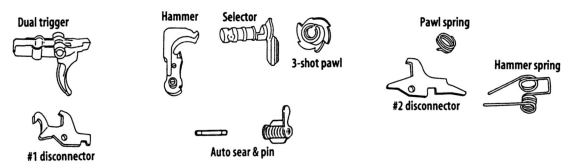

The Rhino Replacement Parts 3-round burst kit is designed to replace the automatic parts on older selective-fire AR-15s. The kit will upgrade the rifle so that it gives the user a choice of semi-, auto-, or burst-fire modes. (Illustrations unless otherwise noted taken from *AR-15/M16 Super Systems* by Duncan Long. This one courtesy of Rhino Replacement Parts.)

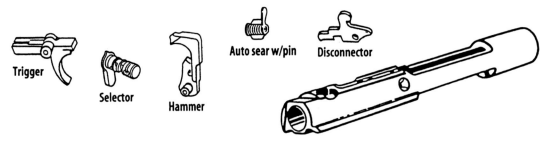

The Rhino Replacement Parts auto-fire kit allows the repair of selective-fire AR-15 rifles. (Illustration courtesy of Rhino Replacement Parts.)

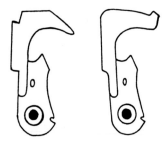

M16-style hammer (right) can be altered on a grinding wheel to the Colt A1 style (left) with some careful work.

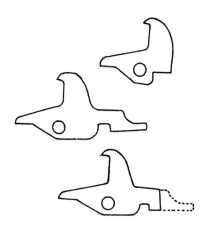

IM16-style disconnector (top left) with "tail." Creating a Colt A1-style disconnector (top right) requires drilling a new spring hole in the trigger. A better bet is to grind off the tail of the disconnector (bottom); this same style is also used on the new A2 civilian Colts.

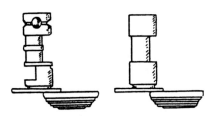

M15-style safety/selector (left) and Colt AR-15 style (right). Complete alteration of the M16 style isn't possible, but it can be made legal by grinding off the central rim that normally engages the tail of the automatic version of the disconnector.

Legal drop-in sears have a serial number that is registered to the owner with BATF. However, no further registration of newly made sears is allowed. Those who want a legal "drop-in" must purchase one made before 1981 that is already registered and pay the $200 transfer tax. These legal sears are advertised from time to time in *Shotgun News.* Prices range from $132 to about $1,000 each!

As with many weapons that have an exotic image, full-auto AR-15s are not nearly as fine a fighting instrument as you might hope. Before deciding on anything beyond a legal AR-15 carbine with 16-inch barrel and folding stock, try to find someone with a full-auto version who will allow you to fire it. My guess is that more and faster strikes on a target can be made at virtually any range with the semiauto than with a weapon you might wish to own only for its perceived glamour.

BIBLIOGRAPHY

Long, Duncan. *The AR-15/M16 Practical Guide.* Boulder, CO: Paladin Press, 1985.

_____. *AR-15/M16 Sourcebook.* Boulder, CO: Paladin Press, 1992.

_____. *AR-15/M16 Super Systems.* Boulder, CO: Paladin Press, 1989.

CHAPTER

AK-47s

10

In times past, when concern ran rampant through the land regarding possible war with Communist invaders, it was fashionable to own an AK-47. This was not an entirely ignorant survival plan if a person assumed that he might be called on to scrounge ammunition from the enemy.

Times have changed dramatically. We now see that there was little to fear from foreign governments thar might have wished to invade the United States. Many men of action are rethinking their personal defense strategies, perhaps including ownership of a rifle that in the near future could be difficult for which to find ammo.

Yet AK-47 rifles have justifiably built a worldwide reputation for reliability and durability. This one specific rifle carried by a person with dirty canvas shoes has become the symbol of those whose goal was the domination and subjection of the producing class.

The weapon's extreme simplicity, along with the fact that the design does away with numerous parts found in almost every other rifle of its type, has earned the AK-47 an honest reputation for reliability. With fewer parts to break, warriors operating in an extremely primitive environment have found they can keep most of their AKs functional.

Some seemingly insignificant design features contribute mightily to the AK's reliability. A whole handful, for instance, of sand or mud will scarcely foul an AK because of its inordinately heavy bolt. Most users never realize that this is one reason the AKs keep working when logically they should not.

The change handle located on the right side of the receiver can do double duty as a forward assist, doing away with the need for a complex forward assist. The safety-selector lever on an AK doubles as an ejection port cover, and the weapon simply does not have a bolt hold-open function. This makes it somewhat less convenient when cleaning or clearing a bad round, but, as a result, from nine to 11 different parts are simply absent from AKs.

The Federov *avtomat* was much like today's modern assault rifle. Had Communist bureaucrats spent less time hassling the rifle's inventor and more on developing the weapon, Russia might have been decades ahead of others in small-arms development. (Illustrations taken from *AK47: The Complete Kalashnikov Family of Assault Rifles* by Duncan Long.)

During World War II, Germany produced what many consider the first of the modern assault rifles. One of the best of these was the MP44, which was later redesignated the StG44.

Traditionally this simplicity has meant extremely low prices for AKs. Within the past year, I was offered 25,000 AK-47s (at $25 U.S. each) located in a warehouse in Managua, Nicaragua, but refused because the price was too high. Artificial scarcities due to import restrictions have significantly hyped prices in the United States, but, on a worldwide basis, new AKs are trading for considerably less than $25 each.

Kalashnikov rifles have influenced weapons development around the world for about 40 years. Its ifluence has not been to the level of AR-15s but it has been significant, nevertheless. Many soldiers have seen and fired this rifle and no other. Irregular soldiers traveling to miscellaneous places around the world must know how to deploy and care for AK-style weapons lest they be put at real disadvantage. Fortunately, the design's simplicity contributes to ease of training. Absolute grass-shack African natives have become fairly proficient with this weapon, whereas something like an AR-15 might have been well beyond their capabilities.

The history of the AK-47 can only be understood in the context of a Communist society. Were it not for gritty Russian politics, the first assault rifle in history would have been developed in the land of the bear. Vladimir Federov invented a self-loading rifle while on assignment to the czar in 1918 or 1919. Ironically, this rifle was initially designed to use a reduced-power rifle round similar to ones developed in Germany in 1943 and 1944.

Federov's rifle was produced only in limited quantities for use by Russian infantrymen on their western front at the very end of World War I. Little

is known about this terribly cruel piece of history, either in the East or West, but we are certain that this rifle did little to equip a horribly ill-supplied and neglected army. Federov did not make a very good Communist; after Lenin assumed control, Federov's work was given low priority, and he himself was jailed for a time.

Starting in 1925, a Soviet committee was set up to search for a modern, self-loading shoulder weapon. This people's committee, however, made a fatal error in deciding to retain the obsolete 7.62x54R cartridge—a decision made because of huge stocks of ammunition of that caliber still on hand. Retaining this old, obsolete rimmed cartridge for a modern, state-of-the-art weapon was the ultimate in military stupidity.

By 1939, with war increasingly imminent, various committees had tested and rejected quite a number of different Russian designs. Virtually in desperation, a Tokarev-design rifle was finally adopted. It was overly complex to manufacture and too heavy, and it severely taxed available supplies of Soviet raw materials.

Shortly thereafter, U.S. M1 carbines began showing up on World War II battlefields. Soviet planners expressed amazement at the huge numbers the United States was able to push out into the field in very short order.

Meanwhile, design experimentation in Germany was given high priority. Work started on assault rifles in Germany during the 1930s came to fruition. By 1943, a machine carbine characterized by cheap, quick steel stampings and cheap, automatic-screw, machine-made barrels was successfully deployed against the Russians. It is lost in history who actually

The third version of the AK-47 with milled receiver and the stock attached directly to the receiver.

The AK-74 with side-folding, sheet-metal stock; this stock allows the use of 40-round RPK-74 magazines with standard rifles.

The AKR Krinkov is made for use by officers, tank crews, special forces, and the like. This weapon has a greatly abbreviated gas rod and barrel as well as the metal folding stock of the AKS-74.

The Valmet M2's bullpup design would appear to be the next stage in the development of the Kalashnikov rifles, but poor sales suggest that the need for such a rifle on the world market may not be great.

The Valmet Hunter is a Kalashnikov rifle barely disguised in hunting garb. This attractive firearm's low barrel also makes quick follow-up shots possible.

took note of this innovation, but the design obviously influenced some Russian committee person.

Not being one bit reluctant to copy others' success, the Soviets started a search for an intermediate-powered rifle round and for a simple, cheap, mostly stamped, highly engineered weapon design to take advantage of this technology.

At this time, a weapons engineer named Simonov brought out a prototype weapon that eventually became the common SKS. The design's heavy weight, fixed magazine, semiauto-only fire, and heavy built-in bayonet made it acceptable only in a Communist society where there is no choice. SKS rifles were, in spite of their many serious shortcomings, better than nothing. Strangely, the SKS rifle achieved a fairly high level of acceptance despite the fact that the Soviets replaced it just a few years later with the AK, leading some to speculate that the SKS was intended as a stopgap measure.

When competition and markets are not a factor, strange things happen. For whatever reason—perhaps because the party first secretary was sleeping with Mikhail Timofeyevich Kalashnikov's wife, who knows?—Kalashnikov was invited to submit another design for a standard, military rifle shortly after adoption of the SKS. In 1949, one of Kalashnikov's prototypes, the AK-47, was accepted as the Soviet army's standard, but use of the SKS continued.

AK-47s were a bastardized cross of German StG-44s, the U.S. M1 Garand, and the U.S. M1 carbine! Like many bastards, it was not of sturdy construction. The fact that two years elapsed between design date (1947) and final approval (in 1949) suggests that numerous updates and improvements were undertaken.

Kalashnikov went on in the 1950s to become a senior engineer of OKB, an experimental design and construction bureau in the Soviet Union. In this capacity, Kalashnikov developed literally dozens of

The Valmet M75 family of rifles was created for the export market. Shown here are the metal folding-stock version (top), the standard wooden-stock model (center), and the LMG version, the M78, (bottom). (Photos from *AK47: The Complete Kalashnikov Family of Assault Rifles* by Duncan Long.)

additional weapons ranging from sniper rifles to medium machine guns. Unbelievable as it may have sounded in 1947, all of these weapons were of a common design based on the original AK-47.

By 1951 the Russians switched from a stamped to a milled receiver. Again, anybody's theory as to why this regressive technology was undertaken is as good as anybody else's. Perhaps the comrade who inspected the milling machines thought there was better fishing in the region than where stampings were done.

Changes in 1953 or 1954 were mostly internal, which resulted in making the weapons simpler to build and more durable. By 1959, the Russkies were back to stamped-steel receivers again. Small indentations over the magazine well in the stamped-sheet-steel receiver distinguish this model. Other modifications include a simpler flash hider, gas port holes in the gas cylinder, finger swells in the foregrip, and a few slightly modified internal parts. These new models were named AKMs.

Worldwide, little difference was noted. All these weapons were lumped together as AK-47s. The term AK-47 has become a generic word including all assault rifles whether or not they fire a reduced-sized cartridge, are full auto, or are made from stamped steel. Any metallic rifle with composition stock might now be called an AK-47, especially if it is Soviet made.

AKMs remained standard Soviet infantry issue until 1974 when AK-74s came out. This model resulted from competition engendered by the U.S. AR-15 systems. It is a .22-caliber weapon firing a round similar but ballistically inferior to our .223/5.56mm round. Called a 5.45x39mm, it is much more suited to modern infantry weapons than the older Russian .30-caliber short round. Some wags have suggested that the Russians would have been best served by adopting our 5.56mm round.

For the time this ended the evolution of AK-47s. Most knowledgeable observers believe it is the end of the line for Russian AKs, especially in light of the current political situation there. An exception might be China, where newly developed wealth, competition, and freedom may generate better designs.

Including countries outside the Soviet Union, more Kalashnikovs have been manufactured than any other firearm in history. Our own M1 carbine and the M16 rifle run a distant second and third. Approximatley 55 countries have adopted some type of Kalashnikov, so you are likely to run across them anywhere in the world.

Total production worldwide of AKs is estimated at 36 to 70 million! Bulgaria, Egypt, Hungary, Poland, North Korea, and Romania, as well as the former Czechoslovakia (although internally the Vz58 is quite different from its Soviet counterpart), East Germany, and Yugoslavia have all produced significant numbers of AK-type rifles. The champion producer in terms of numbers, however, is China. Of all nations that make an AK-type weapon, China has aggressively sought export markets for its AKs. It alone has produced an estimated 10 to 20 million AK weapons, which include rifles, machine guns, and sniper rifles. Most AKMs erroneously lumped together as AK-47s sold in this country were originally exported by Norinco of Beijing.

In addition to those for the United States, the Chinese have exported AKs to Iraq, Nicaragua, and the Afghan rebels. One of the reasons revolutionaries prefer AKs over M16s is that AK systems are cheaper to manufacture, easier to train on, and more universally available. Yet many experts insist that M16s are better, more effective, and more reliable.

Several unlikely nations not related to the Communist bloc, such as Israel, Finland, and South Africa, have adopted mostly AK-type shoulder weapons of their own.

In the case of Israel, its rifle is based on an AK design but chambered for a 5.56mm U.S. round. In some regards, Israeli rifles are something of hermaphrodites based on FAL, Stoner 63, and Valmet components. Israel called the rifle a Galil. It works extremely well in tough, dirty, sandy conditions often encountered by Israeli soldiers. Galils were exported or manufactured under license by South Africa, the Netherlands, and Sweden.

Valmet in Finland produced probably the finest AK-type weapon, if fit and finish are any criteria. Valmet designated its weapon the M76. From the M76, literally scores of entirely different families of weapons evolved. These include rifles, carbines, machine pistols, bullpups, light machine guns, and even sniper rifles. These weapons were not conglomerations of something else. Anyone who picks up a Valmet and is familiar with AKs will know immediately what he is looking at.

Worldwide, those wanting quality, well-finished AKs bought Valmets. If for no other reason than because AKs have such widespread popularity, men of action should know how to service and maintain them. Fortunately, this is not difficult for people used to being around guns. At any given time, an AK may not be the weapon of choice, but it may be the weapon you have.

Because of their weight, AKs are relatively easy to fire full auto. On the other hand, it is often said that relatively wimpy 7.62x39mm rounds have produced more wounded soldiers than any other weapon in history. If the objective is to wound rather than kill, thereby overloading the enemy's medical facilities, AKs definitely are the weapon of choice. These big, slow bullets can practically be caught in a first baseman's mitt at 300 meters.

AKs are very easy to turn into full-auto weapons if you have the U.S. semiauto version. This model was initially designed to be full auto, so conversion does not unduly wear the weapon.

Many Kalashnikovs have excellent night sights. Shown here is the Valmet M76 front sight that flips up to give a glowing circle for aiming. (Photo courtesy of Valmet.)

Simply disable the trigger and disconnect either by grinding, tying it back with a paper clip, or installing an outside disconnect lever.

Anyone who has ever been around an AK can tell a mile away with the wind blowing when one is being fired. Their sound is extremely distinctive. Firing one even semiauto will either warn someone away or make him very curious.

Dave W. thought it ironic that he was flying a Chinook helicopter over Vietnam. Married to an American missionary's daughter who was born in Vietnam, Dave considered Vietnam his adopted country, even though he hadn't been back there for a great number of years. In September 1965, a time of significant buildup of American forces in Vietnam, Dave had been on station about four months, flying large doses of our soldiers in and out in his giant machine.

Dave adeptly maneuvered his lumbering giant through a little saddle, intending to put down in a series of rice paddies built about 300 yards down the long, gently sloping hillside. Unexpectedly tall trees caused him to pull up, slowing a bit. As his machine hung in space, someone below rattled the beast's belly with a magazine of AK rounds. Miraculously, none of the sardine-like grunts inside were hit. Dave, however, saw his chopper panel light up like a Christmas tree.

He deftly landed where planned and shut down. The 24-man unit fanned out instantly. Almost as quickly, two Cobras arrived on the scene. Dave did not want to kill the engines completely, but his crew chief insisted.

"Give me 30 seconds to make a quick check," he said. "If we keep running, the machine may self-destruct, and we won't get out anyway."

Severely motivated grunts pushed back into tall grass and trees uphill till a furious firefight erupted. It lasted perhaps 30 seconds.

"One control line damaged but sufficiently intact to fly, one oil line shot out that I can shut off, and one electrical line we can do without," Dave's crew chief reported. "I'll have her ready to fly out in another 10 minutes," he said.

Up on the east ridge, it was miserably quiet. Dave hoped that the VC had pulled out, but he knew that any second an RPG-7 round (although the round is actually a PG-7, most people refer to it as an RPG-7, like the launcher) could come crashing into his machine.

As quickly and invisibly as they left, the grunts were back. "We got a ride out of here?" one man queried hesitantly. "Here is the AK that shot you down," he added. "Got the guy running along the ridge. Seemed to be the only one with a rifle."

Dave still has that AK. He took it home to his place in Ogden, Utah, where he would like nothing better than to display it. But, of course, that is impossible. It may be the only AK in the United States that shot down a chopper. Then, again, it might just be another AK.

BIBLIOGRAPHY

Hogg, Ian V. *Jane's Infantry Weapons*. London: Jane's Publishing Co., 1991.

Koenig, Scofield. *Soviet Military Power*. New York: Gallery Books, 1983.

Long, Duncan. *The Complete Kalashnikov Family of Weapons*. Boulder, CO: Paladin Press, 1988.

CHAPTER

SKS Carbines

11

Like golf clubs, SKS carbines are absolutely and completely worthless for anything other than entertaining their owners. Unfortunately, much of the world wishes to censor and control our entertainment, but this is an issue unrelated to this volume. At first impression, these weapons seem to have little charm, but people who own SKS rifles report great satisfaction.

In my neighborhood, there is a fairly large group of mostly farm and schoolboys, all of whom have recently purchased SKS carbines. These fellows were initially attracted to them by their relatively low price, exotic origin, and—most of all—the large supply of relatively cheap, easily available ammo. Several of these guys have each blasted away more than 6,000 rounds through their rifles—something they could not normally have done even if they hand loaded.

One fellow is an especially frugal farmboy who must work very hard for every penny he spends. I could not have afforded eight cents per round when I was his age, but he has a blast with his SKS, both figuratively and literally. "It makes a nice, sharp 'pop' when fired, and with a 30-round magazine, I can really throw 'em out," he says.

His remark came as quite a surprise to me since the fellow is normally very quiet and reserved. When he and his friends get together to plink, it sounds like Tet all over again. You can almost hear approving chuckles from Norinco people who see ammunition sales soar in the United States as a result of fellows like these. Perhaps in the future, the Chinese planned to give Americans SKS rifles with the intention of making money on ammo sales. This is now impossible because of an edict by the U.S. president prohibiting importation.

"This is cheap, wretched ammo," one of the fellows recently confided. "It is quite corrosive and may soon wear out my rifle." But I pay less than that for .22 mag ammo, and it is really much more spectacular to shoot. There is even some talk of organizing

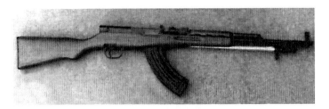

Despite the import restrictions, as of this writing, U.S. citizens can still purchase new and used SKS rifles from a great number of importers. (Photo from *The SKS Type 45 Carbine* by Duncan Long.)

an all SKS deer hunt. Some hunters tend to deprecate 7.62x39rounds, but one must recall that they have about as much pizazz as the venerable .30-30.

"Were it not for .30-30 rifles and open sights," one old sage observed, "white-tail deer in the U.S. would have gone extinct."

The history of the SKS rifle is about as strange as the weapon itself. This is a rifle brought out in desperation as a temporary expedient that acquired a lobbying group that has kept it alive for years, long after it should have become a museum curiosity.

The history is greatly oversimplified, but one can honestly show that Russian arms designers gave the world its first assault rifle in 1916, to replace older Moisin Nagant rifles made during the last days of the nineteenth century. This assault rifle saw only limited production, in part because of restricted fabricating capacity for an admittedly overly complex design and because the design was flawed from inception. It was made for the Japanese 6.5x50mmSR cartridge.

Next, an able firearms inventor, Sergei Simonov, brought out a semiauto rifle that, because of its 7.64x54R cartridge, was not really an assault rifle. It was, however, a small step in the right direction. Soviet generals with huge stores of old, rimmed cartridges still in stock insisted that this be the round of choice. Decisions in that place and time were made by committees of comrades, much like the current government in the United States.

Other faults and defugalities ensured that the Russians had another genuine nonstarter on their hands. Fortunately, the committee could make no decision, and time slipped rapidly by.

In 1938 other trials were run. Again, no real winner appeared among the designs, but the committee selected a Tokarev rifle design as the

most reliable. Many of these models were eventually imported into the United States in the 1960s.

Stalin himself picked this rifle, probably in desperation over the fact that German soldiers were on the very outskirts of Moscow. Wartime circumstances and the Communist system itself caused startup of production to be very slow and uncertain. Eventually, large numbers of Tokarev rifles were produced, but these were never considered successful.

"There is a certain, high quality to large quantities," Stalin said, explaining away the fact that very crude, often inferior products were produced in large numbers for the Russian military.

At the same time, educated by their horrible losses in Finland, Russia adopted a new submachine gun. Called the PPSh-41, it fired the old rimless .30-caliber Mauser pistol round. PPSh-41s were stamped out in incredible numbers, in part because the design made this type of manufacture possible and because only the most basic raw materials were required. Whole divisions of Russians were equipped with PPSh-41 submachine guns.

Fascinated by ultramodern, state-of-the-art German Sturmgewehrs and the reduced-power cartridge they fired, the Soviets, who were still without a suitable first-line rifle, intensified their search again in earnest in mid- to late-1943. As with the PPSh-41, the Soviets required something their rudimentary manufacturing facilities could handle. German manufacturers who were being bombed back to the stone age were good teachers.

At this time, Sergei Simonov stepped forward with a couple of designs he had kept in his top drawer. One was accepted as an interim design. During the next few years it evolved into the standard 7.62x39 caliber SKS rifle as we know it today. Although markedly better than all previous designs and incorporating some manufacturing advantages, these SKS rifles were far from ideal. One might conclude that it took the SKS to rid the Russians of their old .30-caliber rimmed round.

Ammunition capacity of the SKS was limited to 5 or 10 rounds. It lacked a detachable-box magazine (although this can be installed as an aftermarket accessory), and there was no full-auto capacity. This is not surprising when one remembers that initial models held only 10 rounds.

Even at this writing, a nonselective SKS can be made full auto by reworking the weapon's sear. But this operation is seldom undertaken by modern owners because it just isn't practical.

Russia was destined to adopt the AK-47 as its standard rifle in 1947. Why the SKS design stuck around as long as it did is lost in the fog of peace following World War II. Despite its early demise, the SKS rifle was carried by various elite Russian honor guards. It was used extensively along with the AK-47 in Vietnam and was used to supply various rebel forces around the world from Laos to Nicaragua. One commentator claims that no Russian war materiel is ever discarded or made surplus. Perhaps SKS rifles were passed around enough so that everyone who really liked them finally got one!

SKS rifles have been used in large numbers as "homeguard" weapons, perhaps implying that grade-two equipment is sufficient for "National Guard" soldiers in Communist countries. During Vietnam, many U.S. GIs were so fascinated by SKS rifles that they often sent them home rather than the more functional (but illegal) AK-47s. Many a GI claimed SKSs were "very unique."

Current Chinese weapons designers apparently prefer SKS systems to the AK, although their new rifle—the Type 63—has distinct characteristics of both weapons. These characteristics include detachable-box magazines, select fire, rotary bolts, and composition stocks.

A later Chinese design called a Type 68 was made to be faster and easier to manufacture. Other hybrid types have come as quickly as Chinese arms makers could assimilate them into their manufacturing systems. At this writing, SKS rifles in 7.62x39 may have finally reached their apex in the Chinese Type 84 rifle. This is a much-modified and worked-over SKS. It is immediately distinguishable by its ability to use older AK magazines.

China and the Soviet Union, in competition with each other to influence world politics, exported these rifles virtually everywhere. Now, after the collapse of Communism, both of these producing countries export rifles to earn foreign exchange rather than for any particular ideology.

U.S. citizens can, as of this writing, still purchase new and used SKS rifles from a great number of importers. Sales of SKS rifles have, to some extent, expanded to fill the void left by import bans on military AKMs.

Folding-stock versions or unpinned, folding-stock conversions are prohibited, as are some detaching magazines. But these rules are tough to enforce.

Aftermarket products for SKS rifles are generally limited to structural nylon folding stocks and to packages that modify magazines to a greatly expanded capacity. These can either be detachable-box magazines or extra-capacity integral magazines. Currently, permanently attached or extra-capacity magazines (either attached or detachable) installed before November 18, 1990, are legal. One might be tempted to conclude that this type of rule is not enforceable, but the more valid conclusion is that in a police state tremendous latitude for arbitrary enforcement exists.

The cost of a folding stock, which must be permanently pinned after installation, is about $35. Various suppliers are reportedly enjoying brisk sales of these items.

Many SKS owners remove the useless integral bayonet assembly, cutting weight and doing away with a potential seed and weed catcher. With the bayonet gone, aftermarket bipods function a bit more easily.

Surprisingly, SKS rifles are sufficiently accurate to warrant adding a telescopic sight. Placing a scope on an SKS is a bit convoluted, but a number of aftermarket suppliers have come forth with designs that work well. For specific suppliers, check in *Shotgun News* or with a local dealer. New designs hit the market almost weekly, so your best bet is probably *Shotgun News*.

Great numbers of different SKS rifles have made their way to U.S. shores. Most are from China, but others have also come from Russia, Romania, and Bulgaria—and the Chinese even set up a factory in Bangladesh! Unfortunately, unlike with later AR-15s, parts from all these diverse makes, models, and configurations are not necessarily interchangeable. Owners who purchase aftermarket parts, including stocks and magazines, may find that some hand fitting is required. As a general rule, this work is neither complicated nor difficult.

The basic design of the SKS has remained constant for a good number of years now. It is likely, however, that these rifles will be modified to fire 5.56mm/.223 rounds. If this occurs, it will certainly be an improvement of this design. No mechanical or engineering problems hinder this relatively simple alteration. Resulting weapons will be rugged, easily manufactured, effective, and, most of all, very cheap. Competition with Western-built AR-15-type weapons could become severe, provided we are still allowed to own them.

BIBLIOGRAPHY

Hogg, Ian V. *Jane's Infantry Weapons*. London: Jane's Publishing Co., 1991.

Long, Duncan. *The SKS Type 45 Carbine*. El Dorado, AR: Desert Publications, 1992.

CHAPTER

The AR-15 Pistol

12

The concept of owning and using a pistol that fires .223/5.56mm rounds tends to appeal to gun nuts. As a result, numerous firearms designers have come up with their own designs. Currently, at least two companies manufacture AR-15-type commercial pistols, and many have been offered in the past for varying lengths of time. These latter designs were often characterized by high cost and shoddy workmanship. In the United States, you might have one of these qualities and still stay in business, but not both.

Ballistically, using a .223 round in a pistol has a great deal of appeal. The round is infinitely more powerful than whatever is in second place. The design of the .223 was specifically tailored to facilitate function in self-loaders. Penetration, even out of very short barrels, is excellent. Using the same ammunition and magazines in one's pistol as in one's rifle is also laudatory, harking back to the Old West when weapons were often purchased for that reason alone.

If there are problems with AR-15 pistols, they relate to their weight, bulk, and expense. It is difficult to bring any AR-15 type pistol currently available into play with any speed and accuracy. These are not for fast-draw pistoleros. On the other hand, one would—and should—be tempted to fire effectively at far greater ranges with an AR pistol. Users report good, usable accuracy up to 150 yards when a rest is used. Accurate one-handed "pistol" fire is virtually impossible.

AR-15-style pistols sell for as much or more as rifles; this is not always a logical situation, but it is nevertheless a fact of life.

Undoubtedly, a great many more gun nuts would be actively in the market for an AR/.223 pistol if they could somehow circumvent the horrible price, $600 to $900 each. Unfortunately, this chapter cannot explain how to circumvent these cost realities or make an AR pistol for little or nothing. Owners must count on spending between $600 and $800 each, even if they do all the work themselves! This may take some

Two-tone version of the AR-15 pistol makes use of noncoated aluminum parts and chromed flash hider and magazine. Note the Aimpoint dot scope with a tiny BSL-1 laser mounted to it. The barrel can be detached from the gun quickly without any special tools. (Photos from *Making Your AR-15 into a Legal Pistol* by Duncan long.)

Prototype AR-15 pistol made with "in the white" Provost kit. The lightweight Action Arms electric dot scope on an A.R.M.S. mount makes sighting quick and simple.

PK-15 protype with 5 1/2-inch barrel. The charging handle is on the left of the upper receiver and the return spring is inside the cover on top. The pistol weights 2 1/2 pounds empty and has an overall length of 13 inches, which is shorter than the 16-inch AR-15 below it. (Photo courtesy of Tom Provost.)

dedication on the part of some, but it is true that in this technological age the price of some equipment spirals upward mercilessly.

Duncan Long is one of our nation's foremost gurus on matters relating to the AR-15. He has forgotten more about this type of weapon than most of us will ever know. Working with an assistant or two, Long has developed a workable and fairly simple *legal* method of building an AR-15 pistol in one's home workshop. Those who suddenly discover that they absolutely must have an AR pistol and are not either fairly competent gunsmiths or knowledgeable regarding AR-15s should order a copy of Long's book *Making Your AR-15 into a Legal Pistol* from Paladin Press. It contains—in minute detail—all the steps required to put a proper pistol together.

Legal aspects of building an AR pistol are not particularly formidable, but they are almost foolishly exacting. One should plan to follow these procedures as precisely as assembly of the actual parts allows. Those who don't or can't follow these requirements should not consider building a .223 pistol. There is simply no way that these weapons could possibly be worth the hassle and grief encountered from not following a few, relatively easy procedures. Those procedures are, however, quite costly and not entirely rational.

Keep in mind that it is absolutely forbidden to ever make a pistol out of a rifle or to own any rifle less than 26 inches long with less than 16 inches of barrel without registering the weapon and paying a special tax. Yet, it is completely legal and aboveboard to assemble a pistol from brand-new AR-15 parts that have *never* previously been assembled into any firearm.

If a person builds only for himself and not for resale, a federal manufacturer's license is *not* required. Logic, here, involves the fact that the receiver is already manufactured by a federally licensed maker. It (the receiver) must be transferred through an FFL holder, but this is the extent of the restrictions. Owners should carry papers with the pistol at all times showing that it has been made from new parts that were never part of a rifle.

Tom Provost, a gunsmith-tinkerer from San Jose, California, worked with Duncan Long to design and develop an aftermarket kit containing a buffer tube that is shorter than a shorty carbine version of the AR-15. With this kit, one can use a regular, commonly sold aftermarket "shorty" 10- or 16-inch barrel or even purchase a new 6-inch model from Provost to construct a pistol.

Muzzle blast from this really short barrel is said to rival stun grenades—guaranteed to kill all mosquitoes in the area plus any low-flying ducks. You have a choice about twist on these barrels, either 1-in-7 or 1-in-9. Either will stabilize nicely, with even the heaviest .223 rounds.

You can purchase regular 10-inch barrels from Olympic Arms, Olympia, Washington; Quality Parts Company, Windham, Maine; or from any other supplier of AR-15 parts.

When ordering, you must include a letter stating that the barrel and most likely the upper receiver assembly, which logically should be purchased with the barrel as a package, are to be used with all-new parts to build an AR-15 pistol and not an NFA gun. Doing this may take extra correspondence, but be sure that this chore is handled properly. Save copies of your letter to the parts people as well as their invoice for *new,* never-assembled-before parts.

Be absolutely certain that this completed upper-receiver assembly is made up of all-new parts never before assembled into a weapon and that the dealer gives you a written statement to that effect. This may preclude buying any parts for an AR pistol at gun shows. Cost for an upper receiver and short barrel will be about $490.

Write or call Tom Provost about AR-15 pistol buffer kits or about his 6-inch barrel kits at The Accuracy People, Box 24096, San Jose, CA 95144. Buffer kits alone cost about $90. Full upper-receiver kits with short barrels cost about $600, including needed short buffers.

Using the same procedure as above, order a complete lower receiver, less stock and, if possible, the buffer tube and buffer tube spring. This will probably cost about $165.

If you purchase completely assembled upper- and lower-receiver assemblies with assembled bolt carriers and trigger mechanisms, putting the pistol together is dramatically simplified. All you must do is put the upper and lower receiver units together. The short buffer tube assembly is simply screwed into the rear of the lower receiver.

Duncan Long strongly recommends that you use either a rivet to connect the upper and lower receivers or that stock push pins be permanently altered so that regular push pins can never be used. This is to preclude anyone from ever changing the pistol back to a a rifle or anyone from claiming that he has seen the weapon as a rifle. Once made into a rifle, it can never be legally changed back to a pistol. Using a bushed pin hole, a smaller pin held in place by a cotter key creates a pistol that looks a bit hokey but that cannot be changed to a rifle. During these times of intense paranoia, some precautionary measures must be taken.

After the two receiver halves are permanently attached with a rivet, cleaning problems may result.

Firing AR pistols is quite a bit of fun, provided you have ear protection. The discharge sounds very much like a .50-caliber machine gun, especially in the 6-inch barrel version. Recoil, never great in the rifles, is virtually absent in the pistols. Accuracy is OK to very good, if you shoot from a rest. These pistols are tough to use in traditional one- and two-handed stances.

You would not expect penetration with a relatively small .22-caliber bullet that achieves its results from speed to be as great as with rifles, and it is not. At longer ranges, .223 bullets from a pistol really run out of poop.

I have owned two .223 pistols briefly. Both are now on sailboats plying eastern Atlantic coastal waters. They have even traveled with their owners to Europe. One man has rigged a 90-round drum magazine to his pistol. Including a dozen or so 30-round mags, he really has a great deal of very compact firepower should he ever need it. This same owner contemplated building a full-auto AR pistol that would really be a kind of submachine gun. He quickly discovered that there is no way of doing so legally.

As Duncan Long says, partly in jest, "With a 90-round drum magazine and full-auto capacity, this would be the only crew-served pistol."

BIBLIOGRAPHY

Long, Duncan. *Making Your AR-15 into a Legal Pistol.* Boulder, CO: Paladin Press, 1991.

CHAPTER

The Mini-14

13

A significant number of well-qualified men of action who own Mini-14s believe that this is the finest, best-tested, initially trouble-free semiauto rifle ever brought to market. Judging by the number sold and the legion of very satisfied users, it would be tough to argue with this. The Mini-14, many people believe, is an ideal balance of military, hunting, and survival rifle. Further, because they are made domestically, M-14s are not subject to foolish and contradictory import restrictions.

Sturm, Ruger and Company has been our nation's most progressive, innovative firearms manufacturer for several decades. Had the U.S. military not adopted the AR-15 .223 mag, knowledgeable observers believe that a slightly modified version of the Mini-14 could have become standard GI issue.

Ruger's rifle is ideal for both military and civilian use. Few designers have ever done this.

Because of this fact and because of a great host of aftermarket suppliers available, owners can customize to their exact tastes, creating some extremely interesting, functional, and unique weapons systems.

It is not quite accurate to claim that William Batterman Ruger invented the Mini-14 in 1972. Ruger was probably the last of the true genius-class firearms inventors we will see in our country. One of Ruger's most outstanding talents was his ability to put together and guide teams of people who, by feeding off each others' strengths, were able to accomplish dramatic results.

Ruger's Mini-14 team had already invested more than five years' blood, sweat, and tears testing and developing this design when it finally hit the market. Initial sales were to government and law enforcement agencies exclusively. In 1976, with production running along nicely, Ruger finally made semiauto-only Mini-14s available to the public.

Success was not instantaneous, as was true with most other Ruger designs. It took about eight years

The paramilitary 20GB version of the Mini-14. (Photos from The Mini-14: The Plinker, Assault, and Everything Else Rifle by Duncan Long and courtesy of Sturm, Ruger and Co.)

A standard series 181 Mini-14 that has been customized with the addition of an extended magazine, Choate ventilated handguard (which replaced the then-standard wooden handguard), Choate flash suppressor, and an Uncle Mike's sling.

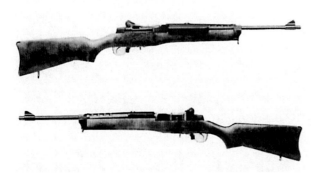

The standard Mini-14 stock has a shape that many find comfortable, but the overall pull will be short for some shooters.

The Choate buttpad can be mounted onto the standard Mini-14 without having to cut the stock. It adds 1 inch to the length of pull, as well as maintaining the curve of the butt.

before Mini-14s really started selling in large numbers. Seemingly, some owners wanted to hunt with them, others viewed them as paramilitary, and a few even thought the cartridge was too small. Ruger worked on a .308 version but dropped this in part because of the .223's acceptance and in part because of functioning problems with .308s.

In 1984 Ruger acknowledged the design's popularity by setting up a separate manufacturing facility just to handle the huge number of rifle orders he had on the books.

Alexander M. Sturm and Bill Ruger started their company in 1949 with the introduction of a radical new .22 auto pistol. Many people miss the Sturm in Sturm, Ruger and Company, assuming incorrectly that Ruger was a play on World War II German pistols. Ruger simply capitalized on good form and function with his pistol, which was in no way a Luger.

Because of Ruger's design genius, which included remarkable, new, cost-saving manufacturing techniques, his original .22 pistol dramatically undersold the market in terms of price and quality. As a young man running a trap line, I recall as clear as yesterday thinking that here is a good, reliable pistol I can purchase for less than a week's wages. If my memory is correct, my first Standard Auto .22 cost $28.50 in about 1954!

Alexander Sturm passed away before he could see the fruits of his investment, but other Ruger designs followed his .22 in rapid succession. Today, Ruger's stated goal is to bring out one new design every year. At times, Ruger's new designs are mostly cosmetic, but in others they are definitely trend-setters. Ruger's 10/22 rifles, for instance, are thought by many experts to be *the* benchmark .22 against which all others should be measured in terms of reliability, ruggedness, accuracy, price, and aesthetics.

Primarily, the Mini-14 is as reliable as it is because it is not really a new rifle design. Instead, this weapon is a hybrid of previously perfected, excellent designs. Both our M1 Garand and M1 carbine heavily influenced Ruger's thinking on this rifle—Garands for their trigger assembly and bolt camming arrangements, and carbines for their light weight and smaller, reduced-power cartridges.

Simplified manufacturing techniques reminiscent of those of the AKMs are used in Mini-14s, but no design components carry over directly from the AK family to the Ruger rifle.

The Ranch Rifle version of the Mini-14 is ideal for scope mounting, thanks to its integral scope mounts. The iron sights can be retained for emergency use should the scope become damaged. (This photo and the one below from *Mini-14 Super Systems* by Duncan Long and courtesy of Sturm, Ruger and Co.)

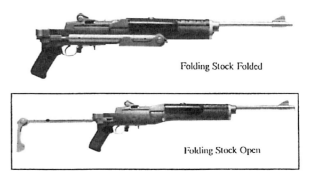

Folding Stock Folded

Folding Stock Open

The Ruger-made folding stock folded (above) and open (below). Currently, it is somewhat of a collector's item; therefore, readers are advised to trade off the stock and purchase a more easily modified folder if the length of pull doesn't suit them.

The original rifle to which the lineage of the Mini-14 can be traced is the U.S. M1 Garand created by John Garand. Various versions of the rifle include the standard M1 (top three rifles and the rare M1-D sniper rifle, bottom of photo). Rifle second from bottom is a standard M1 with a commercial scope mount that replaced the rear sight assembly. (Unless noted otherwise, photos from *The Mini-14: The Plinker, Assault, and Everything Else Rifle* by Duncan Long.)

These rifles were initially offered to civilians with 5-round magazines so as to conform to laws in some states regarding hunting with extended-capacity magazines. Police models came with 30-round capacity magazines. Civilian users needing greater capacity could modify standard AR-15 mags or, preferably, purchase some of the 30- and 40-round models offered by aftermarket houses.

These rifles' dependence on quickly changed, high-capacity magazines rather than internal clips is heavily influenced by the U.S. M14 design.

Ruger has now more or less stabilized Mini-14s into two main designs—Ranch Rifles and Mini-14s. Ranch Rifles are specifically designed to accept and operate with scope sights easily and effectively. Internally, they have a slightly different buffer system that reduces already light recoil, and they throw their spent cases down to the side, away from the scope. Ranch Rifles were made in .222 Remington for export to places where military cartridges—.223 caliber (about the same as .222 Remington), and 7.62x39—are prohibited. In the United States, .222 Remington Ranch Rifles are collectors' items. All Mini-14s are offered in .223 caliber.

Ranch Rifles are also available in the Russian 7.62x39 caliber, sometimes called Mini-30s. These would be about like a semiauto .30-30 deer rifle. In both cases (7.62x39 and 5.56/.223 caliber), American owners should never fire even modestly corrosive surplus ammo in their rifles. AKM and SKS military rifles are manufactured with chromed barrels and gas ports and can be effectively cleaned after the use of corrosive ammo. Most of Ruger's rifles, however, are made of steel and will deteriorate unless they are cleaned thoroughly.

Within these two broad design classes, Ruger has offered a number of variations, including stock types, folding stocks, and stainless steel, as well as paramilitary and police models. Some models have even come with bayonet studs as standard equipment. One can only wonder who Bill Ruger figured would use a Mini-14 with a bayonet.

Basically, there are only three distinct Ruger .223 rifles if all cosmetics are stripped away: the Mini-14 semiauto sporting rifle, the Mini-14 police/military model, and the Ranch Rifle. More Mini-14s have probably been dressed for success than any other weapons, with the possible exception of AR-15s.

After purchasing a large capacity 30- to 40-round magazine, users usually start looking at aftermarket stocks. Both Choate and Ram-Line offer excellent to almost classy models of folding stocks which, unlike SKS folders, do not legally have to be pinned open. Their cost is about $65. No special tools or ability is required for installation. Basically, they are a drop-the-barreled-action-in-and-tighten-the-screws arrangement.

In theory, Mini-14 barrels could be shortened to about 13 inches without affecting function. Muzzle blast is increased by this alteration, while penetration and long-range accuracy suffer a bit. Mini-14s chopped to 13 inches with folding stock installed would constitute an extremely handy, deadly cross between a rifle and pistol. Regrettably, Ruger does not sell component receivers that can be built into long-barreled semiauto pistols legally.

Bullpup stocks designed for Mini-14s have great appeal. These kits work with chopped flash guards, but the resulting package is just barely a legal 26 inches (if that), even without fooling with the barrel. Nevertheless, gunshop owners who put these packages together report great interest in bullpups on the part of gun nuts who see them.

Until relatively recently, assembling bullpup firearms was a difficult, convoluted program that had to be undertaken on a custom, one-at-a-time basis. Now the Muzzlelite Company has a structural nylon, clamshell-type stock that can be installed on a Mini-14 action in an hour or less. Some gun nuts not accustomed to packages of nuts, bolts, springs, and miscellaneous small parts will still find assembly convoluted.

Unfortunately, you must purchase a new Ruger Mini-14 and discard the stock when converting to a Muzzlelite bullpup. You must add the price of a rifle to the $100 stock package. The end product is very nice but quite costly. It is, however, a great treat to own—provided a total of about $500 including rifle, stock, large capacity mag, and sling does not turn one off.

Laser or scope sights are easily installed on either a basic Mini-14 or a bullpup. Most owners who experiment with lasers eventually retire them since their use in broad daylight is limited. Regular scopes mounted on the relatively thin, flexible nylon bullpup carry-handles are also marginal. Mounted on Ranch Rifles themselves, scopes have some utility.

Ruger's open sights are accurate, rugged, and suitable for many uses. Open sights on the bullpup housing are adequate but certainly not target grade. In this case, you are in a cul-de-sac. Open sights are just OK, and a scope mounted on the handle doesn't hold its zero well.

Although a bullpup stock package on a Mini-14 provides a very powerful, compact, and attractive package, keep in mind that you are bumping into absolute legal minimums with these outfits. Shortening the barrel of an issue Mini-14 or camp rifle to 16.5 inches, for instance, results in a total package less than 26 inches long, below the legal minimum for a non-NFA rifle.

A close acquaintance living in a far western suburb of Chicago made his living raising deer- and elk-size wild game. His principal herd was Sika deer, of which he had about 80. Poachers from the heavily populated areas surrounding his game farm caused continual grief. His first deterrent was heavy rubber pellets loaded in shot shells. Judging by penetration tests on 1/2-inch plywood, these projectiles would have stung pretty good! But the fellow's attorney advised against actually using them.

"If anyone was ever seriously hurt, or said they were seriously hurt, a horribly expensive legal wrangle would result, especially if they were kids," the attorney advised. Being from the "rock salt" era myself, I had little sympathy.

Next, we put together a Mini-14 with an ominous black Muzzlelite bullpup stock *and* a MWG-brand 90-round drum magazine. Mostly, the

1. **Connector assembly mounting screws**—secure connector group mount to receiver frame.

2. **Connector assembly mount plate**—assembly base for the complete connector group mechanism.

3. **Selector index plunger**—locks the selector lever into the desired index for the type of fire (semi- or full auto).

4. **Selector index plunger spring**—powers the selector index plunger.

5a. **Selector index plunger and spring housing**—contains the selector index plunger and its spring.

5. **Selector lever**—controls the desired type of fire. The lower arm restricts the upward movement of the sear trip lever when set to full-auto position.

6. **Selector index plunger pull knob**—must be pulled in changing selector indexing for the type of fire required. Pulling the knob will disengage the selector index from the index hole so it can be moved from one position to the other.

7. **Connector bar and rocker lever rivet**—connects both parts permanently as one unit. Both ends of rivet heads must be flush to the external surface of the countersunk hole so the assembled parts will lie flush with the assembly plate when assembled.

8. **Rocker lever**—acts as a bridge between the connector bar and secondary sear trip lever.

9. **Connector bar**—the key part of the connector group. The bar is operated solely by the slide cocking handle during forward recoil.

10. **Connector bar from screw support nut**—mates with the connector bar from screw support.

11. **Connector bar from screw support**—assembled through the slotted end of the connector bar. The screw secures the front end of the connector bar to stabilize and prevent it from wobbling during operation.

12. **Trip lever assembly screw**—secures the trip lever to mount plate.

13. **Sear trip lever**—pushes the secondary sear connecting pin rearward when the selector lever is set at full-auto position. It acts as a mechanical trigger during full-automatic operation. If the selector lever is set at semiauto, the tripping lever only moves up and down and does not pivot rearward.

14. **Selector lever assembly screw**—secures the selector lever unit to the mount plate.

15. **Rocker lever assembly screw**—secures the rocker lever unit to the mount plate.

16. **Replacement secondary sear connecting pin**—makes contact with the tripping lever during full-auto operation each time the slide closes forward. This part, when pushed by the sear trip bent arm, will automatically release the hammer during full-auto cycle of operation.

17. **Replacement secondary sear**—replaces the original facotry sear so that it can be operated by the connector group mechanism for selective firing. The replacement sear need not be removed, as it will funciton as well as the original with or without the connector group mounted on the receiver frame.

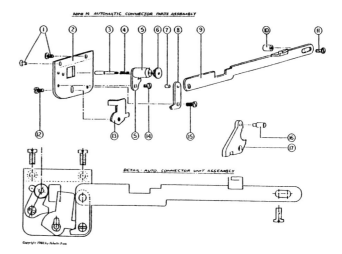

Mini-14 automatic connector parts assembly. (Illustrations taken from *The Mini-14 Exotic Weapons System*.)

fellow carried it around in his pickup for show. For a while, it seemed as though just letting people know about the gun would be sufficient. But it wasn't.

A flat, slow, muddy creek ran down through his property along which the herd of Sika deer usually ran. Very late one evening, several young men boldly climbed over the 8-foot chain-link fence, shot one of the does with a .22, and started gutting it.

My buddy, covered a bit by a little patch of woods, grabbed his bullpup and crept to within about 150 yards of the young men. It was not difficult because these guys substituted a brazen attitude for any finesse. They were still along the creek when he got in position, but full dark was fast approaching. No one was acting as lookout.

Even in the failing light, my friend's silhouette was obvious on the little knoll as he sat there with his bullpup. On an even cadence he started pumping rounds into the muddy flat creek. His first salvo was about 10 feet left of the group. Mud and water flew in every direction.

His second was to their right, sufficiently close that the wind carried the spray over the young men. For an instant, they just huddled there in fear. My friend got up and started toward them. When he did, they broke and ran like the proverbial turpentined dog.

Later this same fellow asked about altering his Mini-14 to full auto. It was after 1986, and there was no way to make the conversion legal. I talked him out of the job. Full auto in a Mini-14 is a dream

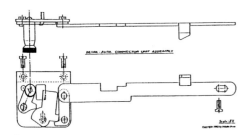

Machinist's drawings of detail of auto connector unit assembly (not to scale).

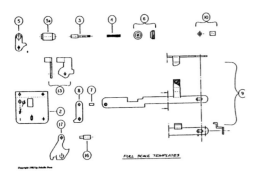

Templates (not to scale).

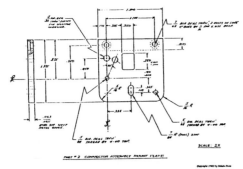

Part #2, connector assembly mount plate (not to scale).

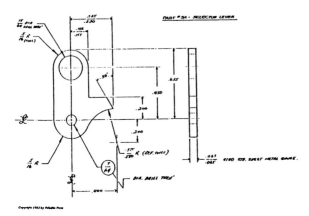

Part #5A, selector lever (not to scale).

of many but may not be practical even if you choose to disregard the law.

The Mini-14 Exotic Weapons System (available from Paladin Press) has machinist's drawings that show how a home builder can fabricate and install the 17 or so parts required to produce a good, workable Mini-14 select-fire assembly. Some of these parts are simple store-bought screws and nuts turned down for this specific application, but others of these parts are complex.

Estimates are that it would take a reasonably adept and determined man of some skill using a hacksaw and file about five working days to make these parts and fit them into their required subassemblies. After that, my guess is that it would take a day or two on the range just to tune and fit for reasonable functioning. That is too much fooling around and expense just to replace a trigger finger, which can be more effective, I finally convinced my friend.

Nevertheless, for those who find the concept of a select-fire Mini-14 intriguing, machinist's drawings for this conversion are included here.

As mentioned, commercial Mini-14s are fine, trouble-free systems, as long as you don't use corrosive surplus ammo. It won't happen overnight, but this cheaper ammo will eventually trash any commercial semiauto made without a chromed gas port and piston assembly.

As of this writing, the Mini-14s and Ranch Rifles are the most ideal combination of hunting, survival, and paramilitary weapons available in the United States. And future restrictive gun laws may preclude anything better from coming along. Given their relatively low price, it seems that everyone should own at least one of these incredible weapons. They are bound to dominate the market for the foreseeable future.

BIBLIOGRAPHY

Long, Duncan. *The Mini-14: The Plinker, Hunter, Assault, and Everything Else Rifle.* Boulder, Colorado: Paladin Press, 1987.

_____. *Mini-14 Super Systems.* Boulder, CO: Paladin Press, 1991.

The Mini-14 Exotic Weapons System (revised edition). Boulder, CO: Paladin Press, 1989.

CHAPTER

AR-7: Half Pistol, Half Rifle

14

During the early-to-mid 1960s, Cliff and Dennis Stover, brothers then living in Kokomo, Indiana, started what became an annual event. Early every fall, they drove about 350 miles just about due north to Sault Ste. Marie, Ontario, and continued to wherever moose hunting was good that year. Initially, they hired an Indian guide with a boat, but eventually they simply took their own boat and their own chances of finding a moose. This pleasant tradition continued until the 1980s when the Canadian government made it virtually impossible for a nonresident to secure a hunting license and tag.

Some years, the Stover boys shot a moose, and some years they didn't. They did, however, discover that Canadian soil where they hunted raised truly large numbers of delicious-eating grouse, called "partridge" by the Canucks. Basically, there were three kinds of partridge: a red-eyed fool's hen they could snare with a shoelace and pole, a very large chicken-size blue partridge that was both wary and scarce, and the ubiquitous common "partridge," which we Yankees call ruffed grouse.

Often, two or three of the latter would stand on old logging roads, picking gravel or counting cars. They were often so numerous that the brothers tried to line them up, getting two with one shot. On one occasion, Dennis shot 36 of the birds, bringing to grass more pounds of meat than Cliff, who elected to look for the wily moose that day.

The brothers and their accompanying friends would have liked to take their pistols with them while hunting moose, but quickly discovered that, for some unknown reason, Canadians are extremely paranoid about sidearms. As mitigation against this obvious mental disorder and in an attempt to salvage some good, usable meat from among the obvious plenty, the Stovers purchased Armalite AR-7 rifles. They used a light saddle strap securely buckled around the small of the pistol grip and snapped a spring-loaded D-ring onto their belts. In this way, the little, light AR-7s carried just about

The AR-7 was designed from the start as a survival gun and makes an ideal .22 rifle to carry along in a backpack for camping or to keep in a car or airplane for emergencies. The barrel (which can be taken off the receiver by unscrewing the threaded ring), magazine, and receiver all fit into compartments in the hollow stock. The buttplate then slips over the stock to hold everything in. Total length of the package is just 16 1/2 inches. (Photos from *AR-7 Super Systems* by Duncan Long and courtesy of Charter Arms.)

like pistols. It took perhaps 40 additional seconds to draw and assemble their "sidearms," but this didn't count for much in the total scheme of things.

Eventually, the Stovers got sufficiently practiced with their AR-7s that they were able to shoot two or three partridge on the ground before the others flew off. They were even able, at times, to make wing shots with these .22s at what is admittedly a fairly difficult flying target.

They shot partridge of all kinds, ducks, and an occasional beaver and mink, whose skins they brought home as souvenirs, when given the chance. On one especially memorable occasion, the brothers were motoring their steel canoe along shore, slowly looking for moose when they came across an otter out for a swim. It took a bit of stealthy pursuit, but eventually they were able to plug the little fresh-water critter in the head. It was the toughest critter they ever tried to skin, the Stovers recall.

Their AR-7 bird shooting ended in a most unfortunate fashion. One fall they got into a very large flock of Merganser ducks. All together they dropped six or eight of the large birds. It was very near freezing, so they simply pulled off the heads and stripped entrails out. At home, their wives dutifully roasted up the critters after finishing the dressing operation. As anyone who has been around these toothed monstrosities will attest, God did not intend for them to be eaten by humans. At best, they taste like shoe leather dipped in sardine oil. As a result these were the last birds from Canada these ladies ever tried to prepare. The Stovers simply gave up bringing any birds home after a few years.

Armalite 7, .22 caliber, semiautomatic rifles are the second in the series of dramatically modern weapons designed by forward-looking armament engineers at Fairchild Engine and Airplane Corporation, Hagerstown, Maryland. AR-15-type weapons, as previously mentioned, were the first, and by far the most successful, weapon system designed around modern alloys and mass-manufacturing techniques. There are many similarities between the two.

George Sullivan is credited with coming up with the idea of using a minimum number of aluminum alloy die-cast parts and a fiberglass stock for this extremely simplistic little rifle. Eugene Stoner, later of Stoner 63 Systems fame, seems to have been the principal inventor of both the AR-5 (a very small, lightweight .22 Hornet bolt action) and the AR-7.

Radically new and different, Armalite first sold this little clip-fed, semiauto for $49.95 in 1959. This price reflected both the weapon's uniqueness and quite a high profit for the company.

Despite what now seem like excellent prospects for commercial success, Armalite decided to spin off its AR-15 to Colt, and then in 1970 Armalite sold its second-best design, the AR-7, to Charter Arms.

Charter hit the market in the United States with its widely promoted AR-7 just at the time that survivalists were making the most dramatic impact on our arms market. These people wanted a sound, light, rugged, easy to carry and hide, simple to maintain, quiet and accurate, and cheap to shoot .22 LR system. They instantly found it in the AR-7. After smoothing some rough edges, Charter produced thousands of AR-7s equal or superior to the original Armalites.

Again, aftermarket manufacturers followed the money by offering accessories not originally available from the manufacturers. AR-7 owners thought these add-ons were important.

As is true with many modern weapons designs, the biggest complaint about the complete system involved magazine function and reliability. Know-ledgeable owners talked about having to treat original AR-7 magazines like eggs because they were considered so fragile. Reliability was sometimes poor and capacity for a semiauto was ridiculous (eight rounds!). Owners quickly discovered that without good magazines they had very little, and in the case of AR-7s, magazines were definitely the weak link.

Fortunately, Feather Enterprises, Ram-Line, Eagle, and several lesser-known houses immediately saw their opportunity. For instance, Ram-Line's 25-round magazine is a marvel of fit and function. The cost is only about $10 because of modern injection-molding manufacturing processes. Full-auto versions of the AR-7 are completely impossible without these magazines.

In some cases a bit of fine tuning is necessary. AR-7 owners of some models report that, for extremely flawless function in either semiauto or full-auto mode, they must slowly, carefully custom polish the guns' loading ramps with a fine rat-tail file.

AR-7s, as the Stover brothers discovered, are surprisingly accurate out to the limits of a .22 LR fired in a rifle so light that it becomes the only .22 rifle in which one can feel recoil. Scopes can be easily mounted on existing AR-7 receivers by use of simple, 1-inch tip-off mounts. Scopes dramatically improve the shooter's ability to hit distant targets, while dramatically reducing portability. The Stover brothers found the weapon too light to use off-hand with a scope.

Taking the scope off and on à la James Bond in Istanbul does not cut it. Fine accuracy, superior to using issue open sights, is only possible if the rifle is sighted in again after each disassembly.

Mitchell Arms, Sherwood International, and Choate Machine produce one-piece composition stocks for AR-7s. They are all neat, rugged units, but they sacrifice the knock-down, out-of-sight portability that is otherwise the AR-7's strong suit by installing a large fixed stock.

If you must own a silenced weapon, an AR-7 is made to order. They work well on standard, low-velocity ammo, and the owner can easily replace the suppressed barrel with one that does not have telltale muzzle threads. Even better, it is easy to purchase a new silencer-only barrel that is covered by a jacket of plastic or aluminum pipe. The only problem is securing these full-length silencers to the barrel. Some owners have epoxied jackets in place, and others use friction collars secured by hose clamps. Either way, a full-length silencer is much more effective than a barrel-end add-on.

In any case, it is easy to purchase a number of new barrels from Charter Arms so that a silenced version can always be kept safely out of sight.

To take advantage of the work it had done on the AR-5, Armalite devised the AR-7 Explorer rifle. Shown here is a Charter Arms AR-7 with barrel, receiver, and magazine ready for storage in the gun's hollow stock.

Since accessories were designed for the AR-7 fit the Explorer II pistol as well, there is a large number of accessories available for the pistol. As a result, the Explorer II owner has the option of addding accessories such as this Tasco rifle scope and Ram-Line 25-round magazine. (Note the d-i-y epoxy and wood finger rest added behind the trigger guard to improve the "pointing" of the pistol.)

As this photo shows, the AR-7 and Explorer II lend themselves to custom modification, so shooters can easily create unique guns all their own. The top rifle sports a Sherwood International Convert-A-Kit, while the lower gun has been modified with homemade grip plates made from scrap wood.

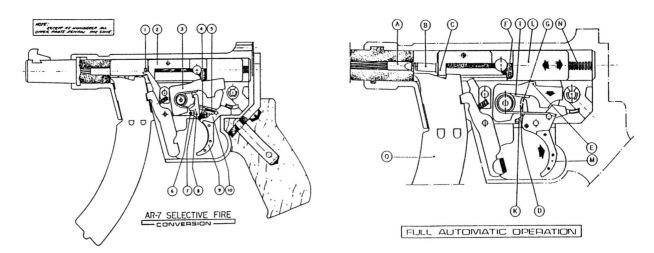

AR-7 SELECTIVE FIRE CONVERSION

FULL AUTOMATIC OPERATION

AR-7 selective-fire conversion. (Illustrations taken from *The AR-7 Advanced Weapons System*.)

1. Extractor—same specifications as the factory part except for more forward hook to compensate for firing-pin protrusion.
2. Fixed-type firing pin—replaces the factory retractable firing pin.
3. Sear—replaces the factory hammer. Uses the same spring that powers both the hammer and trigger.
4. Trip spring plunger—powers the trip mechanism.
5. Strip spring—powers the plunger rod.
6. Tripping shoulder—a cross pin that pushes the trip finger to disconnect the trip from sear engagement at the end of pull, producing semiauto operation. Pulling the pin out will instantly convert the gun to full-auto operation, thus acting as the fire-selector mechanism.
7. Trip—connects with sear. Acts as bridge between the sear and trigger.
8. Trip pin—retains the assembly of the trip to trigger.
9. Trigger shoe—widens the lower section of the trigger. Can be riveted on both sides of the trigger or brazed.
10. Trigger—replaces the factory trigger. Accommodates the trip assembly.

Full-automatic operation.

A. Barrel chamber
B. Top round
C. Firing pin
D. Sear hook
E. Sear lug
F. Bolt-shoulder pathway
G. Trip hook
J. Selector
K. Trip toe
L. Bolt
M. Trigger
N. Spring tension
O. Magazine

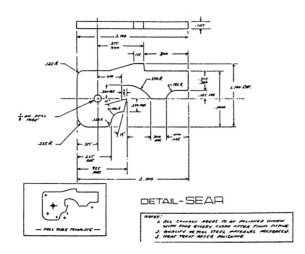

Detail of sear.

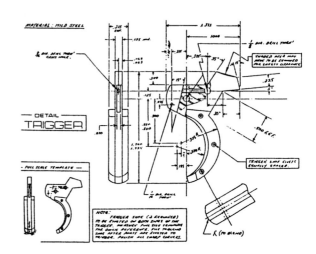

Detail of trigger.

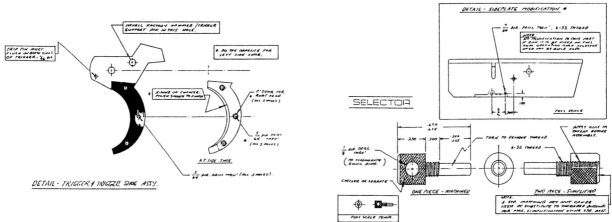

Detail of trigger and trigger shoe assembly.

Selector.

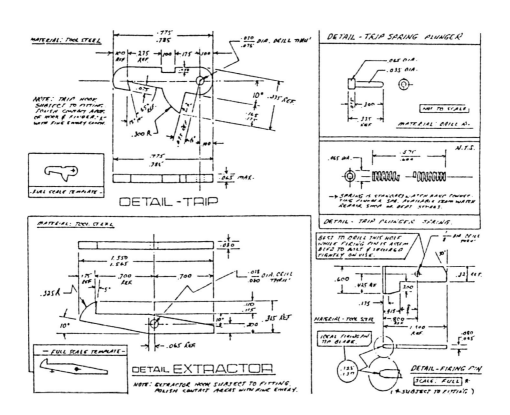

Detail of firing pin (not to scale).

Jon Ciener makes a very nice commercial silencer for AR-7s. Simply purchase the barrel and silencer package, which is installed on the AR-7 receiver like any other barrel. The cost is approximately $465, not including a $200 tax stamp. All of Ciener's silencers are extremely effective.

A few add-ons, such as flash hiders and barrel shrouds, can be adapted to AR-7s from other weapons. Some owners like the way these items doll up their rifles, while others consider them to be "gingerbread."

For a time, U.S. literature was full of do-it-yourself information on converting an AR-7 rifle to a pistol. This is a legal conversion if all-new parts are used. Responding to this perceived need, Charter Arms brought out an AR-7 pistol, the Explorer II, in the early 1980s. It was big and clumsy, but not nearly so bad as it first looked. User reaction to the Explorer II pistol was underwhelming, to say the least. By early 1988, virtually all of Charter's Explorer IIs had been dumped on the surplus market at distressed prices.

Enough time has probably elapsed so that Explorers have become collectors' items. Interest in building an AR-7 pistol may evolve again. Those who have owned both can only wonder. It still seems that those wanting an AR-7 pistol are best served by finding an older-model Explorer in *Shotgun News*. Making an AR-7 pistol is a convoluted process.

If you have the time, money, and inclination to own a questionable firearm, it might be fun to construct an AR-7 submachine gun. This is done by screwing a short pistol grip onto the rear of the AR-7 receiver and placing a front-hand grip halfway up the barrel.

The easiest way to install a foregrip is to purchase a Choate or Eagle barrel shroud and bolt the grip to it, rather than to the barrel.

If you are an advanced gun tinkerer willing to patiently play around with and tune your weapon, alteration to full-auto select fire is not unduly difficult. Function is not flawless on this or any full-auto .22, but, given its rate of fire and lack of recoil, it is a formidable weapon.

Many possible conversions exist, but simpler ones that do not unduly impinge on the visible receiver seem best.

Full-auto conversion is accomplished by making a sear, trigger, trip, and trip-spring plunger. Trip-spring plungers are inserted in a tiny hole drilled in the weapon's receiver when semiauto fire is desired. (See page 148 for detailed drawings of these parts.) These parts are constructed from relatively thin, short steel ranging from .080 to .125 of an inch thick.

Careful workers, with only a fine file and hacksaw (but starting with stock of the correct thickness) and the attached drawings, can make these parts in a matter of days.

Under current law, these full-auto AR-7s cannot be made legal. An owner must decide if utility is best served by a small, easily concealed and carried grouse and duck-getter, or a full-auto, ammo-eating toy. I use my AR-7s on edible game.

AR-7s have had a dramatic influence on survival weapons in the United States, and this influence probably has not yet run its course.

Patent rights to the AR-7 have now expired, and it is possible that some "strange" versions may come on the market. Norinco in China, for instance, has been very diligent about grabbing this kind of opportunity. They have not shown up yet, but we may see collapsible AR-7-type weapons made in .380 ACP, .25 ACP, or even 9mm. Seemingly, the market is ripe for an intermediate weapon, somewhere between a .22 rimfire and larger .223 or .308s. Only time will tell.

BIBLIOGRAPHY

The AR-7 Advanced Weapons Systems. Boulder, CO: Paladin Press, 1990.

Long, Duncan. *AR-7 Super Systems*. Boulder, CO: Paladin Press, 1990.

CHAPTER

The Mighty Spud Gun

15

The following report was on the local police radio. A number—perhaps 30 to 40—fraternity boys on campus were firing muzzle-loading guns of some sort at each other. It is difficult to understand how the caller knew they were fraternity boys. As a matter of record, she didn't get the muzzle loader part right, either.

The dispatcher on duty handed the call to a sergeant, who immediately rang up the sheriff, asking for assistance. Two cars from the sheriff's department and two city police units converged on the south campus along Greek Row. They were unable to coordinate with members of campus security who were out rattling doors.

It was almost as good as the movies. One car stayed back a block in case the supposed miscreants tried running in that direction. As it worked out, the guy in his car was the only one with any credible observations.

Whatever the situation on the ground before the arrival of the gendarmes, it shifted rapidly thereafter. Instead of continuing to battle each other, the young men formed an instant alliance—no doubt created by necessity—against "the law." Before they had stood in opposing ranks three deep, separated by about 80 yards. Now, they were four deep with several in the rear who seemed to be fooling with ugly, black, plastic-looking contraptions. Quickly, the first rank was filled with men with pipes under their arms and giant smiles on their faces, facing down a gentle, grassy slope toward the authorities.

Police cruisers, each with two disembarking officers, were lined up on the adjoining tree-lined street below, perhaps 120 yards distant.

The fraternity men behind the front rank stepped back a bit. Most of those behind were fooling around with their pipes, with unusual fervor and diligence.

At the command of "fire," an estimated seven of the nine devices—according to the officer across the block—discharged with a deep, throaty rumble one would expect from a larger, heavy muzzle loader. There was no smoke and little flash, but many large projectiles went arcing out over the grassy area toward the men in blue. A few of the projectiles were launched on their high trajectories with accuracy and would have achieved a stunning blow had they actually struck anyone. Others had too much elevation and sailed out to the police cruisers. One projectile splashed off a hood, leaving a shallow dent.

Someone among the young men coordinated events. Immediately, a second echelon of perhaps 15 stepped forward, forming a second firing line. At the command they too let loose. Some of these projectiles splashed to the ground in front of the police. They looked down incredulously. They were being mortared by devices that hurled potatoes!

No one had been hit, as yet, but there was plenty of confusion and consternation. Had it not been for the single observer across the block, an accurate after-action report would have been impossible.

As the ranks of schoolboys formed for a third volley, some of the officers began to unsnap their side straps. The sergeant couldn't see everything, but what he could see was worrisome. Quickly, he hit the siren and lights, and pulled out his loudspeaker.

"All right," the sergeant hollered. "You are all under arrest!"

A third much more ragged volley followed, but this time instead of falling back to reload, the group broke ranks and fled. No one was arrested or even caught, but one unlucky fellow lost his piece in the melee. Later the police posed triumphantly with the captured device on the front page of the local rag.

Other than harassing police officers or fleeing to resist arrest, one could validly question any basis for making a legal pinch. These fellows were not discharging firearms within the city limits. They didn't even have firearms. As the police admitted later, they were being fired upon by devices they hadn't encountered before, called "spud guns." At the name implies, common potatoes are used as projectiles. The propellant is nothing more than aerosol hair spray or a few drops of lighter fluid. Ignition resulted from the spark of a barbecue grill lighter.

One can throw tennis balls, apples, pears, beanbags, or any other similar half-solid, slippery projectile from these devices. It just happens that potatoes work best. Their density, size, and natural lubrication all are ideal for a spud gun.

After repeated firings, heat from the propellant creates a kind of fried potato odor, and after the device sits in the corner, a rank smell gradually grows. Otherwise potatoes are quick, easy, cheap, and effective.

Construction of a spud gun can range all the way from detailed and expensive to extremely simple and cheap. Anthony Lewis, in his Paladin Press book *Bazooka—How to Build Your Own*, outlines complete construction techniques for a very complex, relatively expensive device that is really little more than a spud gun. Lewis fires his device using home-mixed powder as a propellant and an electrical bridge wire to detonate. However, he is content to shoot reusable, soft tennis balls.

Jeff Baker and Thomas Tribble instruct readers how to construct a tennis ball mortar from tin cans in their Paladin book *Homemade Mortar Construction Manual*. In either case, tennis balls do not have the whomping power of a 4-ounce spud traveling at 350 fps.

These two latter devices are mostly on the other end of the cost/complexity scale and do not, in my opinion, encompass the basic, natural charm of firing potatoes out across the countryside. At this writing, a number of people are deploying spud guns throughout the country. In fascist lockstep, our authorities wail about the fact that no law prohibits or controls ownership of a spud gun, but we ought to pass one—quick. As far as I know, no one has been hurt with a spud gun, but California and New York already require registration. Texas has arrested some spud gun owners as having zip guns, because spud guns fit the Texas legal definition for zip guns. The BATF has ruled that spud guns are not a firearm or destructive devices because they do not fire fixed ammo.

In my youth, it was common for kids to fashion a stout but springy 3-foot-long stick with which to launch pears and apples. During the fall fruit season, those living in small towns never knew when a missile might come careening through the trees. Using these as an arm-extender, and given a bit of practice, we could hurl a big, old apple 150 yards or more!

As an added feature, we often poked a giant Zebra firecracker into the rotted apple or pear. One kid threw, one kid lit the firecracker fuze, and another snuck down the block to act as a kind of forward observer/fire control director. This guy had to hide behind a big elm so that we could see him but people at the target could not. Thus positioned, we attempted to zero in on the neighbor's open porch. After a little practice, we were able to throw the missiles over a line of trees across one other house and a city side street so that detonation occurred over the victim's porch.

On several notable occasions we were able to cover the porch with pear sauce without the owners ever finding out who was responsible. Although we were never found out, the homeowner simply called a halt by building a roof over his porch. No doubt the lady of the house had always wanted a covered porch. Our antics simply speeded up the process.

Building a modern spud gun is relatively easy if you're willing to settle for nonexploding projectiles. We haven't found a reliable and cheap method of lighting explosive rounds.

Chances are the local plumbing supply has already sold parts for many. On several occasions, I have discovered that plumbing supply clerks have their own ideas about construction of spud guns or that, when presented with a list of parts, they already know what the buyer has in mind.

Use common Schedule 40 black plastic ABS pipe. This stuff is quite tough and able to take the pressure of exploding hair spray. Reports of equipment failure are almost always apocryphal and wholly undocumented. Common, single-layer plastic pipe is fine.

Have your plumber cut a piece of 4-inch pipe 16 inches long. This is the breech. Using regular ABS plastic pipe glue, securely fasten a 4-inch-to-1 1/2-inch reducer in one end of the breech pipe. Glue a 42 inch length of 1 1/2 inch plastic pipe into this reducer. This is the barrel.

On the back of the breech, glue a 4-inch cleanout fitting. By unscrewing the cleanout plug and charging the chamber with propellant, you have armed the device. That's all there is to it. The total cost for all these parts, many of which will come from your plumber's scrap heap, is about $15.

Discharge is accomplished by purchasing and installing a gas barbecue grill sparking device. Sparkers have a long wire lead that makes holding and aiming a bit easier.

Into the middle of the breech, drill a 3/16-inch hole (or one as small as possible) in which to insert

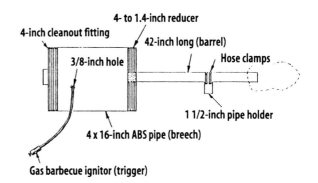

Homemade spud gun. (Illustration by Ragnar Benson.)

the sparking end of the lighter. Glue this fast with multiple layers of well-dried plastic cement. Some spud gun builders have drilled this hole too large or have placed it on one end of the breech, resulting in poor ignition or an ignition system blowout. Detonation should be as sharp a bark as possible. Aiming is done completely by manual calculation while holding the breech under one's arm. Sights are mostly impractical because of the spud's high trajectory and erratic flight.

If a blowout occurs, it may be necessary to epoxy or fiberglass the ignitor back in. If the breech is torn up, with holes larger than a dime, start over with new pipe. These devices are not expensive.

Some owners prefer to fire their guns from atop their shoulders, as with antitank rockets. In this case, a convenient foregrip should be put in place. It definitely does not work to place a T-fitting in the barrel pipe so as to have a downward extension. These T-fittings bleed off too much of the propellant gas even if sealed at the bottom.

Secure a foregrip by cutting slots in a short piece of 1 1/2-inch pipe and fasten with two hose clamps.

Cram the apple or potato projectile solidly into the barrel so that some material is shaved all around. Do not use a projectile that is too small to seal all the openings in the barrel. The fraternity men used an old shovel handle cut just to the right length to ram the spud down to within 6 inches of the chamber. One ramrod was sufficient for several devices.

Unscrew the cleanout plug from the breech *after* the spud projectile is in place. Blow heartily into the open chamber. Place two drops of lighter fluid from a 4-ounce long-nosed can into the breech and blow again. During the heat of battle, it is easy to forget to screw the plug back all the way into the cleanout.

If you don't, you may lose several threads on the cleanout plug. After a time, the plug will no longer screw into and seal the barrel, if it is allowed to blow open frequently.

Aerosol hair spray works just as well if not better as a propellant. Use as little as possible and do not blow into the breech a second time with hair spray.

Discharge should be fairly resolute, but expect some misfires and squibs. These are common. During the police incident, about 80 percent of the devices fired at any given time. Hit the sparking device several additional times if a misfire occurs and then, if necessary, unscrew the breech and recharge.

About the only maintenance is to keep carbon and potato gore out of the rear threads. After prolonged use, it may be necessary to replace the sparking device. Bad smells can be kept down by pouring a cup or two of water through the gun—as long as the sparker does not get wet.

Spud guns are inaccurate as weapons. They are recreational devices, having about as much utility as tennis racquets. After a bit of practice, you can throw spuds 150 yards with plus or minus 10-yard accuracy. One trick is to always use similar-size projectiles. This device is not sufficient to reliably send a spud through a bay window 100 percent of the time, but it is certainly good enough for government work!

Rush Limbaugh opines that in our restrictive, overregulated society we may eventually face a five-day waiting period on the purchase of potatoes as a result of widespread use of spud guns. If so, at least in this case, owners will be able to grow their own projectiles.

CHAPTER

A Great .22 Handgun

16

Significant numbers of men of action do not believe that a handgun is necessarily an essential part of a good working arsenal. Reasonable men can differ on this issue. It is a matter of personal preference, based entirely on one's experience. But general agreement exists that if a person does use a handgun, the first choice should always be a .22 LR model. Some owners find a larger centerfire pistol of value, but certainly not before you have secured and mastered a .22.

The .22 rifles tend to be significantly less expensive to purchase and shoot than do big-bore centerfire pistols. Even including handloading, it is much cheaper to practice with .22s. Unless you have a government to purchase ammo for you, this becomes a significant factor when doing the year or two of practice required to become reasonably proficient. Also, .22s tend to be easier to maintain, less subject to breakage, and, in real life, much more versatile than centerfires. It is rare, indeed, to hear

of a trapper, for instance, who carries anything but a .22 rimfire. Trappers don't have all the answers, but my inclination is to go with the professionals who use an item daily as a tool.

My Uncle Dugan killed at least half a dozen black bears by shooting them in the ear with his Stevens single-shot tip-up pistol. On one occasion when I was telling this story, I failed to also mention that all these bears had, at the time of their demise, one foot solidly planted in a big, ugly steel bear trap! Sometime later, the man to whom I related my uncle's bear-killing escapades pulled out his Ruger Standard Auto under a treed bear and commenced to kill it deader than a democrat, much to the horror of his companion.

After this admittedly dangerous incident, I have never failed to tell the full story. In Uncle's case, had the first shot been ineffective, the bear was not going anyplace or doing anything.

My first personal contact with Ruger Standard Auto pistols was in an article in the November 1950 issue of *Fur, Fish and Game* magazine.

Although Ruger's new pistol bore a passing resemblance to the old 9mm Luger shown here with its military holster, the .22 pistol was in fact quite different in operation and was designed with modern industrial techniques in mind.

The first ad for the .22 Ruger pistol appeared on page 58 of the August 1949 issue of the *American Rifleman*. A good review in the "Dope Bag" section of the magazine augmented the ad's pull. (Illustration and photos from *The Ruger .22 Automatic Pistol* by Duncan Long and courtesy of Sturm, Ruger and Co.)

I don't recall who wrote the review, but the fact that the weapon worked flawlessly on the author's trapline impressed me mightily. I vividly recall that the pistol held well, shot accurately, and was, the reviewer said, much like a German Luger. The writer in this latter case was in error, thinking that this radically new handgun was designed with a German Luger in mind. Yet this myth was with us for a number of years.

Ruger's first advertisement for his radical new pistols appeared in the August 1959 issue of *American Rifleman*. Coincidentally, Julian Hatcher wrote a favorable review in the same issue. Being a noted and respected gun expert, Hatcher was believed when he said that this was a remarkable new pistol design, of highest quality, but selling for a relatively modest price. By the New Year, Ruger had sold his original production run of 1,000 guns plus another 100 his small staff was able to fabricate. Back then, delivery was made legally by parcel post.

Through these many years, Ruger Standard Autos and their predecessor, the Mark II, have become the most popular .22 pistols ever produced in the United States, and probably the entire world. Well over one million have been produced and sold. Don't, however, count on finding a used Ruger pistol. Used Standard Autos are virtually non-existent; those few still around come with a "new" price. Once a person purchases a Ruger Standard Auto, he finds that they never break, need a tune-up, or become obsolete. Nothing better has come along in spite of the fact that these models have been out so long that their patents have expired! There is no reason to sell one.

My daughter received a Ruger .22 for graduation in 1979. Although she seldom uses it, she still has the gun and can think of no reason to sell it.

William Batterman Ruger, born in 1916, was one of those "overnight successes" that take 20 years to develop, for which our country has been justifiably famous. He was born and raised in Brooklyn by fourth-generation German immigrants. In spite of living in the city, Ruger was able to own and shoot guns and enjoy the great outdoors.

Early on, Ruger took an interest in machine shops and machining processes. Initially, his love of metalworking and firearms and his ignorance of history caused him to reinvent the wheel a couple of times. Ruger's first two firearms inventions turned bolt-and-lever action rifles into semiautos, an invention tried decades before.

During the early 1940s, Ruger worked at the Springfield Armory and the Auto Ordnance Corporation. When he applied for jobs at Colt and Savage, they both turned him down. Natural entrepreneurs have a way of gravitating to their own companies. Some prove to be idea people alone, while others have great management skills. Ruger had his own concern by 1946. First he designed and manufactured woodworking tools, and then he went into the design of firearms, which was really his first love. Through the early years, most of Ruger's jobs appeared to be failures, but in each case he learned.

While living in Southport, Connecticut, he became friendly with his neighbor—one Alexander M. Sturm. Sturm was a relatively well-to-do gun collector/visionary who financed a joint-venture company to produce Ruger's first pistol (a Standard Auto.) It is sobering to realize that today, no matter what level of genius was represented by Sturm and Ruger, Southport's planning and zoning laws *alone* would have stopped the two job-creating entrepreneurs dead in their tracks.

Ruger drew on all of his experience in designing and producing his radically new and different pistol. It had relatively few parts, required very little final assembly, and was made with new, highly automated processes. Just like the Maytag repairman ads, repair and replacement at Sturm Ruger was virtually nil. Nobody had to do it. Spare parts were reportedly kept in a shoe box.

Orders for the nice-shooting, nice-looking new gun quickly outstripped the little factory's ability to produce. The initial price was $37.50 factory direct, undercutting the competition by more than $20 at a time when the minimum wage was $.75 per hour! Ruger did not have anything but Uncle Sam's postal service in place to handle distribution. All other competing pistols sold in the $60-to-$80 range. Ruger's modern manufacturing techniques and simple design beat the others so badly in the marketplace that many who held on to this way of manufacturing went bankrupt.

Gun nuts today pine for the good old hand-machined steel guns of yesteryear, but there simply are not enough of us who can afford these types of

William Batterman Ruger.

The Ruger pistol has become one of the most popular .22 automatics ever made because of its high quality and low price tag. Shown here is a late production model of the Standard.

The Mark I 5 1/4-inch-barrel version of the Ruger pistol was only available for a short time.

The Mark I Bull Barrel, introduced in 1964, has a nontapering 5 1/2-inch barrel with a front sight base attached by screws to the top of the barrel. The right view of the pistol is shown.

The Mark II Bull Barrel was introduced in 1982. The 5 1/2-inch barrel gives the pistol a forward balance, which is desired by many target shooters, and the added mass helps reduce recoil.

weapons to support these types of makers. Gun companies that held to the old, obsolete techniques simply disappeared.

Sturm passed away in 1951 while Bill Ruger was out of the country hunting. Physically, the partnership was terminated, but psychologically it is very much alive, even today.

I cannot accurately recall the circumstances of my first Ruger Standard Auto purchase, including whether it was new or used. I am certain, however, that it was in the mid-1950s that I bought it to carry on a trapline and that I paid less than $30 for it.

Standard Autos are strange in that absolutely all they do is function flawlessly and accurately. Barrels do not dismount, so silencer installation is difficult. Back when it was legal, they were sometimes converted to full auto, producing a reasonably reliable submachine gun. But these are certainly only toys, having limited practical application even for men of action who like strange and different guns.

From the basic design, Ruger went on to offer a target model with 6 7/8-inch barrel and micrometer-adjustable sights and a surprisingly popular model with a heavy "bull" barrel. Later, other variations were offered, but the basic 5- and 7-inch models remain most popular.

Sales of Standard Autos reached a million units in 1979. Many were sold to the U.S. military both for use in Vietnam and for training soldiers. Ruger also brought out stainless-steel versions of the Standard Auto. Other makers who relied on machining rather than casting, stamping, and welding had production problems with this material because it has traditionally been too "grabby" to tool.

Today, Ruger Standard Autos have evolved into a Mark II Standard Model in both 4 3/4- and 6-inch barrels. There also is a stainless-steel Mark II in both barrel lengths. The cost is about $165 for blue and $215 for stainless. Both come with extra magazines. Newer Mark II pistols are indistinguishable from older models to casual observers. Differences include a bolt-stop, hold-open mechanism; an easier-to-insert magazine; better trigger mechanism; and shallow scallops cut into the rear of the receiver that allow a better grasp the bolt.

As it has since the late 1950s, Ruger still produces both a heavy- and a longer-barrel target model in the Mark II. Blued models run about

$190 to $200. Stainless target models cost from $240 to $255.

Ruger's marketing plan from the inception was to produce one new variation yearly and completely new designs every couple of years. At present, Ruger is rumored to be working on a completely new centerfire auto that will use a .28 caliber "Baby Nambu"-type round, and may also have a .22 WMR model of the Mark II Standard Auto in the works.

As mentioned, if men in this business require a pistol, the first one should probably be a .22. Ruger Standard Auto .22s have earned the sterling reputation they enjoy. You receive more bang for the buck in every way with one of these models. One million satisfied customers can't be wrong.

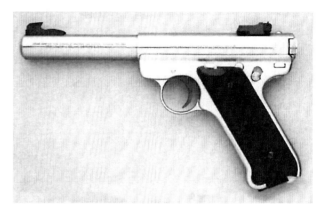

The Mark II Bull Barrel in stainless steel was added to the Ruger line in 1984. It has a 5 1/2-inch heavy bull barrel.

BIBLIOGRAPHY

Long, Duncan. *The Ruger .22 Automatic Pistol.* Boulder, CO: Paladin Press, 1988.

CHAPTER

The Grendel P-30

17

Perhaps it is too early to say, but gun owners may have recently witnessed the introduction of a new concept of firearms design that in years ahead will be viewed much the same as original Spencer carbines, Model 97s, Colt 45s, .22 Rugers, or Glocks. Win, lose, or draw, the ultramodern design and construction features of the Grendel P-30 seem destined to make it a benchmark. Men of action, however, should proceed with some caution because they are dealing with a model that is essentially a prototype.

As I loaded my P-30 pistol, I felt much as Confederate soldiers must have felt after enduring seven volleys of fire from newly introduced Spencer carbines at the Battle of Gettysburg. The P-30 looked no bigger than a standard-size Beretta or Heckler & Koch 9mm pistol, but the magazine capacity was 30 rounds of Winchester magnum rimfire rounds! Not .22 LRs or even .380s, but high-velocity, hard-hitting .22 WMRs.

At 30 rounds per magazine of ammo having muzzle velocities of 1,450 fps and 186 foot pounds

of energy (fpe), you could easily conclude that if the second magazine were required, you were in a war, not a firefight. Thirty rounds, for those who haven't thought about it, leaves 13 extra after the owner of a Beretta M-92 expends his first magazine. In this case, .22 mag ammo shoots flatter, has more penetration, and is easier to control than the 9mm. Federal, for instance, found that its .22 LR penetrated only five 3/4-inch pine boards, while its .22 mag went through 11.

Grendel P-30 pistols and their near cousins, target and laser models P-30L and the P-30LM, are the brainchild of George Kellgren, president of Grendel, Inc., Rockledge, Florida, about 25 miles east of Orlando. Cut somewhat in the same mold as 9mm Glocks, Grendel P-30s are all made from high-quality LaSalle stress-proofed steel and Zytel structural nylon. They have a futuristic, tooled nylon feel and look, much like the Glock.

Approximately 9,500 P-30s of all types have been placed on the market by the 20-employee Grendel crew since it first cranked up operations in August 1990. Sales may have been slowed a bit by the firm's decision not to use distributors and its

The Grendel-30 is destined to be a benchmark in the firearms field. (Photos by Ragnar Benson.)

The Grendel models are the brainchild of George Kellgren.

lack of an advertising budget. Few gun owners in the nation are aware of the company's existence.

At approximately $225 for the standard P-30 trail-type pistol with 5-inch barrel, $280 for the P-30L with a slightly more accurate 8-inch barrel, and $295 for the target version with an 8 1/2-inch barrel and muzzle brake, one could validly conclude that part of the Grendel's charm is its price. In this era of $400 to $600 pistols, well-made and classy models for half the price are attractive.

Yet shooting tests demonstrate that the P-30 design is truly unique. Its empty eight is 21 ounces, and a loaded 30-round Zytel magazine adds only 6 ounces. Even carrying an extra magazine, the P-30 is a long-distance patroller's delight.

The trigger pull is unique. It is definitely auto-like. Creep must be taken up to a point where the pull is very firm and crisp at about 3 1/2 pounds, about appropriate for a pistol of this weight. Hammer fall is very short and positive. Eighteen-inch groups at 60 yards, including all 30 rounds, are common, right out of the box.

Firing the pistol is like something out of *Star Wars*. Obviously, the user can go on and on, firing more rounds than most rifles carry. Recoil is evident, but not a major consideration. Full-size grips allowing a firm grasp seem to assist the shooter. Certainly, bounce is far less than a on 9mm. The single largest problem, in my experience, involves the incredible muzzle blast. In my estimation, the Grendel with its .22 mag ammo would be impossible to fire either indoors or without earmuffs.

After firing 800 test rounds without any significant problems, I can conclude that the pistol is reliable as long as Winchester or Federal ammo is used. My old favorite CCI ammo seems better suited in its mag configuration to rifles and carbines, where burn rates are more nearly suitable. It also becomes apparent that .22 mag ammo is extremely dirty. My experience indicates that the piece must be cleaned every 200 rounds or malfunction may occur regardless of the make of ammo. Of the 30-some P-30s I have tracked, about six have had to go back to the factory for repair. They break firing pins, lose their ability to hold the mags, and sometimes just don't cycle. That's the price of a prototype, I figure. But not a high one. All Grendels are unconditionally guaranteed forever.

The Grendel P-30 is a fluted, unlocked chamber, blowback design with fixed barrel, leading—it seems—to extensive mechanism fouling. Fortunately, disassembly for cleaning is extremely quick and simple. You need only unscrew the barrel sleeve, pull out the recoil spring and barrel bushing, pull the slide back and up, and all parts are available for scrubbing. Owners with limber wrists find it easier to rethread the barrel sleeve on reassembly, but even this is a minor problem compared with that of some other pistols, even those of modern design.

The safety is an ambidextrous type, rotating on the hammer axis pin. When engaged, the safety both disconnects the sear and blocks the hammer.

Because of the gun's modest weight and the fact that the safety rotates down to fire, I find that until I became familiar with the P-30, the web of my hand tended to move up on recoil, inadvertently reactivating the safe mechanism. Thirty-two other owners of P-30s in my area do not have this problem, leading me to believe this problem is of my own doing.

The sights are a windage-adjustable front blade, with a fixed square rear notch. Moving the front sight is easy, but it was unnecessary on my pistols. Filing the front blade or deepening the rear notch could easily be accomplished at home if it is necessary.

Other than very incidentally klutzing the safety a time or two, I have had only minor problems with the Grendel. It functions well in mud, snow, water, and rain if you keep the internal components clean. The design seems to inherently protect operating parts. After 400 rounds, one of my pistols developed a glitch unrelated to cleaning, which I reported to the factory. All Grendels are covered by an unconditional, full-lifetime, no-questions-asked guarantee good for the original purchaser. When I called the factory on its 800 number, a representative explained that I might have broken a firing pin. To find out for sure, he priority-mailed a new pin to me.

It seems that, as many manufacturers do, Grendel contracted for all of its firing pins. There were absolutely no problems among the first batch, yet some firing pins in subsequent batches appear to be improperly heat treated, leading to occasional breakage. But it was impossible to predict which pins would break. Grendel is developing more sophisticated techniques of assuring the quality of the hardening process in order to deal with this problem.

As a result of its using Allen screws, the pin was replaced in less than four minute, even though I initially had no idea how to proceed. Use of nicely blued, aesthetically contoured Allen screws to assemble the pistol may put off some gun enthusiasts unwilling to move into 21st century designs. Civil War generals reacted similarly to their revolutionary rapid-fire Spencer carbine in 1863.

The overall look and feel of the Grendel is very pleasant. It is sufficiently eye-catching that absolutely every gun nut I have shown mine to has purchased one. Grendel P-30s look very much like Astra 600 autoloaders except for the thicker grips. Several females with small frames have fired our

After firing 800 test rounds without significant problems, I can conclude that the pistol is sufficiently reliable as long as I use Winchester or Federal ammo.

Grendel's P-30s are fluted, unlocked chamber, blowback designs with fixed barrel.

Grendels without problem or discomfort. It is a nice, pleasant handful without being anything more.

Acquiring a Grendel in the P-30 series is not a particularly simple undertaking. Presently, the factory produces only for back orders, rotating among their various designs one week to the next. Grendel also produces a carbine and a .380 backup pistol for the civilian and police markets.

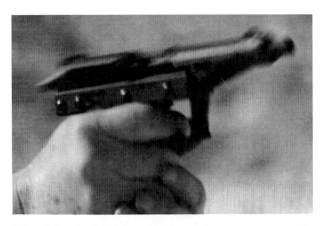

When firing the Grendel, my hand tended to move up on recoil, inadvertently causing me to reactivate the safety.

All sales are factory direct to dealers, there being no distributors with weapons in inventory. One must have his dealer order from the factory and then simply be content to wait 40 to 50 days for the next production cycle. At times, this becomes excruciating since it seems obvious that, once these pistols become widely known for their large 30-round capacities, they will probably suffer the same political future as the streetsweeper and the striker.

Because of their low-rust, low-maintenance, mostly structural nylon manufacture, Grendels will probably find their way in large numbers into boats and airplane emergency bags. Given the gun's light weight and magazine capacity adequate for most four- or five-day missions, my guess is that those that can get one for this purpose will do so. At just over $200 each, the Grendel is within the budget of many gun enthusiasts in the United States. As soon as they are widely known, two things will likely happen: they will go up in price dramatically, and tens of thousands will be sold.

Ammo for the Grendel is available in most discount sporting goods stores at about $5 per box of 50. The WMR at $.10 per round compares favorably in price to factory-new .380 ammo at $12 per box of 50 ($.24 each) and standard 9mm ammo at $15 ($.30 per round). Reloading empties or, in some cases, locating a supply of surplus military ammo is the only way of lowering the price of shooting these larger calibers to the level of the WMR. If cost is the only consideration, .22 LR ammo is still much cheaper. Currently I pay about $1.50 per box of 50, or $.03 per round. Five hundred rounds of .22 mag represent incredible firepower and weighs 3 3/4 pounds; 500 of 9mm weigh 11 pounds!

The Grendel's only drawback as a survival weapon is the rimfire ammo, which ranges from difficult to virtually impossible to reload. Magnum rimfire pistols would be rendered suddenly and completely obsolete if Winchester and Federal were ordered by the feds to stop manufacturing the ammo. As part of the cost of ownership, I have purchased 500 rounds ($50 worth) of ammo. If I use a box from inventory, I immediately replace it with another. In the interim, we have what appears to be one of the truly unique and more practical pistols to come down the pike in the last 30 years.

CHAPTER

The .22 Rifle

18

Bill Ruger thought that developing a new superreliable, rugged, and accurate .22 rifle was important enough that he assembled a high-powered design team 18 months before the rifle was due on the market in 1964. This is a tribute to both Ruger's organizational abilities and his capacity as an engineer to recognize the weak link in a complex system.

"It is the magazines," Ruger said. "Without good mags, the best firearms system will flounder."

Early in his firearms design career, Ruger worked with Savage 99s that used Mannlicher-type rotary magazines. He was unsuccessful with his Savage semiauto modification but continued to wonder why a compact, efficient, rotary-cartridge-fed design had not been successful in the United States.

As kids, our standard rifles were Marlin 39s, first built and sold in this country in 1892! We favored these rifles because they had extended-capacity magazines; were reliable with shorts, longs,

and long-rifle ammo; and were accurate. Often, we used our Marlin lever actions to shoot English sparrows off the top of our hip-roofed barn. From the shop door, it was an incredible 120-foot shot on a 2- or 3-square-inch target. Using only shorts, we often dropped two or three sparrows in a row.

Some of our friends appreciated Marlin lever actions because of their long, heavy barrels. Even without silencers, .22 Shorts were very quiet in these rifles.

However, all lever actions are complex, subject to malfunction, and expensive to keep up. Old-fashioned, tooled-steel manufacturing techniques were costly then; today, they are prohibitively expensive. Most of us saved for years before we got our first "real" .22 rifle.

After several years of firing two boxes of ammo or more per week in all kinds of conditions, our Marlins became grimy and worn. This was especially true for the kid using his father's or uncle's gun, which had already been around a while.

One of the most popular .22 rifles in the world, the 10/22 is very reliable and has a wealth of aftermarket accessories. Owners of the 10/22 can quickly transform a standard model (like the lower carbine) into a high-tech "combat-style" firearm without any special know-how or gunsmithing work. (Photos and illustration from *The Sturm, Ruger 10/22 Rifle and .44 Magnum Carbine* by Duncan Long.)

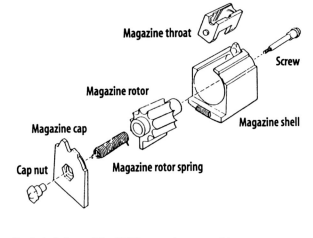

Exploded view of the 10/22 magazine assembly.

As a result, we became proficient at cleaning and adjusting these complex mechanisms. It took skill and patience to keep a .22 going in those days.

Times change—often violently. I vividly recall the summer of 1964 when Sturm, Ruger introduced its revolutionary 10/22 rifle—so named because it had a 10-round magazine and was a .22 cartridge. This was the company's first .22 rifle and, to an extent, bucked contemporary trends. Buyers, however, accepted the new Ruger design because of the success of Standard Auto .22 pistols.

I recall remarking on the gun's limited 10-round capacity to a gunshop clerk. He told me to purchase an extra magazine, thereby boosting capacity to a more effective 20 rounds. That was good advice, except that these rifles were so popular that extra magazines were unavailable. I was also shocked to hear that price of extra magazines at that time was $10.95—when they were available. The price probably reflected Ruger's philosophy of placing major emergency emphasis on the weakest link.

The trend at that time was to tube magazine semiautos with "floating bolts," allowing one to shoot shorts, longs, or long rifles intermixed. Apparently Bill Ruger was more visionary than we supposed. The .22 ammo has survived as the most popular cartridge in the world, the very same round for which 10/22s were designed.

With this cartridge, many 10/22 owners claim they have *never* had a feeding problem or jam. One noted gunsmith claims that he has never experienced a jam with a 10/22, including home-workshop full-auto conversions involving nothing more than grinding down the sear. If his claim is true, that is remarkable! (This includes regular, standard, and high-velocity long rifle ammo.)

As a result of their modern design, reliability, accuracy, and low price, Ruger 10/22s have become the standard modern boy's gun. Traditionally, we older duffers have favored single shot or rifles that must be levered before each shot. But it apparently takes only marginally more self-discipline to keep from pulling a trigger than from racking a lever. There is such a thing as careful marksmanship with semiautos, I am told.

Gun nuts have questioned Bill Ruger's use of a heavy solid-steel barrel on 10/22 rifles. Obviously, the reason is to provide a more accurate, more controllable weapon, and 10/22s are extremely accurate. As a result, mounting a high-quality 1-inch scope on a 10/22 makes good sense. You can use standard 7/8-inch tip-off rings or, by using a Ruger of Weaver baseplate, go up to full-size, 1-inch scopes.

Ruger 10/22 barrels are reasonably easy to dismount in a home workshop. This is not a job to be attempted in the field, but barrels can be removed from the action by taking off the weapon's stock and removing the two-barrel retainer V-block screws located just forward of the receiver.

Ram-Line produces a composite steel-fiberglass barrel weighing about 16 ounces less than original Ruger barrel. You could thread the original barrel

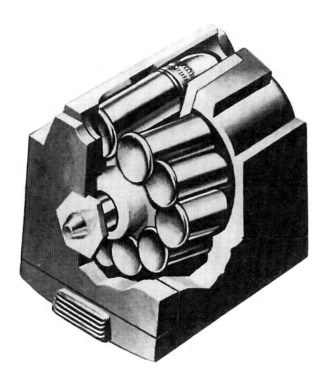

This cutaway drawing shows how ten .22 rounds wrap around inside the magazine's rotary assembly.

Ram-Line makes excellent extended "banana" magazines (the 30-round model is shown on the left and the 50-round model on the right). These magazines have a special pair of coiled springs that keeps pressure quite low on the cartridges (and makes loading easy). Double-column cartridge storage in the magazine makes the length of the magazines relatively short. (Photo courtesy of Ram-Line.)

for a silencer, replacing it with the light 16-inch fiberglass model for about $40!

Perhaps because of the 10/22's incredible reliability, commercial silencer makers have often built on its actions. Until the Gun Control Act of 1986, it was also popular to commercially convert 10/22s to select fire.

Substituting a shorter, lighter barrel makes good sense if you intend to go the next step and install a nylon stock. Ram-Line and Choate Machine & Tool make excellent, rugged folding stocks for 10/22s. Their folding mechanism is use-, abuse-, and weather-resistant. Large buttons activate the long-lived folding mechanism. The cost is about $100 each. These folders include an integral pistol grip, which is a nice accessory when deployed one-handed with a short, light barrel.

Ram-Line also sells a takedown kit that turns a 10/22 into a component rifle similar to an AR-7. Large knobs make it possible to quickly remove the barrel from the receiver without tools. This modification will fit nicely into Ram-Line folding stocks. This package is extremely compact and easily concealed.

Perhaps it goes without saying, but 10/22 owners who have come this far require large-capacity magazines over and above those offered by Ruger. Fortunately, this is not the chore it once was.

Ram-Line manufactures structural nylon mags in both 30- and 50-round capacities. They are driven by pairs of special coiled springs, which effectively, but not rigidly, keep pressure on the contained cartridges. As a result of these soft springs, loading is not a difficult task. Yet, Ram-Line also produces a structural nylon crank-type automatic loader that speeds reloading considerably.

In addition to Ram-Line, Bingham, Mitchell Arms, and Condor also offer large-capacity magazines. Gun nuts seem to prefer Ram-Line because of its magazine's shorter length. However, Mitchell's magazines work on a wind-up spring principle and, because of its teardrop shape, are not all that cumbersome.

Choate stocks are quickly unfolded or folded by pushing down on a small thumb button at the top of the pivot point. This section releases the stock so that it can be automatically locked open or closed. A barrel band allows the ring to be removed easily. (Photo courtesy of Choate Machine and Tool.)

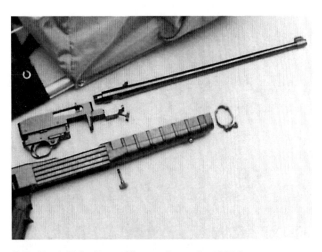

Ram-Line's Take-Down Kit transforms the 10/22 into a takedown rifle similar to the Marlin Papoose or AR-7. The Ram-Line kit replaces the stock and barrel bond screws with knurled plastic knobs (which allow the gun to be fieldstripped without a screwdriver), and the 10/22's barrel block is replaced with one having a knurled knob, making it possible to remove the barrel from the receiver without tools. (Photo courtesy of Ram-Line.)

Those who envision their 10/22s as select-fire assault rifles must use extended-capacity magazines. At 1,000 rounds per minute, one gentle squeeze of the trigger rips out a standard Ruger magazine. High-speed photos graphically show empty brass arcing through the air with only 3 or 4 inches separation.

Wayne Thornbrugh of Orofino, Idaho, has produced a legally altered 10/22 select-fire

conversion. His company was thriving until the Gun Control Act of 1986 shut it down. Thornbrugh has written a short book exploring in detail how he made these conversions; the book contains excellent working machinist's blueprints. The author claims this conversion can be done in an amateur shop using a minimum of hand tools, files, and hacksaws. Some amateurs like myself view the conversion as quite complex.

Both the issue 10/22 trigger housing and the bolt must be altered slightly. Four somewhat complex parts must be hand fabricated. These include an auto sear, auto sear spring, arrestor release cam, and arrest release lever. You must also manufacture a trigger, trigger sear, and select-fire lever, all of which must be turned and fitted to the entire assembly.

It seems certain that this system would work well, but it also seems obvious that one cannot reasonably produce these parts in a home workshop. Those with both machine shop skills and tools, as well as a burning desire to own a select-fire 10/22, are best advised to purchase a full copy of the publication *Select Fire 10/22* by Wayne Thornbrugh from Paladin Press.

Now that Ruger also produces its 10/22 in stainless, a man of action is best served by using this rifle as an inexpensive super-reliable, accurate workhorse. There is always more for the .22 rifle to do than you would initially suppose. As we found out early on, having a reliable common .22 rifle is very important. But if you have a place for a .22 assault rifle, there is probably no better design from which to start.

BIBLIOGRAPHY

Long, Duncan. *The Sturm Ruger 10/22 Rifle and .44 Magnum Carbine.* Boulder, CO: Paladin Press, 1988.

Thornbrugh, Wayne. *Select Fire 10/22.* El Dorado, AR: Desert Publications, 1985.

CHAPTER

Crossbows

19

Interest in crossbows seems to develop in inverse proportion to an individual's ability to purchase or make real firearms. Most reader correspondence I receive about crossbows comes from places in this world where ownership of firearms is difficult.

People who live in places where the right to keep and deploy a gun is limited view crossbows as their only hope for any kind of effective weapon. This explains, in part, my many letters from England, Australia, Canada, and Germany. Some of the writers' remarks are quite caustic about the fact that I am negative about using crossbows in any serious real-life context.

In 1984 when I agreed to do a book on crossbows as survival weapons, I believed that a dedicated, experienced woodsman could fool around with them long enough to become proficient. But I quickly found that many obstacles must be overcome before a crossbow can really become a usable weapon.

Previously, my only contact with crossbows was through an older brother who worked with them off and on for years, and this was long ago. Now, I reasoned, modern materials and design must have alleviated most inherent crossbow weaknesses. But, as a more philosophical correspondent pointed out, "Crossbows cannot be effective because there has never been a serious national campaign to either ban or register them."

The history of crossbows is fairly well known. Because Alexander the Great had an official, though often very glib, chronicler, records of the first use and deployment of crossbows is fairly well documented. Winners do write the history, but in this case history could have been very obscure. We are fortunate to have any written record at all.

At the time of the invention of the crossbow, Alexander was contending with Scythian archers along the banks of the Syr Darya River north of the Himalayas in an area that today is probably in China. Scythian soldiers were excellent longbowmen who could shoot with proficiency as they

The author shooting a crossbow. (Photos and illustration from *Bull's-Eye: Crossbows* **by Ragnar Benson.)**

A modern crossbow.

Modern materials applied to designs thousands of years old have made crossbows more functional and reliable.

galloped across the steppes. The Greeks really had no good way to contend with this organized horde of Scythian soldiers.

The favored Scythian strategy was to ride into an area of rough ground where the archers were somewhat protected from Alexander's footmen and shoot with their powerful long bows out over great range, "discomforting" Alexander's massed troops. Later, Alexander acknowledged that few Greeks could even draw the stubby little Scythian bows, much less shoot them accurately, because they were so powerful.

In response to these random missiles flying in from nowhere that his troops could not handle, Alexander brought up his trusted engineers. They designed and built several "great" windlass-cocked crossbow machines that threw standard Greek javelins with accuracy. Thus armed, Alexander placed some of his troops at river's edge under a protective layer of hand-held infantry shields.

Scythian archers, thinking they were out of reach of the Greeks, converged into little clusters while they continued to fire away. Alexander fired his javelin guns, producing immediate and grievous casualties among the surprised Scythians. Enough were killed by the javelins that they withdrew about 500 yards, allowing the Greeks to approach unmolested. When the Greek formations attacked, the Scythians were out of arrows. The ensuing rout broke the enemy, opening the way for Alexander's disciplined soldiers to conquer the region.

Much later, Roman soldiers became masters at engineering. To a great extent their cleverness at producing effective machinery of war paved the way for their world domination. Roman engineers used a few machines to hurl iron javelins, but generally Roman soldiers did not use bows and arrows until later.

During the dark ages in Europe, crossbows were deployed extensively as a means of doing each other

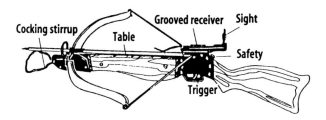

Parts diagram of modern crossbow.

The distance between a crossbow string on the table at rest and cocked is called the draw distance. It is generally better if the bow gains its power over a longer stroke. Heavier, longer arrows have more stability.

in more effectively. It is, however, important to realize that as soon as firearms of *any* kind appeared on the scene, crossbows disappeared. This is in spite of the fact that early firearms were incredibly unreliable, inaccurate, and difficult to use.

It is tempting to conclude that crossbows were poor performers because of the primitive materials and workmanship of that era, rather than because of basic design deficiencies. But this is simply not true.

In preparation for writing *Bullseye*, I bought or borrowed five different models of modern crossbow. I could have kept any of the bows I borrowed for testing. In the end, I sent all of them back to the makers except for one, for which I actually paid cash. A few years ago, I disposed of it as well by sending it to the landfill!

One of the best uses of an improvised weapon is to use it on a temporary basis to secure a real weapon. I can't imagine anyone walking around with a crossbow and not drawing a huge amount of the wrong kind of attention. As demonstrated by the number of little wars going on around the world, our next conflicts will likely be fought in the cities, not in the jungle someplace. In the deep woods, crossbows are difficult or impossible to maneuver with.

I know where virtually every deer on my mountain beds down. In winter they congregate into little, easily hunted yards. Yet it took weeks of steady hunting before I was able to get a deer with a crossbow for my book. It took many deer before the bolt finally flew true to the target. Branches, tree limbs, and underbrush knocked and scraped noisily on the cumbersome device. Any bolts recovered could not be fired again, even if they hit nothing solid but the ground.

When I finally did connect at 50 feet, the bolt sailed right through the critter, which then ran 300

yards downhill before dying. Big, powerful crossbows, I found, are a waste. They were tough to cock and fire, whereas more modest devices kept the bolt in the deer, killing it in a more humane fashion. Range for both was 50 to 70 feet max, no matter how powerful. There was no reliable accuracy past 70 feet. In one case, a new bolt completely missed a 4 x 8-foot sheet of plywood from 25 feet. Two of five hit the plywood on average at 25 feet.

Crossbows do work fairly well when feeding fish from a small boat—you do not have to worry about noise, slow reloading, and dirt and leaves getting caught in the mechanism. Crossbows are fairly noisy when discharged, but this does not trouble the fish.

On one notable occasion, I broke four strings in four shots in a row. When contacted by phone, the manufacturer told us that although breaking that many strings in series was uncommon, it was not unexpected. Homemade replacement strings fared

The top of the crossbow is known as the table. The groove holds the bolt in place, assisted by a spring-steel bolt keeper.

Safeties on crossbows are automatic. When the string hits the trigger mechanism, the safety is automatically engaged.

Prod or bow ends are protected with nylon or leather caps. Using a crossbow without these protective tip caps will dramatically shorten the string's already short life.

out leaves and dirt, a goat's foot cocking device, pliers, and heavy gloves are the minimum extra support equipment required.

It is true that members of primitive societies often use crossbows. I have been with many of these in Laos, Burma, Malaysia, and northern Thailand. Yet one must not succumb to the mindless tendency of some modern Brahmans to worship these societies for their primitiveness. Most modernize as fast as circumstances and economics allow when they are given the chance.

The old adage of "it's not whether you win or lose, but how you look while in the game" comes to mind. What really counts for men of action is being effective and staying alive, not playing around with some ineffective, primitive weapon because it's "neat." For that reason, there are no plans to build a crossbow in this chapter. If some readers are still unconvinced, a number of plans are on the market in other places. They take 60 to 80 hours to build, not including construction of bolts.

Huge quantities of mail have come in regarding my contention that one can build a primitive but workable firearm more easily than a crossbow. Remember, crossbow triggers must hold great force mechanically. As a result, they tend to be heavy, unreliable, and subject to breakage especially when made at home. Effective strings, as I have mentioned, are extremely difficult to manufacture. Bolts, even when machine manufactured, are marginal in quality. I cannot envision anyone making effective bolts by conventional means in a home workshop.

no better. It wasn't worth the time and expense to make them, and it was too expensive to buy them.

It also became painfully apparent while hunting that crossbows are far from quiet. After a single shot, all deer ran off even though winds were favorable. In covert circumstances, expect crossbows to attract about as much attention as a .22 LR in a long-barreled rifle.

You must practically convert to a traveling hardware store when using a crossbow. Numerous extra strings, wax, an old toothbrush used to brush

As I have continually maintained, it is far better to spend your time making a simple slip-pipe shotgun, setting game snares, or building mantraps than in venturing into the vast swampland of homebuilt crossbows.

Certainly, I would alter my opinion, including placing an addendum onto this chapter, should new and better evidence come to light. In the interim, I see no practical purpose for crossbows.

BIBLIOGRAPHY

Benson, Ragnar. *Bullseye*. Boulder, CO: Paladin Press, 1985.

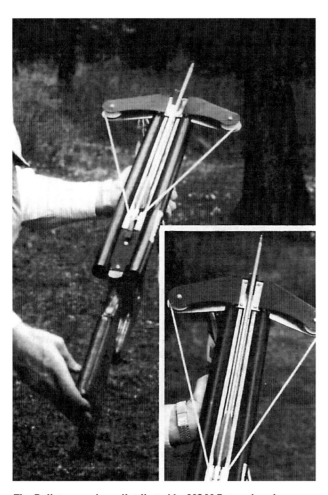

The Balista crossbow distributed by **M&M** Enterprises is powered by heavy rubber tubes and does not have a cumbersome bow or prod. It has a self-contained cocking mechanism and a trim, light design. Hopelessly inaccurate on land, these bows work best underwater.

CHAPTER
Blowguns
20

An Ecuadorian Indian, with skin more cream-colored than one would have supposed, stealthily crept up on a group of small monkeys eating in a fruit tree. His life under a thick canopy of trees in permanent twilight was more responsible for the light skin than any racial heritage. This man may never have seen a full, open sky unless it was while he was on one of the wide-open rivers.

The hunter was not only fearful of his quarry fleeing to the tops of the 60-foot trees, but also of the critters using their natural defense mechanisms that included raining fecal matter down on a ground-based foe.

The hunter, in this case, was in the very upper headwaters of the Amazon River, perhaps a four-hour drive and three-hour walk into the bush from Quito. Slowly and carefully, he extracted a long, sliverlike piece of bamboo from a small, woven-reed box he carried on a sling. With great precision, he spun a small dab of wild cotton onto one end of the dart. An extremely small piece of colored feather tied into the cotton marked the dart as his own, in the event controversy arose over who had made the shot.

Again exercising extreme caution, the man poked the long, slim splinter into a very small glass bottle containing what seemed to be a frayed piece of hemp lying in a thin, milky liquid.

Still keeping his almond eyes fixed on the small monkeys, he pushed the dart into a 5-foot long wooden tube. Slowly and carefully, he extended the tube through leaves that hid him. For an instant he froze. Then a kind of hollow, wooden, pneumatic pumping sound sprang back at me. I glanced furtively around for snakes.

A monkey shrieked once and climbed chattering to the top of a tree, its baby still holding on for dear life. Others of the group simply disappeared. When the light was just right, you could see a thin dart sticking in the monkey's back. For a few moments, it reached around trying to extract the projectile. Quickly, however, a numbness came over the

The power of the blowgun is obvious in this photograph. Three darts were shot from a distance of 15 feet through a homemade aluminum blowgun. All three easily penetrated this 3/8-inch plywood. (Photographs from *Blowguns: The Breath of Death* by Michael Janich.)

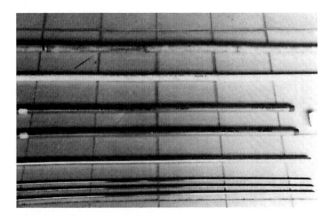

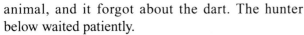

Raw materials for blowgun barrels include (from top to bottom) bamboo, PVC tubing, threaded PVC tubing with coupling, aluminum tubing, and brass tubing.

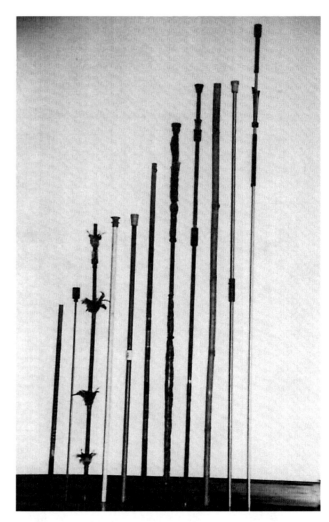

A collection of commercial, traditional, and homemade blowguns. The shortest is 3 feet in length; the longest is 7 feet.

animal, and it forgot about the dart. The hunter below waited patiently.

After perhaps five minutes the paralyzed monkey, with baby still clinging, fell out of the tree. Being careful not to injure the real quarry, the hunter tapped the bigger critter on the head with the butt of his knife. He ate the larger monkey, sold the juvenile to a middleman in Napo, who in turn sold it to a man in Quito, who also resold it. Chances are excellent that if the small one is still alive, it is in the United States.

This was the first and last time I have witnessed a blowgun being used for anything other than practice on a corkboard. I still don't know for sure whether blowguns have a place in a man of

action's arsenal; perhaps without good poison, blowguns are ineffective.

We do know that from a range of 15 feet modern commercial blowgun darts will penetrate about 2 inches through a 3/8-inch piece of plywood. They will reliably kill rats, smaller cats, and tree squirrels, but their absolute range in calm air is 45 feet.

The problem with blowguns is that, as near as can be ascertained, there is virtually no effective dart-injected poison, such as South American curare, available in North America. No plants or natural trees supply a material, and other than distilling nicotine sulfate from difficult-to-obtain insecticides, there is nothing among our common

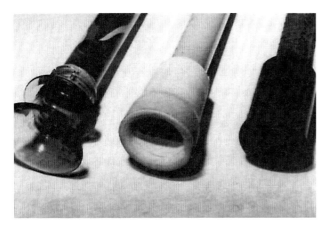

Mouthpieces for homemade blowguns include (from left to right) neck of plastic soda bottle, hollowed-out rubber crutch tip, and 35mm film can.

Homemade dart materials. Stopper materials include paper and adhesive tape (for paper cone darts), corks, wooden dowel, golf tees, and cotton balls. Dart shafts can be made of nails, bicycle spokes, spring steel, or bamboo chopsticks.

agricultural chemicals. Succinylcholine chloride, often used by archers on deer, is not practical. More than can be carried on a blowgun dart is required for a kill.

Blowguns are not particularly easy to learn to shoot well. Those deciding to deploy them will find that they must spend several months of almost daily practice till they become proficient enough to actually hit a cat- or rat-size target. Blowguns can be accurate, but shooters who hit small targets at maximum range must spend years practicing.

Even then, reliability suffers. Blowguns only function well in environments where there are no winds. Every culture that depends on blowguns lives on the forest floor beneath a thick canopy of trees where there are no breezes. When given a chance, blowgun users always seem to prefer rifles.

On the other hand, blowguns are extremely inexpensive to build and shoot. There is virtually no situation in this country where a blowgun and darts could not be home manufactured. They are silent and not terribly suspicious if only modest efforts at disguise are employed. Workable, 2-foot blowguns could be carried in a sleeve. From 10 feet, they can put a 4-inch steel dart deep in an enemy's neck.

Modern factory-made 3- and 4-foot aluminum blowguns with excellent mouthpieces and a generous supply of darts sell for about $25. Most of us have seen them at gun shows, usually touted by a man who could shoot (or does one blow?) well at modest ranges. Those who purchase blowguns at gun shows or by mail order will require some of the

following information, because darts have a way of disappearing quickly.

Blowgun tubes run from .40 on up to about .625 inch in diameter for the J.W. McFarlin "Magnum." Any piece of plastic, aluminum, or wooden tube between those sizes will work, provided of course that you construct appropriate darts to go with the tube.

Longer 5- and 6-foot models are easiest to shoot accurately but are, of course, much more difficult to carry discreetly. Longer models damage easily and, in the case of plastic pipe, are often not rigid enough to be accurate. Owners who wish to do serious work must have absolutely straight blowpipe tubes.

Some makers couple two 3-foot sections of pipe, using a long strip of overlapping pipe that becomes a solid union. Some sanding and fitting may be required to do this, but shorter sections are easier to carry and replace if damaged.

Experienced users suggest that about 5 feet is the correct length, balancing utility, portability, and accuracy. Longer 6-foot models are best left to true professionals living in the jungle.

Mouthpieces on blowguns are just as important as barrels and darts. Novice builders sometimes do not appreciate their utility. Excellent serviceable mouthpieces are made from the neck of a plastic soda bottle, a hollowed-out rubber crutch tip, or a 35mm plastic film canister. All must be cut and trimmed to fit over the blowgun tube.

Use heavy epoxy, Goop, or silicon bathtub caulking to secure the mouthpiece to the tube.

With a very light piece of thread, dangle a small filmy feather from the tube's exit. Blown in the breeze, this feather becomes a windage gauge.

Blowgun darts or projectiles can be made from a variety of materials ranging from simple finishing nails and a piece of cork to spring steel skirted with plastic sheeting. The size range is 1 1/2 to 24 inches in length. Unlike Indians on the Amazon, modern, urban blowgun users make up all their darts at home before seeking the quarry.

Spring-steel wire 1/16 inch (.063) in diameter (available in hardware or hobby shops) is probably best, given penetration, range, wind-bucking ability, and availability constraints. A length of 4 to 6 inches works well, provided that you start with wire that is absolutely straight and remains that way. Sharpen the nonskirted end on a grinder or whetstone. A 6-inch dart blown into a soft, man-size target will cause a grievous wound even without poison.

Stoppers are made from glued paper treated with hair spray, plastic sheeting, golf tees, or even new-age plastic beads—if you can find light, hollow types of correct diameter. Heat the steel shaft with a match and quickly poke it into the bead. When the plastic hardens, it will secure the steel shaft.

Paper stoppers can also be coated with clear nail polish or lacquer to give them extra body. Use whatever is convenient to coat the little cover that is glued to the steel wire. Some makers simply roughen the steel shaft a bit with a Dremel tool and wrap a small cotton ball on the rear end. These are OK, other than the fact that the cotton damages easily.

Set aside a small section of extra shaft tubing in which to test dart stoppers for fit. Some users crimp a small split-shot fishing sinker onto the rear of the dart, providing additional mass to aid penetration.

Professional blowgun users, who commonly use poison, often place a diminutive broadhead on the dart. They cut two-thirds of the way through the shaft just below the head, which is liberally coated with poison. When the target animal is hit, it will break the shaft, leaving the poison tip embedded deep in its flesh.

At this point, it is difficult to predict whether blowguns are similar to crossbows or if they

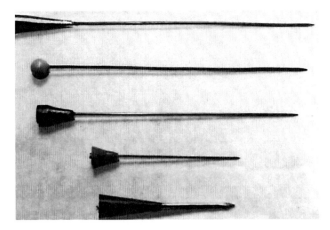

Examples of steel darts. From top to bottom: a homemade spring-steel dart with paper cone stopper, a commercial bead dart, a homemade steel dart with a golf tee stopper, a commercial cone dart, and a dart made from a finishing nail with a paper-cone stopper.

actually have practical field utility. Those who become extremely proficient with these devices may be able to take pigeons off a roost, rabbits out of the garden, or squirrels out of the buckeye tree in complete silence. Blowguns are also easy to build in a variety of circumstances and could act as a psychological deterrent to human intrusion under some circumstances.

In dense forests or confused urban environments where some concealment is possible and no other weapon is available, they might be effective. Peashooter-length blowguns accurate to 15 feet are extremely deadly, and the psychological damage inflicted on an enemy by their use can be tremendous. Just contemplating having a 4-inch pin stuck in his neck would make an enemy extremely paranoid.

BIBLIOGRAPHY

Janich, Michael D. *Blowguns: The Breath of Death.* Boulder, CO: Paladin Press, 1993.

CHAPTER

Surreptitious Weapons

21

It may seem too dumb to be true, but the following really happened as closely as possible to the way in which I am about to tell it. These events occurred less than a year ago right after the state in which I live changed its laws to make it much easier to get a permit to carry a concealed weapon.

A fellow wearing a heavy belt and buckle walked into the county sheriff's office. The buckle was one of those designed to carry a North American Arms 5-shot mini-revolver. In this case, it was a matter of being the best place to hide a tree that is obviously in a forest. The weapon was right out in plain sight. This guy wanted to apply for a permit to carry a concealed weapon! In this instance the shcriff's deputy was alert. The fellow was placed in custody for carrying a concealed weapon without a permit.

Eventually the prosecutor refused to proceed on the basis that this weapon was not concealed. In my state, carrying openly is not a violation.

Throughout the ages, men have looked for new and clever methods of carrying some kind of weapon. Some of these devices were deviously brilliant, while others were of doubtful value. Cleverness now, the reasoning seemed to suggest, precluded unpleasantness later.

During the Middle Ages, for instance, a few people carried poison capsules inside special compartments in rings, the idea being that the ring was big enough to use as a brass knuckle and that the dose was instantly available should it be required. Today we are a bit more technologically advanced. Knives have been built into rings, long thin pins, and even .22-caliber pistols. Some rings even have hidden handcuff keys built into them.

Knives, guns, and handcuff keys are very cleverly hidden inside belt buckles. Most of these devices are machine manufactured, and some are of top-quality construction. *Soldier of Fortune* magazine and *Shotgun News* often run ads for these devices. Many are so good that you must pay close attention to discover them.

From India we have a claw-like device that attaches to two opposite fingers worn on the inside of

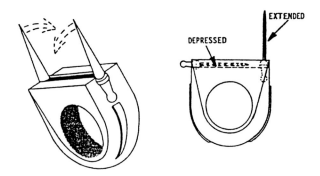

This guardian ring will release two sharp projections in a switch-blade manner. The spikes are approximately 3/8-inch long, and when closed they fold across the face of the ring. By applying pressure to the ring with the thumb, the spikes are released into an upright position. (Illustrations taken from *Hidden Threat: A Guide to Covert Weapons* by Mark Smith.)

the hand. As long as the wearer's fist is closed, these claws are hidden and retracted. On opening a hand, a set of deadly sharp claws is exposed for deployment. Like many of these devices, fist claws are obtained from specialty knife or martial arts suppliers.

Many surreptitious carriers of deadly weapons prefer small pistols of the type the not-so-smart friend carried in his belt buckle into the sheriff's office. These might include a device that looks identical to a telephone pager, but contains a small pistol inside rather than electronics. These days, one would be well-advised to be suspicious of anyone who carries two pagers.

There are small leather holsters that look exactly like wallets with trigger-finger holes that neatly hide small pistols. Some wallets contain special knives—disconcerting, to say the least, to the bandit who asks for a victim's wallet only to have his throat cut or his head blown off. Another neat holster is sewn into a front shirttail. This is a very innovative place to hide a pistol, but it's unhandy when one must deploy quickly with pants still securely in place.

Placing a firing device in a common fountain pen has always been popular. Given current fads that have brought back thick-barreled fountain pens, we may see more of these, and they may become much more clever. Pens have been made that fire .410, .38, .32, and, of course, .22 rounds. A pen firing a .410 round would truly be a heavy-duty assassination device.

For a number of years, these pen devices were produced legally in the United States. While they

were available, few people purchased them, validly reasoning that their practical uses were limited. Later—after being declared illegal—demand soared, and mechanical magazines such as *Popular Science* and *Mechanics Illustrated* often carried ads for the home builder.

Flare pens are sometimes legally offered today, perhaps under the assumption that these can be modified to fire ball ammo. Turning a common steel cigarette lighter into a .22 single shot also has been around for a long time, and advertisements for plans used to be common. Today, with the advent of throwaway plastic lighters and the rapid decrease in smoking, these devices might not be as unobtrusive as one would hope.

Workable firearms that discharge a single round have been built into chair and table legs, key chains, billy clubs, tire irons, tire pressure gauges, and even smoking pipes. Some of these designs are desperate measures done by convicts or other similarly restrained people, but would tear a large hole if deployed. Police in St. Louis were shocked to report a vehicle shock absorber modified to fire a 20-gauge round!

Weapons locations other than on one's immediate person are often unique. A farmer working rural areas of Mexico built a hidden compartment for his pistol behind his pickup glove box. In New York it is common for some folks to hollow out the area under a car's armrest so that a pistol can be hidden there. In another well-documented case, some especially paranoid people carefully secured a double-barrel shotgun inside the driver's side door of the auto. One wire pulled the safety, and another discharged the piece. All the driver needed to do was open the door slightly to aim and then blaze away at anyone walking up from behind.

But auto owners are not the only paranoid people. Both motorcycle and bicycle owners have been known to build shot shell discharge mechanisms into their vehicles' handlebars. Presumably, the discharge merely scared people off rather than doing bodily harm.

We aren't sure if they are being custom made or are part of a factory's production someplace, but several knives attached to the bottom of motorcycle gas caps have come to light. These are relatively large dagger blades brazed to the standard gas cap. Their length depends on the depth of the tank.

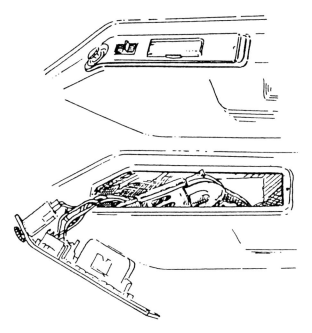

An armrest has hollow spaces that can easily conceal a weapon or contraband.

Vehicle air bags have become a real plus for men of action. They are easily dismounted from the center of a vehicle's steering column and can be disassembled, modified, and reassembled with carefully cut foam rubber, holding a small automatic or 2-inch barrel "revolver." When needed, the cover can be popped off and the loaded pistol deployed almost instantaneously.

Police estimate that a great number of these devices are being employed in high-crime areas. It is even claimed that they are being commercially manufactured in larger cities.

Until relatively recently, it was possible to purchase very tiny firearms no bigger than 2 ounces in weight and 1 1/2 inches in length. These weapons fired a single-pin-fire round capable of propelling a single number 8 bird shot through about 50 pages of a phone book. People disguised these as cuff links and tie clasps. The ammo was supposedly only blank, but manually loading a single small bird shot was possible. These devices look like firearms and are easy to detect unless carried hidden in a turnback cuff, behind a tie, or in a bra.

Several hundred years ago, jailers developed keys that were actually muzzle-loading pistols. This is a fairly easy proposition given the size of ancient keys.

In modern times, several keys have been manufactured that actually fired .25 caliber ACP rounds! Other keys have had short knives built into them that, if deployed, would have really upset the victim without much effective damage.

Other common devices are used to conceal firearms. Up until the late 1920s, knives firing .22 shorts were commercially manufactured. Some were clasp knives with little, short barrels that popped out, and others were pistol-like affairs built into larger belt knives.

My grandfather owned and often used an old German walking stick that fired either a .410 cartridge or a .45 long Colt. These were not the correct cartridges for which the device was made, but, in the absence of the antique German round, they functioned well enough. Grandfather could wield the stick itself skillfully enough, but in a pinch he always had his one shot. On one occasion, he took it to the park where insolent crows sat in trees, thinking themselves safe from harm. Grandpa fired once, and after that the crows never stuck around when he appeared with his stick.

I have always wanted one of these devices, but home building is not particularly easy, and, of course, in our own culture everyone is already suspicious of a walking stick. Perhaps building a gun into one leg of a crutch might be effective. Or even better, building a cartridge-firing device that can be slipped into a chair leg might have commercial value.

Shooting-type walking sticks were never popular, but those with knives or spikes are commonly available today. Sword umbrellas are now advertised in many men's magazines, and, if memory serves me, there was once an umbrella gun on the market.

Small handguns of many types such as mini-revolvers or even small automatics can be worn behind a wide tie or suspended inside a shirt. Cram a cleaning brush of sufficient diameter to stick in the barrel, and hang this from a shirt button or any other place in the pants leg, inner thigh, or shoulder. The weapon can be quickly pulled from the brush holder to deploy.

On several notable occasions, firearms have been concealed in specially designed shoulder bags, suitcases, briefcases, file folders, or jewelry boxes. In some cases, the guns were secured in place so as to shoot effectively from inside while held from the outside in an innocuous-looking case.

Makers of these devices usually wire the gun in soundly, placing a wire or steel strap extrusion on the trigger so that it can be activated while carrying the container under an arm.

Large cameras are another excellent place in which to hide firearms. No one gets suspicious of a camera that is carried or pointed. The problem is that most modern cameras are much smaller than most modern pistols. Yet a clever but desperate citizen who needs a firearm in a place such as New York or Los Angeles might keep this option in mind.

Some Middle Easterners recently traveling to Frankfurt were found to be carrying two fully loaded pistols with extra loaded magazines for each, a silencer, and three hand grenades hidden inside two sealed wine bottles. More sophisticated guards at the White House or international airports would probably discover this ploy, but if someone had to carry weapons in less security-conscious places, cutting open a large wine bottle and filling it with hardware just might work.

Slick, hard-to-detect, commercially produced containers made to look like Pringles potato chip, soft drink, and beer cans in which a person can stash a weapon are also available. These are occasionally advertised in *Shotgun News* or in specialty men's supply catalogs. One could pack along an authentic-looking can of Coke containing a small pistol, hopefully without raising suspicions.

Our grandmothers were also imaginative about weapons they carried in their era. Pistols among women traveling on public conveyances were common, and we have all heard stories about long hat pins used as weapons. Some women carried long butcher knives in special holders sewn into their heavy, full-length dresses. Others carried pistols in their muffs—leading to the term "muff gun" still used today for a very small pistol.

Currently, women need be even more innovative about self-defense because laws often favor the attacker rather than the victim. Specially made high-style women's purses are made with an easily accessed hidden compartment for a pistol or can of Mace. No doubt many women still carry hat pins, large knives, and other such innovative devices as cans of aerosol oven cleaner or a handful of change inside a piece of nylon, when absolutely nothing else is available.

Some big-city police units have encountered ladies of the street carrying lipstick tubes with 2 1/2-inch razor-sharp knives fastened inside. These extrude when the base is twisted in its normal function. Authorities do not know whether these are commercially available or are custom made with epoxy glue and hobby/craft knife blades.

This same kind of user carries combs containing knives. Some were originally switchblade combs and look like combs until activated.

Mexican nationals have been observed bringing with them a regular religious medallion-type cross in which a 3-inch knife is hidden. This is sufficiently popular that at least one major U.S. knife maker has it in its catalog. At first glance, the cross appears to be just another piece of religious jewelry. Many have, no doubt, been smuggled on board many commercial flights.

Almost everyone would agree that it is not wise to go to dangerous places unarmed. Given this basic fact of life and the fact that some of us must occasionally go to dangerous places, the best weapon is still one's mind. In that regard, thinking up ways to carry good, effective, pack-along weapons is desirable. Most weapons covered in this chapter are extremely clever, requiring only modest home workshop skills to produce. This material should get creative juices flowing so that those in need can always come up with their own appropriately clever systems.

BIBLIOGRAPHY

Smith, Mark. *Hidden Threat*. Boulder, CO: Paladin Press, 1989.

CHAPTER

The Future Infantry Weapon

22

Shortly after its adoption of the AR-15-type weapons (i.e., the M16A1) in 1967, the U.S. military began a search for its next infantry weapon. At first, efforts were minimal, but as the years rolled by, the search intensified. Thirty years is the average lifespan for basic infantry weapons in the U.S. Army. Although it seems like only yesterday—to some of us—when 5.56mms were adopted, it is now time for a change. Although we can't say for sure, our next infantry weapon will probably represent a change as radical as 1873 Springfields did when the United States first adopted cartridge firearms.

Unless conservative military planners decide on half measures in an attempt to avoid the inevitable, our new rifles will be made of structural nylon and fiberglass produced in injection-molding machines and containing very little steel. Wooden stocks and brass cartridges will be ancient history. What seems like extremely radical changes would not have been

possible had the mold not been broken with the introduction of AR-15-type designs.

As a result of many studies costing millions of dollars, our military planners finally decided late in 1989 what they really wanted next in an individual combat rifle. On the surface, their wish list represented the ravings of idiots. They required a system that had the following characteristics:

1. It would be a complete system that could be built up or down into individual combat weapons, squad automatic weapons, submachine guns, officers' sidearms, and even grenade launchers.
2. Given the fact that only 47 percent of the shots taken at an enemy are actually aimed and that proportionately few rounds actually produce casualties, the new system must allow more hits on targets out to 300 meters. This could include better sight planes, smart electronics sights, or vastly increased ammunition capacity.
3. This advanced rifle must have a minimum

capacity of 100 rounds and weigh, fully loaded, no more than 10 pounds.

4. It must effectively fire rifle grenades without alteration, additions, or special cartridges.

5. These rifles must be mass producible at low prices, using inexpensive materials. Affordability in times of diminishing military budgets was determined to be critical.

6. Rounds fired by this radical new weapon should be designed to engage the enemy out to about 300 meters principally, but must also be effective up to 600 meters. In general, this is taken to mean that any new round must be sufficiently accurate and powerful to consistently hit and penetrate an enemy helmet at 600 meters, even though most fire would be on targets out to only 300 meters.

Weapons designers call these criteria a "blivet," meaning that they are being asked to stuff six turds into a four-turd box. Initially, most knowledgeable people claimed that these standards could not be met unless some basic laws of physics were altered. How could you fire a grenade from a rifle, for instance, using standard ball ammo? Yet being given a blivet is common in military procurement.

Surprisingly, to a great extent, most of these seemingly impossible goals have been satisfied or overcome by current designs. Not all solutions are 100 percent, but work goes on. Remarkable alternative types of technology have emerged that already have produced notable improvements in combat rifles.

Unfortunately, it is also common for those speccing military hardware to change their minds frequently. By so doing, they give designers moving targets that are even more difficult with which to contend. Weapons designers lead frustrated lives, dramatically influenced by the fickle finger of fate.

Colt Firearms is an excellent example. From the onset of operation in 1847, they have almost always had some models to sell to the U.S. government. Because Colt's bread and butter has been U.S. military sales, they have been sensitive to shifting needs and priorities. Currently, Colt has a prototype that satisfies some of the current U.S. military requirements, but perhaps not to the extent of other makers who may be further along in this business.

As one might logically suppose, Colt has an upgraded, enlightened, improved version of its M16A1 on offer. Called an M16ACR, it has an improved foregrip handguard along which users can better sight. As is often common, this is an extremely simple improvement, but it does increase hit probability dramatically on the part of shooters not really using the weapon's sights.

A remarkable new muzzle brake cuts flash and recoil, while reducing full-auto bullet dispersion. Auto fire is damped down to a more easily controlled 450 rounds per minute. Complex three-round, burst-fire mechanisms are history.

This weapon is small when collapsed. The rear stock is adjustable to six positions, both to fit the user and to produce a small, easily carried package. The stock has a cheekpiece recommended after extensive "human engineering" studies had been conducted by Colt.

Probably the most dramatic improvement to hit probability resulted from the perfection of the duplex cartridge. This round has two piggy-backed bullets, a 33-grain bullet nestled behind the first of 35 grains. One bullet arrives on target a bit high, the other a bit under point of aim. As a result, faulty estimation of range might still result in a strike on target. This concept holds a great deal of appeal for U.S. military people who otherwise would have had millions of rounds of obsolete 5.56mm ammo in storage should some other rifle and caliber be adopted.

Changing to other weapons configurations is accomplished by adding or removing heavy barrels, larger-capacity magazines, specialty launchers, stocks, and, in some cases, special optic sights. The weight of any one of these possible configurations must run under 10 pounds, even for vehicle-mounted machine guns.

This Colt does satisfy some of these criteria, but it is probably not the optimum weapon in the terms originally specified. The M16ACR may be a compromise that military planners can live with till a more radical design is more commonly accepted.

Some really weird designs are already out there. In some cases, they are even being used by large, credible military organizations. Before looking at these, it is interesting to look at some more conventional designs. But, remember, conventional is in the eye of the beholder. Fifty years ago, any of these "middle ground" weapons would have been viewed as hopelessly radical. Given the more conservative nature of our military-rifle buyers and the deep commitment to the status quo, one of the following more conventional designs may actually be our next infantryman's rifle.

Aero-Jet General and Ford Aerospace have jointly produced a prototype advanced-combat rifle, the AUT XM70. At first this partnership tried to crack the nut of producing more accurate, effective flechette-type ammo. They dropped this in favor of a reduced-weight, aluminum-cased cartridge fired in a more stable weapon. Users could carry more ammo that dispersed less when fired, producing additional strikes on target, AUT designers reasoned.

One of their cartridges, a 5.56mm round, fired at 4,600 fps. At this speed, it was ideal for snap shooting at moving targets. Soldiers who estimated speed and distance poorly were more likely to get a strike on target because of the bullet's relatively straight, fast flight. Recoil from regular 5.56 rounds was reduced 25 percent, allowing less shot dispersion.

Lightweight, large-capacity magazines on the SM70 provided for almost belt-fed ammunition capacity that also contributed to the likelihood of hitting the target. Some recoil reduction resulted from the XM70's radical new flash suppression. Its weight fully loaded is about 9 pounds. Construction consists of metal stampings and plastic composition stocks.

Developers claim the rifle is central to a great family of different weapons that could be built around, and with, the main components. Because the design is experimental, few if any of these possible variations have actually been built.

American gun nuts, alert to new weapons designs at a time before then-President George Bush's import ban on assault rifles, may recall Steyr AUG rifles. This is a bullpup-design rifle made of some steel and structural nylon. It was introduced in 1978 by Steyr-Daimler-Puch AG of Austria. Originally, Steyrs worked on a flechette and sabot round. The flechettes fired at 4,900 fps, again doing away with the need to estimate lead on moving targets out to 600 meters. Mid-range trajectory was 13 inches, dramatically increasing likelihood of a strike on target.

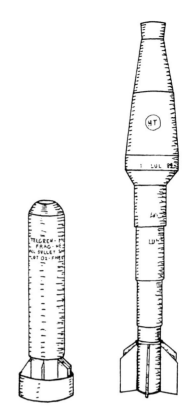

Fabrique Nationale's Bullet-Thru (left) and Luchaire's bullet-trap unit (right) are two modern rifle grenades that enable a soldier to deal effectively with lightly armored vehicles, bunkers, or similar obstacles normally protected from rifle fire. (Illustrations taken from *Combat Rifles of the 21st Century* by Duncan Long.)

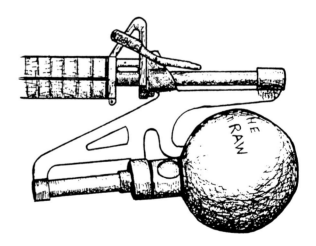

The Rocket Assisted Weapon (RAW) can be aimed and fired quickly and easily. Such a weapon might some day greatly extend the capabilities of a rifleman.

Early German prototype with single 50-round metal magazine (1987). (Photos supplied by Ragnar Benson.)

German mountain troops field-testing the G11 (1981).

G11 with reloading unit attached (1986).

Early prototype of G11K2 (1989).

Weapons were lightweight (7.12 pounds) and handy (30.7 inches), having virtually no accuracy-spoiling recoil. The weight of the flechette cartridges was half that of the conventional 5.56 round.

Modular buildup or -down to a number of different configurations was also possible. In the United States, AUGs were offered in 5.56mm—not flechette! All the AUGs were reliable and accurate, and they were a bit more conventional looking than many other designs.

Meeting modern criteria for grenade launchers will not be nearly as difficult as originally supposed, no matter which rifle is chosen.

Fabrique Nationale (FN) and Luchaire's have, to a great extent, solved the problem of firing rifle grenades from modern combat rifles using standard ball ammo! They have developed extremely effective antipersonnel and antiarmor rounds that

will drop on virtually any rifle barrel. A hollow tube runs through the device with baffles set for whatever ball ammo is being used. No special grenade blanks are required.

Another remarkable grenade-type weapon has been developed by Brunswick Defense of Costa Mesa, California. It is called a Rocket Assisted Weapon (RAW) and can be fired from virtually any infantry rifle. Hot gases from a standard ball round fired in a rifle on which a RAW is affixed light a small rocket engine that carries more than 1.25 kilograms of high explosive to a target. Detonation produces a "squash-head" effect, powerful enough to take out a wide range of hardened battlefield vehicles.

Up to 200 meters, you have a line-of-sight situation. You simply lins up the rifle sight and fire. Accuracy is very good. Flight time to a 200-meter target is 1.9 seconds. Because it is really a rocket-

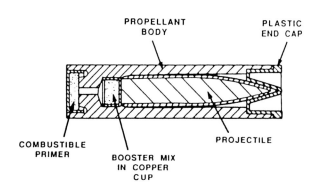

PROPELLANT BODY   PLASTIC END CAP

COMBUSTIBLE PRIMER

BOOSTER MIX IN COPPER CUP

PROJECTILE

Cross-section of the G11 "telescoped" cartridge with a bullet resting in the propellant body. The booster mix propels the bullet forward into the bore a fraction of a second before the powder is ignited. This helps prevent gas from traveling ahead of the bullet. (Drawing courtesy of Heckler & Koch.)

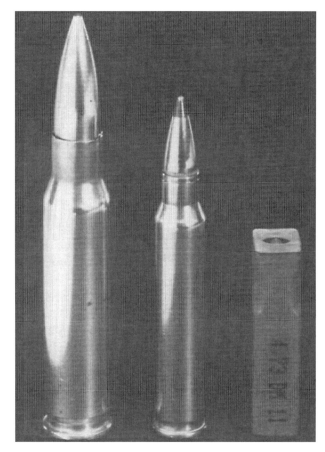

Left to right: 7.62mmx51mm NATO; 5.56x45mm NATO; 4.73x33mm caseless.

driven spherical projectile, crosswinds are not a significant factor. Although the round is insufficiently powerful to take out many large tanks, it will knock a tread off the heaviest vehicle. The telltale rocket signature is virtually nonexistent.

Given these remarkable leaps in rifle grenade technology, virtually any shoulder weapon is a grenade launcher without special cartridges, adapters, or sights. But, meanwhile back in the prototype lab, other incredible things are happening.

After World War II, two German weapons engineers, Edmund Heckler and Theodor Koch previously attached to the Mauser-Werke, left Germany to start a new company in Spain. Apparently, they didn't have firearms exclusively in mind at the start. But guns were their first love, and now Heckler & Koch (H&K) is one of the most innovative weapons factories in the world. In Spain, the pair perfected the CETME. This modern design based on World War II technology previously pioneered by H&K sold well around the world.

Eventually, H&K moved its factory back to Germany where they produced a number of innovative small arms. During the late 1980s, the German government decided to leapfrog ahead of U.S. M16s by adopting the remarkable new G11.

German military people laid down criteria very similar to those adopted by the Americans. During most of the 1980s, weapons' designers tended to consider these specifications to be complete fables. However, H&K took up the challenge. And although not everything is perfectly in place, it comes closer than all others.

The keys to producing a much lighter, more powerful rifle having dramatically increased hit capacity, H&K reasoned, were to greatly increase cartridge capacity, reduce recoil, and develop better human engineering for the weapon. This is only possible, H&K said, if we can perfect caseless ammunition.

Caseless ammo was researched extensively in the United States and Europe till the early 1980s, when almost everyone except H&K threw in the towel. H&K's approach (which, in retrospect, proved remarkable) was to produce guns for new ammunition, not the other way around. This may be a minor point to some, but it's earthshaking in practice.

Meeting weight, size, and ammunition-carrying capacity required that H&K go to a bullpup configuration. Without the hazards of empty brass being ejected out of a side port and of large, clumsy magazines dangling under one's chin, bullpup designs made even more sense. Initially, it was H&K's plan to stack rounds for the G11 in horizontal columns above the receiver. But this weapon in its final configuration did not have a conventional receiver, bolt, and chamber for the ammo to be placed above. In terms of current designs, this is the only way to describe ammo placement.

The rifles themselves were made almost entirely by injection-molded plastics. Barrels were made on automatic screw machines coupled to injection-molding machines, which resulted in a very highly automated manufacturing system. As such, there was no receiver, chamber, and bolt. A kind of floating chamber tipped up after each discharge. After the round slid into this device, it tipped back into alignment with the barrel, becoming a chamber. Rounds were stacked above, side by side in plastic magazines with bullet pointing down.

Ammunition for the G11 rifle is right out of *Star Wars*. A 51-grain, .20-caliber bullet is surrounded by a cube of compressed, tough, plastic-like material. You have to look in the end to see the bullet tip because a glued-on plastic endcap covers all but the tip of the bullet. Primer material is made of the same "powder" used in the body of the round, except that ground glass is added to the powder to assist detonation.

When the round is struck by the firing pin, combustion takes place in the specially formulated primer mixture, igniting a booster mix in a small copper cup within the round. This booster throws the bullet out into the barrel. A microsecond later, superhot gases from the primer and booster ignite the main propellant charge, thus propelling the bullet. By so doing, the barrel is sealed against propellant gas leakage without having to seat a bullet forward in a chamber. Ammunition, as a result, is extremely compact—about half the weight and length of conventional cartridges.

The propellant and primer contain no common nitrocellulose gunpowder. "Dynamite" Nobel took a material called Octagon and treated it to burn as a propellant. This treated material is called Nitramine and can only be detonated by superhot temperatures. Nitramine can be safely molded and shaped with automated machinery, and it will not cook off in a hot barrel.

The propellant and primer are consumed during the firing process. The plastic bullet cover and copper booster cap follow the bullet harmlessly out the barrel.

Recoil of the G11 is virtually nonexistent. Cyclic rate is mostly kept around 450 rounds per minute (rpm). On burst fire, the rate is boosted to 2,000 rpm! At that rate, all three projectiles have left the barrel before the shooter feels any recoil. The power of the round, which travels at more than 3,000 fps, is said to provide terminal ballistics comparable to 7.62 NATO rounds. Accuracy is about 3 inches at 300 meters.

Perhaps the system's greatest advantage is its magazine's location and carrying capacity. Each magazine holds 45 rounds, weighing a total of about 1/2 pound. Three extra magazines are piggy-backed in immediate reserve along the weapon's top buttstock and receiver area.

Loading units of 15 rounds each are carried in plastic belt holders. These can be inserted in the ready magazine any time. Clear plastic windows allow the user to monitor the ammo supply. The total weight of the rifle and 45 rounds is just under 9 pounds. The length is about 30 inches, and the weight with all 135 rounds in place is about 10.5 pounds!

The cost to manufacture using highly automatic machinery is said to be extremely modest. No one is talking publicly about the cost of caseless ammo, but a few commercial hunting rounds put on the market have retailed for well over a dollar each. However, these prices may not indicate very much about the cost to manufacture in large quantities for military use.

The only problems to surface so far with the ammo involve some cooking off and deterioration from rough handling. H&K claims these problems have been solved by coating the rounds with a varnishlike material.

Throat erosion in the floating chamber becomes serious at between five and six thousand rounds, but new, space-age ceramic technology is said to have solved some cartridge erosion problems. Barrel wear is about average for military rifles in general.

Because of the G11's incredibly high cartridge capacity, it can easily double as a squad automatic weapon (SAW). One could validly claim that every soldier with a G11 and packful of ammo has a SAW. Hit probability is increased dramatically because of low recoil, increased magazine capacity, and the straightline sight plane.

Worldwide, the trend in various armies is to fire toward the enemy rather than at one target in particular. Assumptions continue to be made that targets will be engaged successfully at shorter ranges.

This remarkably weird-looking H&K rifle answers most or all of the criteria set down by the U.S. military in 1989. Reliability, given its closet system design, has been said to be extraordinary. G11s even float!

The G11, however, is not U.S. made and would require massive tooling away from our present traditional brass cartridge system. Germany has, in a limited sense, adopted this rifle for some special units in its army and navy. Norway, Holland, and Italy are said to be seriously considering the G11s.

At this point, it is difficult to predict whether this rifle will become our next infantry rifle. After 25 years with the AR-15, it's certainly time for a change. Yet, 100 years ago, we were still using mostly a single-shot rifle with a large hammer because it was configured "like a muzzle loader." Change, in retrospect, has already been traumatic.

BIBLIOGRAPHY

Hogg, Ian V. *Jane's Infantry Weapons 1990-91.* London: Jane's Publishing Group, 1990.

Long, Duncan. *Combat Rifles of the 21st Century.* Boulder, CO: Paladin Press, 1990.

CHAPTER

Combat Shotguns

23

Turning a shotgun-type weapon into a true military weapon has been contemplated extensively by many excellent thinkers. Unfortunately, it is much more difficult than most gun nuts would first suppose. At least since 1873, when trapdoor Springfields were turned into forage guns by field armorers, there have been some attempts to use scatterguns for military purposes.

Yet forage guns designed to put prairie chickens in the pot are not really military weapons, other than the fact that military personnel operate them. Pot-filling shotguns were carried by our military personnel to every war, but mostly as personal weapons, property of the officers.

Shotguns intrigue armorers because of their ability to produce strikes on target without precise aim, their perceived flexibility to deliver different kinds of munitions, and the ease with which inexperienced soldiers can be trained to use them. But shotguns as we presently know them lack the range, penetration, and cartridge capacity to qualify as modern combat arms. Just carrying around enough ammunition for a shotgun would be a major problem for a shotgun-equipped infantryman. Yet it is not for lack of trying that modern shotguns are only used in special cases for warfare.

Some reports indicate that shotguns were used in the Spanish American War and the Philippines insurrection by troopers fresh off our frontier. Perhaps this is true, but after-action reports mentioning shotguns as being decisive—or even important—are extremely scarce. Recent readings of reports filed by Americans on Mindanao in the early 1900s do not mention shotguns at all. Most actions were undertaken at relatively long ranges and were decided by U.S. soldiers, who were then excellent marksmen.

An estimated 30,000 shotguns were issued to U.S. troops serving in Europe during World War I. One would have supposed that new Browning-design pump 97s would have been extremely effective trench-warfare weapons, but these guns' unique weaknesses as true military weapons prevailed. The ammo was too tough to pack around, the design too subject to fouling, and the stoppage and range far too limited. There are reports that Americans shot enemy passenger pigeons, deflected hostile grenades, and put "unclaimed" chickens in the pot, but again few after-action reports mention shotguns as being decisive.

America entered World War II mostly against its will. Japan attacked unprovoked, and Germany reaffirmed its treaty with Japan by declaring war on the United States. Initially, it was a come-as-you-are-when-called affair. Our military swept up what weapons they could from commercial sources, including a great number of shotguns. Mostly, these were Winchester Model 12s and 97s fitted with 20-inch barrels, bayonet lugs, and ventilated handguards. It is amazing, in retrospect, that our military reasoned that merely adding a bayonet lug created a military weapon, when added ammunition capacity with better potential was really the critical issue.

Shotguns found few willing users in North Africa and Europe, but in the heavy jungle country of the South Pacific some of their inherent weaknesses were mitigated. Our marines thought shotguns were the cat's meow for breaking up banzai charges and for triggering Japanese ambushes. Some GIs estimated that as many as two out of five Japanese small arms cartridges were duds. Combat, in these circumstances, was close, swift, and deadly.

Fighting in Korea took place over ranges too great to be practical for shotguns. The few scatterguns deployed were used to guard prisoners and keep civilians from pillaging supplies. In Korea, the Chinese used the tactic of surrendering in large numbers as a ploy. As a result, our soldiers were sometimes kept from doing their jobs while they dealt with prisoners more numerous than they.

More than 100,000 pump shotguns were purchased by the U.S. government to be sent to Vietnam. The plan was to distribute them in the hamlet defense program. But central government officials feared their own citizens as much as the Vietcong and refused to allow distribution. In regular combat, great numbers of shotguns were used by both the army and the marines in Vietnam. These included Stevens 520As, Stevens 620As, and

venerable Winchester Model 12s in military configuration. Shortcomings of shotguns as combat weapons were somewhat mitigated, but only through the efforts of some of our design and supply people.

All-weather plastic cases replaced paper and brass rounds, increasing reliability dramatically. Plastic shot cores and wads increased range a bit. It is sobering to realize that many gun nuts alive today have never seen an old, original paper shot shell case or experienced their propensity to swell and go dead after exposure to common battlefield conditions.

Military people finally identified the fact that available shotgun designs, especially in semiauto, were unreliable and subject to numerous mud- and debris-related stoppages. The range was still too short, guns were too heavy especially when fully loaded, and ammunition capacity was woefully limited. Recoil was severe; penetration (especially on modern body armor) was very limited; and, even with the excellent resupply capabilities found in Vietnam, sufficient ammo was difficult to pack around.

But stringent, seemingly impossible military criteria have been overcome by bright, young scientists in the United States. Shotguns have a great deal of charm *because* they do the one thing military planners always request: out to the limits of their range, they dramatically increase the probability of hitting the target. This is, of course, the first priority of soldiers on the line.

Various military contracts were initially designed to discover lighter, more reliable shotgun ammunition with materially increased range. Many original concepts were dead ends, but some interesting work was accomplished. Sabot rounds, for instance, traveling at speeds of 4,000 fps were tried in an effort to defeat armor at 150 meters. Effective grenades and tear gas rounds specifically designed for shotguns were introduced. Multiple flechettes were loaded in newly designed, smaller, lighter, special high-performance rimless magnum rounds. Other cartridges were loaded with exotic razorlike multiple projectiles, all in an attempt to make modern shot shells more efficient and to increase range and penetration while maintaining hit potential. It was some of these programs that led to development of the 40mm grenade system, including M79s and M203s.

Those in the firearms design business spent considerable effort developing new, more reliable

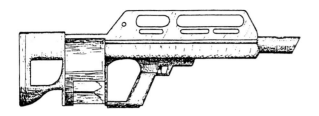

The Pancor Mk3A-1 Jackhammer has a bullpup design. However, unlike most other bullpups, it can be fired by either a right- or left-handed shooter. (Illustrations taken from *Streetsweepers* by Duncan Long.)

semiauto designs. Many proved to be quite good. Franchi, for example, worked on a bullpup shotgun that uses special, high-performance Magnum .410 rounds fed through large-capacity magazines.

As a general rule, commercial shotgun designers failed to note one of the most pervasive deficiencies. Most modern versions of scatterguns held at most 9 rounds of 12-gauge ammo, and most makers wanted owners to make do with a 5- or 6-round capacity.

Many aftermarket suppliers made an excellent business of supplying magazine extensions for popular models. Yet some makers still sell semiauto guns with nothing more than a 3-round capacity for which no mag extension kits are feasible, and many of the limited numbers produced are not even offered. Some of these semiautos function flawlessly, but only for 3 rounds?

To a large extent, both gun nuts and the military were forced to rely on regular commercial makers for their weapons. Producing a shotgun strictly for the military is risky and often counterproductive unless a manufacturer has a firm contract in hand. Commercial production, including possible sales to civilians, dramatically spreads the risk of developing a system that military people claim they want but that may never *exactly* meet ever-changing criteria and for which they end up never placing orders.

In conclusion, shotguns are awkward weapons with limited current ability for use as real military weapons. But they are a weapon with great potential for accomplishing the most sought-after military goal: to easily and consistently produce strikes on target when deployed by confused, scared, and inexperienced soldiers.

No doubt other more efficient, more cleverly designed shotguns will "surface" as we move into the 21st century. However, there are a number of good military-type shotguns currently on the market. These are not perfect, but they are state of the art, as we know it. This is especially true considering the fact that 125 years ago about all we had were double-barreled guns using paper cartridges.

The following is only an overview of the current military shotguns available, not a complete compendium. Given our strange, contorted gun laws, it is impossible to predict whether you will be able to purchase these weapons by the time this appears in print. It is equally impossible to guess whether other, better designs might suddenly come on the market. No matter what happens to gun rights in the United States, combat shotguns will no doubt be similar to machine guns: they will be readily available to those who are willing to both pay the price and break the law.

Ruger is an excellent example of an ambitious gun designer that currently has no military-type shotgun available. It would seem logical that Ruger would come on the market with a model to fill a void while avoiding current import restrictions on military shotguns from abroad. Use of currently available, extremely efficient 8-gauge industrial shot shells might be the basis for a valid new design.

Some current military shotguns are extremely expensive. "Cheap" is probably not the correct term, but perhaps it is fitting to first mention several models that are relatively inexpensive.

Seven-shot Mossberg Model 500 Persuaders, standard with synthetic stocks and pistol grip, are an excellent value at approximately $170. Maverick Arms has an efficient, light 8-shot bullpup design. This model is essentially a Mossberg 500 with a compact, factory-installed bullpup stock. Its current price is about $207. These may not be military weapons in some people's eyes because they are pump actions, but they are some of the most rugged models available.

First of the highly engineered semiautos is the AAI close-assault weapon designed specifically for the military. A special long-range, 12-gauge flechette round is part of the AAI system and is integral to this model's meeting design criteria. The weapon has a composite-stock, 12-round box magazine and is built of die-cast parts very similar to those of the AR-15. Advanced recoil systems chop recoil to about M16 levels. Makers claim that at least three of their flechettes will produce disabling strikes on man-size targets at 150 meters.

Only select-fire models are now produced, thus dramatically limiting commercial sales to Americans. This model could alter military shotgun tactics dramatically. It corrects many of the problems that have traditionally afflicted shotguns used in warfare.

Another excellent military-type shotgun currently available to Americans is the 12-gauge Benelli 121. It has an extended 8-shot magazine and an extremely fast, long-recoil operating system that will handle almost any loading. Its design is in general rugged and reliable.

As a result of the buffer spring mechanism located in the buttstock, folding stocks cannot be installed on Benelli 121s. Yet Choate Machine sells an aftermarket pistol grip that makes handling in combat a bit easier.

Benelli Super 90s are the next generation after Model 121s and perhaps the only Benelli series currently available new in the United States. Super 90s are 12-gauge, 9-shot semiautos with tough composite plastic stocks. If you wished to mix 3-inch mag rounds, Super 90s would work without a glitch, but tubular magazine capacity would be cut to 7 rounds. Light 12-gauge trap loads work only sometimes in this versatile weapon. Test any ammo before the situation gets serious to be sure.

Recoil on these light (7.25 pounds) guns is pretty hairy, but as the man said, most of us carry our weapons more than we shoot them. As with Benelli 121s, Super 90s cannot be fitted with folding stocks.

Special pistol grip stocks, called SWAT stocks, are offered by Benelli. As a rule, any Benelli must be purchased new. Owners must specify a SWAT stock when they order their guns if this is the model they want.

Some gun nuts theorize that owning a super-reliable semiauto shotgun with extended magazine that also looks like a commercial hunting gun is wise. Should assault rifle hysteria ever extend to shotguns, these owners reason that they and their "hunting guns" may be spared.

Those adhering to that philosophy should consider the Franchi 48/AL. This a light, reliable weapon. However, magazine extensions must be

The South African-made Striker, with its spring-powered cylinder, borrows heavily from the Manville gun. It has a sheet-metal folding stock, and a small optical aiming system can be added to the gun. Another plus is that the design includes a shroud over the cylinder. All these features greatly aid performance in a dirty environment.

custom built by a gunsmith, and no folding or pistol grip stocks are available.

Of current combat shotguns currently on the market, later models of Franchi probably come closest to meeting combat criteria.

SPAS-12 Franchis are mild-recoiling, gas-operated 12-gauge semiautos that come standard with pistol grips, composition stocks, and 9-shot magazines, and can be purchased with folding or removable buttstocks. These remarkable weapons can be used as pump actions if the owner has special-purpose ammo such as rubber projectile, gas, or exploding rounds he wishes to deploy reliably.

One criticism of the SPAS-12 involves its complexity. At first glance, it appears bewildering with its dual interlocking safeties, magazine cutoffs, bolt stops, and adjustable foregrip. However, if you use it only as a semiauto till function smooths out, it is not nearly as formidable. SPAS-12s are also quite heavy and resemble assault shotguns in appearance.

As a compromise, Franchi has released a LAW-12 semiauto that is not just dramatically simpler and lighter than a SPAS-12, but is also very reliable. LAW-12 guns are not terribly common at this writing, but they are available for those who root around a bit. Expect to pay approximatley $450 to $500 for either of these models.

USAs-12 combat shotguns are made by Daewoo of South Korea. Originally, these were open-bolt, select-fire, gas-operated weapons. The shotgun is constructed much like AR-15 with its many stampings and trademark carrying handle. This is a very rugged weapon that comes with both 10-round box and 20-round drum magazines.

As of this writing, civilian models are available for about $1,000, not including magazines. The weight, loaded, is well over 10 pounds. No folding stocks are currently offered.

Two basically similar versions of windup revolving shotguns have come on the market accompanied by great controversy in the United States. Both originated in Rhodesia and were designed by Hilton Walker, who took the design to South Africa when his country collapsed. In South Africa, Walker perfected a weapon that used a revolving drum much like a revolver that held 12 rounds of 12-gauge ammo. After completion of the design, he attempted to bring the weapon to the United States for commercial sales.

Windup revolving shotguns have a bit of charm in that they will function reliably with a vast variety of different ammo. This seeming advantage is not as great out in the field as could be hoped. Once empty, these guns are extremely wearisome to reload. Unlike with tube magazines, which are themselves sometimes inconvenient, you cannot continually push a few fresh rounds into revolving-drum magazines. These magazines must usually be totally emptied before each round is individually punched out and replaced.

Revolving shotguns are intrinsically cantankerous and subject to jamming from the least bit of muck, dust, or debris. Of the two current models in production in the United States, streetsweepers came on the scene first, but are far less sturdy. At $400, they also sell for about $150 less than strikers, but the latter are better built and more closely approximate those originally developed and tested in South Africa. Both have recently been ruled illegal by the BATF.

In either case, speed of firing and reliability are not nearly as good as one would hope. Weight and price for both are quite high. Having used both extensively, my plan is to use more conventional, purely military types of shotguns such as the Benelli Super 90 or a Franchi SPAS-12.

Reportedly, other much more experimental designs that use radically improved ammo are in the works. Whatever model you choose, it should be only an interim step until either new laws preclude any additional purchases or some radically new models come on the market.

Of all weapons, shotguns are long overdue for significant leaps in technology. Although nothing radical or dramatic seems to be on the horizon, change is inevitable.

BIBLIOGRAPHY

Hogg, Ian V. *Jane's Infantry Weapons 1990-91.* London: Jane's Publishing Group, 1990.

Lesce, Tony. *The Shotgun in Combat.* Boulder, CO: Paladin Press, 1984.

Long, Duncan. *Streetsweepers—The Complete Book of Combat Shotguns.* Boulder, CO: Paladin Press, 1987.

CHAPTER

Shotgun Deployment in Combat

24

Tony Lesce raises interesting and thought-provoking ideas in his book *The Shotgun in Combat*. Usually, when you think of shotguns in combat, scenes of hundreds of Winchester 97s in the hands of U.S. troops at the Argonne come to mind. Those who have experienced 97s as well as the incredible spring mud in Europe can only wonder how these lowly trench fighters ever kept their pump-action scatterguns operational. In terms of working environment, World War I was designed specifically for bolt actions.

They may be apocryphal, but other after-action accounts from that war indicate that someone, perhaps unofficially, in a French machine shop, redesigned at least one Maxim water-cooled .30-caliber machine gun to fire 12-gauge shot shells. Belt-fed, brass-cased shot shells, the story goes, were fired at about 500 rpm.

You would have hated to be part of the supply column for that one weapon alone, but if true, no attacker—day or night—could have come through that wall of buckshot unscathed. Admittedly, this

weapon may only have been a fantasy of some desk-bound officer, yet the concept does stimulate the interest of gun nuts.

Attached to the front of a small punt and used on ducks, it would have been truly amazing if the weight of ammunition or dead ducks did not sink it, and if nosy authorities were kept at bay.

At any rate, in his book Lesce seems to confuse domestic self-defense with actual soldierly use of shotguns. Homeowners standing in the breach, with shotgun in hand to protect the family, may not immediately be able to tell the difference, but—in terms of order, mission, supply, and personnel—differences do exist. Ambiguous areas in this logic surface when one looks at old Western gunfighters who often used shotguns to blow away opponents. One could say this was law enforcement, or domestic violence, self-defense, recreation, or—when involving large numbers of participants—military use. In reality, it was probably none of these.

Twelve-gauge number 4 buckshot loads 27 pellets per round and has 2,079 foot-pounds of total muzzle energy. Double 0 rounds load 9 pellets having 1,099 fpe. Don't, however, conclude that 4 buck is a better load, Lesce cautions. This is good advice for those who tend to flip through loading manuals looking for the last fps of velocity when what really counts is available energy *at* and *in* the target.

Anyone using a shotgun for anything serious should expend at least a box of ammo shooting into paper, water, or snowbanks, so that he knows precisely what to expect from the loads at various ranges. This is for both shot concentration and penetration.

It is best to purchase man-size paper targets so that the exact number of pellets hitting the target can be discerned. Some users load number 4s, buckshot, and then slugs in their shotguns in an attempt to increase effectiveness. Lesce calls these Dutch loads, but given the limited ammo capacities of most shotguns, mixing in actual range and penetration tests may prove less than ideal.

Lesce agrees with many other experts that range, penetration, and killing power are maximized for 12 gauges from about 30 to 50 yards. In times past, 30 yards or 120 feet was thought the maximum for a 12 gauge, but modern plastic wads have increased the scale a bit. Pressures and velocities are greater in some unthought-of rounds. A .410, for instance, will impel number 4 shot farther into a telephone directory than a 12 gauge. The likelihood of hitting that directory with fewer shots in a .410 round is dramatically decreased, however.

Shotgun silencers are commonly available for .410 shotguns in the United Kingdom, and in longer-barreled guns they are reportedly quite effective. Weight and size constraints limit the use of silencers on 12 gauges, although, contrary to the author's experience, they have been tried extensively.

Increasing kill potential by mixing rat poison in the shot load is suggested. Although this device may give the victim of a glancing or long-range wound a serious infection, it may also make him so mad that the shooter will be forced to do the job correctly the next time. One can only wonder how smooth shot could carry sufficient poison of any kind in quantities needed to incapacitate a victim. Forming poison into pellets also won't work because of the limited range and penetration of the material. Plain, old lead is—by itself—poisonous if left in the wound any length of time without medical treatment.

An old, old trick that increases a shot shell's range involves pouring melted paraffin or beeswax into the shot column inside a round. The resulting mass fires much like a slug that will break up on impact. Although sometimes done back in the era of paper cases, this device is seldom employed today. Modern plastic wads and factory fiber-filled shot charges seem to work better than paraffin filling.

Another ancient trick involves drilling a 1/4-inch hole into the front of a 12-gauge slug into which a .22-caliber short or blank is inserted. The destruction of thin-skinned targets when this round strikes and detonates is impressive.

Lesce did a great deal of work testing the actual (not theoretical) penetration of various shot shell loads. He built a large rack onto which he could place sheets of standard 1/4-inch wallboard. He then tested by firing into double wallboard separated by common 2 x 4-inch studs similar to those in most home wall interiors.

At 10 feet, almost any small shot or buck load penetrated both sheets of plaster board. Rounds of buck fired at 30 feet also easily penetrated both layers of wallboard, even when fired at an angle. Small shot at this range was trapped between wall one and two—exactly what police users of shotguns are counting on. No consideration was given to the results of multiple rounds striking in basically the same location or, most important, to the impact on a shooter who discharges such a blast in a small, closed room.

Both small shot and buckshot fired at even very short ranges had little effect on concrete blocks, with only surface scarring resulting. Slugs might crack unsupported, unfilled blocks, but even if the strike occurred at an empty hollow section, penetration is unlikely.

For defense (combat) situations, shotguns are said to have an advantage in five specific areas:

1. Stopping power. At relatively short ranges, the shotgun is superior to most pistols and many rifles.
2. Intimidation factor. Staring down the huge bores of a 12 gauge or hearing a pump gun racked makes quite an impression on a person who where he is not supposed to be in the middle of the night.
3. Easier, more certain shot placement. True enough. If it weren't for limited range, poor penetration, and bulky ammunition, shotguns would have been standard military issue years ago.
4. Popularity of the ammo. Lesce validly concludes that aside from .22 LR ammo, 12-

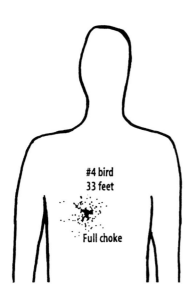

#4 birdshot at 33 feet, full choke. Because the pellets are larger, they have more sectional density and better carrying power than the #8 shot. They would be effective out to a longer range. (Illustrations taken from *The Shotgun in Combat* by Tony Lesce.)

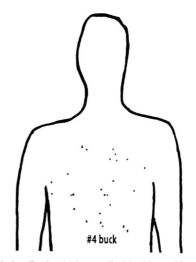

#4 buckshot fired at 30 feet, cylindrical bore. Many people believe that #4 buck is the best all-round load, and looking at this pattern, it is easy to see why. The 27 pellets [all of the following targets were shot at 27 times] are evenly scattered on the target. This can be compared to 27 hits with a .24-caliber pistol. The heart, lungs, and various blood vessels would be damaged. Additionally, #4 shot is heavy enough not to be seriously impeded by heavy clothing, as would #8 shot at this range.

gauge shells are the easiest ammo to purchase virtually anyplace in the world.

5. Shotguns are some of the last weapons taken by gun grabbers. Many shotguns look like common hunting weapons.

Police often use shotguns in place of billy clubs to discourage, restrain, and block belligerent assailants. At times, shotguns are also used to fire smoke or gas or to lay down suppressive fire so that those fired upon keep their heads down and do not move. Even at extreme ranges, they are said to be effective for this mission, provided the user gets the elevation and trajectory down.

Shotguns are of limited use as home-defense weapons, Lesce points out, unless you take the time to plan specific deployment. Know where the weapon is kept, where others in the family will hide, where ammo is kept, and who in the family will be coming back late and might be mistaken for an intruder. Lesce validly points out that a homeowner who knows his house and how he will protect it has a great advantage over an intruder, but says nothing about what you should do if the police are intent on killing you and your family—a terrifyingly frequent occurrence in modern America.

Lesce does point out that you can find good refuge in the kitchen or bathroom where metal appliances will afford some protection against shot and fire. Bathtubs will withstand a blast from a shotgun at very short range, for instance. Whatever you plan, these routines must be rehearsed with your family, Lesce emphasizes.

Perhaps 50 percent of the use of a gun for home protection involves a shotgun. Lesce attributes at least part of this popularity to the fact that shotguns are relatively cheap and easy to learn to fire effectively. The actual operation of pump and semiautos can be relatively complex if you are completely unfamiliar with any firearms. A shotgun is said to be intimidating even if an intruder only hears and sees them. In terms of actual shot range and penetration capabilities, they can be deadly effective.

We can only hope that homeowners do not have to engage in combat and that this instruction for them is at best a bit miscalculated and not in any way prophetic.

BIBLIOGRAPHY

Lesce, Tony. *The Shotgun in Combat*. Boulder, CO: Paladin Press, 1984.

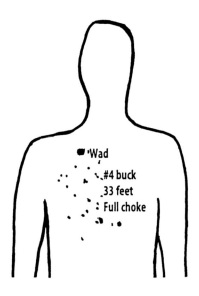

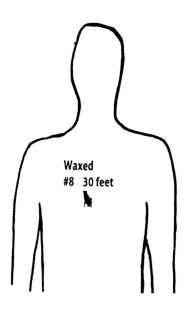

#4 buck, 33 feet, full choke. Characteristically, the pattern is tighter with the full choke. In this photo the hole made by the wad can be seen, although at this range the wad would probably not have enough force to make a lethal wound. The shot, however, would. The pattern, slightly off center here, would hit both lungs, the heart, and the major blood vessels in the center of the body. A head shot would not only involve the brain and the eyes but would severely lacerate the windpipe and the blood vessels in the neck, again causing a fatal injury.

Fired at 30 feet, the improvised slug looks like this. Notice that most of the shot held together—only a dozen or so scattered. They would have held together even better if epoxy instead of wax had been used.

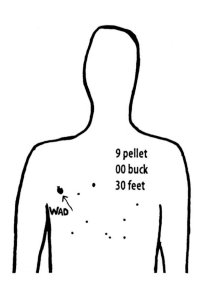

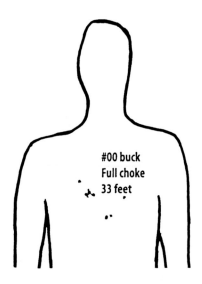

9 pellets #00, cylindrical bore, 30 feet. This is the pattern made by a standard 00, the favorite police load. The pellets are scattered enough to involve the heart and lungs and would surely penetrate any likely clothing worn by the subject. The wad, whose impact can be seen in the upper left, can penetrate paper at this range, but not much more. 00 is noted for penetrating car bodies, not surprising considering that the pellet is .33 caliber and weighs 54 grains.

9 pellets #00, full choke at 33 feet. The pattern here measures slightly more than half the diameter of that fired from the gun without a choke. The concentrated lethality of the 9 pellets striking in an area only about 6 inches in diameter is apparent in this photo. There are only 7 holes; two of them are elongated, suggesting double impacts. These pellets are heavy enough to cause severe damage by breaking off pieces of ribs and thereby generating secondary missiles. Notice that the small diameter of the pattern dictates careful aiming, particularly if all you have is a simple shot.

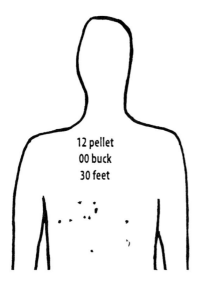

12 pellets "magnum" load, cylindrical bore, 30 feet. The little used "magnum" load for the 12 gauge has 12 pellets instead of 9, but travels at the same velocity. The pattern is about the same diameter as the one made by the regular load, but it is denser, if an increase of 3 pellets can be labeled as more density. There is one double impact visible in the center of the pattern, right in the region of the heart. The deadliness of the "agnum" load is beyond question, without implying that the regular load is in any way puny. The increase in recoil is severe, making the load far less popular than the regular one.

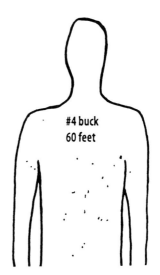

#4 buck at 60 feet, cylindrical bore. There are only 23 hits visible in this photo, which leads one to believe that 4 went someplace else. The pattern is wide enough to have been capable of engulfing two subjects if they had been standing side by side. The lethality would have been uncertain, however. In this case, the hits are evenly distributed between the chest and the abdomen. In the unlikely event that the hits in the heart and lung area did not do the job immediately, the hits in the soft, unprotected abdomen would ensure death from peritonitis within a few days, if untreated.

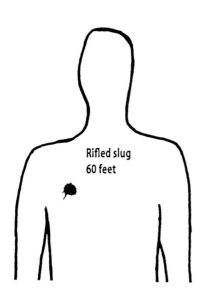

Rifled slug, 60 feet. 400 grains of lead traveling at somewhere over 1,000 fps means impact and wound. In this case, the slug would crush ribs and penetrate the lung, causing a severe wound with massive hemorrhaging, with additional damage from secondary missiles. Caution: A rifled slug should not be fired from a gun with a choke because there of the danger of overpressure and damage to the choke.

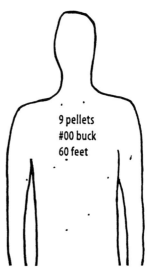

9 pellets of #00, 60 feet, cylindrical bore. In this pattern, the hits are well scattered, with 2 up near the throat, 1 in each arm, 2 in the abdominal area, and the rest in the chest. Again, the pattern is scattered enough to hit two subjects standing side by side. The effects would be serious, even if the 9 pellets were divided between two subjects. As shown, the effect would be a sure fatality, unless a medical miracle were performed, because the tissue destruction would be widespread and severe, hitting several vital areas at the same time.

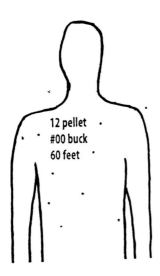

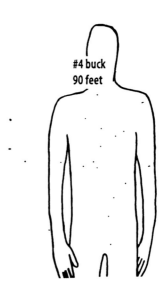

12 pellets of #00 at 60 feet, cylindrical bore. The scattering effect is such that the "magnum" load resulted in only 9 hits on the subject. Another hit would have been recorded if the aim had been slightly lower. Nevertheless, the 9 that did hit caused lethal damage. This load, with more pellets, would have been slightly more effective than the 9-pellet load if split between two subjects. Mitigating this is the battering effect of increased recoil.

#4 buck, 90 feet, cylindrical bore. At 90 feet, the scattering is pronounced, and two subjects standing side by side have been well peppered. #4 buck is still capable of causing serious injury at this range, even though the velocity of the pellets has fallen off a lot. They may not be able to penetrate the rib cage, depending on the clothing worn by the subject; however, the unprotected areas would still be terribly vulnerable.

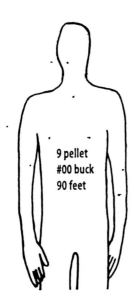

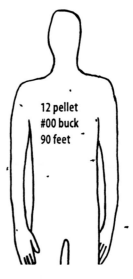

9 pellet #00 buck at 90 feet, cylindrical bore. 7 hits, 3 of which are in vital areas. This pattern shows a good scattering, enough to hit another subject standing beside the first. A shotgun with a full choke would have concentrated the pattern more for enhanced lethality, but a tighter pattern means more careful aiming, as well as precluding taking out two opponents at that range.

12 pellets "magnum" load, 90 feet, cylindrical bore. Of the 12 pellets, only 7 hit the subject, and only 9 are visible on the paper at all. The 12-pellet load scatters more, making it more suitable for use against multiple opponents. Notice that there is no impact from the wad visible. The wad, being large, light, and of low sectional density, has a very poor ballistic coefficient and does not reach much beyond 30 feet. Of the 7 hits shown here, only 2 can be said to have hit in vital areas, causing immediate serious effects. Nevertheless, 7 hits taken together are very serious in their cumulative effect.

CHAPTER

Combat Handguns

25

A tough, street-smart 60-year-old woman worked nights as the attendant in a 24-hour self-service gas station/convenience store. She had the security of a somewhat hardened cash register area from which to work as well as the fact that the store was situated in one of the city's larger shopping centers.

Because this tough old broad had seen it all, she took seriously reports of armed robbery and murder at all-night marts similar to hers in the area. As a result, she went to a local sporting goods shop where, with her own money, she purchased a Browning .32 ACP auto pistol and two boxes of ammo. Because she realized her own limitations, the woman went out in the country and practiced away one box of ammo. With the remaining ammo, she loaded up her "piece," including the spare magazine. All went into her purse.

Exactly two weeks later, while working her regular night shift, a man appeared to stagger and

fall into the pump area. She left the relative security of her office to go out to see if she could help. On coming up to the fellow, he poked a sawed-off double barrel in her face.

Still at gunpoint, she accompanied him back to the office to retrieve the cash box. After grabbing the night's receipts, he told her he felt he had to kill her.

At that moment a car pulled into the station for gasoline. Momentarily, the shotgun-wielding thug was distracted. Knowing it was now or not at all, she dove for the little auto in her purse. He turned and fired once, missing her. The blast from the huge gun in so small a closed space temporarily stunned the stickup artist. She rolled on the ground behind a desk, quickly brought her pistol up and fired twice from a range of about 5 feet. Only one round hit the guy, but it was enough. It entered from the left side of the chest, punching on through to his heart. By the time police and emergency people arrived, the guy was history.

Was this combat pistol shooting? Certainly, the lady maintains it was, even now several years after the event. However, combat shooting in the traditional sense usually involves young men of one country's military service pitted against young men of another's. During the last 40 years of this century, the definition has blurred as crime has run rampant and guerrilla wars have proliferated. In that regard, any one of us might instantaneously be called into combat.

Recently, many average gun owners have come to feel that they and their weapons are all that stand between them and plundering criminals of both the civil and political persuasion. They have banded together into what one may term "guerrilla groups seeking mutual protection." In this regard, many pistol owners are seriously practicing what were previously arcane skills of combat shooting.

Like other weapons categories, such as shotguns and assault rifles, the pistol type with accouterments defines the activity. To some extent, requirements for combat pistols are even more stringent than those for shotguns and rifles. Wins and losses are measured in tenths of a second. Pistols by nature are weapons of extreme speed used at relatively short ranges. A number of studies evaluating a huge cross section of pistol altercations have indicated that the average range is only 7 feet!

Eugene Sockut probably has as much actual on-the-street combat pistol experience as any man now living. As a result of surviving numerous shoot-outs, Sockut is an instructor for the Israeli military and police. He has also taught combat pistol craft extensively in the United States.

All of Sockut's recommendations, which come firsthand from serving on the streets of the West Bank, are extremely interesting. He maintains, for instance, that the most important aspect of a combat pistol encounter involves the spirit of the person thus engaged. Sockut would agree that the lady at the convenience store displayed a fierce fighter/survivor mentality; she had an intense desire to prevail, doing so with a popgun of a weapon.

"Keep your equipment simple," Sockut says. He uses twin 1911 Colt .45s stuck between a double leather belt! He chose the Colt .45 auto because he thinks it is still one of the most reliable manstoppers available. He does not encumber himself with holsters. Extra magazines are interchangeable for both pistols. During the heat of battle, he doesn't have to concentrate on anything except shooting.

Sockut validly points out that your backup weapon should be identical to your main weapon. Thus, you can avoid carrying two types of ammo and magazines, and—most important—learning to shoot two different weapons.

Combat pistol practice is undertaken so that one learns to shoot instinctively with extreme speed and without benefit of sights. Sockut advises placing man-size targets on standing racks set from 1 to 7 yards from the person doing drills. He recommends drawing and firing at the small center ring on each silhouette target.

"Try one or two quick shots, attempting to place rounds in the kill zone as much as possible," he says. "It is important to shoot at a very small point on the actual larger target if one hopes to ever become both very fast and accurate. Keep at this drill until both accuracy and excellent speed are achieved.

"After this, set up two or even three targets in a small 1- to 7-yard semicircle. Practice accurately hitting these in order of importance as imagined attackers. At first, draw and shoot only once at each target. After accuracy improves, try double tapping each of the two or three silhouettes," Sockut recommends. "Always try to hit a small spot within the kill zone rather than being content to hit *somewhere* within the big target."

This sounds very simple at the short ranges Sockut recommends and at which experience suggests the primary work of the pistol will be undertaken. Sockut also suggests adding distractions such as loading the shooter down with packages, positioning chairs or barrels to represent innocent bystanders, and simulating multiple, partly obscured assailants as the shooter becomes proficient.

"Before using live ammo, spend hours dry firing," he says. If you do not become glass smooth and very fast, tragedy will result the first time you try this for real on the street.

Mike Jennings was one of the first to suggest using instinct combat or point-shooting methods in his 1959 book, *Instinct Shooting*. He pointed out that in all likelihood, early West pistoleros were instinct shooters when they actually used pistols. But Jennings' book institutionalized the method as a valid combat-shooting technique.

Chuck Klein has worked both as a full-time police officer and a sheriff's deputy. During the 1950s and 1960s he was an avid civilian target shooter. By 1970, it had become increasingly clear to Klein that uniformed officers who successfully withstood armed assailants were *not* doing so by deploying conventional draw, crouch, aim, and fire techniques. His book *Instinct Combat Shooting* became something of a classic when it first appeared in the early 1980s. It pointed out that you must learn to draw, point, and fire accurately in mere tenths of a second.

Klein became something of a guru on the technique of instinct combat shooting, while Chuck Taylor became the authority on equipment as a result of his book *The Complete Book of Combat Handgunning.*

Technique and equipment converge when Klein maintains that it is important to purchase a combat pistol capable of shooting at least 600 full-power rounds per year, as well as thousands of lighter loads without wear or damage. This same pistol must endure hundreds of hours of dry firing without wear, Klein says.

High-quality pistols perform this role easily, Taylor maintains. "One must purchase a high-quality pistol as the first phase of learning combat shooting," he says.

Universal agreement exists among experts that debate will continue at least two to three more decades, but that semiauto pistols are simpler, more effective, less subject to breakage, and contain more firepower—they are just generally superior to revolvers. Those genuinely deploying pistols in a combat role most often use semiautos, experts agree.

But no matter which type of handgun with which you decide to become proficient, custom handgrips are important, the experts claim. Even though the grips tend to be expensive, owners with custom grips always get their hands on their pistol in exactly the same manner. Form-fitted grips are ideal in that your fingers are always in the same place. Without constant hand placement, good instinct combat shooting is virtually impossible.

Long, often harsh, experience has taught Klein that one absolutely must practice and learn to place his forefinger in a ready position along the trigger guard until the absolute last instant before firing. At times, the moves are virtually simultaneous, but a you must not touch the trigger until you are certain that you will shoot. Klein says that this maneuver

can take as much practice as getting your pistol out of the belt and rounds in the black in a split second.

Unlike many instructors, Klein believes that a main service pistol out on display in its holster must be sufficiently secured against unauthorized removal and that the backup pistol is the only practical speed combat weapon. He might not disagree with Sockut that they should be the same make, model, and caliber.

Instantaneous pistol removal is always done with a single, continuous, circular motion. Never use a stop-and-start motion, experts say. Once started, hand, gun, and arm must clear the holster—continuing on in one motion toward the target, till the arm reaches the limits of its travel or—in a two-handed posture—hand meets hand. At the instant of meeting or arm extension, the shot is taken. Experts can put four or five rounds in a 4-inch circle at 7 yards using this speed-draw technique.

Body posture, according to most experts, is not critical to shooting as long as balance is maintained and you achieve good results. In terms of stance, start with a common, left foot slightly forward, weight balanced, knees slightly bent, perhaps with a Weaver or modified-Weaver two-hand-hold stanceuntil you develop your own unique stance.

Like fighting of any sort—with pistol, knives, shotgun, or rifle—none of this is of any value, experts contend, without a positive mental approach, including an intense desire to win based on extremely high levels of concentration.

Concentration leads to focusing on a small spot on the big target rather than on pistol or its sights. By watching the target, you can more reasonably expect to get off a quicker, more accurate, effective round. Experts use the analogy of throwing a ball at a running receiver or of striking a nail with a hammer. Successful combat shooters instantly identify the smallest target central to the main target and go for it. This may be a tie tip, button or button holder, or the attacker's hand. Focus provides the correct distance and the correct intent of the attacker.

After hours of dry firing and range practice with live ammo, Klein recommends that serious shooters build a moving target that uses a pulley, power drill rope, and spindle with pulley. He tapes a pop can to the scope and allows the drill to pull it along. Practice drawing and instinct shooting on these moving targets, Klein says, after becoming proficient with stationary silhouettes.

Chuck Taylor has been in more than his share of shooting scrapes, including ones from which he did not walk away. As a result, his experiences and recommendations are valid even though they differ a bit from *Instinct Shooting* pistol practices. As mentioned, Taylor looks to equipment more than some, and he claims to use pistol sights even though he acknowledges that handgun contests are quick, close, and brutal.

Taylor uses a pistol as smooth as a worn cake of soap and one that has a crisp, breaking-glass-rodlike trigger let off. He prefers either smooth or checkered wood grips without finger grooves or indentations, especially on semiautos, which, he feels, may be a bit faster from the holster.

Sights or trigger guards with any sharp corner, hook, or protrusion should be avoided he says. Sights must be high and large enough so that they are instantly obvious. Rear sights must be correspondingly rounded with enough notch so that the front can be picked up without thinking about it. Adjustable sights, Taylor says, are needlessly complex and should be left for hunting and target guns.

Keeping combat pistols very simple implies that you not use double-action automatics, he claims. Taylor avoids ambidextrous safeties but likes extended safeties that enhance speed of deployment.

He is ambivalent about checkered back frames, saying they seem to add little to speed, their use being only a matter of personal preference. Yet checkering the steel frame under the front trigger guard is a defensive advantage, the author-expert claims.

On semiautos, Taylor suggests having a gunsmith bevel the magazine well so that reloaded magazines insert faster and easier even if done unsteadily in the heat of combat. Trigger shoes on either autos or revolver are dangerous and clumsy, he maintains. Narrow, smooth hammers are always preferred to wide, checkered ones that have a maddeningly common propensity to catch on something, he says.

Taylor intends to carry his main service pistol in an open holster providing for both safety from unauthorized withdrawal and for fast combat deployment. As a result, he spends a great deal of time evaluating various makes and types of holsters. He admits that accomplishing both goals is extremely demanding for a holster. Unlike Klein and Sockut, Taylor draws from his regular service holster. His top recommendation for performing this almost-impossible dual role is a Milt Sharks #1AT holster.

Sockut carries his extra magazine in a specially made, open-ended leather cuplike holster. Taylor recommends double-ended pouches that lie close to the body. Both agree that the choice of mag carriers is important only as long as the spare magazines are held securely and that they are actually carried. Sockut, of course, strongly urges that magazines be interchangeable in all weapons carried.

All experts expend a great deal of time and energy evaluating the concept of relative stopping power of various combat handgun cartridges. Evan Marshall and Edwin Sanow have written the definitive volume on this subject, *Handgun Stopping Power*. As a result, relative stopping power is no longer a theoretical concept. In this volume, they minutely evaluate thousands of actual street reports involving use of virtually every handgun caliber. They look at actual effects on the recipient party, calculating the percentage of times a specific round and specific bullet actually stopped an assailant.

These are not mathematical models or hypothetical gelatin block tests. Rather than killing power, they evaluate one-shot stopping power whereby persons fired upon stop whatever it was that they were doing as the result of suffering that one shot. As one might expect, larger .45 Colt, .45 ACP, and .44 magnum-type rounds do the best job of settling the issue as the result of one strike on target. Yet even relatively wimpy .32 ACP rounds achieve good results in 50 to 60 percent of the cases using only one round.

Unfortunately, the authors did not include .22 LR or .22 Magnum rimfire rounds. Although these two rounds are not combat calibers, pistols firing them are what people are most likely to own and shoot most accurately.

No matter which pistol, caliber, and accessories you choose, universal agreement exists that there must be good, solid strikes on targets and that generally the first shooter to achieve these is victorious. We also know that after years of using

.380-caliber pistols, European police are now upgrading to more powerful, standard 9mm models.

A police officer who, having served 26 years on a small, rural Indiana city force, came into a gunshop in North Manchester to have his .38 special worked on. It seems he carried his service revolver loaded all those years, but never had the occasion or desire to fire it while on duty or at practice. The rounds in his revolver were green and so corroded he could not turn the cylinder or punch the rounds out and almost could not swing out the cylinder.

Ultimately, his pistol had to be disassembled and the cylinders soaked in penetrating oil for a week or so before a gunsmith could die-press the dead rounds out.

There's no doubt that this situation was unique, reflecting gentler, more rural times. Today, law enforcement personnel and many gun nuts must take rapid deployment and instinct pistol marksmanship very seriously. Many exercise great care in the selection of guns, holsters, and accessories. Competitive events that mimic actual combat are available to virtually everyone. Like hunting or shooting trap or skeet, combat shooting is only one of the many areas of specialization in which gun owners can engage.

BIBLIOGRAPHY

Cooper, Jeff. *Principles of Personal Defense.* Boulder, CO: Paladin Press, 1989.

Klein, Chuck. *Instinct Combat Shooting.* Boulder, CO: Paladin Press, 1992.

Marshall, Evan P. and Edwin J. Sanow. *Handgun Stopping Power.* Boulder, CO: Paladin Press, 1992.

Mullin, Timothy J. *The 100 Greatest Combat Handguns.* Boulder, CO: Paladin Press, 1994.

Sockut, Eugene. *Secrets of Gunfighting Israeli Style.* Boulder, CO: Paladin Press, 1991.

Taylor, Chuck. *The Complete Book of Combat Handgunning.* Boulder, CO: Paladin Press, 1982.

CHAPTER

Knife Fighting

26

People who know about such things claim that virtually no professional knife fighters exist in the United States today. If you were unfortunate enough to encounter one of the very few who have experience fighting with knives, your chances of survival are practically nil. The only exception might be a well-trained, experienced person with a good sidearm. Invoking the old adage about being so dumb that "he brought a knife to a pistol fight," one could say this was not really a genuine knife fight.

In times past, before the advent of firearms, significant classes of people took the time to learn to effectively wield blades—both large and small. These included road agents and bandits who used their skills to make a living; common citizens who took exception to this economic activity; soldiers in pursuit of their profession; and, in the case of people such as Native Americans, Afghan tribesmen, and Vikings, as a means of harvest, plunder, and self-esteem.

Fighting knives developed by ancient (as well as current) blademasters were designed to cut, thrust,

or, more commonly, to do both. As strange as it may seem, some knives in use today do only one job well. Fencing foils are good examples of thrusters, while popular Gurkha knives are mostly thought of as cutters.

Sharp, durable edges are a necessity whether you wish to cut, thrust, or do both. Modern technology has contributed mightily to improving both quality and longevity of blade edges. Today, we can commonly have both tough and durable edges, whereas until relatively recently only one was obtainable at a time, unless the owner was willing to go to astronomical expense.

To evaluate a knife, hold the blade with the edge upturned, allowing light to reflect from the sharpened edge. If a thin, white line appears, the blade edge may either be inferior or simply require a great deal of finish honing. In either case, owners should get to work putting on the necessary edge with which to do the work or proving that the particular steel is not adequate for the test ahead.

Almost certainly no reader will engage a modern Gurkha soldier in a knife fight. If the unlikely happens, be encouraged by the fact that their blade design is considered far from ideal, it being one that evolved with their warrior culture. Only in this regard is it a successful pattern. Picking a pattern to suit each person is a highly individual endeavor. Design can be a scramasax, butcher, Japanese tanto, bowie, stiletto, or Fairbairn-Sykes. Without a knife-fighting culture to set rules, you are free to pick whatever design appeals to you most. Good, effective professionals have successfully used all of these designs.

Regardless of the design, great attention must be paid to the handguard. Those who genuinely plan to use their blades in a serious fight must be certain that their knives have handguards that will keep their fingers off the edge after a tough, slippery thrust and that can be counted on to keep the opponent's blade off their fingers during a violent check.

Two fighting knives are in view from my desk. One is an old but not ancient Finnish knife with large handle and pommel, but absolutely no handguard. The other is an exact replica of an ancient Viking knife. It also has a small, smooth handle, which—given the size of the blade—would be very dangerous in rough service.

Both have excellent steel blades sharpened to a fine edge. Yet I would not so much as butcher a steer with these knives lest my hand slide forward and I lose fingers to that fine steel and edge.

After handguards, handle style is most critical. Experts believe that although many valid blade designs exist as part of usable fighting knives, only two handle variations are worth considering. These are Japanese or straight handles and Saber-type handles. The latter are characterized by a small knob (pommel) or lump on the end of the handle that assists in holding the blade in tough conditions. The size of the handle is also critical. It must adequately fill your hand so that holding security requires as little effort as possible.

In feudal Japan where truly sharp blades were an extremely serious business, prospective sword buyers required that some proving demonstration be made. Skilled professionals called *tameshigiri* cut through as many as seven cadavers in one great blow. It is not known how or under what circumstances these poor deceased were recruited. Use of cadavers today is probably prohibitively expensive and not socially acceptable.

As an alternative, you can test modern fighting knives by clamping the edge of a layer of 64 sheets of regular newspaper to a workbench. At the 4-inch mark on the blade, touch the edge to the paper at a 45-degree angle. Holding the secured paper with the left hand and exerting only modest pressure, pull the knife through the sheets. Apply identical pressure from start to finish. Do not stop the cut or saw the knife. Knives with edges fit as fighting knives will pull through the newsprint cleanly and easily.

Assuming that this test is successful and that you wish to really test your new blade, double the newsprint to 128 sheets and pull the blade through again. It seems incredible, but truly worthy fighting knives will slice right on through.

Professional users of fighting knives had very little disagreement about blade length. This is surprising because one class of people used their knives as an adjunct to swords and the other simply used them in the melee. The important factor in all cases was to use a blade long enough to reach into the victim and do genuine damage. In modern times, blade length is decided to a great extent by what the owner can conveniently carry and hide. Still, the age-old consensus exists that effective fighting knives are about 7 1/2 inches long.

Street wisdom suggests that you should run toward a man with a pistol and away from one with a knife. If there is a kernel of truth in this adage, successful knife fighters must keep their blades hidden until the very last instant before the moment of truth.

One can carry a fighting knife on a belt, in a holster, under the armpit either handle up or handle down, in a boot, or in a false bottom in a loose pants pocket. Users disagree as to what constitutes a perfect carry, but general agreement exists that it is seldom in a boot. If I were to hazard a guess, I'd guess that most serious users probably carry either in an upside-down underarm sheath or, in the case of a modern switchblade, in a special pocket sewn into a jacket collar behind the neck.

Probably because it has been illegal for so many years and because it has not generally benefited from modern improvements in metallurgy and design function, the switchblade tends to be dismissed by many experts as a valid fighting tool. Recently, some custom switchblade makers (mostly supplying the police and military) have started to alter the perception of switches as cheap Mexican toys.

Instead, significant numbers of users have adapted more cumbersome, difficult-to-learn-to-use-well Buck Folding Hunter knives into their strategies. These are excellent, well-made, lockbacks that fulfill the same role as switches but at a much greater cost in deployment time, practice, and skill.

Having put together a suitable knife (including blade, edge, handle, and handguard with a workable carry system, you must commit to hundreds of hours of practice. More rigorous, realistic practice is always best. From this practice, you should evolve a fluid, smooth, lightning-quick deployment.

In one form or another, serious knife fighters must devise a plastic, wooden, or rubber mock knife with which to make their thrusts and stances as realistic as possible. Most experts who have actually been in knife fights claim that even those with relatively modest practice experience will consistently whip those with no experience in knife fighting. As mentioned, very few people in the United States have actual, practical experience at knife fighting, giving the few who do an inordinate advantage.

A great deal of controversy seems to surround the selection of an ideal knife-fighting stance. Some recommend a left-foot-forward, one-quarter crouch stance while others prefer the right-foot-forward method. Those who have been in the most knife fights seem to prefer using the strong hand and corresponding leg forward while the weaker hand acts as a block or parry. A few, perhaps those with the least experience, even suggest that you switch hands as well as grip in a fashion that will keep an opponent off guard. Most people have a special aversion to actually engaging in knife fights that will be exacerbated by their opponents' switching hands while maneuvering for a thrust, these people claim.

The bottom line is that you really should not switch hands and grip and that the knife should be carried close to your body in the strong hand while the other hand serves as a block and, in some cases, a decoy. In all cases, the crouch should provide as much flexibility and balance as possible. How you best determine this posture is by using a training knife of wood, plastic, or rubber with which you can try as many different postures and ploys in as many

The saber grip is the most commonly taught knife-fighting grip. Although it looks practical and functional, its shortcomings become painfully obvious when you make hard contact. (Unless otherwise noted, photos from *Knife Fighting: A Practical Course* by Michael D. Janich.)

different circumstances as possible. These might include mock fighting on stairs, on a sandy beach, in a room full of furniture, or in a high-grass field. Those who continually suffer potentially fatal cuts or stabs from fake knives should improve their basic techniques. All experts agree that only a little practice can help develop a good individual system.

Invariably, those who practice find that they use their weaker arms to fend off blows, distract their opponents, and attempt to lock up the knife wrist of opponents. The knife itself is generally held close to the body. Seasoned knife fighters learn to snap their wrists around so that those trying to grab their knife wrists suffer immediate cuts, some of which can be serious.

The actual grip on the knife depends a great deal on the circumstances of the fight. In general, experts recommend only using a kind of "saber" grasp with thumb forward, at the handguard. This grip allows you to work your knife in from below, snap the wrists against grabs, or swing it wildly from above in great powerful circular motions. In tight, crowded circumstances, this may not be practical.

As a result, some experienced knife fighters point out that the often deprecated ice-pick hold is effective. This grasp was commonly used by some of the best professional knife fighters ever to go to war. In fact the ice-pick or Indian grip gets its name from a group who used it. Although not normally considered to be a sophisticated hold, it is practiced where concealment, surprise, and instantaneous deployment are vital and for use in a military situation where crowding moving bodies precludes any other grip. Ice-pick grips are tough to dislodge, and you can hold a relatively long knife with blade pointed more or less up your wrist

Ice-pick grip with the edge in. This limits the grip's effectiveness. (Photos on this page from *Knives, Knife Fighting, & Related Hassles* by Marc "Animal" MacYoung.)

Ice-pick grip with the edge pointed out. The knife can be used to stab, slash, and even punch when held in this manner.

without being seen from the front. An adversary will never grasp the wrist of a person using an ice-pick hold.

All experienced knife fighters agree that only one thing counts. It's not size, strength, reach, or specific types of equipment. It isn't even fighting spirit and stamina. Most real knife fights are over in 30 to 40 seconds. *Practice alone provides the margin between victory and defeat.* Of course, this also says a bit about spirit and the desire to prevail. Those with limited spirit won't practice.

Experienced fighters know by reading their opponents if they will actually have to fight. Very hostile people intent on getting it on will hold their mouths tightly. Their skin will drain to a deep gray color, and their heads will be pushed forward in an aggressive manner. If you are not able and willing to go toe to toe with such an individual, take the first opportunity to depart.

Since knife fighting is much more primitive than virtually any other combat in which you might engage, you might actually use a fierce countenance to scare off an opponent. This is known as putting on a "war face."

War faces are characterized by hostile, aggressive, continuous eye contact with the intended victims. In all cases, your pupils should contract dramatically. At times, one cannot fake or put on this "face." It comes from deep within and is motivated in great part by a tremendous urge to dominate that circumstance.

Those dealing with such people and with knives learn to watch the knife, not the owner's snarly face. As discussed, few people in our culture know this or have spent the required hours practicing.

About 12 years ago, a man with extensive knife-fighting experience—gained mostly in reform schools, jails, and penitentiaries—found work in security at a large Southern nightclub. He was called on to handle many different disturbances in the club.

One night, a bartender asked him to settle what everyone thought was a minor disturbance between three burly truck-driver-type patrons of the club and the club owner. The rowdies had consumed too much booze, and the club owner had forgotten to have the band play a special song they wanted.

It became immediately obvious to the bouncer that he had to get the three drunks out of the crowded club before a serious problem developed that could hurt business. He tried sitting and talking to them, buying them drinks, and even swapping stories—all to no avail. The three truck drivers were intent on a fight.

The bouncer then announced he was going outside and that the three should join him. He turned and started walking out. For some reason, the three followed, proving that the best bouncers are also excellent students of human nature.

On the way down a relatively long wooden corridor, a waitress ran by telling the bouncer that all three had knives in their hands. The bouncer had a Colt .32 ACP pistol in his pocket, but because of his past record was extremely reluctant to use the handgun under almost any circumstance. Shooting someone would very likely put the guy back in the joint, no matter who started what or who was at fault.

Just as they came to the exit, the bouncer rammed hard left into one of the men at his side and hit the one on his right front as hard as possible with the pistol on the top of the head. He then hit the man on his left with the little chunk of steel. The third man, two steps ahead, would have received a similar blow but stepped ahead and avoided it.

As the front man recovered from his surprise, he lunged low and hard at the bouncer who deflected the knife with his weak hand. Simultaneously, he clobbered his huge opponent with the pistol, cracking his skull.

The first recipient was now recovered sufficiently from the booze and the blow to try again to cut the bouncer. Breaking away from one of the patrons, who had tried to hold him and who suffered severe cuts on his legs as a result, and springing onto the bouncer's back, this assailant cut the bouncer on the shoulder. The bouncer grabbed his knife arm and threw the guy down, braining him solidly twice more with his improvised knuckles.

At this, all three men ran out of the club and down the street. The bouncer went to the emergency room, where it took more than 40 stitches to close him up. The three belligerents went to another hospital for their treatment. One required a steel plate in his skull and was hospitalized for almost six months. Another man was in the hospital for three

No matter how proficient you may become at fighting with a knife, this is still the best solution when confronted with the prospect of a knife fight.

weeks. One of the three walked away that night, heavily bandaged.

It took months of police investigations and insurance company paperwork plus thousands of dollars in attorneys fees before that matter was finally resolved—in spite of the fact that the three attackers were extremely well known as troublemakers.

Successful knife fighting is a relatively delicate balance that involves practicing a lot, picking the proper equipment, correctly reading your opponent, and having the heart to carry the matter through to a successful conclusion. Just remember that legal and physical ramifications can be severe. Wise people don't get into very many knife fights no matter how good they are. No matter who wins, everyone involved will spend time with police and attorneys. Virtually everyone in a knife fight gets cut. For some, the cut is worse than others.

BIBLIOGRAPHY

Janks, Harold and Michael H. Brown. *Bloody Iron*. El Dorado, AR: Desert Publications, 1978.

MacYoung, Marc "Animal". *Knives, Knife Fighting, & Related Hassles*. Boulder, CO: Paladin Press, 1990.

LaTourrette, John. *Warrior's Guide to Knife Fighting*. Medford, OR: Psychology Publication, 1988.

Sanchez, John. *Slash and Thrust*. Boulder, CO: Paladin Press, 1980.

CHAPTER

Balisong Knives

27

Legend has it that yo-yos of the basic type that kids play with as toys were originally conceived as weapons of war in the Philippines. Confirmed reports of their use in combat are scarce, but one has to give some credence to ancient lore.

Time, place, and accidents of history can produce strange and often convoluted weapons. Use of these weapons can, at times, attract a great number of dedicated, almost like followers of a cult. Gurkha knives, claymore swords, and AK-47 rifles are examples that come immediately to mind. As it happens, weapons such as these evolve in an atmosphere where they are the best, with only limited, weak competition from other systems. It also helps when several notable users become remarkably proficient with a specific weapon. The use of sail pegs among ship-boarding parties in the late 1700s is another excellent example.

Balisong knives definitely fall into the category of arcane and unique weapons wielded by a warrior

class who took the time to learn to use these devices well. Filipinos believe that invasion of their islands by the Spanish around 1520 marked the beginning of balisong development. Spanish occupiers prohibited the ownership or carrying of any weapon. Eventually, Philippine resisters developed a relatively long knife that folded in such a way that it was hidden innocuously within its handle. These knives were carried in pants pockets, leather belts, shirt collars, or even as miscellaneous items in bundles of sticks or trays of bread. Even today, a plain balisong lying on the dresser does not look ominous. Originally, they were also disguised as combs, chopsticks, or pens and were carried in books or rolled newspapers.

Colloquially, they were referred to as butterfly knives because of the wing-like folding of the handles. Eventually, a great mystique sprang up around these knives, taking on many aspects of the martial arts. During the mid-1980s, a Filipino airport guard watching similar Moro knives being off-loaded from a plane for shipment to the United States told the

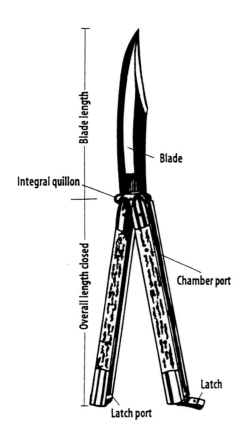

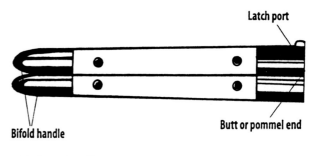

Balisong handle.

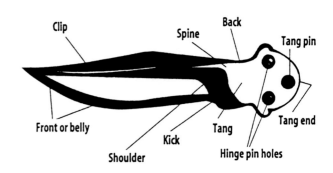

Balisong blade.

Open balisong. (Illustrations and photos taken from *Balisong: The Lethal Art of Filipino Knife Fighting* by Sid Campbell, Gary Cagaanan, and Sonny Umpad.)

writer that "those knives are so dangerous they will cut right through a chain link fence."

This, in turn, leads to legends that great masters with balisongs can defeat up to 29 enemies single-handedly by using their deadly blades.

During and after World War II, balisongs were cleverly handmade from all kinds of available material, including truck and jeep springs, vehicle body parts, crashed Japanese Zeros, jack handles, and steel runway mats, to name just a few weird sources of raw materials. Most of these knives were very sturdy with long, deadly blades that had an excellent reputation for holding an edge. It helped mightily as balisong legends evolved that Filipino makers avoided a Mexican reputation for shoddy, cheap tourist items. At the same time, some Filipino martial arts masters really became extremely proficient with balisongs.

Returning GIs brought balisongs back to the United States in fairly large numbers. Thousands of miles from their place of origin, the knives became even more legendary as rumors of their tradition and spiritual deployment spread. Roughly, these legendary tales resulted from an intense fighting spirit and desire to practice with these knives to the point of extreme proficiency. Any modern knife fighter realizes that no matter what the weapon of preference, fighting spirit is 50 percent of the matter and dedication to the discipline is at least another 40 percent. Luck, equipment, and terrain probably contribute the last 10 percent.

The use of a balisong is said to be in peaceful coexistence with nature. When threatened, practitioners are supposed to attack only the closest targets who pose a threat to their survival. Experts claim, for example, that they would only attack the hand of a knife-wielding assailant rather than going immediately for a body thrust, even if one were possible. By so doing, the discipline teaches, an attacker has the opportunity to withdraw after receiving some damage or, as an alternative, suffer lethal blows to vital organs. Use of these knives is said to

The bufferfly knife can be used in a manner very similar to that of the ancient Okinawan weapon known as the nunchaku (two sticks connected by cord or chain). The butterfly knife, once it is flipped and spun, can generate speeds up to 150 MPH and cause severe damage to the temple, eyes, or throat.

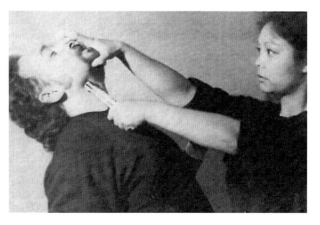

Any portion of the butterfly knife—pommel, tang, bifold handle ends, or blade section—can be used to strike the pressure points.

be almost exclusively defensive. In that regard, closed balisongs are often used as sort of short clubs or as a set of knucks.

Masters insist on long training periods designed to filter out those with poor self-control unworthy of balisong skills. Generally, training is done with longer sticks, taking much the same form as stick fighting, or as an alternative with short balisong-length mock daggers.

Even today, most balisong knives are custom made or produced in factories having very short runs. A few strictly tourist models are currently seen, but, in general, the quality of even these is quite good—not as good as in Japan and Korea, where knives and swords have been venerated for generations, but quite good.

One can only wonder why balisongs evolved in the Philippines instead of the much simpler, easier, and perhaps more effective switchblades as in Italy and Germany. There is no question that each knife accomplishes the identical objective of concealing a blade that can be instantaneously deployed. But whereas one can learn to effectively deploy a switchblade in a matter of months, mastery of a balisong takes years of practice.

Balisongs, for those unfamiliar with them, comprise a split-hinged handle that rotates and folds to completely enclose a relatively long, thin, yet sturdy blade. In the United States, 1950s-type switchblade laws have been broadly interpreted to include gravity-type balisongs. Principally, these rules affect the

importation of knives from Pakistan and the Philippines, where cheaper labor allows good hand-finished quality, which is necessary for good balisongs at acceptable prices.

Although interpretation of these laws on the part of customs agents is questionable, not enough is at stake for any business to make it worthwhile to fight them. Slightly more expensive models made in the United States are available without hassles. These are ordered by mail from major domestic knife distributors.

Deployment of a balisong can be as fast or faster than a switchblade or virtually any other conventional battle blade. Because of their protected nature, balisongs do not have to be deployed from a sheath. Deployment is a very showy affair, calculated to strike genuine fear in the heart of an opponent. In addition to its show, balisongs make a sort of ominous clicking sound as they are opened. Some experts liken it to the sound of a pump shotgun being racked in a dark room. There are oncerns that it would be tough to deploy speedily in rough terrain, and especially in a crowded room. A fighter should have his balisong out and open well before a genuine hand-to-hand melee starts.

Speed deployment is achieved either by grabbing from the front of the knife or with two fingers on its base. In either case the wrist is rotated and snapped, opening the knife. Only one half of the handle is pinched between the fingers until the knife has rotated, with the second half snapping into the

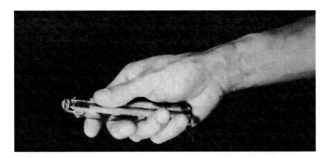

Step 1: Back-hand wrist flip. Pop the latch with the little finger.

Step 2: Flip the handle with the latch outward with a quick flip of the wrist. As the blade clears the gripped handle, reposition the fingers around the handle.

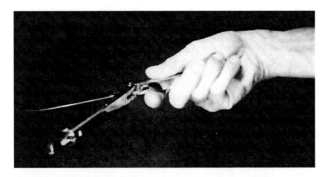

Step 3: Rotate the handle a half-turn counterclockwise (opposite direction if wielded with the other hand). The motion should be smooth and continuous.

Step 4: When the counterclockwise rotation assumes the position in the photograph, begin a backhand (toward your body), upward flipping action.

Step 5: With a downward wrist motion, the weight of the loose handle is redirected toward the fingers.

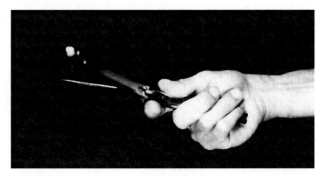

Step 6: At that moment, an upward flip occurs, and the loose handle is returned to the waiting fingers.

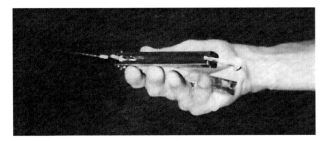

Step 7: The fingers are then opened to receive the handle. The grip is maintained with the meaty part of the thumb and the folded palm.

Step 8: When the flip is completed, the fingers are repositioned around both sections of the bifold handle.

owner's palm. As mentioned, this is a very fast maneuver after some practice, and it is benefited by the fact that no sheath is used. After practicing, you can speedily open a balisong carried virtually anyplace and grasped on the half-handle anyplace. As in drawing a pistol, opening is done in one great fluid, smooth, circular motion. It is similar to speed pistol drawing and shooting, and it helps immeasurably to have seen this operation performed a time or two. Most GIs stationed in the Philippines have seen young girls and women speed-deploy balisongs as part of a cultural show. These women are quite good at this operation, but most have no idea of how to use their blades to cut an opponent.

When circumstances do not allow users to swing their arms, skilled practitioners may pop their knives open by flipping a handle half with their little fingers. As the swinging handle half comes round, the user grasps it with a strong thumb-over saber-type grip. Balisongs are used to both thrust and cut.

As a knife is flipped open, a skilled user simultaneously assumes a fighting stance. In general, this stance involves a saber hold with the strong hand and the weak hand and arm in a slightly forward position. The fighter is in a small one-quarter crouch with the knife arm held close to the leading leg. In all cases, excellent balance must be rigorously maintained. The actual precise, fighting posture is said by balisong practitioners to be unimportant in contrast to developing a specific stance that works well for the individual. In this regard, the entire discipline is a bit flexible.

Experienced balisong fighters make extensive use of wrist snaps and changing hand positions during actual combat. Their starting grip is always a saber, but that may change rapidly as they expertly roll their knives around in their hands. Their imme-

diate intention is to inflict wounds on either the knife hand or guard hand of their antagonist. Balisong practitioners always hope that, having inflicted what might be considered to be minor wounds, their assailants will think of urgent business elsewhere.

Balisong deployment is a martial art form, especially when the knife is used unopened or in a limited sense. Severe martial arts-like rules govern one's use of a balisong:

1. Read an opponent's eyes for intentions while keeping his entire body in the peripheral vision.
2. Always maintain balance and solid footing.
3. Use continuous movement to elude and fool an opponent.
4. Employ terrain and range to advantage.
5. Never overcommit, drop your hand, or get trapped in one position.
6. React only when accuracy and outcome are ensured.

It is said that in an actual fight, balisong practitioners absolutely must rely on extensive past training to hold fear in check and to evaluate an opponent. Knife fighting is universally accepted as one of the most dangerous, disagreeable types of personal combat. Balisong experts agree that it is no different for their discipline.

BIBLIOGRAPHY

Campbell, Sid, Gary Cagaana, Sonny Umpad. *Balisong: The Lethal Art of Filipino Knife Fighting.* Boulder, CO: Paladin Press, 1986.

CHAPTER

Mantrapping

28

Just as it is vital to know the tactical difference between caching and storing, it is equally important to know the differences between mantrapping and booby trapping. Booby trapping, for those who never thought about it, involves the use of modern, usually sophisticated detonators, explosives, and other manufactured devices. Mantrapping involves using only primitive materials found out in the country. Theoretically, one can expect to take only an ax and knife out into the bush and use these to construct effective antipersonnel traps. As a practical matter, mantraps require huge amounts of both labor and creativity. In other words, they require one person who knows what he is doing and a great number of manual laborers to install the trap.

Construction of mantraps is not undertaken as some sort of funky, new-age accommodation with the soldier of fortune. People definitely do not construct mantraps for the same psychological reason that they eat berries and twigs.

Mantraps are put in place when an aggressor impinges on your territory and there simply are no components available with which to build viable booby traps. In this case, you substitute cleverness for modern manufactured materials and, by doing so, implant real fear and caution in an enemy intruder. Clever, well-placed mantraps can soak up a tremendous amount of your pursuers' time and energy, while also giving them a genuine feeling that they are striking at an otherwise unreachable enemy who has all the advantage.

Mantraps can theoretically be built anyplace. I recently tested that theory by building several good, workable mantraps that protected a long driveway in Long Beach, California. We built the trap as part of a television news special that questioned and explored the curiosity of mantraps in an urban society.

We constructed our traps at the secluded home of the program director. One involved little more than rolling round concrete "log"-type parking lot barriers to the top of a rise in her long driveway. They rolled smartly down the little hill and would

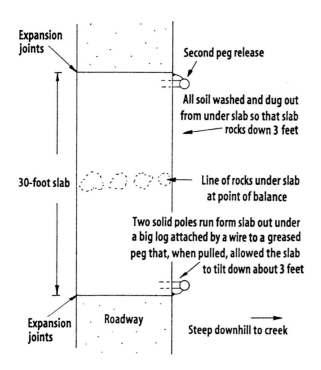

NPA guerrilla trap. (Illustrations by Ragnar Benson.)

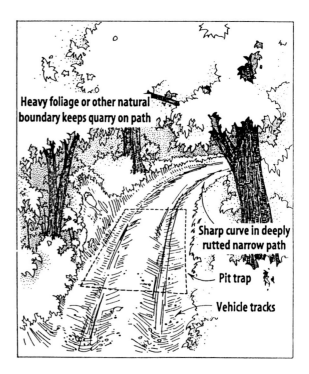

Pit trap location.

have taken out even a fairly large truck. The hold-back trigger, in this case, was nothing more than a simple figure four activated by both a concealed wire to her garage and a trip wire down the lane. I wanted to take down the phone company's lines to use for the trap, but she insisted that we go to Ernst to buy needed supplies.

She readily admitted that the second trap she triggered as she safely drove past would have easily and effectively handled pesky motorcyclists tearing up and down the private lane whenever she left the gate open. Were it not for current liability laws, she might have actually deployed the device as a lesson-creating deterrent rather than just filing it for the news segment.

In this instance we purchased 1/16-inch airplane cable for our trap. Again, we could have appropriated a utility company's wire or even made something from hemp fibers or indigenous vines. The natural materials wouldn't have worked as well, and our goal was not to be environmental, but to have the traps perform well and be effective. The idea is to use whatever materials are at hand in a sort of "live off whatever is on the land" mode. (Snake traps are an excellent example. I first ran into these in an old,

abandoned warehouse in Thailand. They are tremendously effective, the plan being that anytime one comes across a large snake—poisonous or otherwise—you catch it. A poisonous snake placed in an airplane or truck will cause incredible disruption that may lead to snake bite casualties or even crashed vehicles.)

In the case of the driveway wire trap, we rigged a segment of cable between two stout steel posts across the drive so that one could drive over the thin cable hidden in a concrete expansion joint unseen and then, using a broom handle, push a heavy pole off balance, thus pulling the wire taut between two posts. The cable was stretched tight right at neck level of someone riding a motorcycle and was virtually invisible. Because of the weight-activated feature, the setup cable might have had some slack when hit hard, but a car driven even at 35 to 40 MPH would probably take some impact from the cable. Motorcyclists arrogantly racing around would certainly lose their tops.

Another definitely unnatural "natural" trap in the Philippines is based on many of the same principles as the wire and works just as well. This device could only be set up where concrete slabs making up a paved road were hand poured segment by segment rather than continuously by a machine.

New People's Army (NPA) guerrillas dug out and under one sheet of concrete, which was about 10 feet wide and 30 feet long. Patiently, using great care, they found the center balance of the slab under which they positioned a thin line of 6-inch rock. An estimated 30 men worked two nights until the weight on either end of the slab caused it to tilt down almost 3 feet! Much of the digging in the gravelly underside was done using water pumped up from a creek below that sluiced supporting gravel out from under the slab till only a foot or so on either end held it up.

Smooth, well-greased wooden pegs were placed on either end of the free-tilting concrete slab so that a few days of normal traffic would not expose the nature or presence of the device, other than a hollow sound when crossing. To these pegs, builders attached heavy posts that stood upright innocuously along the road. Although builders anticipated using the device in only one direction, pegs were rigged on either end so that the slab would tilt either way.

The NPA' guerrillas' plan was to drive across the slab as they left Cagayon de Oro with government forces in hot pursuit, slow down enough when clear of the slab to push the post over, thus pulling the stabilizing wooden peg. These guys ambitiously envisioned trapping a second close-following vehicle that would run into the banked uphill rise of the slab after it was tilted by the first vehicle.

As it worked out, the lead vehicle chasing them out of town ran into the trap right on schedule. It was a 3/4-ton Ford truck, painted olive drab and similar to ones our National Guard currently uses. Unfortunately, the slab did not swing down as far as builders had planned. The 3/4-ton truck hit the forward wall, bounced pretty good, and actually came up onto the second forward stable piece of pavement, where it dragged bottom heavily and bent the drive shaft slightly. The second vehicle was able to stop without incident.

Obviously, these two traps are not particularly sophisticated. They require tremendous amounts of manpower and ingenuity, but no one had to acquire such materiel of war as detonators and explosives.

A simple, well-concealed pit dug into a frequently traveled road detour around an obstacle blocking the main road into which an enemy drives his vehi-

cle is an excellent example of a mantrap. All you need (in addition to being alert to the opportunity) is a pick and shovel. Roll some old tires over the trap cover to give the impression of recent travel. You can remove the obstacle and allow normal traffic through until the enemy is expected, when the road is then closed for repairs again. It is even possible in this modern era to simulate little water-filled ruts in the road by use of a sheet of plastic.

Clever surprise and concealment are vital to any mantrap. Study the lay of the land meticulously before installing a trap. Then go to great lengths to work with the topography, blend the trap into natural surroundings, and put everything back exactly as it was before work started. Be cautious about screening with cut branches, which will shrivel and look different in a couple of day. They can be replaced periodically, but a skilled opponent will still know the difference.

In the case of most overhanging drop weights, concealment is not overly important. The only part of the trap on the ground is the trigger, which can easily be screened by bending over a branch or bunch of long grass. Screening overhead can be done by tying up or back a leafy branch or rigging a weight to swing in from behind from a distance through light foliage.

As a general rule, the more disorderly an environment, the easier it is to hide a drop weight. It is, for instance, relatively easier to rig a falling piece of steel in a junkyard than to set that same chunk of iron to fall on an intruder in a pristine wood.

In the woods, you might have to bait a target into an area that is "naturally" unnaturally cluttered, with items common to a woods. There are lots of logs in a logging deck, for example, that could be induced to roll onto an intruder. Match trap to setting and remember that in an unduly cluttered setting even a very watchful person will overlook things.

Several times in my life I have seen examples of mantraps set on hillsides where rocks or long, heavy logs have been set up to roll down, squashing targets. Big, heavy logs are best, in my opinion, because they thoroughly wipe out everything in their path. However, really big logs are extremely tough to move into an uphill position.

Rock, on the other hand, can be moved one at a time over relatively long distances. Even a modest 25-pound rock will really brain someone if rolled

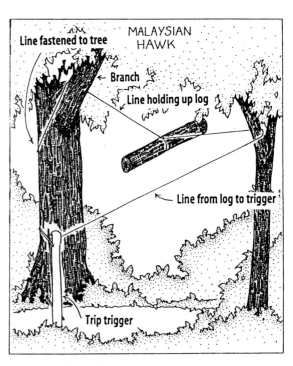

Heavy beam with wire attached to top, balanced next to steel post. Post is pushed over by driver who wants to set the trap.

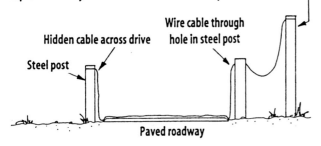

Hollywood movie producer's mantrap. (Illustration by Ragnar Benson.)

Malaysian hawk trip-stick trigger

from even as few as 10 or 15 feet. The trouble with rocks is that they roll, bounce, and fall somewhat haphazardly.

I have one close friend who survived tons of falling bouncing rock simply by standing still in the downfall. Incredible as it was, not even one little pebble hit him. This definitely would not have happened had the bad guys rolled logs.

Much has been written about attracting a target to a trap. Use of bait is the correct but socially unacceptable term to use. In at least 95 percent of the instances where mantraps have been successful, they have been cleverly laid out in places where intruders normally travel or can be enticed into traveling. A well-used path through the mountains or in town through an alley cleverly set up with garbage cans is an excellent example.

Often, however, bait will put a target on alert. Sometimes bait can be used to bring a target close but not right up to a trap, maybe as much as 50 feet away. Humans may come over to look at a valuable firearm, pair of binoculars, or item of food, but they will be vigilant while doing so, especially after one of their group becomes a casualty.

In the movie *Crocodile Dundee,* Croc used

about the only piece of bait that will work a first time without arousing suspicion when he put out an item of women's underwear to attract bad guys to his trap. This works extremely well in virtually any culture—once. Seeing a buddy get squashed or fall onto a bed of punji sticks after going over to look at a bra or pair of panties will immediately alert an enemy.

However, traps in trails and paths cause intruders to become slow, inefficient, and paranoid while traveling them. Even if they stay off trails, progress will be slow and laborious. Intruders never know if a trap lies in wait 100 feet or 100 miles or one footstep from them. In every case, progress will be slow and painful for intruders having suffered even one minor incident with a mantrap. In this case, one can skillfully place decoy bait about, making intruders even more hesitant.

In all cases, the core issue of mantraps is their trigger mechanisms. By nature, triggers must hold back tremendous loads that are also easily and quickly released. These triggers must be such that the maker won't be killed during assembly. Sometimes it is feasible to mitigate your problem slightly by swinging a heavy load rather than dropping it: use a second line that holds the load back but not up, or by using two triggers under a heavy pile of rocks or logs. But, generally, it is difficult to reliably contain enough energy to do harm. As you get further away from manufactured products such as nails, wire, and rope, these challenges become especially severe. Using only vines, homemade rope, and forked branches to construct triggers is challenging.

In general, effective triggers must be

1. Simple
2. Foolproof
3. Unaffected by the normal range of weather normal to that region
4. Made of common, easily obtained materials
5. Easily hidden
6. Not inherently identifiable as a trigger by an intended target

My favorite trigger, which can be placed almost anyplace in a woods, is a swinging trip stick, shown on page 224. Using it, you can hold back tremendous loads while still using very light, easily hidden trip-stick material. Place both pivot pole and trip stick quite low in a path at a place where overhead brush and branches temporarily obscure the path floor and trip sticks.

A second favorite trigger is the peg and nail, shown at right. This is another sensitive trigger that can hold back a very heavy load. The peg-and-nail trigger also can be adjusted to be unusually sensitive; just include a safety rope the first few times you play with these triggers and actual loads. These are extremely simple triggers to build.

Halve the load on the trigger by throwing the rope holding the load over a tree limp. Both friction and basic physics help in this case. Remember, it takes less force to hold a load back than to pull it up, again arguing in favor of swinging rather than dropped loads. Yet if you wish to successfully swing a load into a target, much thought and great care must be paid to timing.

Target and load used to whomp the target absolutely must come along at the same time. The best way to do this is to swing the load along the path so that the target can be encountered for several feet *along* the route of travel rather than swinging across where more precision is required. Always walk the trail and calculate load-swinging time.

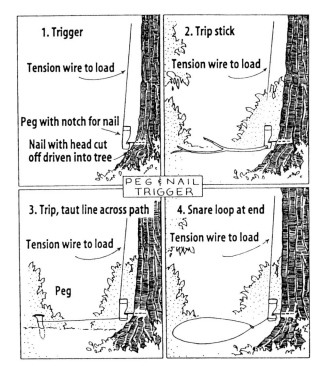

Peg-and-nail trigger.

Some mantrappers use a simple trigger called an eye and pin with rollers. Simple eye-and-pin triggers seem to bind up frequently, but if you use a couple of steel pin rollers run along a hardwood base, this trigger can be sensitive enough. (Detailed drawings for this and other triggers can be found in my book *Mantrapping*, listed in the bibliography at the end of this chapter.) Generally, these are extremely simple triggers to deploy, but they are direction sensitive. Pull them the wrong way and they may not even trip.

All they require is a hole in a wall, or a steel eye, a rope, and a pin with two rollers. Anyone who can screw in a steel eye can place one of these triggers.

One of the most successful triggers I have seen deployed was in the mountains of northern Kenya, near the Sudanese border. It was set by Somali guerrillas called *Shifta*.

A small sensitive trigger pulled a much bigger, more insensitive trigger. This was accomplished by balancing a big, relatively long pole at the edge of a steep path where the pole could fall down when tripped by an intruder hitting a trip stick. A small cable attached to the heavy pole ran back to a large platform full of round rocks, held uphill by a massive pin on a roller. When the pole fell, it pulled the pin on tons of rock that could not have been otherwise contained.

Mantraps are interesting and almost fun to set up if one has some help. They tax the ingenuity of the setter, especially when few tools and materials are available. In that respect, they cost virtually nothing other than one's time, which may be extremely cheap in some circumstances. Intruders who suspect traps will be very cautious out of their home territory. In many instances, it is effective to take a crew and sneak in one night to set up a trap right in an enemy's backyard.

On the down side, mantraps often claim innocent women and children as their victims. Sadly, they seem to pay the least attention to their surroundings. An alternative is to place traps out away from settlements if done in the country. Mantraps also work well in cities or wherever one has access to an uphill lay and something that weighs a lot and rolls easily.

Those who build their own mantraps are more likely to stay out of the other guy's traps—another good reason for being aware of this technology.

BIBLIOGRAPHY

Benson, Ragnar. *Mantrapping*. Boulder, CO: Paladin Press, 1981.

_____. *The Most Dangerous Game— Advanced Mantrapping Techniques*. Boulder, CO: Paladin Press, 1986.

Whitney, Lyle J. *Robot Warriors—The Mechanics of*

CHAPTER

Hostage Negotiations

29

Boobytrapping. Miami, FL: J. Flores Publications, 1989.

Probably all of us owe a great debt to the hippies of the 1960s and 1970s who identified the imminent, horrible dangers of unbridled government power. Early on in our country's history, George Washington said that "government is the power to destroy. Like fire, government can be a wonderful servant or a fearsome master."

Conditions wherein hostages are taken almost certainly will involve government. In our current environment of increasing government force, people can easily assume that if they are in a hostage-negotiating situation, they will be negotiating with government authorities. In reality, there may or may not actually be hostages involved. In several notable recent examples, government officials maintained there were hostages when there weren't.

The following tale is put together almost entirely from the recent activities of a state health and welfare bureaucrat; the actual conduct of federal officers at Waco, Texas, and Ruby Ridge, Idaho; and from a procedure manual originally published on hostage negotiations by the U.S. government secured under the Freedom of Information Act. Virtually everything that follows actually happened or is a matter of official policy. It illustrates what one may be up against better than a simple listing of procedures.

A young couple with a son, age 9, and a daughter, 6, lived on the edge of a fairly large city. Their home, a large old farmhouse, abutted a low, swampy area on two sides. The total land area they owned was about 10 acres. It was a measured 5.6 miles from their house to high-rise office buildings comprising the core of the city. The nearest neighbor lived a minimum of 600 yards away.

Partly because of the couple's religious convictions, the mother stayed home tending a vegetable garden, making their clothes, home-schooling the kids, and occasionally cleaning houses or barns for cash payment. The father had originally worked as a tractor mechanic, but as the area became more cosmopolitan, had begun working as a small engine mechanic on small estate and garden tractors. He also supplemented their food supply greatly by shooting rabbits, pheasants, deer, and an occasional elk as circumstances permitted.

A young professional woman living in the area took it upon herself to use her weekends and days off work to canvas the community for potential legislation that would make recycling compulsory. With her blank petitions she stopped at the young couple's place one Sunday morning. She found no one at home, although none of the doors was locked.

Later, just past noon, she noticed a car in the drive when passing the house again. She pulled into the drive and approached the couple and two children who were probably returning from church because they were all dressed up. She noted how everything, including the family, looked very plain but scrubbed and neat.

After introducing herself, the canvasser was immediately invited in by the gregarious, vivacious wife. In the course of their pleasant 10-minute conversation, the professional lady discovered several disconcerting things about the family.

For starters, they were completely, absolutely but pleasantly uninterested in recycling. They mentioned that they felt the issue was something of a religious/faith issue not supported by any facts. But that if she—the petitioner—was interested, that was fine with them.

She also discovered to her horror that a number of guns were kept in the home within sight and reach of the children, who otherwise paid no particular notice to these firearms. She presumed these guns were used to kill animals.

Last, she observed a number of textbooks, blackboards, and other school-related materials that strongly suggested that the two children were not attending public school. The visitor was far too discreet to mention any of these concerns. Because she worked as a full partner in a local CPA firm, she was able to judge that the little rural family lived fairly well in spite of a limited single income. Surroundings in the home and the fact that the housewife admitted that they threw little away and that their grocery bill was only about $200 per month reinforced that opinion. At one time, the young housewife claimed she paid only about $300 per year

for cloth to make all their clothes. About the price of one evening out, the young CPA thought.

As she drove back to the city, the young CPA thought about the encounter, eventually working herself into a slow burn. Day care alone for her kids came to about $1,500 per month. Including taxes, house payments, groceries, clothes, and child care, she spent about 101 percent of her $48,000 salary. Obviously, these were some kind of religious nuts because they didn't "believe" in recycling. She decided to do something about them.

After thinking about it for a week or more, the CPA approached one of her friends from a feminist group who worked for health and welfare in the child-protection office. "They are abusing those little kids," the CPA dutifully reported, "by forcing them to stay home where they avoid productive association with other kids. They have weird religious beliefs, and there are dangerous guns all over that house that are probably used to kill little animals, traumatizing those children."

After double-checking to be sure that no children of that name were enrolled in public school, the woman from child-protective services decided to drive out to see the couple's house for herself. The young housewife met the bureaucrat at the door. After explaining who she was and why she was there, the bureaucrat asked if she could come in. Young housewife asked who had reported them for child abuse and was curtly told that "the department never gives out that information, and that no court action could ever secure it." The young mother was adamant that the bureaucrat come back when her husband was home, in spite of heated threats from the child-protective lady.

While they talked at their door, the bureaucrat spotted a legal Colt AR-15 rifle hanging on the wall. Back in her office, she phoned the BATF, reporting a suspicious-looking "machine gun" in a place where they had had reports of child abuse.

From this point, events moved very quickly. At home, the housewife explained her version of the visit to Dad after he returned from work, while they were out in the garden hoeing weeds. They were both confused about the lady from child-protective services. While talking they looked down their rural road to see four clean, new-model cars coming up to their home in a convoy. An estimated six or eight burly men jumped out of the rigs, heading quickly for their house. All carried several weapons.

As they double-timed toward the old farmhouse, one of the BATF agents accidentally discharged his shotgun into the hard gravel ground, inflicting a nasty surface wound from ricocheting rock and shot. Thinking they were being fired upon, the other agents began firing their weapons randomly into the old home.

Young dad scooped up his two children and, with his wife, ran frantically for the house. Inside he immediately sent his kids down into the basement. Quickly, he got out his .30-30 and a .22 pistol.

Outside, the agents immediately and somewhat frantically radioed in for an ambulance and to report that one of their men was hit by gunfire and that they now had a hostage situation. The BATF director heading the party had his office patch through a call to his headquarters reporting that they were being fired upon and that a suspect had taken two small children hostage.

He requested immediate deployment of a Threat Management Team. Because of his recent training, the director asked that he personally be appointed as incident commander of the team. Because this fellow's office was already a regional investigative center, and because the automatic assumption is that anyone with hostages is either mentally disturbed, a criminal, or a terrorist, all his requests were granted instantly.

Inside, the terrified homeowner watched as the burly men surrounded his house and lay there with weapons pointed from about 200 yards. Finally, it occurred to the fellow to call the sheriff, whom he knew personally. He was just starting to talk when his phone went mysteriously dead. He had no way of knowing that one of the first official duties of an incident commander is to disconnect the hostage taker's phone. It was important that this criminal talk only to the hostage negotiator who became the only point of contact for the "criminal."

Soon the five member negotiating team members consisting of team chief, record keeper, intelligence coordinator, and two extra negotiators arrived. All reported to the incident commander, who knew that his career hung on having this situation properly resolved. Because this seemed to be a small incident, they did not call out other available specialists including linguists, mental health,

extra military personnel, or civilian telephone and utilities experts.

The incident commander did talk about cutting off power to the house as a means of harassment but decided to wait because the child hostages wouldn't have water from the property well to drink if there was no power to run the pump.

The negotiating team chief instructed his intelligence coordinator to immediately rent two big van-type U-haul trucks. One became their headquarters, in which a number of phones on separate lines were installed, and the other was to privately interrogate and interview witnesses and suspects as needed.

The record keeper's job was to maintain a detailed chronology of all negotiations, including things sent in to the hostages and promises made by both sides, as well as requests. A great wall chart was set up to record major events. The record keeper brought along a tape recorder to assist with these chores. A separate log was kept of all promises and deceptions that could be destroyed if the project went bad.

The intelligence coordinator's duties included collecting all available information from local sources about past records, explosives, personalities, firearms and likely responses of the criminal. If some of the hostages were released, it was his duty to interrogate them before putting them in jail for the duration. One of his first chores was to see about locking the kids in jail should they emerge from the house.

In another city, several additional members of the hostage rescue team, including two well-trained U.S. Marine snipers, packed their gear for the short charter flight to the hostage crisis. Because women hostage takers are known to be irrational and often more determined under these circumstances, they were instructed in their rules of engagement to shoot the wife as soon as possible after their arrival at the site.

Back at the farmhouse, the phone rang. The father thought it strange but answered anyway. He was told that the caller was from the government and that they could talk about anything, but he wanted to know if everybody was OK and to assure them that if they needed anything to let him (the negotiator) know. The father somewhat angrily asked if this guy was a psychologist, preacher, or a police officer. They guy may have been only a simple tractor mechanic, but his guess was right on.

As it works out, hostage negotiators are virtually never clergy or trained counselors. Usually they are middle-aged, mellow police officers with lots of street experience. All are trained at the U.S. Army military police negotiators school at Fort McClellan, Alabama. They go through a two-week intense course and, if successful, periodically receive additional three-day refresher courses. Their duty is to manipulate the subject and to buy time so that additional personnel and equipment can be brought up.

Negotiators are chosen who

1. Display common sense and good judgment with an ability to organize one's thoughts
2. Can speak to and not down to people
3. Are deliberate thinkers and speakers who are always in control, while continually alert to the surroundings
4. Have an exceptionally self-disciplined, mature, and emotionally stable character
5. Are patient, good listeners but also good talkers with a talent for salesmanship
6. Are excellent actors able to lie through their teeth for the good of the cause

Negotiation team members are expected to carry the following basic equipment to their "assignments":

1. Civilian clothes and coveralls
2. Handgun and ammunition
3. Concealable body armor
4. Camera kit
5. Complete Rolodex with pertinent names and numbers
6. Binoculars
7. First-aid kit
8. Hand-held radio for team use only (in all cases, land lines must be used, if possible, to prevent subject or media from listening in)
9. Bull horn and portable computer or typewriter

Negotiators are cautioned to always use phone lines to talk to the hostage taker himself, not someone else, including one of the hostages. Negotiations should never be done face to face, by loud voice over a distance, or through a third party. In all cases, the hostage-taker must be forced to talk *only* to the negotiator.

Other special group equipment not the responsibility of each team member includes the following:

1. Tables, chairs, lights, and a blackboard
2. Night vision devices and periscopes
3. Gas masks useful when CS or CN gas is ordered by the incident commander
4. Bomb blankets and covert (sniper and hidden) weapons
5. Various types of covert listening equipment, special telephones and remote TV transmitters
6. Tape recorders, video recorders, telephone pickup microphones, and telephone headsets
7. Complete, well-stocked lineman's/electrician's tool kit containing hundreds of different pliers, splicers, screwdrivers, and different pieces of testing equipment

The negotiator told the father that he was concerned about everyone's safety and that he wondered why the man ran for the house and barricaded it when the agents pulled up. The father didn't know that it is official negotiating policy to assume hostages are of no value once the "taker" is surrounded, and he was especially curious because his kids were all that was of value to him. He answered that he had run because he was being fired upon and that if the negotiator would come up to his door unarmed or restore his phone service so he could talk to the press, he would be pleased to work something out.

The hostage negotiator knew these requests were impossible but lied and said he would do his best to get them cleared through the incident chief. He was buying time so that more members of the hostage response team could arrive and they could safety shrink the perimeter. They also needed to keep pesky members of the media away before they became a problem. At this time, the father had not fired a shot or displayed a weapon to the agents. He was, however, armed.

In a few minutes the negotiator was back, saying, "Sorry, I was denied permission to come to the door for face-to-face negotiations."

After using these broad opening statements, the negotiator began his attempts to keep the dad in a problem-solving mode. The negotiator assumed the father was holding his children hostage for some strange social reason, which would surface if they just talked long enough. The father, in the home, worked on the assumption that these strange people were trying to shoot him and his wife so they could forcibly take the kids.

Now, whenever the father made a statement such as, "My children and I are afraid of being shot by your agents," the negotiator echoed back his statements without comment. This was the negotiator's application of indirect counseling whereby all he did was repeat statements.

About the only variation occurred when, in his molasses-barrel voice, the negotiator asked, "Do you know how upset you sound?"

As the night wore on, the negotiator sometimes lapsed into a posture of agreeing and sympathizing with the father. This was his attempt to develop a bond of trust between himself and the father. Being basically a simple person not used to being shot at and lied to, father became increasingly suspicious—to the point of paranoia.

Often, the negotiator also lapsed into long periods of silence broken by several minutes of acknowledging the hostage taker's feelings. He tried to keep the father busy clarifying meaningless facts and statements. Until he caught himself up short, the father spent five to ten minutes at a time making long, unproductive, and often foolish explanations regarding the exact type of food the agents were willing to allow in. The negotiator still wanted the father to rail against agents in an attempt to exhaust himself.

When the dad said he did not want cigarettes sent in because he thought smoking was unhealthy and did not thus indulge, the negotiator found 15 questions as to why the hostage taker felt that way. The father suppressed his rage over the assumption that he was a criminal hostage holder, knowing that his kids were in much more danger from the government agents than from himself. At one point, he seriously considered sending the two children out but his wife pointed out that then both of them would probably be shot and that his kids would be given to others to raise. They decided to keep the family together.

The negotiator never trusted the father, although he went out of his way to make him think he did completely. In that regard, both men played the same game. Talk went on all night. The negotiator attempted to build trust, listen to his problems, and generally deploy all the psychological techniques he had been taught. Generally, these negotiating tricks were the following:

1. The negotiator tried to limit the situation by involving only those participants currently involved. He attempted to decrease stress and anxiety with the passage of time. It had not yet occurred to him that the father did not believe he was holding his kids hostage.
2. The negotiator planned to build time into the process so that additional tactical numbers could be assembled, while the father could supposedly calm down, think about his situation, and evaluate alternatives.
3. The negotiator wanted to give his intelligence team time to interrogate friends and neighbors and to allow his electronics people to install remote spike microphones and TV cameras in the home to monitor the family's activities.

Many of the people interviewed by government agents took great umbrage at being rounded up in the middle of the night. Basically, the news media were kept uninformed about the incident, the only information coming from the government at the 1:30 a.m. news briefing.

The morning papers carried an exclusive story quoting the environmentally active CPA and the child-protective services worker about machine guns and child abuse.

During the night, agents successfully deployed remote cameras and microphones at the house.

At first light, government agents wearing heavy flack jackets and helmets ran up with shovels, hoes, and a four-wheel-drive jeep to destroy the family's carefully tended garden. This was done as part of their own personal revenge over one of their members being shot and as part of a psychological campaign to convince the hostage taker his position was hopeless.

Inside the negotiator's command center things started to turn to worms. The interrogation of friends, neighbors, and relatives turned up no real dirt on the family. A pattern evolved demonstrating that these were simple, hard-working, strongly religious, only somewhat educated, and not-very-articulate people who really did not know what was happening to them. Their basic rural mistrust of government added to their bewilderment and discomfort.

After a night of televised news showing only hypothetical machine guns and parroting the official government line, some of the media people were finally starting to ask embarrassing, tough questions. As the day wore on and the media were also able to talk to friends and relatives, some of these questions were definitely hostile to the government.

Intelligence based on the electronic eavesdropping equipment reported a basically bewildered and confused mom and dad, desperate with concern for their two children. There were family prayers and long talks with the kids about the dangerous situation they were in. One of the stated (public) goals and principles for negotiators is to get those being held out safely. The negotiator and incident commander privately discussed the inescapable emerging truth that they had the wrong guy and that the weapons he had inside were almost certainly all legal. They were also fearful the media would find the agent who shot himself in the foot and secure a statement to that effect from him. It also became apparent that the family was so terrified of the government that they would never come out.

Quietly, a decision was made that this obviously bungled operation could not be made public. The original tactical team was quietly withdrawn and dispersed to diverse parts of the nation. Explosives were brought up from a nearby infantry installation and a demolitions expert who knew nothing real about this situation was assigned to blow in one side of the house. The blast instantly killed all inside.

After burning the rubble, the negotiator, the incident commander, and what remained of the government team dispersed to their various offices. They assumed that although the outcome was not perfect, they had done their jobs pretty well as trained.

That year, after the environmentalist CPA paid more than 50 percent of her salary in state, local, and federal taxes, seeds of doubt regarding effectiveness of government problem-solving began to form in her mind.

BIBLIOGRAPHY

Get 'em Out Alive: Hostage Negotiating Teams. Boulder, CO: Paladin Press, 1990.

The Spokesman Review, Spokane, WA. August 20, 1992 through October 29, 1993.

Videotape of David Nevin, defense attorney for Kevin Harris. (Harris was tried by U.S. government for the murder of federal marshals, after a standoff at the home of Randy Weaver.)

CHAPTER

Electronic Perimeter Defense

30

University of Idaho College of Law Seminar. September 2, 1993.

Hardly anyone, except perhaps a few politicians, will deny that protection of one's property is mostly a matter of personal responsibility. Citizens cannot sue the police or the city if officials refuse to respond to a crime in progress or if their response compounds the crime. Yet these same officials often attempt to prevent law-abiding citizens from defending their own property.

Being personally responsible for crime prevention is not a revolutionary, new philosophy. But it has been only slowly and grudgingly acknowledged by liberals now in power. Taking responsibility to stop crimes against property has created several observable phenomena in our society. Government statisticians, for instance, establish that more than 50 million homeowners keep guns. It is also true that the business of installing and servicing burglar

alarms has exploded in recent years. Apparently, property owners reason that if we cannot penalize thieves for taking our goods, perhaps we can help prevent the theft.

Modern burglar alarms systems are fascinating because increasing demand has led to new levels of sophistication. When viewed in total, these systems are formidable. When viewed in their component parts, they are not really all that complicated.

Electronic perimeter defense vis-a-vis the modern burglar alarm is little more than two simple electric circuits and a control box. One circuit, much like a simple trip wire, maintains a constant electrical power supply that, if interrupted, triggers an alarm. Numerous switches in this circuit act as sensors if someone should try to violate this trip wire. This circuit is constantly monitored by a control panel that sends an electronic signal to a bell, siren, or light if one of the sensor switches is tripped. A warning that someone is in the wire is supposed to alert the owner and discourage the intruder. The intruder will try to defeat this system by eluding the

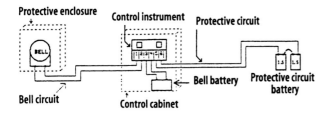

Protective enclosure   Control instrument   Protective circuit

BELL

Bell circuit   Control cabinet

Bell battery   Protective circuit battery

A basic burglar alarm system consists of three separate segments: the bell circuit, the control panel, and the protective circuit. (Illustrations taken from *Tricks of the Burglar Alarm Trade* by Mike Kessler.)

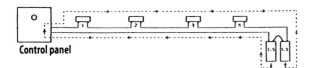

Control panel

The phantom line of arrows depicts the flow of current from the battery, through the entire protective circuit (including the protective circuit relay in the control panel), through each of the sensors, and back to the battery. This diagram is representative of a simple, straightforward installation, such as a row of four windows on the same wall.

trip switches or disconnecting either the alarm or the control box.

Both the alarm circuit and protective circuits have their own independent power supplies. Usually, but not always, these circuits contain batteries that do their job independent of a 110-volt power supply. Were this not true, a stay-behind burglar might simply disconnect the power supply to a building's burglar alarm, thereby disabling the entire system.

Modern burglar alarm protective circuits may be more than just perimeter defense. They may be composed of sophisticated infrared and motion detectors, broken-glass detectors, or simple magnetically held power-interrupt switches. Once a switch is opened, interrupting the protective circuit power supply, the control panel will send a signal through the bell circuit, causing it to ring. Some perimeter switches that rely on movement, slight temperature changes, and sound are really area sensors used well inside a facility's perimeter walls.

Confusion or sophistication, depending on one's point of view, of total burglar alarm systems occurs when these circuits and switches are multiplied and layered one over the other. Modern designs may make use of genuine perimeter defenses, such as

broken-glass detectors or electric eyes at windows and doors, but also deploy numerous circuits within the premises containing ultrasound-type, wide-area detectors.

As these devices become progressively complex, finding someone who can install, debug, and maintain them is often difficult. A favorite trick of burglars is to disable a burglar alarm so that it sounds when turned on by the owner as he leaves in the evening. Then his choice is to try to find somebody to service it at that late hour, spend the night in the shop, or leave the system disconnected. Smart burglars do not strike till the third or fourth night that they have managed to "disconnect" one of the electronic protective perimeter switches and when owners are thoroughly suspicious of and disgusted with their systems.

Disabling the alarm may seem to be the logical, best place for a relatively unsophisticated, unlawful intruder to start if he wants to be discreet about his intrusion. If it's a matter of a simple bell or siren, clipping the power lead from the control box seems appropriate. To thwart this relatively easy procedure, burglar alarm owners conceal alarm wires inside a wall, place alarms up in difficult-to-reach remote places, wire in multiple alarms on different circuits, including some out in the parking lot, and use special antitamper alarm boxes having self-contained batteries. Most of these also have internal sensors that ring the alarm if someone fools with it.

Foiling the alarm portion of these systems becomes much more difficult and time consuming than one would first suppose. As a result, the greatest effort by intruders is spent in trying to disable one or more of the perimeter defense detectors. As mentioned, when reduced to simple parts, these are nothing but on/off switches. When the power circulated in the protective circuit is switched off, the control box closes a circuit to the alarm.

These circuit sensors can be as sophisticated as passive-light detectors or as simple as spring-loaded door-and-window frame switches that open when doors or windows are. During business hours when people must use the doors, most systems—other than some in remote warehouses or attic crawl spaces—are turned off by a key at the control panel.

Small magnets are sometimes placed inside door frames that hold switches closed but that cannot be seen by intruders. Protective circuits have been set

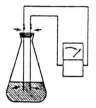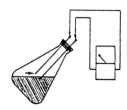

The principle of a mercury switch is illustrated here. On the left is a laboratory flask that is partially filled with mercury, a highly conductive, heavy liquid substance. Two rigid wires are passed through the cork in the flask and extended downward into the mercury. The probes of a meter (set to read continuity) are attached to the external ends of th two wires, indicating that the mercury is conducting an electrical current between the two wires. On the right, the flask is shown tilted to one side, withdrawing one of the wires from the conductive mercury. As indicated by the zero continuity reading on the meter face, the effect is identical to that of opening the contacts of a switch.

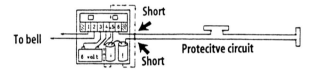

The current flow has been diverted by the short, returning by the shortest possible path to the battery. Electricity flows with incredible speed from negative to positive and will always follow the shortest possible route.

up with common leaf switches that open when pressure is released. These are often placed under cash register safes, major appliances, or other items that may tempt thieves.

Motion-sensitive switches similar to common household mercury switches can be used to hold a circuit till tripped. Intruders who manage to enter the premises undetected and locate these switches can short-circuit them by using a length of 22-gauge wire.

A few of these switches, such as foil on the windows and vibration sensors on property line walls, are easy to identify and circumvent. Foil on windows is either cut, destroying the circuit, or is shorted out with a bit of wire. Vibration detectors used to keep thieves from chopping through a wall can often be gummed up with spray paint or they can be shorted out.

Problems for intruders involve the fact that in nonpublic or semipublic (as in jewelry stores where access is restricted) places, they have a devil of a time identifying all of the switches and getting to them—especially if they must start on the outside.

In times past, burglar alarm installers made extensive use of simple little devices known as "traps." Sometimes, these were nothing more esoteric than trip-wire affairs that pulled a circuit open when an intruder walked or pushed through. Simple traps guarded heat ducts, wall shoots, skylights, and even some hallways. Because these devices could easily be taken down when their access doors were in use, and because they were inexpensively made of little more than black wire or fish line, they were very popular. Each, however, had to be snapped back in place each night or after each use of the portal they protected.

In more modern times, photoelectric detectors ("electric eyes") are used in front of banks of windows, down hallways, and on loading docks. These devices are extremely difficult to defeat if they are properly installed. Modern electric eyes make use of pulsed, infrared beams invisible to human eyes. Intruders cannot set up mirrors or use flashlights to defeat these switches. Some photoelectric detectors are cleverly built into look-alike wall receptacles. If you could identify these systems before running afoul of them, you might find the lead-in wires and short them out. Many of these and other devices are installed with wires running under a moldboard or even completely out of reach in the side wall. Look for wires, but don't be surprised if they are out of sight, especially in newer, more sophisticated systems.

Microwave motion detectors that transmit a beam of focused radio wave energy are currently the most sophisticated interior sensors. Absolutely any movement (even a cat or rat) inside the radio beam opens a circuit, sending a signal to the bells and whistles. Signals from microwave detectors cannot be seen or heard by humans.

Transmitters are usually located in far corners on or near the ceiling, where as a practical matter they are tamperproof. Their Achilles' heel is the fact that any movement within the premise will trigger an alarm. Owners often weary of false alarms caused by cats, rats, or sparrows.

Since microwave motion detectors operate on

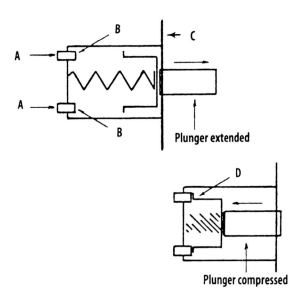

Plunger extended

Plunger compressed

Operationally, a plunger switch is no different from the spring-loaded button used to ring a doorbell. Pressing the button closes a pair of internal contacts, completing a circuit, causing the bell to ring. When the pressure is released, the contacts release.

roughly the same frequency as police radars, one can use a common vehicle radar detector to determine their presence. Without practice, it is tough to detect microwaves without triggering the alarm. Look for these devices in locations characterized by long ranges and wide open spaces, such as gymnasiums, warehouses, and some parking garages.

There are other problems with otherwise perfect microwave detectors: they are very expensive; they often drift out of adjustment; and they tend to over-penetrate to adjoining rooms, where movement triggers the alarm. Owners get tired of responding to false alarms in the middle of the night. As a result, installers may place these units in places where they can be reached more easily for periodic adjustment. In this case, a would-be intruder may spin the adjustment dial at a time when the system is turned off. When the alarm sounds at closing time when turned on, owners often just leave the whole system off, providing an excellent opportunity for an intruder.

Ultrasonic and infrared detectors make up the last two categories of modern sophisticated and protection devices, commonly deployed in burglar alarms. Ultrasonic devices, as the name implies, broadcast signals above the range of human hearing into large open areas such as grocery stores, ware-

houses, stores, and other similar buildings. Receivers tuned to this signal quickly detect any disturbance of the signal. They are sometimes falsely triggered by ringing phones, small animals, and the chronic noise of banging water pipes and heating ducts. Some ultrasonic alarms are advertised as having an added effect of driving off rodents and certain insects.

Passive infrared detectors are simply supersensitive heat detectors. Modern units are reliable and will detect either an increase or a decrease in temperature within their area of protection. Even an intruder wearing a space blanket will trigger the alarms because of a drop in ambient temperature.

These units' weakness involves the fact that smart intruders may raise room temperatures to about 98 degrees (body temperature) so that the switches cannot quickly accurately differentiate between a slow-moving intruder and high ambient temperatures. The trick, of course, is to raise building temperatures without running afoul of this or other detectors.

A friend, now long deceased, worked as a gunsmith in a large firearms superstore in the east. He was a crusty, old fart possessing very few socially redeeming qualities. As part of his duties as gunsmith, the guy packed around a loaded, cocked Colt .45 auto. He said it was safe because he had installed one of his own special safeties. We reckoned that this guy was just itching to get a shot at a holdup man.

Although primitive by current standards, the place did have a burglar alarm system with foil-protected windows, and compression-switch-equipped doors, windows, and skylight. More than 1,200 guns remained in stock as part of the salable supply of merchandise. By an absolute quirk of fate, some of us who worked as clerks in that joint discovered that several of the windows and the skylight had been tampered with. Some portals were unlocked and some sensing alarms had also been shorted out with small jumper wires. We were sure that someone was going to try to break in rather than that the windows had been left unlocked inadvertently. Back then, there were no such things as sophisticated, infrared, or ultrasonic area sensors; perimeter switches were all there were.

We turned the system on, and, as you would expect, it powered up without fault. But, of course, at least three key sensors were shorted out. After much talk, our gunsmith—who really wanted a legal reason to try out his .45—agreed to spend the night in the store.

Nothing transpired that night nor the second. But the third night was a charm. Two young men climbed onto the store roof and came through the skylight. They were in the store perhaps two minutes before the gunsmith-gunslinger got the drop on them. I was surprised that the old guy didn't realize a life's ambition and shoot the two, but apparently they surrendered meekly. Perhaps our man realized down deep in his heart that it would have been murder to shoot—even if it was legal.

Our local police came and hauled the pair to the slammer, but a judge let them out on bail. They both disappeared into the ether. We installed double-sensor switches on every door and windows including foil on *all* glass and plunger switches on everything that swung open. No one tried us again, probably in large part because of the hot air generated by our gunslinger-smith who "really wanted to shoot those varmints!"

When installing a new burglar alarm perimeter defense system, you must use great care to harden, scatter, and diversify actual bells, whistles, and lights used as alarms. You must also hide away under lock and key the system's control box so that it cannot be found and immobilized. Modern systems capable of resisting efforts at compromise by clever intruders absolutely must contain both a tripwire perimeter defense along with sophisticated, often costly, interior area sensors.

Systems of this type cost hundreds of dollars if you buy components, a roll of wire, and a control box and do it yourself. Or the same system can cost tens of thousands if it is done by a professional, especially if all inside-the-wall wiring is specified.

Mike Kessler has written an excellent book, *Tricks of the Burglar Alarm Trade*. It is specifically and carefully put together so that an absolute novice can follow what is a very complex assembly operation. Anyone with a serious perimeter-defense problem would be well advised to learn in detail what Kessler has to say.

BIBLIOGRAPHY

Expedient B & E, Tactics and Techniques for Bypassing Alarms and Defeating Locks. Boulder, CO: Paladin Press, 1992.

Hampton, Steven. *Security Systems Simplified*. Boulder, CO: Paladin Press, 1992.

Kessler, Mike. *Tricks of the Burglar Alarm Trade*. Boulder, CO: Paladin Press, 1990.

CHAPTER

Taps and Bugs

31

Bugs are microphones hidden on premises where valuable information may be collected. Taps are devices placed in or on a phone system. Between the two, with their many variations and nuances, all electronic surveillance takes place.

Both bugs and taps can be hard-wired in, make use of radio transmission to carry their information, or—in rare instances—be combinations of both. Both radio and hard-wire-carried information go directly to a manned listening post, a repeater that picks up and resends the information across town to a better-hidden, more remote listening post, or to a specially built, slow-running, long-recording tape recorder.

In many instances, phone taps bleed off conversations to a surreptitious third party. Usually, they send their signals on down a phone line or another special line set up specifically for the purpose of listening. Taps operate on their own power supply—usually batteries—or pull their power from the phone company. Conventional wisdom suggests that

it is easier to uncover taps tht draw off a small amount of power. A number of radio broadcast tapping devices exist that can send telephone messages up to a mile to common receivers.

Hybrid devices exist that are both phone taps and room bugs (transmitters). These are called hook-switch bypass units or infinity transmitters. They are reasonably priced at around $400. Some are hard-wired into a phone; others are installed by simply unscrewing the speaker, removing the "issue" microphone, and dropping in one's "special" device.

Tales—perhaps apocryphal—suggest that these devices were originally perfected by jealous, suspicious German husbands, who installed them in their wives' bedside phones. By so doing, they could call Germany from Greenland or wherever to hear everything going on in the room. Both domestically and in a business context, Germans—of all nationalities—seem to be the principal users of electronic eavesdropping equipment. Most well-made, sophisticated, off-the-shelf bugs and taps came from Deutschland. They even have standard phones with built-in infinity transmitters that defy detection.

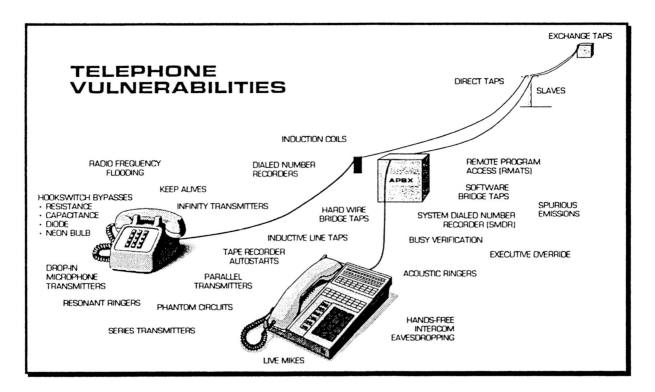

Telephone vulnerabilities. (Illustration taken from *Hands-On Countermeasures* by Lee Lapin. It is copyrighted by Murray Associates.)

An absolute first priority when dealing with electronic surveillance, according to *all* experts foreign and domestic, is to assess the threat level accurately and honestly. Honestly think through the issues of who wants to listen, for what reason, and what will listening to me get them? Investigators universally agree that even in this age of easy, uncontested divorces, the most common surveillance involves domestic issues. Such items as spousal extracurricular activities or perhaps custody of children are the most common situations where electronic surveillance is employed.

Second are civil matters related to workers' compensation, welfare fraud, insurance fraud, and myriad other little scams that small-time individuals try to perpetrate on big government or larger companies.

A third category about which investigators are often very close-mouthed—probably because it is lucrative, fairly easy work—is electronic surveillance on behalf of business or political clients. This includes industrial espionage, political campaigns, and business situations where one partner is pitted against another, perhaps in a hostile takeover. In Germany, for instance, where thousands of dollars worth of surveillance equipment is sold annually, an

automatic assumption is usually made that all of this is done in a business context. Domestic espionage seems to have dropped from sight in Deutschland.

Government agencies employ very sophisticated state-of-the-art electronic equipment and make up the last major category of user. These are the ones with alphabet names such as the IRS (Internal Revenue Service), DEA (Drug Enforcement Agency), SEC (Securities & Exchange Commission), and FDA (Food & Drug Administration). If you have a problem with these people that leads to electronic surveillance, it is serious indeed. Many private investigators will not become involved if they suspect one of these heavyweight agencies or will simply claim they cannot find the bug or tap.

Contrary to popular information, not everyone can run sophisticated electronic surveillance equipment. Effective use requires the services of an experienced, trained, well-equipped "techie." In the marketplace, these people are not common, especially given the fact that it takes between $35,000 and $50,000 worth of complex, often delicate equipment to get into the business.

Federal agencies such as the FBI, Marshals' Service, DEA, and IRS are not particularly constrained by equipment budgets, and they can pay going rates to employ needed techies with top-of-the-line skills. Private investigators universally agree that, if someone has this category of antagonist after him, there is very little he can do to discover and neutralize its equipment. It is simply too good, and those agencies have access that is virtually impossible for common citizens. They can, for instance, flash their badges and gain instant access to company central switchboards, apartment complex phone systems, and even many small businesses.

Good, well-run, profitable crime organizations sometimes have sufficient money to hire the appropriate techies to handle their electronics intrusion problems, but even these smart people always assume that their clients' rooms are bugged and that the phone is tapped. Wiseguys make it a working principle never to speak about sensitive matters in a closed room or on an open phone line.

For about $300, those who require them can purchase phone scramblers that, when required, are placed over existing phones, causing all incoming and outgoing conversations to be hopelessly garbled for anyone listening in. Every member of the cooperating group must have his own scrambler. It is also claimed that these devices are effective when used with cellular phones.

Scramblers convert normal speech to electronic gibberish. Most have in excess of 50,000 different codes that can be changed from time to time or even conversation to conversation. Yet one would suppose that all these devices could be compromised by a sophisticated listener who could also purchase his own scrambler or use computers to break the electronic coding.

Surreptitious listening devices (either taps or bugs) are generally located either by using expensive, often difficult-to-operate, electronic sweeping devices or by deploying an intelligent, well-organized, professional, physical search of the premises. The physical search must be under the direction of skilled personnel who understand, from long experience, the limitations and capabilities of electronic surveillance.

Knowing which devices are on the market and where they could likely be hidden helps dramatically when searching an office or residence for taps and bugs. Most experts claim that the physical search is more important than electronic counter-

measures, but black-box-type electronic countermeasures have more sex appeal.

Presently, for instance, there are on the market tiny microphone transmitters, with ranges of approximately 1,000 feet, factory-built into ashtrays, coffee tables, cigarette lighters, calculators, functional fountain pens, electric wall outlets, and digital clocks. Self-contained microphone transmitters that run on button batteries for as long as 3 1/2 days, about the size of a five-stick package of gum, are commonly available. These can be glued to picture frames, under tables and chairs, in the base of clocks, under desk tables and chairs, under desk trim, to the back of books, into light fixtures, and tens of thousands of other nooks and crannies. They work best if placed high in a room far from interfering motor hum, such as that from air conditioners, overhead projectors, and humidifiers.

Cluttered surroundings provide greatly increased opportunities to secrete small surreptitious electronic listening devices. Many operate best if a tiny wire antenna can be folded out straight from the device. Their placement in the corner of a room with antenna fastened down on a molding is common.

These little transmitters can be hidden inside anything from a teddy bear to a Bible. The unsuspecting carry these gifts back to their own inner sanctums where they divulge all of the secrets till the batteries run down. It is always important that a careful analysis be made of all gifts and supplies received from outside sources when doing a physical search of the premises. Replacement of worn batteries in surreptitious transmitters is a formidable problem. Yet it is still a very common surveillance ploy to provide bugged gifts to those from whom electronic information would be helpful.

This device is especially common in cases where access to a target's home or office, even for a few minutes, to plant a bug or tap is not possible. To get into a home or office to plant a bug, try inventing a social or business call; bribing the custodial crew; or posing as a repair man, delivery person, pastor, or consultant visiting on a professional basis. Pros report that numerous bugs have been planted by security people actually working as double agents.

Common-looking telephones with built-in infinity devices can be substituted by people posing as telephone repairmen. Other devices drop into or hook to a phone in a matter of seconds and are available if one can just have these few seconds unobserved. Those looking for bugs and taps should take apart existing phones to examine them closely. If there is any doubt, take apart another phone and compare the two. In some cases it is virtually impossible to identify infinity devices if you have never seen them before.

Downline phone taps can be placed almost anyplace in the line accessible to someone with a wire splicer. They rely on both batteries and power from the phone and can send their interrupted messages by wire or radio. In that regard a phone tap can be placed just about anyplace accessible. A thorough search will involve looking all these places.

Other than very sophisticated government taps, experts can usually detect their presence on line using power meters or radio frequency meters. Sometimes it is possible to tune a wideband radio to the tap's or bug's transmitting frequency and get a loud, impedance howl when the radio is carried close to the transmitting microphone. All this can be more difficult than it would seem, especially if the tap is installed way downtown at the phone company's switch, which is probable if government agencies are involved.

An associate in the phone business in New York City points out that almost every time he opens a junction box in the basement of a large apartment complex he finds several abandoned taps, left there by some unidentified, long-departed snoop. Apparently, more toney residences are likely to have greater numbers of taps. Whenever he needs a tap, he rummages around in various buildings' telephone connection cabinets till he finds one to his liking. Some devices worth hundreds of dollars are simply abandoned, perhaps because the original owners found out what they wanted, the batteries wore down, or the client paid for a device that was too much trouble to retrieve.

Successfully hiding a bug in a room takes a great amount of hands-on practice. In many cases, bugs do not pick up good, usable information and transmit it successfully to those in need of it. It is easy to place a bug in the wrong place so that the sound of people nervously drumming their fingers on a table or the humming of the water cooler drowns out an important speaker. On one occasion we thought that planting a bug in an overhead light would work, but a defective neon light foiled us: all we got was a hum with garbled speaking in the background.

There is *always* a possibility that someone will inadvertently stumble across a radio-transmitted conversation. Most listening devices are somewhat tuneable in that one can electronically tuck the transmission very close in against an existing station. But even though a delicate receiver is normally needed to receive these transmissions, someone can stumble across a transmission and recognize the voices.

Another big problem in our complex world occurs when the conference day is delayed or a key person fails to show up. We have also had our radio mike batteries poop out before anyone important arrived to talk.

Some installers use 24-gauge type wire to run their bug transmissions to another nearby office, perhaps one floor below, or even, as in one case from a political office across the street, to a rental office.

One excellent listening device clamps firmly onto an outside window. It will pick up virtually all conversations in that room, including one side of a phone conversation, broadcasting them across the block to an eavesdropper. They are simple, effective devices and are not particularly costly. But how does one install such a radio or change batteries every three days on the 30th story of a high-rise? Hardly any high-rise windows open. Installation would require the services of a window washer or cat burglar.

Probably the most common broadcast frequency used by bugs and taps is the regular commercial FM band falling between 88 and 108 MHz. Also, many professional surveillance people use regular 2-meter FM frequencies falling between 141.000 and 149.990 because this range has a great many unused, tiny side bands, and these radios are available in great profusion right off the shelf. In days gone by, it was sometimes common to use high-power transmitters in conjunction with bugs. The transmitters required heavy batteries that lasted only a few hours and were relatively easily discovered. Now, technology made common during the past 20 years allows users to switch to very low-power, sensitive sending units. Often these low-power transmissions are "smuggled" in against those of TV, taxi dispatching, paging, or whateve—and they are tough even for experienced countermeasure people with scanners to find.

Electronic surveillance requires not only great skill on the part of the techies who are into this sort of thing, but infinite patience as well. A recent *Wall Street Journal* article noted that FBI agents bugged a suspect's house for seven months before hearing just one sentence that made them suspicious. Only government agents could possible sit through all the drivel they must have heard for seven months in order to get one incriminating sentence.

I was once involved in a bugging operation within a large company. We wanted to know what top management's plans were for a project on which our division was working.

It was reasonably easy to get a small, commercial FM transmitter into the main conference room and glued under a large table with the broadcast antenna discreetly taped to a table leg. Other than a great deal of initial bumping and scratching, pickup was good, *except* for the key executive who stalked around the room as he spoke. It was maddening because his voice often faded just at a time when he made crucial comments. A loud-mouthed secretary also interrupted often, preventing us from hearing important statements.

We sat for hours listening from an office about 300 feet down the hall. Finally, because this real-time monitoring precluded us from getting any work done, we bought an extended-play tape recorder. It had a voice-activated system by which conversations were compressed to the few hours of what was actually said in that room, without sitting for hours monitoring silence. Then, when all looked good, our transmitter batteries went dead: before we replaced them, a key meeting took place.

Nagging doubts persisted as to whether we had missed some important parts of the conversation. As it worked out, our division was eventually sacked. We knew the real reason why we were let go, and we knew three weeks before anybody else. Our bug didn't stop us from being canned, however.

Probably, given any kind of half-serious, real-life situation, it is *not* effective for a regular non-techie to purchase a tiny bug and 2-meter receiver to do his own surveillance or countersurveillance. Equipment for those who want to see if they are techies is available from a number of suppliers who advertise in such electronics magazines as *CQ* or in *Shotgun News*. It is *not* illegal to own bugs or taps; it is only illegal to deploy them. But technical and mechanical problems are usually too complicated for amateurs to overcome, even if simple, basic, low-priced equipment is used.

Some equipment is not only expensive, it is also ineffective even in the hands of experts. The industry is plagued by overinflated claims regarding performance and application. Usually, it is only those who use or talk to those who use this equipment on a daily basis who can sort out reality from the hype. Many techies rely heavily on components and equipment they purchase at Radio Shack.

One Radio Shack device is ideal for those of you who want to fool around a bit with electronic surveillance to see if you have a talent for the game. Start by purchasing a relatively inexpensive Radio Shack wireless intercom. It is also known as an electronic baby-sitter and is nothing more than a device that plugs into a wall outlet and has a microphone that picks up regular room conversations. The conversations are sent out along existing power lines to another like unit. There are no radio receivers, separate electrical lines, or tunable transmitters to fool with.

These are sensitive units small enough that they can be neatly hidden under a table or bed, or even on top of a picture frame. You could spray paint it to match the color of the room trim, hide the power cord in a corner, and mount the box up on the ceiling in one corner of the room. Most people will never catch it.

Wherever it is mounted neatly and officially, run a dark-colored power cord from the intercom to a wall socket. These microphones can even be hard-wired into a power socket by drilling a hole in the wall and dropping the cable through to the power source. Modern units operate through an amazing number of switches and transformers that were barriers for older models. You can then expend your amateur's energy working with long-play, voice-activated recorders and other, more common electronic devices.

Another relatively easy beginner's device useful against unsuspecting, unsophisticated targets is a telephone infinity transmitter. Purchase the type that is simply dropped into the telephone headset speaker. The cost is about $350 by mail order from either German suppliers or U.S. makers. They are very easy to use. Usually, you call a targeted number, let the phone ring once, blow a whistle, and then hang up. The device keeps the line open, and everything said in the room can be heard.

Those of you who have a tough job with limited equipment may still wish to hire a professional. How do you find that person? It is best to talk to your attorney, who in turn will put you in touch with his best private investigator. This person will always know a number of electronics techies.

These people, if they are any good at all, will charge at least $500 per day. The value of their work precludes them from giving specific references. Based on the foregoing, general information, you can at least talk to these people. Be certain to specify specific objectives, such as three weeks' continuous recordings of both sides of your business partner's phone conversations or a recording of the

December 12 board meeting. Risks still exist because what is undertaken is illegal and it is terrifyingly easy to spend huge amounts of money with very little to show for it.

In this business, only the government is always a certain winner.

BIBLIOGRAPHY

Keep It a Secret. Boulder, CO: CEP, Incorporated, 1990, videocassette.

Lapin, Lee. *Hands-On Countermeasures*. San Mateo, CA: Intelligence, Inc. 1993.

_____. *Hands-On Electronic Surveillance*. San Mateo, California: Intelligence, Inc., 1992.

CHAPTER

Lockpicking

32

Picking locks is very much like playing the piano. Some people do it much better than others. It is also impossible to do either well without a great deal of practice. Some people have natural talents for the game while others won't make acceptable "wires" after even years of practice. Similarly, one absolutely must have a great deal of real hands-on familiarization, much more than one will receive from reading this chapter.

Expert lock picks generally use two basic tools: a lock pin feeler—or pick—and a torque-producing turning wrench. Within these two broad classes of tools there are dozens of little variations. Generally, experienced users settle on one or two of each, but keep up to a dozen others in their tool kits just in case they need them, or for theatrics. Picks and turning wrenches are available from locksmith supply houses or are fairly easily made at home.

Picks are long, slim spring-steel fingers with various different types of ends used to reach in a key

slot and gently manipulate pins or wafers inside a lock. My favorite is a finger that reaches back into the thinnest of key channels. Others are those whose ends are ball-shaped, diamond-shaped, serrated, and even pointed. I favor long, thin fingers with a 70-degree turn because it seems easier to manipulate one pin at a time with this tool.

Turning wrenches are flat pieces of spring steel bent in an L-shape. They are used to bring slight pressure on a lock cylinder while the pins are moved up and down. The theory is that all locks come with a bit of play, allowing for manufacturers tolerances and the random inclusion of dirt, dust water, and ice in the mechanism.

Applying exactly correct pressure on the cylinder and holding it for perhaps 10 or 15 minutes until all of the pins have been worked is the tough part. Too much pressure on the cylinder destroys sensitivity; too little allows pins that are slightly out of line to fall back down, temporarily thwarting efforts to pick that lock. Starting with the toughest (most out-of-line) pin, each is pushed up till the cylinder shear line is reached and that pin pair is held, in a ready-to-open position, by tension on the turning wrench.

When I was first learning lock picking, our instructor gave each of us a pin-and-cylinder lock from which we removed all but one pin set. Pin-and-cylinder locks are the most common locks. They operate on the concept that five sets of double pins will be minutely and correctly raised by a key so that all the varying-length pins push their mates exactly up to a line between the rotating cylinder and the pin raceway above, allowing the cylinder to turn.

Because pin carrier holes in the cylinder and upper lock body cannot be drilled exactly true with one another, pin-and-cylinder locks are pickable. As mentioned, one raises the tightest pin first with the lock pick and gently holds it on the shear line with the torsion wrench while the remaining pins are felt out and similarly moved up.

Theoretically, all locks with key channels are pickable, but in actual practice the game is sometimes not worth the candle. Some lever tumbler locks used in bank safe-deposit boxes take an expert about 25 minutes per keyway to pick. Most of those locks have dual keys, causing picking to be especially difficult.

Lever-tumbler locks are totally different from pin-and-cylinder locks, on which I believe everyone should start their career as lock picks. Carefully unscrew the back keeper plate from a door-type pin-and-cylinder lock. It is possible to look in and see the pins, getting a rough idea how they are mechanically constructed. Hasp locks, which also may have pins and a cylinder, are die-stamped together. You can look in the front of these locks, but taking them apart is usually much more difficult, although more desirable, because they are inexpensive and portable.

No matter which type, take a pin-and-cylinder lock apart over an egg carton or soft rag, so that all the pins fall safely into a container. Place one pin set back into the lock, slide the cylinder back into place, temporarily tape the cylinders in place, and start by picking that one pin.

After mastering tension and pick so that the lock can be opened in a few seconds, place two pin pairs in position. The order in which these pins are arrayed in the cylinder will now be thoroughly mixed, therefore the key will no longer function. An inexpensive lock has been "sacrificed" for the sake of practice. Keep working till all five pins are back

inside the cylinder. If it is important that the same key be used again, sort through the pins till only those that rest flush on the inserted key are used on the bottom in the cylinder.

When the trial lock can be picked with impunity, find another pin-and-cylinder lock to practice on that has not been previously taken apart.

Some locks require a different type of pick, more similar to a passkey. Foremost among these are old warded-bit locks. These extremely simple locks are seldom seen today where anything serious must be secured. Either use skeleton keys purchased from hardware stores in sets of three or a stout piece of wire with a sharp L-bend in the end, used to manipulate the bolt.

Anyone confused by this instruction should take one of these locks apart. Two screws and it will be immediately obvious how to turn the little L-shape rod to pull the bolt back.

Small, cheap hasp locks often found on luggage are called warded locks. These are locks that have convoluted stops built into the mechanism's keyway. A flat key sufficiently wide to turn the rear catch mechanism is prevented by the wards from being turned even if it can be inserted in the keyway.

Some locksmiths make a big mystery of these locks. Basically, you must make and carry a long, thin, tube-like passkey with flat paddle end that avoids the stops, because the shaft is narrow. Correctly made, this key will manipulate the catch mechanism at the back of the lock with its "big-paddle" end. Some of these "passkeys" have ends with two paddles rather than one or a hollow tube key body that fits in an internal pocket in the lock. No big mystery here. These locks are seldom picked, except in dire emergencies and using an L-shape piece of wire. Usually, you make or purchase a set of passkeys for these little locks, carrying them around from job to job.

Look at keys from several small, suitcase-type warded locks and then fool around with the locks a bit. Usually this is enough to reveal how these locks might be handled.

Some luggage has three combination wheels that must be set to a predetermined three-figure combination. At most, 30 minutes is required to open these by trial and error. Set the first wheel at one, the second at one, and run the third wheel one through nine. Keep repeating till success is yours.

In 1818, the British government offered 100 pounds (a princely sum in those days) to anyone who invented a pick-proof lock. As a result, Joseph Brahmah invented and patented the first lever lock. He also offered 200 guineas (a guinea is 1 pound plus 1 shilling) to the first person to pick his lock. An American named Hobbs succeeded, but it took about 30 minutes. Hobbs used a small spring-steel tension wrench and a single finger pick to do the job. Lever locks have between three and nine wafer-thin plates riding at differing heights that will strike an internal stop, thus preventing the slide bolt from opening, if a key does not properly hold these little plates at correct height. As mentioned, these locks are used in bank vaults, some cabinets, office equipment, and a few expensively built doors. They are generally not worth picking.

Because these are difficult locks to pick and most people have neither the training nor time to handle, a special sheet metal screw is usually screwed into the keyway used to pull the core out of the lock or the door off the box. A specially designed tool much like an impact wheel puller is employed. It isn't picking, but at least one is inside the lock.

Under most circumstances, these are not locks you are likely to have to open, except, perhaps, very cheap varieties on suitcases and file cabinets. Then, given only two or three tumblers, you can validly make an attempt using a special, thin L-shaped turning wrench and a single finger pick that reaches back inside.

Disk-tumbler locks are somewhat like pin-and-cylinder locks in that a blocking member is raised up out of a bottom groove in the lock body by the correct key. These disks cannot be raised so high that they move into a top groove where it again prevents the cylinder from turning. Disk-tumbler locks are mass-produced in great numbers for hasp locks, desks, cabinets, residences, and shop doors, as well as for some autos.

Each of these mechanisms has no more than five disk tumblers, and each disk has only five different slots stamped in it. Translated, this means that a key will have only five different heights cut into it. Pick these locks by looking into the key slot while manipulating each disk in turn up out of the lower channel. You'll quickly learn the five heights that the wafers could be pulled up to. Slight pressure on the turning wrench usually holds the disks in place, but you may also have to start with the toughest wafer first, as in regular pin-and-cylinder locks. Since these locks are usually quite sloppy by reason of their cheap mass production, they are not particularly tough to handle.

Raking is a subset of a procedure in delicate picking. Wafer-tumbler locks are subject to this procedure. In this instance, you take an S-ended pick and rhythmically pull it over the wafers while maintaining considerable pressure on the turning wrench. Because these are simple locks with relatively few internal parts and wafer positions, raking often opens the door.

Making keys by impression is a valid opening technique. Yet, like lock picking, this is a very difficult skill to acquire. You are best served by learning to pick locks first before moving on to impression key making.

Impressing a key requires finding the correct key blank for the lock being worked on. A small, rat-tail file with which to cut the key is also required.

Slide the key into the slot and, using a set of pliers, severely turn the key back and forth just to the point of bending. Remove the blank, examining the top carefully. Tiny, light, worn spots should be evident. If not, polish the blank with very fine steel wool and try force-turning again.

File down on the marks gently. Insert the key and roll it again. Gradually, you will work down to the place where pins or wafers no longer bind against the key, opening the lock. It is a tedious, delicate process. Marks on the key are tough to see, especially after the first few file cuts. File on only one impression at a time.

Some locksmiths gently tap their key blanks from the top with a small mallet while turning the key to produce better marks on the key blank blade. Others file the key blank thinner, believing that this will allow better marking.

Tubular cylinder locks are found on most vending machines, coin-operated washing machines, and as key locks on dispensing services such as key-lock gas pumps. These locks are nothing more than rotating-pin cylinder locks having as many as eight sets of pins, rather than the customary five found on most pin tumbler locks. In this regard, and because of their round configuration, these locks are considered more difficult to pick than flat-pin cylinder locks.

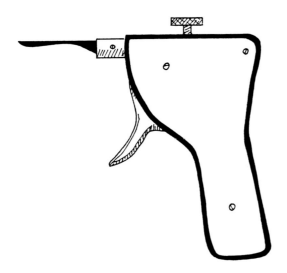

A lock-picking gun based on the Segal patent.

Skilled, practicing lock picks find that tubular locks are often as easy to pick as regular pin-and-cylinder locks, provided you have the correct tubular lock-picking tools used by locksmiths. Otherwise you must use a straight pin and circular turning wrench, which can be very difficult.

These special tools are available from advertisers in *Shotgun News* and from most locksmith supply houses. Usually, you will require three different diameters of tools to fit the various lock sizes you may encounter, and the tools cost about $60 each! As an alternative, tubular locks are quickly drilled out with a half-inch bit if you can survive the fact that entry has now obviously been accomplished.

Sidebar locks are a specialized version of disk-tumbler locks. They are commonly, but not exclusively, found on automobiles. Many disk-tumbler and pin-and-cylinder-type locks are also used by vehicle manufacturers.

Sidebar locks are very simple. They are constructed of disk tumblers housed inside the lock, having U-shaped notches in their sides. When the correct key is inserted, the key aligns the disks so that a spring-loaded sidebar moves out of the cylinder into the plug. This core plug is now free to rotate inside the cylinder.

Probably because these locks are simple and cheaply made for quick construction, they are time consuming to pick. It is impossible to hear or feel the wafers align with the shear line.

Locksmiths either drill or pull these lock cores and replace them with new core and key. They also

experience modest success raking these tumblers by using an S-pick and fairly heavy turning wrench, as previously described. Some people become proficient enough to open an auto in a matter of seconds.

Other methods are available for those who must get autos started (these will be covered in subsequent chapters). Because of an epidemic of auto theft, car makers are upgrading their locks slightly, making them more difficult to pick.

Devices known as pick guns are available on the retail market from locksmith suppliers. These tools thump pins inside a lock, when a special blade is inserted in the lock and a trigger is pulled. As with billiard balls, the first pin stays in place while the second is bounced up above the cylinder sheer line, allowing the lock cylinder to be turned.

Although these gizmos do occasionally work, most users feel that they are greatly overrated and will not open most locks most of the time. Pick guns will sometimes open disk-tumbler locks in an action similar to raking, but generally they only work on pin-cylinder locks that can be "bounced." A type of this tool can be made at home from heavy spring-steel wire, or it can be purchased from locksmith supply houses for about $85.

Contrary to what one may have wished, there is no quick, easy tool that can open locks without a great deal of practical, self-acquired skill. I personally have picked a number of locks, but have never become really good at it simply because I do not invest the time and energy practicing and studying the art. After the initial two-week course of study, it was too easy to allow exigencies to intervene.

BIBLIOGRAPHY

Hammer, Carl. *Expedient B & E.* Boulder, CO: Paladin Press, 1992.

Lockpicking. Little Falls, NJ: Locksmithing Institute of America, 1967.

Mannerly, John. *Pick Guns.* Boulder, CO: Paladin Press, 1989.

The Wire, Eddie. *The Complete Guide to Lock-Picking.* Port Townsend, WA: Loompanics, Ltd. 1981–86.

_____. *How to Make Your Own Professional Lock Tools, Volumes 1-4.* Port Townsend, WA: Loompanics, Ltd. 1981–86.

CHAPTER
Interrogation
33

"It is my legs that need medicine, not my eyes," the young Samburu warrior pleaded. Anthrax sores on the fellow's legs were serious enough, but I was intrigued by his eye that he held tightly closed. Gently, I pulled up the eyelid and peered in. A perfectly good, seemingly functional eye looked back out at me.

The mystery was solved by talking to members of the fellow's family. It seems a witch doctor had cursed his left eye, telling the man that he now had to keep it closed forever. A couple of shots of lumpy, vet-grade penicillin cured the anthrax, but the eye atrophied and eventually died regardless of anything I could do. This was and still could be rural Africa at its anthropological finest.

In some regards modern, trendy interrogation techniques developed by Western witch doctors having sanitized, politically correct titles such as psychiatrist, psychologist, or even social worker, are about as effective as those used on my young African friend. If one really believes, he may very easily become the victim.

Since these techniques cannot be replicated in any type of controlled laboratory environment, they cannot be considered science, no matter how strongly or with what fervor perpetrators support them. Significantly, DEA, BATF, IRS, and FBI agents (to name a few) have accepted these techniques wholeheartedly. Defectors from these agencies indicate that these techniques are used on citizens with impunity.

Supposedly, these new, modern interrogation devices will indicate whether a person is being truthful—during a tax audit, traffic stop, or drug bust, for instance. However, no matter how one uses them, these methods are extremely subjective, and often contradictory, in nature.

Long, expensive symposium-type training sessions have become mandatory for those working in our federal agencies who interact with people who may have reason to be less than truthful or may not

177

Although interrogation techniques used by those in authority are not new, attempts to make them into a science and the focus of their viciousness seem inappropriate to many Americans. (Photo by Ragnar Benson.)

wish to tell big brother anything at all. Average citizens may have a great deal of concern about these techniques that, as stated, are entirely subjective: that is, whether or not an interrogator "feels in his bones" that the person he is confronting is guilty and thus will thus look hard enough to find indicators to substantiate his feelings. Many federal agents brag that they can tell in the first 20 seconds of an interrogation whether a person is guilty or not, just by how they feel about the victim.

Under the title of "kinesiology," this type of interrogation assumes that most people will reveal their deception by nonverbal clues. The trick is to be well-trained and smart enough to identify these nonverbal clues, which may include such obvious signs as biting one's lips, failing to respond quickly to questions, or even blinking excessively. Although some of these signs may indicate simple nervousness, others may actually point to a pattern of deception, the witch doctors claim. The problem is that increasing government intrusion into our personal lives virtually guarantees that sooner or later all of

us will encounter someone from our government "here to help us" who will attempt to use these devices on us. As in all cases of this sort, one's best defense is education.

You will know that you are involved in kinesiology-type interrogation techniques when you are told by official government representatives to report to some sort of questioning center at a precise hour. This type of interrogation is never undertaken in familiar surroundings or in a comfortable, carpeted, furnished office. When motel rooms are used, for instance, an inspector may take out the rug, move in straight-backed wooden chairs and plain desks without fixtures.

On arrival, you will encounter hostile, suspicious, unsmiling stares from reception personnel. There will be no chitchat, only curt, unsmiling responses to small questions.

No matter how disrupted your personal schedule may be, late arrival for these interviews is considered prima facie evidence of guilt. An early arrival—more than 15 minutes before the appointed time—is also suspicious. Most experts in counterkinesiology advise showing up 10 to 12 minutes early with a good book or magazine. Showing up early without something to pass the time is always suspicious.

Be doubly suspicious of a kinesic interview if the receptionist makes a crack to an interviewer that his 3:00 "tax avoider" or "drug pusher" has arrived, or otherwise applies stress to what is already a stressful circumstance. If the interrogator's room is extremely stark, with few pieces of furniture and a completely clean desk, and 1) you are asked to sit in a stiff, straight-backed, armless chair; 2) the interrogator sits right in front of you, or 3) the distance between him and you is minimal, you are about to experience a kinesic interview.

It sounds like something out of a B-grade 1930s gangster movie, but the interrogator may sit so close that both persons' legs touch. One way of checking for certain that you are about to be grilled is to move around so that a desk or another chair is between you and the interrogator. If he or she objects, kinesic techniques are confirmed.

One woman undergoing this sort of abuse at the hand of a child-welfare social worker moved several times till the interrogator actually cornered her in against the wall before finally sitting down. She fled the room and filed sexual harassment charges against the worker. Unfortunately, in our present society only sexual harassment produces more immediate presumption of guilt than child abuse.

This woman, having had extensive prior military training in interrogation, did the best thing possible: fighting fire with fire.

In starting out in the interrogation, the interviewer will take great pains to establish a baseline on the victim. This may include random small talk of a most innocuous nature so that he can determine how often you answer after a big swallow, keep your eyes closed or diverted, sit with crossed arms and legs, scratch your head or butt, uncross your legs, or whatever. The interrogator may stare intently at your genitalia in an attempt to fluster and unnerve you.

Many otherwise perfectly natural body movements are read as signs of guilt. Some are contradictory, but that does not seem to be a particular problem for modern psychological interrogators.

Being seen as overly gregarious, especially if one chats nervously during the initial stages of interrogation and as conversation shifts into the main questioning period, is also taken as a sign of guilt. Psychologist interrogators also look closely at this time to discover if you are an introvert or extrovert. Different evaluation techniques apply, depending on whether you are outgoing or basically inward looking.

Counter this ploy by only answering questions and comments offered in a most direct, concise fashion. It is quite difficult for some of us, but you should answer the questions asked in only the narrowest manner possible. Do not volunteer information of any kind or become chatty in an attempt to fill an embarrassing void or pause with conversational noise.

This is extremely important. Skilled interrogators with a talkative victim on hand will simply shut up, allowing long periods of silence to intervene. Japanese businessmen often negotiate in silence, a device that few Americans can handle adequately. If an interrogator responds by parroting or paraphrasing your comments, again be cautious—this is a device known in the trade as nondirect counseling.

At this point, remember to speak quietly, confidently, and only about subjects related to the topic of discussion. Simply relax, let a baseline be established in normal, quiet, reserved conversation. Act naturally without talking very much. Those who talk on and on, interrupt continually, and anticipate questions are always regarded as guilty.

Supposedly, interrogators look for clusters of four signs indicating (in their minds) that you are lying. These responses will be induced by formula questions calculated to create peak stress and anxiety. They may also surface as a result of the color of your clothes—brown is bad, blue is best—length of hair, cleanliness of your clothes and hands, and your general deportment.

Leading questions may include, "Who do you personally think is likely to make a silencer for their rifle?" If one answers, "Just about anybody because they are so simple and easy to construct," a kinesic interrogator will immediately assume you have made a silencer because you are trying to spread the guilt around for so nefarious an undertaking.

Similarly, if he asks, "Did you make this silencer?" and your response is adamantly that you have *not*, this will also be construed as being a sure sign of guilt. At the very least, the interrogator will assume that he is on the correct track. Under these circumstances never protest one's innocence long and hard. Those who do are presumed guilty and will be pressured even harder.

Modern interrogators believe that innocent people want guilty people severely punished and that guilty people want guilty parties to receive counseling, understanding, or help. All direct questions related to guilt and innocence are assumed to be answered in this manner.

At this point, interrogators look intently for signs of nervousness, including licking of lips, hoarseness, nervous laughter, nervous body movements, and rubbing of hands and crossing of legs. If these actions did not occur during the baseline portion of interrogation but do later, you are in big trouble with the interrogator.

By their own manner of dress, facial expressions, shifts in questions, and general demeanor—as well as the size of the furniture in the office—professional interrogators will attempt to dominate an interviewee. They will never show signs of disbelief or insincerity. By intently studying the victim's comfort zone, interrogators attempt to gain advantage. Usually, good interrogators will lean toward the victim to further intrude into his privacy. Any line of questioning that is perceived as uncomfortable to the victim will, at least briefly, be pursued.

Trained professionals claim a 100 percent increase in confession rates using these devices.

Whenever you are at your peak of tenseness, interviewers believe that crossing your legs, moving your hands, or shifting from side to side is almost always a sure sign of guilt. Cracking voices, dryness of the mouth, requests for water, and throat clearing are again considered signs of nervousness in response to stressful situations (e.g., being forced to lie).

Indefinite phrases such as "may," "maybe," "probably he didn't do it," "not possible," or "I couldn't have done it" are also pounced on by kinesic interrogators.

After perhaps an hour of an intense interrogation, a skilled interviewer will start to exhibit some weird body movements, such as rubbing his upper arm, parting his hair with his fingers, rubbing his neck or chin, or any number of others. These are done entirely to determine whether the victim will unconsciously mimic them. Those who do are assumed to have fallen under the control of their interrogator. This device is known in the trade as mirroring. Be alert for it.

Another device used extensively by a professional interrogator toward the end of an especially acrimonious session includes breaking eye contact, pretending boredom, stopping completely to take copious notes, or even excusing himself for a few minutes. Generally, the interrogator will leave the room briefly to take notes. As a counter, one can do the same thing but must do so more subtly than the interrogator. Breaking eye contact or looking away continually before the interrogator does so is a very bad sign (to him).

Skilled interrogators want to determine how much their victims talk with their hands. It is assumed that extroverts use their hands and arms wildly during conversations. Introverts simply sit on them—unless they are lying. An introvert who suddenly uses hand gestures is assumed to be a liar.

Interviewers always look for any hint of a blush, bouncing Adam's apples, and throbbing carotid arteries. People who show up for interrogation and immediately start complaining are always branded as guilty liars—even if the interrogator doesn't know yet what they are lying about.

Interrogators will, in the preliminary chitchat, try to develop common ground from some thin thread of common identification. This may be as distant as "my wife's friend lived in the same city in which you grew up." Be wary of identifying with the agent in

any regard. Be careful how much background information you provide, as already mentioned. Answer only questions asked as narrowly as possible.

When one must say "no" to an agent, do so simply and evenly without shifting in your chair or losing your voice. Look the guy right in the eye, leave both feet flat on the ground, and don't answer breathlessly.

Eye contact is important to many interrogators. Any break may be construed negatively. Also, eye movements that include blinking or shifting—even momentarily—are bad.

Rubbing your chin, nose, or neck during questioning is forbidden. When asked by an IRS agent if you purposefully neglected to include income in a tax return, if you cross your legs, rub your nose, or break eye contact, the agent will tear completely through the return. For trendy kinesics-trained interrogators, it does not matter that no collaborating evidence exists. He will manufacture it if his search does not turn some up.

Victims who lean away or turn sideways to an interrogator are presumed guilty. As you would expect, toe tapping is bad, and victims who slouch in their chairs are presumed to have given up. Those into kinesics will assume they are getting honest, straightforward answers from a chair slouch. Such a person is considered to be under their control. Yet experts advise that you not slouch at least till well into the interview, when it is done completely by your prior design.

Practical, thinking people can readily determine that most of these indicators are fairly bogus and can, as a result, be on their guard against them. However, most people cannot sit for more than an hour without crossing their legs, breaking eye contact, or rubbing or scratching something.

Experts suggest that people try to do as much moving around during the initial benchmark phase of the interrogation and then sit as quietly as possible. Patiently wait out the kinesics-trained interrogator. Never admit anything. When really pressed by an interrogator who gets into your space, react calmly and patiently. Concentrate on something real, such as the the interviewer's chair or the desk to the side. It may help to quietly and secretly slide your foot until it is pressing hard against a table or chair leg.

Some experts believe that one should lie often to lie well. Others are like Abraham Lincoln, who advised, "If you tell the truth, you don't have to remember what you said."

Whenever the interview gets tough—as they usually do—think about something tangible and keep answers quick and crisp. Move as little as possible and sit on your hands if you need to. Relax and understand that this is a giant game of witch-doctorism and get on with it.

Interrogators assume that they will dominate and eventually, using some of their devices, make victims confess. Tell yourself going in that this is what the other guy intends. Knowing what games will be played is helpful. Keep in mind that if the IRS agent already had bankable proof that you had hid income, he wouldn't need to work you over.

BIBLIOGRAPHY

Clifton, Charles. *Deception Detection: Winning the Polygraph Game*. Boulder, CO: Paladin Press, 1991.

French, Scott and Paul van Houten, Ph.D. *Never Say Lie*. Boulder, CO: Paladin Press, 1987.

CHAPTER

Lie Detectors

34

I n spite of the fact that virtually everyone in our society has heard of machines that detect whether a person is telling a lie, very few citizens know much about how these machines actually work, either internally or externally. As you might suppose, acceptance of these devices is cut on a very fine line.

Law enforcement personnel into controlling humans by the easiest method possible generally join with those who make their living administering lie detector tests in approving the tests. On the other side of the issue are those in the legal and business world who have taken time to understand lie detectors. Those who know how the tests work, how they are administered, and something about their past track record have little confidence in these machines. Most knowledgeable people agree that with just a smattering of study and practice the machines can always be beaten.

From spring 1975 till mid-1988 when the U.S. Polygraph Protection Act outlawed many abuses in the employment of these devices, an estimated 4 million people per year were tested. The quality of those administering the tests was said to vary from schlock to reasonably competent.

As all fads eventually do, this one diminished in intensity mostly on its own. Not only did federal law have a dampening effect on lie testing, employers both private and civil came to recognize that even under the most favorable circumstances, test success rates were only about 78 percent. In many cases, determining who was lying by these results was about equal in accuracy to random guessing.

Equally important, as lie detector tests became common and potential victims knew they had to take them, better and more effective methods of neutralizing them also became more widely known. Today, lie detectors are infrequently used except by implicit consent for very specific reasons, such as for Supreme Court nominees. One hears little about them, and of course any information or conclusions garnered from lie detectors remain outside legal use in U.S. courts of law.

Because lie detectors can be beaten by people who know how they work, they are not held in high regard by many in the law enforcement field. (Photo by Ragnar Benson.)

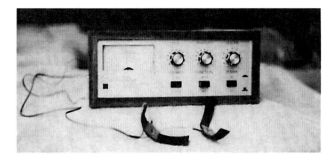

The Galvanic Skin Response (GSR) monitor measures skin conductance. (Unless otherwise noted, photos from *Never Say Lie* by Scott French and Paul van Houten.)

Human interrogation in one form or another has been around since the first kid tried to tell his mother a story. Real, somewhat scientific attempts to use electronic means of discerning the truth were jump-started right after World War II by John Reid. Reid did a great deal of study on involuntary human responses in lying and measuring these conditions via electronic means. Eventually, he published a paper on the proper interaction between sensitive electronic measuring devices and questions given to humans undergoing "analysis." This work was and still is considered a benchmark in the industry.

As currently deployed, lie detector machines cost between $200 (for simple machines) and $5,000 for a five-channel monster affectionately, and perhaps erroneously, known as the "fact finder." No matter what the cost nor how many different human functions they monitor, polygraph examiners know that no machine will work other than randomly unless the victim believes it will. In that regard, more imposing machines induce greater fear and thus more respect in the hearts and minds of those on whom they are unleashed.

Typical lie detector sessions take between 20 minutes and an hour. Businesses and government employees pay examiners between $30 and $150 per analysis. About half the states license examiners. Licensing does not, of course, guarantee fair, honest testing, but it does limit competition, providing greater income to examiners who, on average, knock down between 40 and 50 grand per year.

Polygraph exams are usually administered in sparse, austere little rooms not unlike the interrogation offices previously mentioned. The room and equipment, including the machine, may be rented and set up especially for the occasion. Machines will always be out in plain view on a bare desk where the victim can see wires, gauges, and paper plotters.

Most common are three-channel machines recording heart rate, skin conductance, and rate of breathing. Some machines also record a second breathing rate. Rubber tubes called pneumographs are placed around the test-taker's chest. Wires run from it to the machine.

Heart rate is plotted through a blood pressure cuff placed around the biceps. Skin conductance is measured through electrodes fastened to the ends of one's fingers. Once wired to all of this claptrap, the average person cannot but feel threatened. This is not something one does every day nor would do now, were a well-paying job or legal proceeding not dependent on the outcome.

Those being examined are hooked up and then sat down in the plain, wood armless chair.

Nothing is done by the examiner, receptionist or anyone else involved in the test to calm your nerves. Some examiners are ex-police officers, private detectives, or even ex-CIA employees. However, most are average high school graduates who have taken a six-week training course followed by nine months of apprenticeship.

As with other voluntary forms of interrogation, you must be on time for this interview, lest your examiners automatically assume guilt. Tardiness equals guilt.

During the initial stages—meeting the examiner, receiving instructions, and being hooked to all the wire—try at all times to appear friendly and confident. Cooperate without being glib or even talking very much. Never make insulting comments about the machine, process, or technician. For that matter, do not make any unsolicited comments at all. Since lie detector tests are supposedly voluntary, the operator should have a consent form available for your signature.

Usually, examiners will start with a series of tests calculated to demonstrate the dominance of their machine over an individual. This might include asking you to pick a playing card from a regular deck. You may be asked to not reveal the card but to simply concentrate on it. Examiners will then ask such questions as, "Is it spade?" "A face card?" etc. As part of the test, you will be told to lie to conceal the card's identity. Eventually, the examiner will triumphantly reveal exactly which card you have in your hand.

Experts maintain that this is totally fraudulent. A marked deck is used in a maneuver to convince you that the machine is indeed infallible. When examiners use this device or a variation thereof, they *always* use marked cards. Some will lay their cards out in such a way that their value is known by the inspector. At this point, examiners cannot risk having their process discredited by failure—keep this in mind no matter which initiation scam the technician chooses to use.

Some employ numbers rather than cards, but always know that trickery and illusion are involved. Do not make a big deal about this process. The plan is to pass the test, not prove how smart or well-informed you are. It's better to allow the inspector to believe he is master of the situation.

During the course of the actual lie detector test, three types of questions are usually asked. You must learn to accurately identify these categories of questions. Unless you master this portion of the test, you may not be able to lie like the proverbial Persian rug—undetected.

First are *relevant questions*. These are questions that are directly related to the investigation and are always narrow and specific.

- Did you take the hundred dollars from the cash register the evening of July 23?
- Did you sexually harass the waitress?

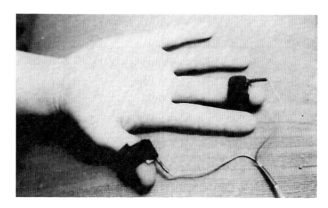

Skin conductance is measured through electrodes fastened to the ends of one's fingers.

- Did you say or do anything to threaten her job situation, as reported in her complaint?

Relevant questions are not hard to spot. They are usually the reason you consented (or have been coerced) to take a lie detector test in the first place. They relate to a specific incident, crime, or complaint.

Second are *irrelevant questions*. These are extremely important questions even though they have nothing directly to do with issues at hand. These questions establish a baseline against which various other levels of response are compared. Be very cautious with these. Differences between these and other questions establish one's guilt.

- Is today Friday?
- Is your name really Luke Carlson?
- Do you really want the job as night watchman?
- Are we in the state of California?

Usually irrelevant questions are easy to spot, but in the case of the second question an examiner may honestly believe his client may not be who he says he is. If you are suspected of hiding a true identity, the question suddenly falls into the relevant category.

Third are *control questions*. These are the tough ones that you absolutely must identify correctly to pass the test. They are very close to relevant questions but not really quite that direct. These questions are calculated to produce a fairly strong response, which is then used as a comparison with irrelevant questions. Since it is tough even for examiners to separate these questions, they are not as common as they once were. Examiners seem to realize that these are wild cards that are tough to decipher in a lie/truth context.

- *Have you ever stolen money from anyone?*

  You would have to conclude that everyone in our society has stolen some amount of money at some time. Those so questioned would immediately wonder whether to truthfully say yes, or to lie, giving an answer the examiner knows is false, producing a questionable reading on the machine.

- *Do you know anyone in the Ajax Company who has been sexually harassed?*

  Obviously, this is a subjective question that is virtually impossible for the average person to answer truthfully if there are more than 30 people employed at Ajax.

- *Is there anything about the incident on January 18 that you have not told me about?*

  If the incident was complex, you could validly wonder if you had correctly recalled all of the details. Your response would reflect that indecision, perhaps including an intense desire to be truthful, even if you do not know in what way to be truthful.

Different examiners have various methods of mixing questions based on training and what they believe has worked in the past. Many honestly wish to gauge the victim's integrity properly against control and relevant questions. Yet anyone forced to endure a test must be alert to the mix, understanding that one type of question forms a standard or benchmark while the other gets the subject riled up and may induce an elevated heart rate, heavier breathing, and different skin conductivity, thus indicating untruthfulness.

Fortunately, you are not at the mercy of the man and his inking machine. Common countermeasures are available that will produce indecisive results or, if mastered, will lead to positive results (you lied like a rug, but the machine couldn't tell).

No matter what questions are thrown out, continue to breathe normally in a measured sort of way. Private pilots learn this technique when flying their light planes too high over mountains with no auxiliary oxygen aboard. Do not hold onto a breath, empty the lungs, or otherwise deviate from a normal pattern established at the start of the test. Focus on this task.

When an examiner asks you something that is obviously an irrelevant or control question, you should make a quiet but invisible attempt to influence the response read by the machine. Probably the best of these is to take a short, choppy breath of air, flex an arm muscle—of the arm not hooked up to the machine—and to pucker your anus hard for five or six seconds.

Other controls include pressing your toes hard against a desk, the floor, or a chair leg; biting your tongue or cheek; or pinching your thigh high up in the crotch.

Obviously, not all these devices are possible when you are being watched closely. One old, old standby involves placing a small tack in the shoe, which you press when control questions are being asked.

All of these devices, if done subtly, create control responses that, when measured against relevant question responses where you attempt to remain as quiet as possible, produce machine readings that at worst are indecisive and at best are identical.

Some survivors of lie detector tests also report excellent results by thinking about their girlfriends or a particularly interesting picture when asked control questions.

Shifting position, coughing, sneezing, or yawning also all work to obliterate a polygraph test. Yet these devices are considered overly blatant in most circumstances. Trained examiners quickly spot these type of ruses, raising their suspicions. It is best to stay with small, covert countermeasures that have some hope of escaping an inspector's eagle eye. Remember that you cannot be judged deceptive if responses to control questions are greater than or equal to responses to relevant questions.

Invariably, questions regarding chemical countermeasures surface. Will a couple of stout belts of whiskey help, for instance? Extensive testing indicates that alcohol, tranquilizers, and such will probably lull a user into complacency to the extent that he cannot effectively deploy the needed mechanical countermeasures. Some questions must be critically analyzed before a response is made. At times, lie detector technicians ask questions calculated to force everyone to lie. Those on Valium or two jolts of corn whiskey may not be sufficiently alert to handle these type of situations.

Some researchers have done a great deal of work evaluating various drugs and their effects on the machine. They discovered that only one—a fairly new drug, trade named Inderal, has potential to best the box. Generically, it is known as a propranocol or beta blocker. Inderal is usually prescribed for high blood pressure. It is not a tranquilizer in the same category as Valium. Inderal has been prescribed by medical doctors in single 40 mg doses as a deterrent to stage fright when taken two hours before the performance. It is also occasionally prescribed as a prophylactic for migraine headaches. However, if you do not have a prescription or cannot somehow bring it in from overseas, it seems unlikely that a physician will prescribe Inderal for a lie detector test.

Excellent controlled tests indicate that Inderal taken two hours before a session in 40 mg doses will provide a 70 to 100 percent deception rate. Those who take time to learn how lie detector tests are administered and also take Inderal in conjunction with countermeasures appear to have maximum avoidance rates.

Successful lie detector operators absolutely must bring you to a high state of apprehension by which they convince you that their machines are infallible. There are even instances on record where examiners have taken common household colanders used to wash vegetables, soldered wires to the back, and run them to a Xerox machine. Inside the copy machine, they have placed a typed sheet reading, "He's lying."

The examiners then sternly sat their suspects down on a bare stool, placed the colander over their heads, and began asking questions. Whenever they got an answer they believed was cheeky or bogus, they hit the machine copy button. Sure enough, out came a note saying, "He's lying." Reportedly, several confessions were wrung from suspects through these bogus methods.

Ideally, anyone who finds he must submit to a lie detector test should have a chance to organize a dress rehearsal before enduring the real thing. In the real world, this seldom happens.

Go in confident that the technician will try to blow a great deal of smoke, that the machines are so inherently inaccurate that their results cannot be used in court, and that they can be beaten by evaluating the examiner's questions and applying appropriate countermeasures.

BIBLIOGRAPHY

Clifton, Charles. *Deception Detection: Winning the Polygraph Game*. Boulder, CO: Paladin Press, 1991.

French, Scott and Paul van Houten, Ph.D. *Never Say Lie*. Boulder, CO: Paladin Press, 1978.

CHAPTER

Drunk Driving Charge

35

Unfortunately, the first contact most men of action are likely to have with the law involves drunk driving. Several factors contribute to this syndrome, including a natural growing process whereby everyone must discover what is important to them personally, how to live and perhaps die with these priorities, and the ever-changing way in which society looks at public drunkenness, including political processes that define misuse of alcohol. Rational men take these things into consideration, even though the law, as one Dickens character once said, is often "an ass."

In direct response to such political pressure groups as Mothers Against Drunk Driving (MADD), many states have recently lowered their statute blood alcohol content levels required for prima facie drunk driving from .10 to .08 percent (e.g., Virginia). In some cases, attempts have even been made to lower standards to .00 for those under 25 years of age. Going by this, just a quick shot of breath freshener or even mouthwash could easily produce a drunk driver. Just a few years back, blood alcohol standards necessary for presumptive drunk driving were .15 percent!

The personal capacity to handle booze while still remaining functionally coherent ranges all over the map. Cases on record document levels of .5 to .6 percent and climbing, and those so loaded could still understand and answer questions in an articulate, reasonably appropriate fashion.

But because of arbitrary "one size fits all" standards, drunk driving is our nation's most common criminal offense. Settling these offenses provides a significant portion of income to attorneys who choose to specialize in this type of law. Legal fees alone are punitive for even minor drunk driving charges. A really important drunk driving case costs from $15,000 to $20,000 to settle. Even modest, open-and-shut drunk driving cases wherein the attorney is not expert at finding loopholes and the client is resigned to his fate, will run $1,500 for legal fees alone.

(Photo by D. Kuhn.)

Drunk driving is also profitable for cops who specialize in this area of enforcement. They pull in extra income from overtime, expert witness fees, and perhaps other fees that legally come their way. Some cops who are good at it can be involved in three or four cases per day. In New Mexico, there have been so many drunk driving citations and the courts are so clogged with cases that cops often are scheduled for two or more testimonies at the same time. Some fortunate defendants have been released because their accuser couldn't show up in court.

Political accolades follow ambitious cops who have an especially aggressive record at taking "dangerous drunks" off the road. It is common practice for some police to stake out notorious taverns known for their crowd of after-work drinkers who get together to discuss business with each other. These police may mark tires and record the make and license plate numbers of vehicles parked at the bar. Often, they sit for hours down the road waiting for the hapless revelers to depart the bar, hop in their machines, and go motoring off for a citation. In California, for instance, it has become standard practice for a nondrinker to go weaving off down the road as a decoy for the police. As soon as that driver is stopped, all others depart safely, knowing that the diligent cop is otherwise employed.

Traffic stops made at points of entrapment are generally for routine offenses such as a loud muffler, blinking taillight, suspected seat belt infraction, and even crossing the outside yellow line. Any excuse will do so long as the officer can pull a suspected reveler over for a closer examination. This closer look, which traffic police attempt to arrange for themselves, is very important.

Those who—for whatever reason—absolutely must drive from a bar, should immediately on entering their auto roll down both front windows and turn the ventilation on full blast, in an attempt to blow away any booze and smoke odors. Cops place great stock in finding smell-type evidence as a prelude to a drunk driving citation. Mitigate this situation as much as possible.

Smart drivers who realize going in that they will be stopping for only a few toddies with the gang and who must continue on, either home or to the next round of toddies, take a few simple precautions. These include pacing themselves in the knowledge that as few as five regular beers or glasses of wine within one hour will legally intoxicate a 180-pound man in a state with a .10 standard. Drinkers can also cut back to five drinks in two hours and be sure to graze heavily on bar food while hoisting the booze.

If you find that you must both drink and drive, you absolutely must eat something, even if it's pickled turkey gizzards. In times past, it was common for some bars to not have so much as a peanut available to munch. Modern court liability rulings have changed all that. Most bars now have something to eat, ranging from stale trail mix to popcorn. (At the turn of the century, saloons commonly put on a spread of free food calculated to entice patrons to drink. This fortunate custom seems to be returning.)

Whatever the situation, experts recommend that you never go into a bar to drink where absolutely nothing is available to eat.

After pulling a cork or two, chug down two glasses of plain water along with two aspirin before leaving the bar. Go into the john and check your appearance in minute detail to avoid appearing disheveled or unruly. Appearance ranks right up there with smell with cops who pull motorists over on suspicion of drunk driving. Some experts even recommend that you suck Hall's Mentholyptus Cough Drops as a means of masking the smell of alcohol on your breath and burning up body alcohol.

After smell and general appearance, cops look for neatly trimmed hair, clean shirt fronts and sleeve cuffs, and the presence of a beard. Flushed faces and glassy eyes alone are also giveaways. These last two are tough to disguise if you have really had six or eight belts with no food. Splash a little water on your face anyway before leaving the bar. It can do no harm.

Slurred, slow, confused speech is a quick, dirty method cops use as an indicator of a score. Generally, they use the opportunity of asking for the vehicle registration and driver's license to determine if the driver delays his answer, shrugs, or uses "ahh" extensively when speaking. Typical American drivers do not know immediately where these documents are located. You can get away with speaking to the cop minimally, but if there is a question when leaving the bar about driving home, have the registration, license, and insurance certificate handy. Cops often use this fumble-search-frustration time to ask a driver, "Been drinkin' buddy?"

The law may also ask permission to do a routine search of the vehicle. These searches cannot legally be done without the driver's consent. Many experts urge that permission always be denied even if you know that there are no incriminating items on board. One driver stopped routinely was carrying his trash to the dump. He consented to a search and was cited for open beer bottles. It took him months of expensive court appearances and letter writing to settle that problem.

Experts also suggest that if you have been drinking that you do not lie about the fact. It's better to answer, "Yes, but I haven't had a drink for two hours, since when I ate two big hamburgers and danced with four different, very wild women."

If they cannot smell, see, or hear any signs of intoxication, law officers may not attempt a field sobriety test. However, if a cop does ask that you step out and do some routine field sobriety tests, you are well-advised to do so only if you are absolutely certain you can pass.

Some wise-ass punks, who count backwards from 20 rather than 10, walk the center strip barefoot, or run round and round the police cruiser when asked to perform much simpler tasks will get hauled in for a Breathalyzer test even if they are stone, cold sober.

Cops want and expect precise compliance. Usually, they do not ask for field sobriety tests unless they are reasonably convinced that they have sufficient grounds to haul your weary ass to the station for a chemical test. Portable Breathalyzer tests are notoriously inaccurate and are not generally admissible as evidence in court.

You can legally refuse to do a field sobriety test. Rather than just refusing, claim extremely bad diarrhea to avoid these roadside monkeyshines.

Although cops cannot force you to take a sobriety test, it is absolutely mandatory under implied consent statutes that you take a chemical test back at the station if it is requested by the authorities. You can refuse, but your license will be summarily revoked.

Chemical tests are administered at police headquarters before you can call an attorney. In most cases, time is *not* on the driver's side. Drinkers who left the joint having punched down six tall ones may not be legally drunk when stopped, but 30 minutes or so later, or just about the time they arrive back at police headquarters, they may really be blitzed.

Generally, the law mandates suspension of driving privileges for refusal to take the breath test, but in some cases this is a desirable alternative. If the DUI is a second offense, or an accident involving bodily injury is involved, legal experts advise, "Don't take the test." Let your attorney sort it out later.

Attorneys specialize. Some Mormon attorneys in my state won't touch a DUI with a bundle of $100 bills. If cited for a DUI, do not plead guilty before talking to an excellent, well-recommended attorney who has a track record of winning drunk driving cases. How do you find a good DUI specialist? Ask your company attorney, the cops, clerks at district court, or an experienced brother-in-law. Many bartenders are knowledgeable in this area. Always check references.

No matter what else happens, experts caution drunk drivers to never, ever plead guilty to a drunk-driving charge in hopes of receiving a reduced sentence. A guilty plea destroys your ability to do any pretrial investigation or engage in any discovery. In many cases, shrewd attorneys can use one or more of several methods to destroy a cop's case during a jury trial, but not if you have already entered a guilty plea.

Without chemical tests, there is little difference between alcohol and other drug-related DUI charges. It is considered unwise to consent to blood or urine analysis under any circumstances, especially if you have used illegal drugs within the previous week. Should a cop suspect other drugs, it may be wise to consent quickly to a breath test that can check only for alcohol before pressure builds to do complete drug tests as well.

As a result of political pressure that validly recognizes that on any given Friday hundreds of legally drunk drivers infest our nation's highways, state and local police have started full-scale deployment of preventive roadblocks. There are a few measures that alert drivers can use to counter this threat. Experts recommend using side streets or roads not likely to have drunk-driver roadblocks. You can legally turn around to avoid a roadblock as long as the turn is not abrupt and does not endanger others. It is best under these circumstances, to turn around without the cops knowing.

Good lawyers who commonly work DUI cases have dozens of little subterfuges they can use to get their clients off the hook. Some are procedural, and some relate to plain old schlock enforcement of the rules by police. Although these devices are often effective, they are always costly in terms of work missed, calories consumed in worrying, and money spent for legal fees.

The best advice, of course, is not to drink and drive. Have a designated driver or call a cab or a friend. Experienced people agree that if you do drink and drive, extreme caution at the front end is better than sharp legal work at the other. Don't drive while exhibiting common signs of inebriation. Park your car down the street in the church lot. Walk from bar to car, get everything in order, and then drive home by a route unlikely to be blocked by the police. Take all precautions that might ameliorate your specific circumstances.

Drunk driving is a valid social concern in this country. A tragically large number of vehicle accidents involve alcohol in some form.

Men of action are generally more interested in true adventures than in coming up with thousands of dollars to fight a legal case that could easily have been avoided. Usually, these dollars are far better spent for guns or explosives.

Yet one still must know how to deal with hard-ass cops earning extra money and publicity in a politically popular milieu.

BIBLIOGRAPHY

Judge X. *How to Avoid a Drunk Driving Conviction.* Port Townsend, WA: Loompanics, Unlimited, 1993.

Taranyino, John A. *DWI Defense Forms and Checklists.* Santa Ana, CA: James Publishing, 1989.

CHAPTER

Caching

36

For several decades now weapons and materiel caching has had both strategic and tactical military importance. In cases where caching played a major role in the outcome of hostilities, it was the Communists who usually made best use of the procedure. This was true in World War II France and Italy and 20 years later in Vietnam. Caching may be one of the few devices used by Communists that men of action may wish to appropriate for their own.

At the time of Nazi occupation of France in June 1940, French Communists were the only effective opposition. In large measure, Vichy French Republicans (meaning those French not overtly sympathetic to the National Socialists but not Communist) were almost indifferent to the Nazi occupation. As long as the Germans basically left them alone, the Vichy French were initially willing to try to accommodate rather than continue to fight.

Later this accommodation turned to opposition, but early on, after the decisive defeat of the French

government, the Communists were the only game in town. It is ironic, in retrospect, that we supported hard-core Communists in World War II, just as there will be a bit of irony to men of action in adopting techniques they perfected.

Some very strange anomalies developed in occupied France. Madeleine, an 18-year-old French girl, was active in a small Communist cell in Paris. She was given the codename of Renee, and to this day we do not know anything more about her other than these names.

Renee and the area Resistance leader were attempting to blow up a bridge when they were discovered by a German patrol. He was shot dead, but she escaped by hiding in the tall brush growing near the bridge. His death left her in charge of their central Paris cell.

Communist cells of the era operated with a life-and-death military efficiency. Orders were given and the results they brought were measured as part of a broad political objective rather than by the impact these orders might have on the individual

Rifles, Sten guns, Bren guns, and mortars are packed into cache tubes for delivery to the French Resistance. (Photos from *Modern Weapons Caching* by Ragnar Benson. This photo courtesy of Imperial War Museum, London, England.)

life, health, and safety of local participants. As is true with army leaders, they looked at hoped-for results after subtracting likely losses, including the loss of entire cells out in some of the districts. Based on these cold, hard calculations, the leaders made their decisions.

The decision to order an 18-year-old girl to kill one German officer made absolutely no sense except in the aggregate picture as a means of recruiting additional cell members, demoralizing the enemy, and letting supply givers in the United Kingdom know that the Resistance could deliver.

When Renee got her orders, she looked around to see who in the cell could carry them out, only to discover she was it. An ancient French revolver cached with a few extra rounds of ammo became her sole legacy from her fallen leader. She retrieved the pistol, wrapped in a greasy cloth, from under a tile in a dead-end alley, and practiced dry-firing one night. The next morning, she took off on her bicycle looking for a Nazi officer.

French sports fishermen had reported that a German Gestapo chief walked Pont de Solferino, a bridge over the Seine, every Sunday morning with Prussian regularity. She leaned her bicycle against a tree and quickly walked up behind the officer, who was strolling with his hands behind his back, contemplating nothing except the obvious sound of a

female approaching over the cobbles. As she closed, he turned, probably to ogle her.

She fired once point-blank in his face. The tough, old Prussian stood like a steel post rather than crumpling from the shot. Perhaps the old pistol rounds were weak. She fired again into his chest. He was still on his feet, although technically dead.

Quickly, Renee bent to retrieve the major's Luger pistol and the few rounds of ammo he carried and placed them in her handbag next to the revolver. After all, British agents in Paris in July 1940 had reported only two rifles and two pistols in the entire weapons cache of all Paris cells! Another weapon from the assassinated officer had tremendous value, especially given the fact that two precious rounds of ammo had been consumed, and no one seemed to be taking any notice of the incident.

Renee was not a trained professional, although she tried to act the part. Jumping on her bicycle, she pedaled off furiously down the stone quay. She heard the car for a second or two before it hit her. Cruelly and roughly, Renee was sideswiped into a broad skid across the pavement. A French Gestapo agent out riding with his girlfriend happened by and took his opportunity to apprehend her.

Later, Renee claimed that the most dangerous part of the mission involved riding back to Gestapo headquarters while the French mistress held a cocked pistol on her. Miraculously, she survived the war. In Paris, French police collaborating with their German occupiers interrogated her for weeks, attempting to learn names of other cell members, her section chief, and her weapon source. Although they tortured and killed another young Resistance member in front of her, Renee did not tell the Nazis anything.

She wrote a history of her involvement in the war in 1956, but the report filed in the archives of several U.S. universities did not even include her real name.

Caching was used again by Communists in Vietnam with incredibly good results—from their standpoint. In terms of providing an excellent advantage over despotic governments, caching has, at various times during the 20th century, proven extremely valuable. There is no reason to believe that this fact does not continue to be true. History is full of examples where a very few firearms and rounds of ammunition have decisively altered history. Fidel Castro, for instance, shot one of Batista's key radiomen with a previously cached sniper rifle. This happened in an early battle during which any reinforcements would have doomed all the rebels, including Fidel Castro.

Many men of action have concluded that caching may provide a needed benefit as the United States continues its slide toward lawless anarchy.

Before you attempt to engage in a valid caching strategy, however, you must know the differences between caching and storage. Some overlap exists, but caching implies hiding weapons, ammunition, food, and clothing that you simply cannot replace or function without and the discovery of which will lead to extreme penalties. Nazi occupiers, for instance, summarily executed any French citizen found in possession of any weapon or explosive, very similar to the BATF action at Waco. As a result, weapons and supplies must be removed from caches only when they are to be placed in immediate action. Existence of caches should always remain a closely held secret.

Storage, by contrast, is an attempt to accumulate needed scarce items in years of plenty. Stored items are ones needed in the future to provide support, but ownership of which is not prima facie evidence of some horrible crime. Storage implies scarcity. Caching implies great secrecy, extreme necessity, and scarcity. Caching may overlap storage in many instances, but storage always implies a flow in and out of materials. Cached items imply life and death for the owner.

Criteria as to which items are stored and which are cached vary dramatically from country to country and place to place. Peasant farmers were summarily executed for keeping food they raised for their families in the early 1930s in Russia. Until 1934 it was not illegal to own military firearms in the United States. The Bible speaks of worldwide famines so severe that owners of food will be killed if they are found storing or caching simple items or food.

Modern technology has dramatically influenced both the ability for caching safely and the ease with which a cache can be discovered. During World War II, great expensive, and often unsuccessful efforts were made to develop aluminum cache tubes packed with cosmoline-soaked weapons, tin-sealed ammunition, and explosives that remained "fresh" and usable over long periods in hostile circumstances. At times, these packages survived, but many

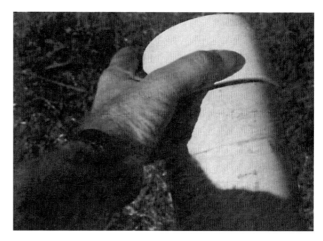

Installing the end cap on a 4-inch cache tube. Most cachers find that 4-inch tubes are too small for anything except ammunition and magazines, but it will hold a tremendous quantity of ammo.

accounts of their complete loss when they were placed in salt marshes, manure piles, or garbage dumps also abound.

Today, we have inexpensive plastic plumbing pipe readily available in every corner of the land This pipe will withstand all sorts of abuse from various elements, including acids, bases, strong salts, and virtually all other natural elements. These relatively cheap, finished cache containers can be placed in ocean estuaries, at the edge of geothermal springs, and even in sewers. Although they do not handle extreme heat or extensive physical abuse well, this failure is seen as minor in contrast to what was available 20 years ago.

The material of choice for citizens who choose to cache is 6- or 8-inch plastic sanitary drain refuse pipe available by the foot from most plumbing sup-

Vertically installed cache tubes are very difficult to relocate. It took great effort to dig this one out, which was in the ground for 8 years.

A new 60-inch section of 8-inch cache tube, ready to be filled with weapons.

Common 8-inch slip-type end cap used with a grease closure on a cache tube.

ply shops. Some novice builders try 4-inch pipe, but they soon discover that bigger is better for everything other than ammunition. For most rifles and shotguns 4-inch pipe is not big enough. Although common in most places, 4-inch pipe is manufactured in both a light and heavy gauge. Heavyweight 4-inch pipe is better if you use 4-inch stock, but it is frequently not available off the shelf.

Cache tubes are generally cut to about 60 inches long, depending on particular requirements. Most rifles (even sniper rifles) will easily fit into a 60-inch length.

Purchase two slip-type end caps of the correct size for the tube. One cap, on the bottom of the tube, should be permanently glued in place with ABS plastic pipe and fitting cement. Some cachers like to use female adapters and screw-type plugs placed in one end of the cache tube. These are relatively expensive, often tough to use in dirty caching environments, and are no more secure than simple grease-sealed slip caps, which can be taken off and put on quite easily.

The best plan is to use an 8-inch posthole digger to bore down 5 1/2 feet, producing a hole for cache tubes. Dig round, perfectly vertical holes that are clean and neat. Any extra dirt must be placed on a piece of canvas or in a bucket and carried off. Once these holes are filled with cache tubes, they are easy to disguise. Even a grass divot will hide them.

In most cases, a 2-foot extension made of 3/4-inch pipe must be added to the posthole auger shaft, allowing you to dig down deep enough to cover a 5-foot cache tube. Tubes must always be buried vertically with the top at least a foot beneath the surface. Modern, ultrasensitive metal detectors are likely to find buried cache tubes unless they are placed deeply in an obscure location.

Run a ring of heavy automotive or water-pump grease around both the tube cap and the tube body at the place where the cap slips onto the tube. Determine that the seal is water- and airtight if the cap builds compression when pushed down onto the tube. At times, internal compression is such that a tiny hole must be drilled in the cap to allow trapped air to escape. It is best, however, to build internal compression inside the tube that will keep water and air out.

Once in the ground, cache tubes cannot be removed except with a great deal of digging and disturbance. Grease-sealed slip caps are a bit tough to remove, especially after they have been underground a year or more. Use a piece of 2 x 4 stud to pry these caps off after removing the soil from the top. All locations must be carefully noted because buried cache tubes are easily lost.

Some small parts or ammunition may fall to the bottom of these long tubes, where they become essentially unreachable. Rather than using a long grabber arm or magnet, consider placing a false bottom inside the tube attached to a rope. You can easily pull up small items from the bottom of the tube as long as the rope isn't also lost down inside it.

Determined enemies will always be able to

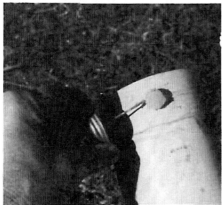

Top: Permanently glue the lower cap on the cache tube using ABS cement purchased from a plumbing supply house. Center: ABS cement used to attach caps to cache tubes. Bottom: 8-inch slip-type cap for cache tube with grease gun used to attach cap.

locate cache tubes. Doubling the distance from a retreat where the tubes are buried makes finding them four times more difficult. Bury them in unlikely, difficult places as far away as you can manage surreptitiously. Think of such places as in swamps, beneath hard-packed gravel roads, in steep hillsides, under rabbit pens, or in sloppy, manure-filled animal stalls. Some cache tube builders sink their tubes in streams or pond, figuring they will snorkel for them when needed.

In dire circumstances, you can hide tubes in fairly hot places (or what could become hot places) such as barbecue grills, incinerators, or chimneys. For these places, wrap the tube in an old space blanket first. Wire this reflective material to the tube rather than taping it or tying it with rope.

Modern electronic metal detectors can reach 12 feet in most soil to find a 3/4-inch steel pipe. These devices are sufficiently accurate that if the "Great White Father" wants to find a cache badly enough, his agents will always do so. It is possible to bury a great many chunks of iron around, slowing the process, but if you become a target, enough people with good, expensive metal detectors will be put on the ground to find the cache.

Defense against this reality involves being tight-mouthed about your caches and burying them several blocks away in the neighbor's flowerbed.

In these days of all-out assault on freedom-loving Americans, a great many items that citizens feel will be vital to their survival will find their way into caches. Under these circumstances, it is important that you do the job correctly, avoiding both deterioration of your precious supplies and detection by the bad guys.

BIBLIOGRAPHY

Benson, Ragnar. *Modern Weapons Caching.* Boulder, CO: Paladin Press, 1990.

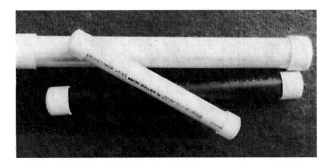

Smaller 1 1/4-, 1 1/2-, and 2-inch cache tubes with slip-type end caps. These are useful for storing scopes, ammo, laser sights, and other small parts within the full-size tube.

Common soil augers of the type used by farmers to set fence posts are available in sizes ranging from 6 to 12 inches. A 12-inch auger should be used to set most cache tubes.

A 3/4-inch common pipe connects the digging head of a soil auger with its turning handle.

Dig down into the ground 5 to 7 inches, depending on the length of the tube. Placing soil on the tarp (right) helps keep the visual evidence of installing the tube to a minimum.

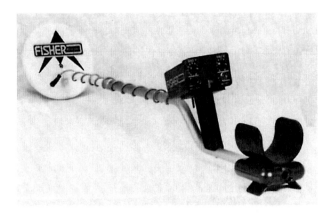

The Fisher 1265-X is a sensitive, deep-seeking, general-purpose treasure hunter's metal detector. (Photo courtesy of Fisher Research Laboratory.)

Sophisticated modern metal detectors like the Compass Scanner can be used under extremely difficult circumstances and can automatically retune themselves for varying ground conditions and earth composition. (Photo courtesy of Compass Electronics.)

CHAPTER

Snipers

37

Those who have given the concept any thought at all generally agree that we have entered an era when proper, precise use of sniper fire will be the deciding factor in many military and paramilitary actions. Because of several modern developments in both armament and confrontational philosophy, this will be true for the foreseeable future.

It was Soviet military planners who first postulated that a soldier is better served directing a large volume of fire *toward* a target rather than a few well-aimed shots at specific targets. Israeli soldiers make excellent use of this concept. Using Uzis, they spray a large volume of fire toward their enemies, causing them to keep their heads down. Advancing Israelis often neutralize enemy soldiers who cower in their trenches and respond to noise alone. In many cases, Israeli fire strikes such terror in the hearts of opposing soldiers that they simply run off.

Stalin, in response to charges of low quality in his armed forces, maintained that "there is a certain high quality to large quantities." Rather than teach marksmanship, which is difficult, Russians taught the direction of large volumes of fire toward a target. In most cases this philosophy simplified training.

Gradually, through the years, our own military drifted away from the concept of individual, accurate, long-range rifle fire pointed at specific enemy targets and looked to see how other militaries were training. Surveys were taken, and the truth emerged that the average U.S. recruit couldn't shoot well. Understandably, training quickly evolved into an exercise where soldiers learned to fire *toward* a target without exposing themselves to return fire.

As all this transpired, it became equally obvious that military operations are more effective if someone specializes in taking out specific enemy soldiers. It doesn't take a military genius to realize that having valuable line officers and noncommissioned officers sniped at from very long range

Springfield Armory's 700 BASR sniper rifle has a camouflaged fiberglass stock with a rubber recoil pad and Douglas heavy barrel. (Photos from *Modern Sniper Rifles* by Duncan Long. This photo courtesy of Springfield Armory.)

has an incredibly demoralizing effect. It can also hamper operations mightily! World War II taught Soviet generals the value of snipers. Although they didn't require their individual soldiers to do much more than make lots of noise, Red generals did start adding great numbers of trained snipers to their units. There is an inconsistency here, but the Soviets failed to notice it.

Soviet equipment, ammunition, and training limited their long-range shooting to distances of 400 to 600 meters at best. As many as one in 12 were designated snipers in the Soviet army. At the time, almost all U.S. soldiers would have qualified as snipers under the Soviet definition.

During the Vietnam War, special U.S. Marine and Army sniper units were formed, using the best equipment available at the time. But psychological factors entered the picture. The United States did not field as many snipers as it could have

logistically, or as planners would have liked, because it was extremely difficult to find enough men of the correct temperament. At Waco and Ruby Ridge, one of the first teams sent in after lines stabilized consisted of government snipers. Seemingly, there will always be government snipers willing to do the work, but their numbers will be limited by psychology and skill.

Modern snipers were also used in recent military situations. Marine snipers in Kuwait used special .50-caliber rifles, and it is reported that they made 2,000-yard strikes on Iraqi soldiers. Barrett, Inc. of Murfreesboro, Tennessee, enjoyed several months of hectic sales as they attempted to fill what then seemed to be unlimited orders.

In retrospect, experts agree that defenders at the Ruby Ridge and Waco would have enjoyed better success if they had had some excellent snipers in their own group—especially if those snipers could have been deployed outside the compound against the government. The final events would probably not have been changed or altered significantly unless these civilian snipers had done their work extremely well. Yet, combined with several other retreat-defense measures to be discussed in later chapters, the outcome might have been different.

Although expert snipers intensely dislike the analogy, successful sniping is—in some regards—similar to hunting. It combines tactics, fieldcraft, and marksmanship into one difficult-to-master, integrated pursuit. Sniping is on the far edge of hunting, relative to mastery of these skills.

Hunters seldom take shots of more than 250 yards, and their targets cannot shoot back. Game animals usually know the country far better than hunters or snipers, evening the contest a bit. In a military context, the struggle is often between snipers and average soldiers who may actually be protected because no attractive targets are among their group. Hunters are almost always better than average soldiers. But to say that sniping is military hunting is untrue. Skills required to snipe far surpass those needed for even the most skilled hunter.

Unfortunately, most people initially think in terms of sniper rifles and little else. Rifles and ancillary equipment are important. To be in the ballpark, a sniper rifle must shoot one minute of angle (MOA), or 1 inch at 100 yards, at a minimum. This degree of accuracy would print 8 inches at 800 yards, or nearly the outside envelope of accuracy with which a true sniper can make do. It is often humorous to hear people flippantly refer to rifle shots made in the 800-to-1,000-yard range as if they are commonly done.

Although 1/2- and 3/4-MOA rifles are available, the price is high. Other than a few exotic European rifles, sniper rifles are bolt actions. Most government agencies, including your local police, use Remington 700/M40 rifles, which come complete out of the box with tuned actions and match-grade heavy barrels. Civilians can purchase 700s as complete rifles with rugged composition stocks as police or varmint specials. They can also purchase 700 actions on which custom barrels are installed.

After several years' hiatus, Winchester is back in the market with an excellent Model 70 model called a Sharpshooter. With a bit of tuning, these

The spring-loaded telescoping legs on this aluminum bipod by Harris Engineering can lock in an open or folded position. (Photo courtesy of Harris Engineering.)

Winchesters will shoot 3/4 MOA. Reportedly, this model rifle is being used by the FBI.

Excellent 1/2-MOA sniper rifles can be made to use Sako actions and custom barrels, if one can survive the tariff. Fewer aftermarket accessories are available for Sako actions with heavy barrels, but most experts agree that if the package can be put together, it will be excellent.

Several aftermarket suppliers, such as McMillan in Phoenix, Arizona, and Bell and Carlson in Atwood, Kansas, offer fine aftermarket stocks suitable for sniper use. It has been a long, arduous march, but, gradually, other makers are coming on line. As mentioned, some major gun makers are even offering complete, out-of-the-box sniper rifles.

Custom builders can sink huge amounts of money into their sniper rifles, especially if one goes for a 1/2- or 3/4-MOA model—only needed if they intend to try shots in the 800-yard category.

Selecting a scope for these monsters can get hairy. In case it hasn't already become obvious, scoping your new sniper rifle will definitely separate a hunter from a sniper. Rather than paying $400 for a top-of-the-line Redfield, for instance, expect to pay a minimum of $800 to $1,000 for a superrugged, extremely accurate tactical-type scope. This scope will probably have a 30mm in tube as opposed to the 25mm found on scopes of hunting quality. These scopes will have bullet drop compensators, large external adjustment knobs that can be read from the rear, permanent metal lens covers, and sub-MOA adjustments. A proliferation of seemingly extra knobs will initially confuse the first-time buyer.

Experts claim that 10- to 12-power scopes are ideal and that variables are okay if they can be found, including genuine sniper features and matte finishes. The style of windage and elevation knobs, along with price, quickly identifies true sniper scopes. Unfortunately, very few acceptable models are commercially available. Sniper scopes need not have internal range finders. Several excellent belt models are available that work well.

Universally, snipers equip their rifles with extendable bipods. Currently, Harris has the U.S. market cornered for this item. It has three excellent styles, one of which certainly would suit the sniper rifle builder.

Any shooter worth his salt knows that just because a well-heeled dude shows up at the range with $3,000 worth of sniper equipment, it does not give any advance indication that the owner can hit targets at 500 yards consistently.

Excellent marksmanship requires in-depth knowledge of the scope, rifle, and conditions on the ground. If the first round strikes 10 inches low, is sighted in at 400 yards, and the scope has a 1/4-inch MOA, what is the proper correction? How will the ammunition perform and how far *really* is it to the target? Either the marksman must use a range finder or become extremely proficient in using sniper range estimation tricks.

At extreme ranges where snipers are most effective, scope adjustments are dramatic. It takes but 18 clicks on a 1/4-MOA scope, for instance, to go from a 100- to 300-yard zero, but 40 clicks going from a 600- to 800-yard zero. Windage adjustments are even more difficult because wind velocities are inconsistent and not easily estimated.

Good snipers become incredible techies with all of their charts, data, and statistics. They practice extensively on various varmints at miscellaneous ranges till they can make frequent one-shot kills on 6-inch ground squirrels or prairie dogs. They also spend several hours a week on dry-fire practice.

One cannot overemphasize how much time is required to study ballistic charts for custom reloading and doing actual field practice. Many experts claim it takes more than a year of daily dry-fire practice, weekly ballistic chart study, and monthly range time to become reasonably proficient at sniper-grade marksmanship. And this happens only after putting in large chunks of time studying equipment, investing perhaps $3,000, and mastering basic hunter/target rifle skills.

In some limited respects, scopes with range-finder reticle, bullet drop compensators, external focus, and wide field light-gathering ability have taken some of the sting out of locating a target and accurately adjusting fire. Nevertheless, sniper marksmanship is a finely tuned blend of academic study and physical coordination. Military-type scopes take time to get used to. Most first-time users find the many knobs and dials incredibly bewildering.

Those who are serious about the business will accumulate dozens of books enumerating many different sniper subjects from scope efficiency to range trajectories, velocities, effects of weather, and even ballistic coefficients. Some, but not all, snipers spend time varmint hunting. All spend time on the range and practicing at home.

Sniper fieldcraft is somewhat similar to sport hunting in that he who knows the country best and has a plan for operating in it generally gets an opportunity for a good shot at relatively modest ranges. Successful snipers spend a great deal of time minutely studying aerial photos and topographic maps of the area in which they intend to work. In cases where the sniper must often change the country in which he works, a great deal of very detailed study is necessary.

Good snipers learn exactly where even very obscure landforms can be found to hide their approach from the enemy. Their scrutiny tells them where to expect their quarry to walk, where all roads and paths lead, and—most important—from which points they can direct undetected fire on an unsuspecting quarry.

Snipers work best in reasonably static military circumstances where they have time to thoroughly learn the country and how the enemy will use it. Trench warfare in World War I, sieges such as Stalingrad and Kursk during World War II, and U.S. firebase camps in Vietnam provided an ideal environment for snipers.

At times, snipers have been dropped into new, strange, remote areas with instructions to take out specific targets. In these cases, snipers use past experience to evaluate maps and photos intelligently, as well as talking to people who have actually been there. On the ground, they realistically evaluate actual conditions as they find them. Good snipers are always willing to adjust quickly should what they see be different than intelligence had suggested.

Because fatigue is a problem, combat snipers usually work in pairs. Equipment, including the rifle, is switched back and forth on a regular basis. One man carries the heavy sniper rifle while another covers them both with an assault rifle. Each man also carries a heavy load of supporting gear, including notebook and pen, rope, flashlight, medical kit, two-way radio, extra camouflage, water bottle, ground cloth, binoculars, field rations, cleaning kit, gloves, tape, sidearm, knife, spotting scope, and, at times, a night vision device. Police snipers generally keep all this gear, plus other personal items, permanently packed in a bag ready for instant deployment.

Fieldcraft also implies effective use of camouflage, including the rifle and scope. Various commercial camouflage suits are available from which to choose, depending on the season and local conditions. According to virtually all the experts, the best all-round sniper-type camouflage is a ghillie suit.

These are earth-colored strips of heavy burlap cloth tied to a nylon net worn as a type of hood or shroud over one's head and shoulders. The fronts of ghillie suits are relatively smooth, to facilitate crawling through brush. Ideally, one would wear both a loose-net ghillie and a regular pair of appropriately colored cammie coveralls. Snipers also wear cammie head nets. Some of these outfits are so good that snipers have slowly, patiently crawled hundreds of yards over bare fields in wide-open spaces without being observed.

For those who have thought of tactics in only a hunting context, sniping tactics are much more cautious. Movement by a sniper team may total only 500 yards per day!

In this contest of skills, it will probably be the men who most patiently and skillfully use good stalking tactics who will win the engagement.

Whitetail deer, pheasants, and coyotes teach us that becoming frustrated, impatient, or scared and breaking cover will invariably lead to loss. Snipers must learn this lesson thoroughly.

Snipers must lurk carefully in the shadows and move slowly, paying great attention to detail. Good men never cross open areas, never take predictable paths, and never leave tracks, trash, or sign.

Patience and caution are the sniper's two greatest skills, explaining in part why one could validly be skeptical of the dude on the range with a $3,000 piece of equipment. Without knowing the fellow personally, it is impossible to know if patience and caution are really there, notwithstanding basic shooting skills.

Target detection is initially tough for snipers. Just as one does not see many deer in the woods the first few years he hunts, a sniper is very likely to overlook his targets. Effective snipers learn to work with partners who can spot a good target among a sea of rock and brush. They must learn to bring their buddies' eyes to the same spot as their own. Those who cannot will not be effective.

Picking the correct target among many possibilities is often difficult. Military snipers are admonished over and over to hit officers first, not relatively insignificant grunts, unless no officers are present or the grunt has the radio. Snipers who stay alive never take more than three shots from one position.

Getting into position requires thinking like the opposition in terms of travel direction, speed, and purpose. When selecting an ambush site, the sniper must choose one that gives him a clear field of fire and provides excellent cover and concealment, as well as a means of escaping unseen.

A well-trained sniper generally spreads a ground cloth out in front beneath the rifle muzzle to minimize telltale dust, brush, and leaf debris flying about after their shot. This muzzle blast can give away a position more surely than anything else. At the shot, the spotter confirms a strike or miss so that subsequent shots can be corrected.

Depending on cover, a sniper might crawl on his belly for hours. Examples are on record of military snipers crawling across open fields, wearing appropriate ghillie suits for more than 24 hours. After a successful shot taken over a ground cloth from a direction the enemy considers impossible, the sniper may take about as long to inch off undetected, leaving basically the same way he came in. In this case, enemy soldiers often refuse to believe that the shot came from an open field. You must always adjust methods of travel to cover available places from which shots can be taken to account for preconceived notions of your opponent.

Snipers about to engage have many, many things on which they must narrowly focus for the shot. These include wind direction, distance, ground conditions, weather conditions, target priority, cover and concealment, and the necessity of keeping precise, sometimes delicate, equipment operational. But always the prime consideration—both while setting up and after a successful shot is taken—is how to get one's raggedy ass safely out of here?

As initially mentioned, good sniping seems to be the tactical method of choice for effectively carrying the battle to the enemy, especially key enemy personnel. Sniping appears at this point to be one of the more effective devices in which the common man of action can engage, yet it requires skill, dedication, and equipment that makes it virtually a way of life. One must take up sniping as an intense avocation spanning a number of years. Those who play at it will never become proficient enough to change the balance materially during a conflict. Nevertheless, for those with the background, skills, time, and money, sniping can provide a deadly advantage. If nothing else, this knowledge will likely keep them out of the hands of government snipers.

One last commonly overlooked but deadly effective element of modern sniper fire must be mentioned. Modern police and military units—especially in the United States—have come to rely on extremely complex technology. This can include jet planes, helicopters, electronic listening devices, night vision, tanks, armored personnel carriers, and many others. Most of these sophisticated weapons trotted out at the drop of a hat can be temporarily incapacitated by a single well-placed sniper round. Usually it is relatively easy to approach these weapons in their park or armory. Always keep in mind that many of these relatively delicate devices can be effectively destroyed by two or three rounds fired from a .300 mag from 500 yards distance, and chances are the attack will be a complete surprise.

It may be that deployment against these types of targets provides a good sniper one of his greatest advantages.

BIBLIOGRAPHY

Long, Duncan. Modern Sniper Rifles. Boulder, Colorado: Paladin Press, 1988.

Plaster, John L. (Maj.) The Ultimate Sniper. Boulder, CO: Paladin Press, 1993.

Senich, Peter R. The Complete Book of U.S. Sniping. Boulder, CO: Paladin Press, 1988.

_____. The Long-Range War: Sniping in Vietnam. Boulder, CO: Paladin Press, 1994.

Ultimate Sniper: The Video. Available from Paladin Press. 1993.

CHAPTER

Disguises

38

I don't know if it is true or not, but the following tale is told about a notorious antiwar protestor during the 1960s who was continually tracked by members of the FBI. This fellow was sheltered by two ladies then in their early 30s who, no doubt, shared his world view.

With gestapo-like precision, FBI people trailed the ladies each day as they left their residence. After a day or two of the game, it became painfully obvious to the women that their every move was monitored. No doubt, the agents hoped they would get a tip about the whereabouts and plans of the targeted fugitive.

These young women resented the obvious, clumsy intrusion into their lives. It is important for the purpose of this chapter to note that these furtive agents stuck out like a white man in an African-American church, even to rank amateurs. Although these young women were untrained, they had absolutely no problem figuring out what was going on or how to eventually ditch their tormentors.

On about the fourth day of being followed, the women packed two largish, purse-type shoulder bags, which they brought downtown to a major department store. Once inside, each went up to the second-floor women's room by a different route.

After 15 minutes, two smartly dressed professional women in high heels and business suits, and with coiffured hair, exited the women's room. They looked exactly like hundreds of similarly attired women spending their noon hour shopping.

Agents at the first floor escalator and at the doors completely missed these women, who exited separately. Officials were fixated on watching for stringy-haired, boot-wearing, sloppily dressed, counterculture types they saw leave the apartment, ride downtown on the bus, enter the store, and go into the women's room.

What wasn't apparent under the long dresses and sweaters was that the women had washed and groomed the night before. That morning, they had packed clothes kept from a previous life, and used them to slip away to other private business elsewhere, completely undetected.

Disguise is about sufficiently changing a person's outward appearance so that he can move

Waiting in disguise at the bus stop. (Illustrations by Bill Border and taken from *Disguise Techniques* by Edmond A. MacInaugh.)

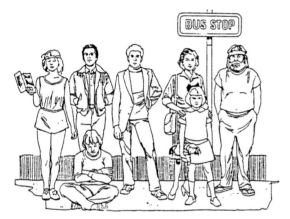

At the bus stop prior to assuming a disguise.

around more freely in situations where he would otherwise be constrained, prohibited, or worse. Other than for one situation on the far end of this spectrum that is covered in later chapters, disguise is *not* about acquiring a new identity.

Disguise also is also *not* about masking identity, as in wearing a ski mask or nylon stocking over one's head. A person wearing a clown suit would not be recognizable other than in his clown identity, but he certainly would not be disguised. A clown suit would never allow slipping through a crowd unnoticed, which, for the purposes of this chapter, is the final proof of an effective disguise.

No matter what personal disguise you choose, always keep in mind the ancient maxim that the best place to hide a tree is in a forest!

Strange as it may initially sound, the very first element of any successful disguise includes a long,

hard look at yourself. What do people see when they look at you? What are your identifying characteristics? It is imperative to evaluate what about characterizes you to other people. Is it size, sex, girth, a full head of hair, a broad chest, a beard, round glasses, sideburns, cotton workclothes, a limp or galloping gait, or, more likely, some combination of the above? Even if it takes a video camera and a brutally honest friend, you must systematically and, at times, mercilessly alter all those identifying characteristics in order of their importance.

If you have good, white teeth, they must be stained brown. If you walk confidently, work at acquiring a stooped shuffle, or put a small pebble in one shoe to acquire a limp. If you seldom smile, begin contorting your face into a permanent smile. Some of these devices are not easy, but all must be identified and appropriately altered.

The most important point to remember when deciding which personality to make yourself into is the kind of trees in the forest in which you must now operate. To use a perhaps obvious example: if no cleaning women or hookers ever get to the third floor of targeted premises during the day, it would be folly to use one of these as a disguise, even if it is otherwise excellent. Placing a wrong personality in a wrong setting may cause security guards to look closely enough to figure out who they are really dealing with.

Most men *and* women of average-build can switch their dress to that of the other sex, immediately masking their identities—provided they pick a type of person that is common to the area. This may be a secretary, grounds crew member, food service employee, deliveryman (if such are allowed in the area), businesswoman, or any other type unlikely to be encountered with suspicion.

Experts warn, however, that a careful job must be done of *not* portraying the image of the disguise as a stereotype. Thai transvestites, for instance, spend so much time studying women and mimicking their behavior that it is soon easy to pick the transvestites out of a crowd. They act more like women than women do!

Stereotyping carries with it a series of subliminal hints that things are not as they appear. Farmers do not chew on a piece of straw or wear boots covered with manure to town unless they are selling cattle. Of all people, they are the most sensitive to removing these little hints that might make them otherwise look like hayseeds.

For example, a young lady worked as a customer service representative for a small-town utility company. It was a plum job for the area, paying extremely high wages. Before moving to the small town, she had lived and worked in a larger city where she discovered the wonders of high-fashion clothes. Every penny she earned seemed to go for what locals thought were exotic clothes. Absolutely everyone knew her on sight. She was the model of decorum but hugely overdressed for the area.

Her stereotypical "big-city, professional woman" look gained her great notoriety in the small town. When she finally did drop this facade and start to wear her clothes, hairstyle, and makeup in a fashion more in keeping with the locals', she quickly faded into the gray anonymity of a basically colorless community, despite the fact that she was a member of an easily recognized minority.

Lessons learned so far for those who wish to successfully disguise themselves are the following:

1. Realistically determine your own identifying characteristics.
2. Know the difference between hiding and disguise.
3. Determine by what steps you can alter your major distinguishing characteristics.
4. Identify a common local trade or social group that you can mimic.
5. Be careful not to stereotype.

Rearranging your image into one that blends in with the crowd usually starts with such external changes as clothes, glasses, hair, and jewelry. If an external sex change is appropriate and you can get away with it emotionally, psychologically, and physically, clothes are your first consideration.

A 5'10", 150-pound female can wear loose bib overalls, large work boots, and a flannel shirt. She may have to bind up her figure a bit to use this disguise, but her biggest hurdle will be summoning enough courage and brass to pull off this scam.

Obviously, a 240-pound, 6'4" male could not dress as a female without attracting too much attention and must think of some other disguise. A bald male might alter his image sufficiently by wearing a wig.

People's glasses always identify them if they habitually wear them. Our female example who became a male farmer would have had to stop wearing her glasses. She would have to switch to more masculine frames if she relied on lenses to see. An excellent disguise might include wearing gaudy, obvious frames with plain uncorrected glass, available in many large drugstores or five-and-dime stores.

Our woman-turned-farmer's next most distinguishing external characteristic would probably be her hair. She would either have to wear a male-style wig in an appropriate "farmer" cut or cut and style her hair in such a fashion. She could shave her head on top, leaving a characteristic male fringe.

In most cases you must also change hair color even if very little remains. Blond and gray hair can be dyed red or black; mousy brown can be bleached blond. This may not always be possible, given some natural colors, but you should always consider making very radical changes to your hair color, style, and quantity.

Keep in mind that placing something as simple as a shoe insert in only one shoe can alter your gait enough to really confuse people.

Given different clothes, an opposite-sex disguise, a dramatic hair makeover, glasses, and a slight limp, all it will take is enough confidence to walk into a post office or store incognito.

Men usually have more trouble becoming women because of scrutinizing stares, which they are unaccustomed to.

Your voice is another immediately recognizable characteristic. Most people have familiar voice tones or speech patterns. It may actually be necessary to plug the nose with clay or place a small marble in the mouth to alter familiar sounds. Also try gargling with Listerine, talking infrequently, using a loud whisper, or talking with a toothpick or cigarette in your mouth.

It may also work to simply talk much louder or softer the few times something is said. If you were talkative as your old self, don't be so now, and vice versa. Affected accents, if handled very carefully, can be helpful.

While working overseas when I was younger, I had several occasions to disguise myself. Commonly, these were hurry-up situations demanding instant improvisation. The plan was to always carry at least a shirt and pants that mimicked

Using facial hair to disguise the triangular face. **Disguising the lean face.** **Disguising the round face.**

those commonly worn by the locals. If possible, I also purchased shoes of the local type. Yet the most noticeable identifier was always skin color. On several occasions, I used common shoe polish to ruddy and darken my complexion. It worked OK for me, but several companions acquired severe skin rashes from the procedure.

Cosmetics that are available in almost all the world's drugstores will do the same job more effectively and safely. ManTan is a commercial product that darkens slightly with minimum fuss, but be sure to wear rubber gloves while applying it and to wash your hands well afterward. ManTan darkens callused or "thick skin" areas more quickly, so an even color can be a problem if application is maintained over a long time.

If you have time, nothing works quite as well as growing a beard or losing a lot of weight. Motivation must be quite high to successfully carry out these plans, but they really do work. Keep in mind that the color of the beard must match that of the new hair.

A couple of my female friends enjoy dressing up as males and going into local small-town stores in search of some weird item or another. They are both fairly conventional, but they have been successfully putting on working men's clothes and wearing male wigs acquired several years ago from GIs home on leave who did not want to show white ears and hair line. These two also affect a Scandinavian accent.

They have been in almost all our local stores, bars, and restaurants. They confess that their biggest challenge has been to remember to go into the correct john. So far they have never been suspected, even though this is a small community where everyone knows everyone else well.

Any of us may need to use a disguise at any time. The rules for good disguise are relatively simple to learn and follow. In this case, knowledge is definitely power.

BIBLIOGRAPHY

MacInaugh, Edmond. *Disguise Techniques*. Boulder, CO: Paladin Press, 1984.

Sample, John. *Methods of Disguise*. Port Townsend, WA: Loompanics, Unlimited, 1984.

CHAPTER

TV Scramblers

39

It's a strange world. Not many years ago, video movie distributors sold their best, most popular movies for prices ranging from $40 to $60 each! At between $2 and $3 apiece for blank tapes to pirate these movies, gray marketers promiscuously and profitably copied all the movies they wanted.

Those with government-granted franchises to sell videotapes of high-priced, first-line movies fought back on two fronts. Copy-protect electronics intercepts were installed on movie tapes, making simple, dual-machine reproduction ineffective. Video electronics makers countered with special filters that cleaned out some of the copy-protect devices. Video producers countered with better copy-protect measures, and so the war escalated, measure against countermeasure.

Most important, in terms of dealing with video pirates, tape producers allowed simple economics to work their magic. From $60, they lowered the price of their videos to $16.

More people, they found, were in the market at lower prices, and distributors did not have the great expense entailed in legally enforcing sales violations that occurred at the higher prices. Illicit copying of movies dropped dramatically. It wasn't profitable for businesses or individuals to pirate videos for $16, and producers still found their profits soaring. More sales, even at smaller margins, equaled more income.

In many regards, cable and satellite TV vendors are in the process of learning similar lessons. They have tried high-tech scramblers and the expedient of lobbying for strong copyright laws through Congress. Now they are just starting to realize that lower prices do the best job of bringing additional customers into the market, cutting down piracy, and yielding the highest profits.

Television came to the homes of thousands of rural, previously TV-less Americans during the 1970s, via TV satellites parked in orbit overhead. TV satellites, placed in orbit, remain precisely stationary above one point on the Earth, where they broadcast back 24 channels of TV programming

Home satellite dishes pull in many scrambled signals. High monthly charges cause many owners to use special scrambler devices that allow them to view all channels after paying a one-time fee for the device. (Photos by Ragnar Benson.)

simultaneously. As time went by, satellite TV vendors who produced and sold programming to home viewers that became hugely more sophisticated and profitable. Continuous news, weather, sports, movies, pornography, nature, and numerous other shows became available.

All that was needed was a ground-based receiving station to pull in these TV signals from satellites out in space. Satellite dishes 6 to 12 feet in diameter sprouted on people's front lawns in regions far too remote to receive viewable local signals. Some economists suggested that agricultural production fell temporarily as farmers adjusted to the junk coming in through their satellite dishes.

As time went by, numbers of viewers banded together into program providers, eventually becoming cable TV companies. Initially, these cable companies were little more than increasing numbers of neighbors tied into the same dish. Members began to make modest monthly subscription payments, and so cable companies grew.

Program providers were not asleep at this time. Those in the business realized that they had to generate healthy cash flows to support the quality programming demanded by cable companies' customers. Eventually, a scrambler system evolved that kept those who did not pay for these programs from being able to view them. Electronics whiz kids put black boxes on the market that defeated scramblers. This scrambler technology continues to evolve in a measure-countermeasure, ratchet-like movement.

Initially, these scramblers engendered unscrambling devices. Measure and counter-measure developed on virtually the same day. Prices for special programs dropped to the point where they now about equal to those of unscrambling devices.

Those who want movies or news on a continuous or part-time basis can call a special telephone number. In return for charges made to viewers' credit cards, satellite program sellers instruct their satellite channels to send down special signals to individual scrambling devices, allowing authorized owners to see programs of their choice. Charges were initially quite high, but owners could pay movie by movie, cutting expenses somewhat. Those with dishes from early prescrambler days screamed their heads off and then went out looking for better gray-market unscrambling devices with which to pirate programs they wanted.

As of this writing an uneasy technological stand-off of sorts exists. Scrambled program owners have developed a unit called a Videocipher II that supposedly is impossible to alter, thereby preventing private citizens from pirating TV signals. Vendors have dropped their subscription prices somewhat. In the interim, electronics engineers in the gray market are working to discover how to alter these new sophisticated TV scramblers so that anyone can purchase a black box useful in surreptitiously unscrambling TV signals. The only hitch is that these unscramblers are getting to be a bit pricey, and no device has hit the market (at this writing) that will unscramble the latest technology.

In the past, people sent their old unscramblers purchased from satellite dish sellers to electronics experts who dealt in the special chips and circuitry needed to pirate TV signals. Converting an old box to private unscrambled use was not tough; it was usually only a matter of replacing an internal module. Scramblers are hooked up to a TV with only a few wires that anyone with a screwdriver and labeling pen can handle.

Those purchasing unscrambling units must not live in the same area as the people who supply or modify their black boxes for them. Gray-market unscrambler dealers almost always advertise their products as "not for sale" in their state of residence. By so doing, they avoid prosecution under local laws. Finding an expert to alter a scrambler box is relatively easy. Look in one of the many consumer electronics magazines found in great abundance at the local newsstand. If past experience is any indicator, they will very shortly be carrying ads for the newest satellite unscramblers. These include *Popular Electronics, Electronics Now, Nuts & Volts,* and *Popular Communications.*

As of this writing, all carried numerous advertisements for cable TV unscramblers that the makers guarantee to function properly. Most offer free telephone consultation, including, in some cases, toll-free numbers. Several sellers offer 30-day free trials or money-back guarantees. Credit card sales are encouraged.

Whenever new scrambler technology comes along, those with the first workable gray-market unscramblers can sell them at the highest prices.

However, these often ingenious devices are not patentable. First buyers are always the competition who blatantly market their own copies, significantly depressing prices. If new technology comes along, prices will spike briefly again. Currently, competition is fierce, with many vendors offering to beat "anyone's" prices. As a result, one might validly conclude that the next quantum leap in technology is about due.

Unlike TV cable, gray-market unscrambler satellite pirates are extremely difficult to detect.

TV cable companies have central maps showing the location of their cable hookups, including types of service purchased and the status of cables running to various subscribers. Average cable systems today have about 4,000 subscribers. About 200 of these, on a statistical basis, will be pirating programs at any given time.

Some subscribers even pirate Disney channels in homes with lots of kids, where money is a problem. Others may pirate programs that viewers do not want people to know they are watching. Reportedly, the Playboy channel is pirated more in some rural Utah communities than all other channels combined.

Cable companies maintain that they have electronic gear that can be used from the street to detect the use of illegal, nonpaying cable unscrambling devices. Experienced technicians claim that this is fiction designed to scare likely nonsubscribers and that, at best, these devices will only work during times that illicit unscrambled programs are actually being viewed. Effective drive-by detectors seem unlikely at this time.

Perhaps in response to being re-regulated by the federal government, which knocked out the most likely new competition for them, cable companies elected to go after their principal competition—gray-market home unscramblers—via the legislative process. Use of markets and competition to lower prices undoubtedly would have worked more effectively, but cable companies apparently reckoned that there was no one out there likely to enter the market with which they had to compete, other than with illicit black boxes.

Prices for services that users thought were basic went up dramatically in many areas. Users came to believe that owning their own unscrambler boxes was the cheapest and best plan. In effect, cable companies trapped themselves when they elected to limit market entry via a government-granted monopoly.

A TV cable unscrambler is far simpler than those required for unscrambling a satellite signal. Almost all dealers who handle unscramblers also carry all types of cable equipment. As with satellite equipment, all purchases are done outside a given area. Ads in common electronics magazines are the best sources for equipment.

Possession of a TV cable in a home does not necessarily indicate that a cable is functional. Often, the cables are disconnected at master panels in apartment complexes or out in junction boxes or poles on the street. At times, desperate pirates must follow wires and open boxes so that individual cables can be reactivated.

Cable boxes atop television sets act something like radios. This box tunes a single program from a complex jumble of signals received from the street into a form viewers can see and understand. Viewers are provided these usable signals based on the monthly fees they pay.

At its simplest, subscribers pay for basic monthly programming while purchasing their own unscramblers so that they can watch more expensive HBO, movie, and sports premium channels. Special tools needed to splice into an existing cable, taking the signal to a "special" unscrambler atop a TV, are available from those who advertise descramblers in electronics magazines.

You do not send your cable company unscrambler off to a gray-market vendor for modifications as is the case with many satellite installations. That can be illegal, risky, and time consuming. Instead, would-be pirates must find which of six or eight major brands of unscramblers their local cable company uses and call their gray-market vendor with that information.

Often this information is unnecessary. Gray-market unscrambler suppliers already know which black boxes are in use in larger metropolitan areas. Usually, they have complete records listing unscrambler brands. Simply use a credit card to purchase either a completely wired, guaranteed unscrambler or, in some cases, new computer chips permitting the modification of the unscrambler. This latter device is much cheaper, but in some circumstances a lot more risky.

Some unscramblers, such as Pioneers, are extremely difficult to home-modify. In this case, expect to purchase a complete, separate, ready-made box in the gray market. As mentioned earlier, prices go all over the map, depending entirely on current technology and who has it at the moment. Expect to pay about $150 for a workable unscrambler as opposed to about $20 per month for premium cable service.

Pirate cable-type unscramblers can be immobilized by an electronic device that people in the trade refer to as a "bullet." This is an electronic countermeasure that deauthorizes a specific unscrambler technology. Gray-market suppliers are aware of this countermeasure. Most advertise unscramblers that are "bulletproof."

Detection of private unscramblers at the consumer level is extremely unlikely. Most "discoveries" result when a disgruntled girlfriend or family member reports the illicit box to a cable company. Some owners cannot keep their mouths shut: they brag incessantly about the free movies they watch.

Some few cable companies simply allow individual thieves to operate unmolested, content to collect fees for the basic service. When they do come down, it is on those who wholesale or retail large numbers of gray-market descramblers. However, cable company executives may elect to come down very hard on selected high-profile individuals if they believe that their actions will throw the fear into other subscribers.

Unscrambling cable TV is relatively easy. Specific techniques vary from region to region, but you need not understand much about electronics to buy good technology. Unscrambling devices themselves are electronically complex and changing rapidly. People who are interested in an unscrambler for their personal use need only pick up current video electronics magazines to find dozens of advertisements for black boxes. Like satellite equipment, many suppliers offer both money-back guarantees and 800 numbers to call for the latest information.

Both in terms of price and flawless function, it is wise to call two or three different suppliers to determine their specific recommendations for your specific application. Price is important but usually not everything. Like the computer industry, technology in the unscrambling business changes dramatically from week to week. Again, the industry is driven by the cat-and-mouse game of measure and countermeasure.

Defeating copy-protect measures on commercial videos is relatively simple. To a great extent, modern video machines used in pairs to copy tapes have handled the problem.

Traditional copy protection is accomplished by adding magnetic strips to recording signals. These strips trick the VCR automatic gain control into believing that an overload imprint signal is present. As a result, copy tapes might suffer a loss of color, blooming in and out, and other distracting defects.

Video stabilizers, sold by Radio Shack and other electronic stores, reverse out and negate copy protection processes. Some of these devices carry statements clearly claiming that they remove video protection from duplicating processes, permitting excellent duplication. Others claim, more legally, that they are designed as simple video enhancers. All these devices work quite well and are priced at under $40 each.

Of all video measures and countermeasures, duplicating movies is the most cut and dried. As with computer programs, makers seem to have given up trying to prevent anyone from duplicating their products for personal use. Most efforts are directed at people who duplicate for mass markets.

In all cases, men of action have the ability to take these electronic matters into their own hands. As in so many other situations, an accumulation of knowledge along with appropriate contacts is required.

It would only be fair to conclude this chapter with a warning from old Charlie Peden, a farmer of excellent skill and reputation in the community in which I was raised. Charlie's wisdom was legendary, and I believed him when he said, "Humans lose one IQ point for every hour they watch TV!"

BIBLIOGRAPHY

Eisenson, Henry. *Television Gray Market*. San Diego, CA: Index Publishing Group, 1993.

CHAPTER

Clandestine Radios

40

Improvised radio-jamming techniques would not initially seem to be a subject with great sex appeal. However, men of action have found that when author Lawrence Myers writes about electronics, his writing is timely, authoritative, and entertaining. We fail to listen at our peril.

An estimated 11,000 nameless, faceless foot soldiers per day were pounded into protoplasm during the Battle of the Somme during World War I. These horrible casualty rates were a direct consequence of trench warfare. Development of weapons of mass destruction temporarily outran the communications capabilities of various units. The only effective method commanders had of controlling and coordinating their men was to line them up to march forward under visual control. As a result, some French, German, and English units suffered some of the greatest sustained casualty rates in the history of warfare.

Today, the opposite may be true. Communications technology may have outrun weapons systems.

However, one could validly argue that modern weapons systems and communications are one and the same. Sophisticated communications play a vital role in military, law enforcement, and transportation throughout our society.

It is generally concluded that he who has the best communications maintains a significant edge.

Governments around the world realize this fact. In Thailand, for instance, all private portable radio transmitters are prohibited or tightly controlled. Illegal ownership brings an automatic 12-year prison sentence in joints so severe that it takes only seven years for the average prisoner to die. Thailand is supposedly a free country, but of course other varieties such as Russia, Poland, Algeria, and Saudi Arabia also prohibit private ownership of radio transmitters.

On several occasions, I carried 2-meter hand-held radios with me on visits to Thailand. Nationals there spent hours listening to palace guard chitchat about the movement of the king from one place to another. After listening to traffic involving

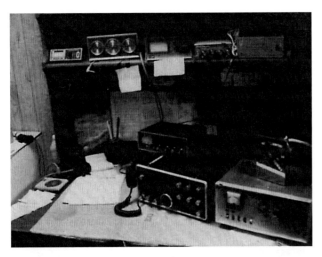

Monitors and transmitters set up in a basic but modest radio-monitoring operation. (Photos by Ragnar Benson.)

everything from going out to see the elephants breed to getting the royal Range Rover washed, I finally convinced my Thai hosts to break into a conversation. This communication directed a courier to get noodles at a carry-out restaurant. Our guy suggested that he not buy at one particular place because the king thought all the waitresses there had fat legs!

I thought it was a hoot, but my Thai friends were scared out of their minds over what they had done. We carefully disassembled the radios and hid them. Those radios never saw Thailand again.

Myers carefully explains in his book that the United States is rapidly catching up with the rest of the world in government regulation, including prohibiting the use of radios or certain frequencies.

Electronic guerrilla warfare is defined as 1) using communications that imitate official communications to confuse and misdirect government officials, 2) using electronic countermeasures to cover and confuse an enemy's radio transmissions, 3) monitoring enemy radio transmissions allowing listeners to know in advance about official actions, 4) using radios to detonate explosive devices or incendiaries, and 5) privately using bootleg radio frequencies to coordinate the movement of men and materiel.

Currently in the United States, it is illegal to monitor certain radio frequencies. One will probably not get caught in using personally modified radio gear to do so. Jamming any radio transmissions or broadcasting spurious instructions is very illegal,

and authorities will try very hard to catch anyone doing anything so dastardly.

Electronics guerrilla warfare starts with establishing covert listening posts. These must be extremely well hidden, yet located in places where there is access to radio signals as well as easy, surreptitious access to the listening post.

The control room must be comfortable and sufficiently large to house power supply, antennas, and radio equipment, most of which must be wheeled into the station. Listening posts themselves are passive, yet many officials here and abroad take extreme exception to being listened to. DEA and FBI agents, for instance, will go to great lengths to see that no one ever listens in on "their" frequencies.

Physically establishing a listening post is very much like putting in a McDonald's: three things are important—location, location, and location. Monitors must be placed where they can reasonably be expected to pick up all the enemy's many mobile, hand-held, and stationary radio transmitters while remaining hidden.

Monitors must continually search for enemy radio transmissions on frequencies not previously identified as being used by that group, monitor all such transmissions made, and provide a log of all frequencies and a summary content of enemy traffic.

Listening stations must be provided with excellent main and backup power supplies, including 110-volt power outlets, 12-volt-battery backup systems, and emergency-generating capacity. Heat generated by these many radio transmitters and monitors may necessitate that provision is made for air conditioners. Adequate space to house some very large antennae must also be provided.

Scanners at the listening post must be digitally programmable, providing for as broad a coverage as possible. Scan speed and sensitivity are important. Until recently, accumulating enough of this type of sophisticated equipment was prohibitively expensive, but this has changed dramatically in the past few years.

Tape recorders must be available to record traffic as opportunities arise. In all cases, logs of radio traffic should be maintained, allowing listeners to learn frequencies, jargon, codes, and likely patterns of use. If one agent always calls in at a certain time from a specific location, it will be valuable to know this.

Four different scanners are normally considered ideal for monitoring the full range of possible enemy communications. First, one is needed to search specific bands for covert transmissions. Second, a priority monitor is needed to cover five to 10 selected frequencies. Third, a monitor should be hooked to a voice-activated recorder set to one or two principal frequencies. Fourth, a continuous-scan monitor cover has to cover 100 to 400 of the enemy's frequencies. These functions can be accomplished using equipment purchased from Radio Shack for about $1,000. In some cases, there will have to be slight modifications to the equipment to enable them to receive certain prohibited government frequencies.

Frequency monitors are actually high-speed radio receivers. They require fairly bulky, sophisticated antennae to operate them properly. Antenna systems developed for the covert operations center must be invisible to even knowledgeable observers. Acceptable results will only be achieved if you tailor your antennae to band and frequencies used by the bad guys you expect to intercept. Antenna length and spacing are critical. Those interested in listening in on government frequencies must identify which frequency range is to be monitored and the antennae designed accordingly.

Experts generally agree that a single, long-wire antenna is probably most effective and easiest to construct. Various loops and pods may also be constructed from this basic system.

Surreptitious antenna construction is very much a cut-and-paste exercise based on materials available, overall need for security, frequency targeted, and the type of monitor and radio one wishes to use. Excellent results have been achieved using metal window frames, existing wire clothes lines, or even metal bed springs. Experienced antenna people claim that nothing replaces wise, innovative improvisation.

Common steel tape measures have been used as antennae with excellent results. They can be pulled out to the correct length, per the markings right on the tape. When you wish to change frequencies, the tape can be shortened or lengthened as necessary. In an emergency, roll-up tape

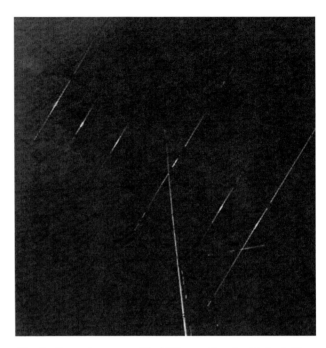

Clandestine antennas must be hidden or disguised to look like common ones. This owner monitors police and military radios with what look like television antennas.

measures are easily collapsed to a small, inconspicuous package. Other clandestine antennas are made from rolls of foil tape, modified TV antennas, and sometimes even by using heat ducts in buildings. Read the instruction book and experiment, experts advise.

Cable leads from antennas to receive transmissions are critical. Improperly done, they might lose a signal or give away the presence of a listening post. Always use the highest grade, thickest, and most expensive cable available. Keep all feed lines as short as possible. These who store their coaxial cable in rolls between antenna and radio can easily lose two-thirds of a weak signal.

Surreptitious listeners are not just gossips. They have a reason for listening. Always have in mind. Keep detailed, accurate accounts of all people who use an identified enemy frequency, their normal speech patterns, a list of their duties, how they go about them, and under what terms and conditions they move their transmissions to alternative frequencies. Learn words and jargon well enough that you could use them. In many countries written logs of this traffic constitutes prima facie evidence of guilt of very serious crimes. You must be continually alert about security.

Should there be the slightest inkling that security at your listening post has been compromised, burn all records and move immediately. Don't wait around trying to decide what to do. Move with dispatch, destroying all evidence of your having been there.

As electronic guerrillas work with monitors, antennas, and, later, transmitters, they discover what types of listening and sending devices are used by the enemy. Some become so proficient that they can accurately predict frequency and radio type just by looking at an antenna! Enemy transmitter locations are eventually deduced by watching radio strength on the monitors. In cases where operation locations may be moved, you can sometimes triangulate a targeted transmitter, learning its appropriate location. In cases of official government antennas, they may not be hidden well. Those who know what they are looking for and have a general idea of location can often pinpoint the exact locations of secret government agencies.

Always be aware that the other guy's antennas are extremely vulnerable to damage once they are located. Sniper fire can easily damage coaxial cable, wire, and dishes. Even a small grenade or mortar bomb can completely tear up a tower or antenna.

From their initial deployment of radios in 1929 through today, police agencies have grown increasingly more dependent on communications. Modern cops don't even stop to tinkle without a 10/7 call to dispatch. Some specific areas on a cop's beat are dead to radio traffic. Tall buildings, steel bridges, or natural soil conditions may preclude police radios from working properly. During the monitoring phase of the operation, this will become apparent and should be carefully noted.

After learning all you can by monitoring the enemy's activities, the next step in the progression of guerrilla electronics warfare involves acquiring transmitters. As long as you do not actually use these radios in the United States, they are not at risk. Once transmission activities or jamming and deception commence, the risks become extremely high. Only those who have done their homework in using monitors should even think about surreptitious transmissions.

Monitor operators will discover many federal agencies transmit their radio messages in scrambled code; this goes for the FBI, DEA, Marshal's Service,

and even, at times, the IRS. It is a serious federal crime to monitor or attempt to decipher these scrambled messages. Even having these frequencies programmed into your monitor is illegal. But jamming these scrambled frequencies is so easy and fun—as well as difficult to detect—that this is usually the place where guerrillas start.

Begin by acquiring suitable sanitized transmitters. Two sources are generally available to serious guerrillas. They can either steal existing radios out of cabs, garbage trucks, businessmen's cars, or even radio supply stores. Or they can be purchased off the shelf at a local two-way-radio shop. In either case, the steel external identification plate with serial numbers must be removed and destroyed. Also clean away any serial numbers painted on the inside of the cabinet. Skilled technicians will still know the make and model, but they have no clue where the radio originated.

Even if you must purchase transmitters, this is not usually a problem. Modern transmitters are incredibly cheap; just compare their prices to those of only 10 years ago.

All radios must be internally altered to broadcast and receive on frequencies identified during the scanner portion of this operation. This is usually a simple matter of installing new crystals. At times, this procedure can become complex and should be undertaken by skilled technicians.

Record any scrambler traffic to be blown off the air. The content will be unintelligible, but this is of no concern. If you use a reasonably high-quality recording of broadcasts based on previously discovered enemy frequencies, sending this garble out again will temporarily lock up the enemy's receivers. Correctly done in very small bursts, it may be quite a while before agency technicians discover that the problem is not malfunction internal to their operations.

Hand-held commercial air traffic send/receive radios are commercially available. If a person wishes to close an airport, he can broadcast bogus instructions to pilots flying into that airport. It will take air-traffic controllers and pilots only a few moments to discover that these transmissions are phony, but the airport will immediately be closed. All flights will be sent to alternative airports. If this is what the guerrilla had in mind, his mission will be accomplished easily. Because these are portable radios, it is difficult for the authorities to locate the guerrilla.

It takes at most two or three minutes of bogus transmission to close an airport. Most experts agree that it is amazing that this does not happen frequently in the U.S. When it has happened, official responses have been massive and immediate.

Covert operators have occasionally monitored enemy radio traffic at times when they know that an official response is in process. Reportedly, drug handlers have anonymously called the DEA to report shipments. By listening to DEA radio traffic, they had learned a great deal about how the agency reacts to these bogus reports.

Several signal-jamming techniques are available. Some entail huge risks; others are worth the risk and expense, just for laughs.

One easy technique involves keying the microphone on a radio broadcasting on an enemy's frequency. At first, the dispatcher will believe it is being done inadvertently by one of the agents. Properly done, it will blank all sending and receiving on that channel, causing great consternation.

Some guerrillas send out low-level noise that is received as an annoying screech. A defective squelch is blamed unless such deception is repeated frequently.

Broadcasting the sounds of birds singing, people applauding, elephants trumpeting, or people laughing distracts and confuses those on a channel. Usually, users who previously thought their channels of communication were completely secure will become paranoid. The paranoia may be translated into a massive effort to find and punish perpetrators. Expect that sensitive directional antennas will be used to triangulate people employing this device.

Outright broadcast deception is a seldom-used means of radio jamming. Novices at electronics warfare tend to think that jamming can only include obliteration of a radio transmission by using an obnoxious noise. But skillfully sending enemy patrols on a wild goose chase, to an ambush site, or away from a planned zone of activity can provide a tremendous advantage. Only those who have thoroughly studied the agency they target can even hope to pull this deception off. When it works, it is dynamite!

Because responses by the enemy will be vigorous, any jamming techniques should be as subtle as possible. Technicians on the other end must be made to believe that their own equipment might be malfunctioning. An excellent method of accomplishing this is to record all enemy radio traffic for several days and broadcasting it back over their discrete frequency. Broadcast both sides of the conversation as received in your listening post. A variation involves broadcasting one agency's recordings on another agency's frequency. An immediate war will develop over their "walking" on each other.

Another variation includes setting up a scanner hooked to a transmitter. Rebroadcast any traffic on as many enemy channels as possible. Every time an agency agent calls, that call will immediately go out on many other official frequencies. Fighting, temper tantrums, and consternation caused by this technique will be monumental. It must only be used infrequently and on a very short-term basis.

Affected agencies will even launch helicopters with radio direction-finding equipment in an attempt to catch anyone actually using these techniques. One way to avoid detection is to set up a battery-operated transmitter at a remote location controlled by an intermittent timer. Taped transmissions can be sent out from time to time until they are shut down by the timer.

Enemy agents will spend a huge amount of time looking for this device. Users will lose their transmitter, battery, and tape recording, which cost about $1,250. But the havoc created will be wonderful—depending, of course, on one's point of view.

BIBLIOGRAPHY

Myers, Lawrence. *Improvised Radio Jamming Techniques*. Boulder, CO: Paladin Press, 1989.

CHAPTER
Medical Care
41

At times, it is difficult to recall that all effective monopolies throughout history have been granted by governments. It is important to keep this in mind when considering something as personal and private as medical treatment for oneself or loved ones.

Private business never earn their monopolies except as a result of bringing influence to bear on appropriate government agencies. Anyone doubting this truth need look no further than the medical profession, including nurses, doctors, and pharmacists. A recent article in the *Wall Street Journal* documented the fact that a nurses' union was upset because some "unlicensed" hospital aides were employed in checking patients' pulses.

When I wrote *Survivalist's Medicine Chest* outlining how one might use veterinary medical supplies in an emergency context, an absolute storm broke out across the nation. "You will cause people to take dangerous risks," some folks wrote.

"Average Americans are not able to assume responsibility for their own health," others scolded.

The assumption throughout this volume has always been that men of action are their own peculiar breed, willing and able to take full responsibility for their own lives, with as little government interference as possible. Certainly, this truth applies to medical care in an emergency, family, or paramilitary context.

Routine age- and life-style-driven maladies are excellent examples. Those of us who do not eat correctly, abuse things such as alcohol or tobacco, or even fail to brush our teeth or wear hearing protection when shooting are taking personal responsibility for problems that will develop later.

Many common illnesses such as colds and flu respond only to rest and time. There is no need to worry about monopolistic sources of medication in these areas.

Other human diseases, including pneumonia, tuberculosis, parasites, pink-eye, skin infections, and bursitis, frequently occur but can be treated

The first stop for those who must take medical matters into their own hands is a good bookstore. Armed with reliable information, you can safely use common and easily acquired veterinary medical supplies. (Photos from *Survivalist's Medicine Chest* by Ragnar Benson.)

fairly easily and effectively with substances available to just about anyone willing to go after them. The only trick is knowing what one is dealing with and where to go for proper medication.

Conditions related to treating accidents up to and including broken arms, legs, poked eyes, knocked-out teeth, gunshot wounds, and other "blood cases"—as MDs call them—can, depending on their severity, be handled by knowledgeable novices. Midwives or med techs might set bones, remove cysts, sew up wounds, or administer remedies for ulcers, parasites, infections, and other common, treatable diseases. Even delivering a baby is generally not tough. Many people still do as their parents did, having their babies at home, attended only by other women friends. The Amish people are an excellent example.

Smart men of action keep on top of conditions such as skin growths, crowns and caps, back injuries, and even double-bypass heart surgery by getting those maladies handled before they are emergencies.

There are five classes of medical conditions with which one must deal:

1. Common medical problems that only time and rest will cure, such as colds and flu.
2. Those that occur as a result of stupid personal decisions including neglected teeth, venereal disease, lung cancer, and obesity. These can be handled by changing one's ways.
3. Medical conditions that are usually curable through potent medications monopolized by those

in power. Examples include migraine headaches, ulcers, malaria, TB, cholera, and pneumonia.

4. Blood cases that one may or may not be able to cure, depending on their severity and the availability of medication. Medical training and skill do play a role in this category. But most blood cases are relatively simple, requiring simple stitching or bone setting. It is validly said that good orthopedic surgeons are really just good mechanics. Without painkillers, these procedures are most excruciating.

5. Terminal cases wherein patients simply use up their allotted time, resulting in death. Death can sometimes be postponed by using modern medications and heroics. This situation implies the use of skills and perhaps medications not available over the counter. The end result, however, is the same, no matter who treats the afflicted.

Obviously intelligent, well-informed, highly motivated men of action address categories one and two through common sense. Three through five also require common sense, but they also require a great deal of information, as well as some fairly sophisticated medical supplies if you are to successfully deal with them.

The challenge is knowing where to get the needed supplies and knowledge required to use them effectively.

First, you must know which drugs and pieces of equipment will be effective. The following reference library recommendations have been developed over a great number of years by knowledgeable survivors. The list has withstood the rigors of on-the-ground necessity.

Better results would be achieved by having someone somewhat medically knowledgeable collect this library, even if that person is little more than a hospital aide or dental hygienist.

Differences of opinion as to which medical books are best to include in a reference library may surface. This is not all bad, as long as these differences are not driven by cheapness or laziness. Listen to those who disagree and can articulate their reasons intelligently; they bring the advantage of having thought through this issue. (If you have any suggestions or recommendations regarding the list, please write to me in care of Paladin Press, P.O. Box 1307, Boulder, CO 80306.)

1. ***Medical Dictionary and Health Manual*** by Robert E. Rothenberg, M.D., 1975, Signet Press, 1633 Broadway, New York, NY 10019.

   This simple, inexpensive paperback dictionary of medical terms lists most of the terms that will be encountered in using other medical texts. Medical texts listed are written for professionals and assume the reader knows the language.

2. ***The Merck Manual***, updated regularly by Merck Sharp and Dohme Research Laboratories, Rahway, NJ.

   This contains complete summaries in technical terms on virtually every physical and medical procedure. Most doctors do not know everything contained in this volume. Purchase the latest edition available and use it to diagnose and treat any medical problem.

3. ***Drugs, Second Edition, Nurses Reference Library***, 1984. Springhouse Corp. Trade & Textbook Dept., 1111 Bethlehem Pike, Springhouse, PA. 19477.

   This essential volume lists all the drugs currently available in the United States, how to administer them, correct dosages, problems, common side effects, and other useful information for people who monitor patients. This book is out of print, but available at some used bookstores. Because of its wealth of information, men of action should expend whatever energy is necessary to secure a copy, including encouraging the publisher to bring out another edition.

4. ***Nursing '90 Drug Handbook***, 1990. Springhouse Corp., Springhouse, PA 19477.

   This later volume replaces the 1984 edition of Drugs, which is now out of print. However, many survivors have and use both volumes, finding the information contained in both to be complementary.

5. ***Physicians' Desk Reference***. Published by Charles E. Baker, Medical Economics Co., Oradell, NJ 07649.

   This very complete listing includes color pictures of virtually every drug manufactured and is revised and updated yearly. Purchase the latest edition possible, either new or used if you can find it. Editions up to two or three years old are still sufficiently current for survival use. The volume does not have much diagnostic information.

6. ***Current Medical Diagnosis and Treatment***, edited by Krupp & Chatton. 1992. Lange Medical Publications, Drawer L, Los Altos, CA 94022.

   This is an encyclopedic-type listing of all body parts (e.g., eye, skin, ear, nose, heart, blood) with a complete analysis of possible problems, symptoms, and recommended treatments. It must be used in close conjunction with a dictionary and drug text.

7. ***Emergency War Surgery***, 1975. U.S. Government Printing Office, Washington, D.C. 20402.

   This is a sometimes difficult-to-find text enumerating various types of injuries and wounds, along with detailed information on how to treat them. This volume, along with Ditch Medicine, is the introduction to emergency military and paramilitary surgery, which we all hope will never be required. It includes extensive trauma and wound information not found in other manuals, and it's in layman's language.

8. ***U.S. Army Special Forces Medical Handbook, ST 31-91B***, 1982. Reprint by Paladin Press, Box 1307, Boulder, CO 80306.

   This is a complete yet easily read emergency treatment manual developed for groups of elite troops working behind enemy lines. This volume is especially valuable because of its information on dental problems and procedures. Possession of this book, along with numbers 6 and 7, equips a novice insofar as is possible to handle intrusive medical procedures, including everything from emergency anesthetic to concussions to abscessed molars to childbirth.

9. ***A Barefoot Doctor's Manual***, 1979. Running Press, 1255 22nd Street, Philadelphia, PA 19103.

   This is the English translation of an official Maoist Chinese paramedical manual and is a very simple, basic text, assuming few medications and facilities for barely literate med-tech workers out in rural areas. When few supplies or pieces of equipment are available, this book could be invaluable for diagnosis and treatment.

10. ***Where There Is No Doctor—A Village Health Care Handbook***, 1990, by David Werner. Hesperian Foundation Publications, Box 1692, Palo Alto, CA 94302.

This very basic, simply written medical text was developed for essentially counterculture or Third World medical workers. This text and A Barefoot Doctor's Manual assume little training or knowledge of medical matters.

11. ***The Ship's Medicine Chest and Medical Aid at Sea***. 1978. Superintendent of Public Documents, U.S. Government Printing Office, Washington, D.C. 20402.

This book was based on actual medical experiences encountered by U.S. maritime services over a period of more than 100 years.

12. ***Ditch Medicine***, 1993, by Hugh C. Coffee. Paladin Press, Box 1307, Boulder, CO 80306.

This manual covers advanced blood cases and how to handle them, using simple laymen's language and techniques. It also outlines the basic supplies required.

13. ***Survivalist's Medicine Chest***, 1982, by Ragnar Benson. Paladin Press, Box 1307, Boulder, CO 80306.

This provides instructions for the use of veterinary medical supplies in an emergency context.

A library containing most or all of these volumes would provide a major boost to any man of action's medical plan. Some of the information is overlapping, but none is contradictory. Even very persistent people will find that accumulating all these volumes will take a great deal of effort.

SI Outdoor Food and Equipment, Box 3796, Gardena, CA 90247 can sometimes help with some obscure or difficult medical titles. Also try any used bookstores in the area and, of course, new bookstores for some titles.

As mentioned, these volumes will discuss some highly sophisticated, tightly regulated medications. Fortunately, several excellent sources are available.

If you know beforehand that specific medications will be necessary, because they are currently in use, a very simple procedure involves trying to buy ahead on the original prescription. Physicians will often allow the purchase of several refills of a drug, especially after being told that the recipient will be traveling for a few months.

Refill as many times as the prescription allows. Some drugs may get stale, but generally druggist recommendations are very conservative. One can

refrigerate or freeze these drugs or plan to take slightly larger amounts as they weaken from age (this requires caution, however; never do this without discussing it with your doctor, pharmacist, or some trained medical professional, or thoroughly researching it in your medical texts). Narcotics seem to be the worst offenders for losing their effectiveness through aging.

If you can secure a copy of a physician's prescription form, it can be scanned into a computer and then used to write prescriptions for oral painkillers such as Tylenol #4s. Injectable painkillers are seldom administered by prescription. Trying to do so could get you caught quickly. Of course, forging medical prescriptions is highly illegal, and you can get in a lot of trouble.

Another workable plan involves going to Mexico or Canada to purchase needed supplies. Rules are changing in these countries, and the selection is not as good as it once was, but it is still worth a try. Travelers to such places as the Philippines or Thailand, for instance, can purchase almost any medication, including many not available in the United States.

Those who cannot travel abroad to purchase medications can have them shipped legally to the United States by regular mail. Given modern phone systems and fax machines, this system is cheap, easy, and legal. Anyone wishing to purchase drugs overseas should read *How to Buy Almost Any Drug Legally Without a Prescription* by James H. Johnson, published by Avon Books.

Although they are used primarily to treat fractures, burns, and skin lesions, and to patch up blood cases, there is no sanitary or medical reason not to use veterinarian-grade pharmaceuticals. This includes using injectable antibiotics for pneumonia, burns, and other infections. Most kids raised on livestock farms are already familiar with use of vet-grade medications on themselves and family members. Vet pharmaceuticals are put up with as much care as human medications. The principal difference is the size of vials of injectables and pills: doses for animals are much larger than for humans. Some eye medications and skin salves are very strong and must be diluted. In this regard, you must know how to read the bottle as well as medical texts in the reference library.

Most convenient vet-grade materials are oral and injectable antibiotics. Vet-grade penicillin, for

Common oral antibiotics and other medications identical to those prescribed for humans are available for pennies right off the farm dealer's shelves. This particular medication is a knockout to diarrhea.

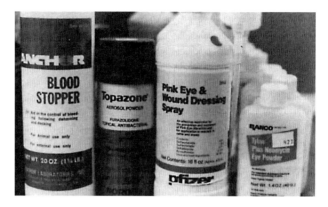

Pink-eye medications, which work wonders in healing wounds, are examples of vet medicines with uses that are not entirely obvious. They contain antiseptics, antibiotics, and anesthetics. Blood coagulants may be useful in treating wounds, too.

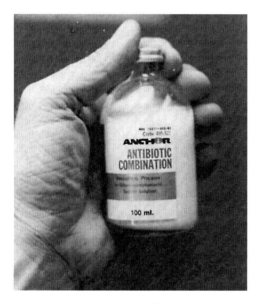

Combiotic, containing penicillin and sulfa drugs, is the old standby for farmers. It currently sells for about $2.50 for a 100cc bottle.

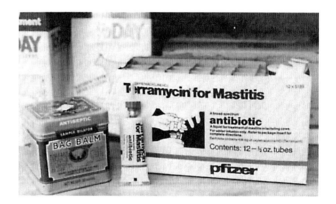

Be alert for survival/paramilitary applications for vet medications that treat seemingly unrelated maladies. Mastitis remedies are useful for eye infections, and Bag Balm works wonders on minor cuts and scrapes.

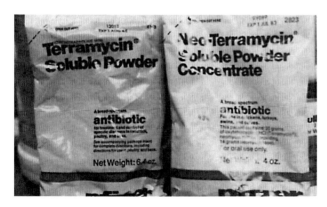

Oral antibiotics are necessary for treating everything from gunshot wounds to plague.

Well-stocked vet supply shelves are common wherever livestock is raised. Even internationally, many otherwise unavailable items can be purchased.

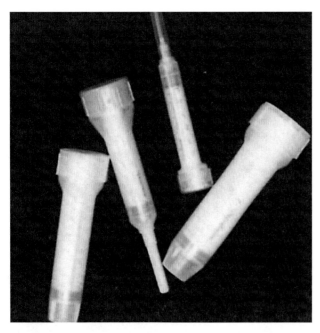

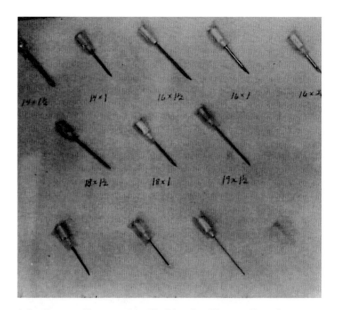

Injection needles are classified by size. The smaller, shorter sizes are best for using on humans.

Plastic disposable syringes cost a few cents each and come in sizes from 2 to 60cc.

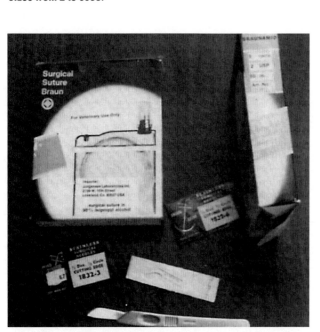

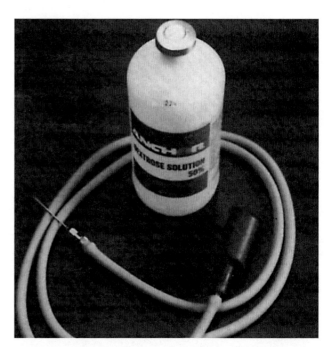

Sutures, scalpels, blades, and hemostats are sold in vet supply houses. The smaller needles are suited for use on humans and must be held with a hemostat or needle holder.

Intravenous devices are used in vet medicine. This simple outfit might work in an emergency, but if you expect to give general anesthetics, you will need a model that has flow metering and valves.

instance, is inexpensive and easily acquired. It is excellent for plague, tuberculosis, pneumonia, and infections from cuts and gunshots. You must consult medical reference books to determine the correct dosage, given the density of the product on hand. You can also use data supplied with the drug that show recommended dosage for hogs of the same body weight as that of the human patient.

Bag Balm, a fine old wound dressing used by dairy farmers for decades to cure minor cuts and chapping, is another common material. Many people already use Bag Balm, but it is a really poor sister among much stronger antibiotic-based skin treatments available in the local farm supply stores in livestock-raising areas. Many such stores are stocked with an excellent selection of vet-grade medications.

Treating serious burns is a common problem for men of action. Several excellent vet products available off the shelf treat burns wonderfully. Use materials containing silver sulfadiazine or mafenide. Trade names are probably Silvadene and Sulfamylon. An aerosol called Scarlex is also effective.

Pink-eye medications work well as topical treatments for gunshot and stab wounds. Treat puncture wounds with pink-eye medication before sewing them up. Tri-sulfa, an extremely common vet product, contains three sulfa drugs effective for treating infections. Common granulated sugar is an excellent wound dressing that often works as well as antibiotics to control infection.

Parasites, internal and external, may be a problem for men of action living in crowded, dirty conditions and eating questionable food. Piperazine works safely and effectively for most internal parasites. Mycodex powder controls fleas. Other vet fungicides work wonders on ringworm and impetigo.

Given our present narcotics laws, it is difficult to acquire a supply of injectable painkillers that would allow you to sew up nasty wounds without convulsing the patient. Yet extensive use of painkillers is risky and best left to someone with professional training.

Vet-grade chloroform, for instance, though reasonably easy to purchase over the counter in the United States, is risky to use even in an emergency.

Chloroform used improperly can easily give a patient pneumonia or kill him outright.

Agricultural vet supply stores are also excellent places to look for disposable syringes, reusable syringes, hypodermic needles, sewing needles, and sutures. Men of action can purchase stainless hemostats, scalpels, and even intravenous kits if they feel qualified to use such gear.

If you are not particularly fussy about resulting scars and the discomfort of the victim, sewing up wounds is not particularly dangerous or difficult. The wound must be cleaned, treated, and then closed so that it drains and has no pockets. (See *Ditch Medicine* for complete details.)

Setting bones is primarily a mechanical procedure and is usually best done by the most skilled auto mechanic in the group. Have the person doing the setting study diagrams of skeletal structure thoroughly before proceeding. For this reason, it may be wise to include a copy of *Gray's Anatomy* in the reference library. Recently, discount booksellers have had these at sizable discounts.

Obviously, those intent on conducting their own medical procedures outside the monopoly imposed by numerous government agencies can do so by using a number of innovative measures. At times, these concepts are not convenient or easy, and, of course, using them throws responsibility for such actions back on the individual personally. And, today, it is uncommon in our society for people to want to assume personal responsibility for their actions.

These do-it-yourself ideas are risky. Proceed only as far as your personal responsibility, knowledge, and external circumstances permit.

BIBLIOGRAPHY

Benson, Ragnar. *Survivalist's Medicine Chest.* Boulder, CO: Paladin Press, 1982.

Coffee, Hugh L. *Ditch Medicine: Advanced Field Procedures for Emergencies.* Boulder, CO: Paladin Press, 1993.

CHAPTER

Auto Pursuit & Evasion

42

On March 16, 1978, Aldo Moro, one of Italy's most famous politicians, was ambushed and kidnapped by Italian members of the Red Brigade as he returned from Sunday Mass. Aldo Moro's case achieved worldwide notoriety partly because he was not found until almost two months later, his dead body stuffed in the trunk of a stolen car, and because he was supposedly protected by a large team of professional guards.

One could argue that Moro's chauffeur and four bodyguards were professionals: they ended up forfeiting their lives in the line of duty. This, however, is only a very superficial evaluation. His chauffeur and the bodyguard accompanying him in his car were killed instantly by extremely short-range pistol fire. Two guards in a follow vehicle were killed by a second pistol-packing team that hit the left of the guards' car. A third guard rolled clear of the strike team but was taken out by sniper fire directed from an adjacent building's third-story rooftop. Experts agree this was a well-planned operation.

Moro was pulled out alive and hustled away in an operation lasting 30 seconds at most. This was not the first terrorist incident of that era. Nor was it unique in its execution. All these terrorist attacks basically used the concept of bringing superior firepower to bear on a target temporarily sealed off from outside help. Attacks on vehicles were favored because vehicles, as in Moro's case, defined the number of adversaries (guards) and they took predictable paths.

Moro's case was especially regrettable in that the same organization had used almost identical tactics to pull off the same sort of operation just six months earlier in Cologne, Germany. In this case, Hans Schleyer was abducted and didn't appear again till his body was discovered in a stolen car parked in a downtown lot. Nobody seemed to learn a thing from either of these attacks.

In both cases, professional drivers were employed who should have had sufficient training and experience to know when something was not kosher. Their duty was to keep their charges out of danger, never exposing them to the enemy.

Both victims were operating on predictable routes in an extremely predictable manner. Both drivers allowed their clients to become creatures of habit, creating ideal circumstances for a trap. Isolating or freezing the intended victim in place for a few seconds was, therefore, not even particularly difficult.

Moro's car was abruptly cut off at a narrow intersection common in residential Rome. His follow car, traveling much too close for its speed, slammed into the rear of his car. The terrorists didn't even require a second vehicle to close the escape route should Moro's driver have had the presence of mind to slam into reverse and get out of there. In this regard the follow car, filled with guards, aided the terrorists! His professional security crew should never have permitted this to happen. But, of course, they were heavily penalized for their neglect.

People who study such things claim that business executives and politicians spend about 17 percent of their time in transit from one place to another. This does not include business trips, but rather is the time spent in autos coming and going to work, recreation, meetings, family, and church. Such vehicles are excellent terrorist targets.

Transport vehicles are often left out in the open in public areas with little protection. When in use, these vehicles are isolated from outside assistance.

The only protection an individual has, if attacked, is whatever is built into the vehicle. The number of persons in transit vehicles is severely restricted, and the maximum number is 100 percent predictable. As a result, terrorists can pick from a selection of good locations from which to concentrate their forces. To make matters worse, terrorists can actually practice to some extent on the actual ground on which they intend to strike. Casual onlookers are seldom suspicious. Under these conditions, it is amazing that terrorist attacks are organized against anything other than a key person's transport vehicle.

A vehicle is the most important component of executive protection plans. A good driver must be trained to use defensive, high-speed, and offensive driving tactics competently. An executive's driver must be absolutely committed to the concept of keeping and, if necessary, getting his man out of danger. A driver should be a coward about ever duking it out with the bad guys. If shooting starts, the driver has already lost 80 percent of his effectiveness.

Good executive drivers spend incredible amounts of time practicing with the same vehicle in which they chauffeur their clients. Automobiles with reinforced bodies, heavy Kevlar floor mats, and bulletproof windows afford the most protection, but they handle differently than other, noncustomized vehicles. Professional drivers learn every nook and cranny of every street, alley, and parking lot along the routes on which they operate. They attempt to bring greater mobility and speed to the equation than the bad buys.

A driver should immediately recognize potentially dangerous or threatening situations and take action to get out of them. An executive driver is always suspicious, nervous, and alert to surveillance, following vehicles, and any other suspicious actions. He always keeps his vehicle buttoned up.

A driver regularly talks over developing circumstances with fellow guards, carefully evaluating situations they notice. It's better to falsely cry wolf a few times than to be trapped by two cars and lose the client. Countermeasures must be undertaken at the slightest reasonable provocation.

Repair and maintenance of the executive vehicle are also duties assumed by the driver. Routine maintenance, such as keeping the engine tuned and reservoirs filled, must never be allowed to hamper safe transport of one's charge. A drive is also expected to be especially alert for any surreptitious entry or tampering. Many maintain inspection checklists that would surprise a novice. These include closely monitoring the spare tire, never driving on less than a half tank of fuel, always checking the exhaust for blockages or explosives, checking the trunk for forced entry, checking wheel lugs for proper tightness, keeping the hood secure, and always being alert for forced entry.

Some drivers are also charged with keeping communications gear in good working order. Responsibility for repairs usually extends only to the drivers reporting any repair problems or suspected problems and seeing that the repairs are made quickly and properly.

When transporting clients, it is imperative that drivers always know that it is more important to know how to detect a trap being executed and avoid it than it is to know how to run through a roadblock or execute a bootleg turn after they fall so far into the trap as to make these maneuvers unavoidable.

Good drivers spend hours practicing on smooth blacktop soaked with oil, so they can properly handle weaving in and out of traffic at high speeds, emergency stopping, and reversing and high-speed backing without losing control. Stability, steerability, maneuverability, and escape routes must always be in mind.

Any special situations, such as detours, accidents, or being boxed in while driving down a freeway, must be analyzed quickly, decisively, and accurately. Good drivers are virtually idiot savants, regarding the streets and roads over which they operate. They know them all and avoid anything unusual, always keeping safe exit havens in mind.

Offensive driving is defined as the violent, sudden, unexpected use of a big, heavy, powerful vehicle against a terrorist to get away or, if necessary, out of a trap. If a threatening vehicle must be rammed, professional drivers do so on one corner so that it can be moved out of the way. Experts slow down a bit, causing the front of the vehicle to drop, relaxing those at the roadblock. They then shift to a lower gear and, at the last moment, accelerate as hard as possible, tearing through at a corner. As soon as they break clear of an attempted roadblock, they try to get out of sight of the bad guys.

Emergency, high-speed turns on narrow roads are done either going forward if enough forward maneuver room is available, or by stopping, reversing to 30 MPH and swinging the vehicle around 180 degrees.

Forward, high-speed turns are done by shifting to neutral at high speed, turning slightly left, and then locking up the emergency brake. The rear wheels will begin to lead the vehicle to the right. As this happens, the driver cuts the wheels a fraction more, simultaneously releasing the emergency brake, slams the vehicle into a lower gear, and applies lots of power, thereby pushing the vehicle around into the opposite direction. These maneuvers take both a lot of skill and practice, as well as great cars. But they are life saving in many circumstances.

Commonly, assassins simply pull up alongside a target car and open fire. Properly done, bad guys will have as many as 15 or 20 seconds in which to expend up to 100 rounds of ammo into a victim's auto. Decoy and trap vehicles are often employed in cooperation with the carload of shooters.

Business laws in Bangkok, Thailand, are often ill defined. As a result, it is somewhat common for a severely cheated businessman to hire a hit team to even the score. It is generally known who in the business community perpetrated the deed, although legal proof is hardly ever forthcoming. This remedy is seldom undertaken and then only in the most blatantly dishonest cases where courts of law are of no help. Knowing that they might be shot for their chicanery has a wonderful, restraining effect on many people who might otherwise abuse their freedom without any attendant responsibility.

Professional hitmen in Bangkok almost always do their work from motorcycles. By so doing, they can escape among the horrendous traffic that characterizes that city. Skilled motorcycle hit teams are extremely tough to react to. They come and go very quickly. The rider-shooter can concentrate on making good shots while the driver slips in between cars and into position.

Defense against these vehicles includes swinging back and forth and changing lanes so that attackers must face forward at long range. If the chauffeur is alert enough to observe a motorcycle approaching, he can swing the heavier, more powerful vehicle into the motorcycle, neutralizing it. He can execute a fast, 180-degree turn or stop suddenly, causing the shooters to overshoot their target. In Thailand, where there are tens of thousands of motorcycles and traffic moves bumper to bumper, no reaction is particularly effective.

Most professional bodyguards feel that hardening a vehicle is important; but, hardening or not, using a trained, experienced driver is by far the most critical element. Adding too much armor will needlessly burden the vehicle, slowing it down and destabilizing it. It can never be known before whether the armor is placed at correct points. Hardening that protects against bombs does little against sniper attacks. Nevertheless, most experts want good, puncture-proof tires rotated at the first sign of wear and perhaps bullet-resistant, one-way side windows.

After that, one may elect to place a Kevlar mat on the floor as protection against land mines and Kevlar or titanium plates in the doors and roof. The cost of these relatively simple modifications will probably exceed $20,000 per vehicle. In cases where relatively inexpensive Kevlar is used on floors, added mats and weather stripping required to keep it dry boost the price.

Increasingly, those who must travel roads in dangerous circumstances prefer smaller, more common automobiles that do not stand out in traffic. Trained drivers are a necessity, however. (Photo by Ragnar Benson.)

In years gone by, executives and bureaucrats who wished to protect themselves did so by hardening their large, luxury Mercedes or Cadillacs. Often done up at great expense, these vehicles stood out like Moses at the crossing. Modern thinking suggests that lightly armored, smaller, common, inconspicuous vehicles of the type often seen on the road make far better transport vehicles for VIPs. These vehicles are quickly lost in a jumble of traffic and do not stand out blocks away.

In any case, it is impractical to armor against an RPG-7 attack. Most terrorists use pistols or submachine guns, suggesting that relatively light, pistol-round-resistant armor be used for side panels in transport vehicles.

Armor, an alert driver, and dedicated men in follow vehicles notwithstanding, it is still imperative to avoid doing something stupid, such as keeping a regular routine in commuting to and from work, driving around with the windows down or even riding in a vehicle with see-through side windows, regularly stopping for a paper or hamburger, or walking the dog at the same time day after day.

Successfully following a targeted vehicle is tougher than novices who have never tried it would suppose. Without prior training and practice, it is just about impossible in heavy traffic. Perhaps this explains why those who never fall into a travel pattern are much more difficult targets.

Vehicle tailing requires a minimum of three vehicles, all with good drivers, who know all the streets and alleys in the region. Each driver must have an experienced spotter riding along, good radio equipment, and a set of binoculars. Proper tail cars are equipped with a battery of light switches, allowing the selection of a combination of head- and taillights with which to confuse the target driver. These vehicles are distinctive, immediately recognizable to drivers being tailed. By switching back and forth, they can confuse their identification as they follow a target vehicle.

All follow vehicles should be generic, not too old or new, and of neutral colors. Tailing drivers and spotters should carry several jackets or shirts to change into, lessening the likelihood that they will be recognized. At times, the passenger should lie down, giving the impression that there is a different vehicle with different driver.

Attempt as much as possible to keep one vehicle way ahead of the victim and one well behind. A third vehicle may pass parallel ahead of both cars or may wait in a place where it is reasonably certain that the victim will pass. Always maintain radio contact.

Any time the target signals a turn, stops, or otherwise undertakes an erratic maneuver, everyone on the follow team must be notified by radio. By so doing, the third vehicle might stop a block behind, from which point its driver can keep the target under surveillance. Other vehicles may wait in a place where it is reasonably certain that the victim will eventually pass. Check by radio.

During sensitive follow projects, the team may elect to follow only halfway, picking up the balance of the journey another day. Tracing routine pattern travel from a predictable office location to a home or apartment quickly becomes a piece of cake!

The toughest maneuver to handle is when the target takes a narrow, deserted road, allowing anyone to see both ahead and behind for great distances. If the target elects to make a sharp U-turn, there is little you can do without giving away your intentions. Without a third follow car in radio contact, the target will be lost.

Like protective driving and guarding, tailing is something of an art. Effective cooperation among practitioners only comes at the expense of great practice and on-the-ground experience.

BIBLIOGRAPHY

Scott French and Lapin, Lee. *SpyGame*. Boulder, CO: Paladin Press, 1985.

CHAPTER

Radar Detectors & Jammers

43

ncredible as it may seem, it has been 20 long years since the feds imposed the double nickel on us. A whole generation has grown up not knowing about freedom of the road. To most citizens, 55 MPH is the established standard. In place of freedom and responsibility, we have a vast revenue-gathering scheme through which our nation's municipalities and principalities are given legal license to force us to pay sums of money way above the costs of collection and accurately calculated to be just under those that will make us fight back. In other words, it is easy to slip over 55, easier still to be apprehended through some shaky technology, and usually easier to just pay up, shut up, and go away.

This apprehension and shakedown of drivers was institutionalized in the mid-1970s when 55 made the venture profitable. Prior to this time, speeding tickets were not much of a factor, other than in a few notorious Georgia and Florida speed traps.

Radar devices were first used in the late 1940s by a few police departments to check speeds. But the insignificantly few offenders apprehended made the practice basically nonproductive. However, things seldom stay the same. Today there are an estimated 220,000 radar units in the hands of those with a vast incentive to catch drivers breaking some foolish laws.

Radar works by sending out a radio wave signal that is reflected off the hard metal surfaces of the target, creating an echo back to the sending unit. Direct (output) and reflected (return) radio beams generate a signal within a radar unit that beams a linear relationship to the speed of the target. At radio frequencies of 10.525 GHz each, 31.4 Hz return equals 1 MPH that the target is moving. Police radar contains relatively simple circuits that calculate this return yielding up a figure in MPH. (Real-time tests indicate that about 30 percent of these figures are inaccurate, but this will be discussed in more detail later.)

Police radar currently comes in 2 1/2 flavors, with some exotic systems waiting in the winds. X-band radar operates at a frequency of 10.525 GHz. K-band radar runs at 24.150 GHz. Newer, seldom-seen Ka-band radar is in the 34.00 Hz range.

Pioneer traffic radars were large, cumbersome, semistationary affairs. Eventually, a few relatively small portable units evolved, some of which had

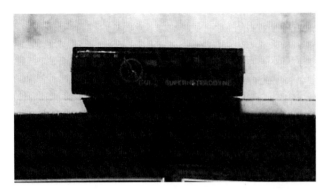

Radar detectors give drivers some protection when driving above the legal speed limit. (Photo by Ragnar Benson.)

instant-on features designed to defeat citizen-owned radar detectors. Often, these early detectors also detected radar detectors.

Modern speed radar units have become much simpler to operate and maintain, but they are still complex. In theory, they can be operated by one person from a moving police cruiser, but so doing requires the dexterity of a fighter pilot. There seems to be a universal consensus that more honest, consistent readings are always made from stationary units, and even these are subject to dispute.

Numerous field tests have shown that speed radar cannot pick out one specific target on a crowded highway, especially at long ranges. Arresting officers make the totally erroneous assumption that radar reads the fastest, closest vehicle. Radar always reads the strongest echo. Small sedans will not register beyond 1,200 feet, whereas large semis echo back good readings at 7,600 feet!

Radar must bounce to work. Signals meant for vehicles may bounce off brick walls, cement abutments, metal guard rails, and even steel billboards, producing really bogus readings. Some portable radar units will actually allow operators to send part of their signal out through the control box, creating great error. Both errors are created by improper aiming, a frequent mistake. As a result, a stationary house was clocked at 20 MPH during tests for a notorious Dade County, Florida, court case. This was caused by moving the unit's antenna while trying to get a lock on a target, something trained users claim never happens, but which field tests have shown to be common.

Moving radar, read from the rear in a following police cruiser, is subject to errors referred to in the industry as "shadowing." The problem here is that accurate target measurements rely on both accurate readings of police cruiser speed and target speed. Moving radar is supposed to compute its own speed. But these readings are often inaccurate themselves. Readings are supposed to track from the road but may inadvertently read from a passing truck. Other times, police car speeds are reckoned to be much lower than they should be as a result of the cruiser's radar fixing on a stationary object too far from the road.

Radio transmissions from sources as diverse as CB radios, police, fire, or ambulance radios; power lines; or transformers have been shown to dramatically affect radar readings. The problem is that many of these causes of interference can be a long way down the road before anyone suspects skewed readings.

Another common error results when police users set a device called an autolock on their radar units. Autolocks are little more than alarms that sound when a vehicle going too fast approaches over a set limit. The guy in the cruiser may be idling away his time thinking about the waitress at the lunch counter and not get it together till another hapless victim approaches who is actually driving well below the legal limit.

Some radar gear takes quite a long time to go from cold start to functional. Contrary to manufacturer claims, this is often true with "instant-on" units. Be alert for errors from this cause as well as all others.

Most radar units are calibrated with a special tuning fork, supplied by the maker. These tuners can be damaged, or, in some cases, calibration is not held to a recognized standard.

None of these relatively common errors happens in isolation. Each compounds the other, piling up errors to the point that you wonder how courts ever take evidence from police radar seriously. Speeding tickets issued on the basis of radar evidence can be beaten, but a competent court battle would probably cost around $40,000. You would have to bring in expert witnesses, depose and study all of the citations issued as a result of a specific radar unit, look at the cops' training, the condition of the unit, road conditions, and the likelihood of erroneous, conflicting radio transmissions, and even bring in weather experts.

One such case did go to trial in Dade County, Florida, in 1979. It was funded by Dale Smith, who became something of a cult hero as a result. The presiding judge was Alfred Nesbitt who eventually concluded: "I find that the reliability of the radar speed-measuring devices as used in their present modes and particularly in these cases has not been established beyond and to the exclusion of every reasonable doubt, nor has it met the test of reasonable scientific certainty."

Judge Nesbitt ordered that evidence from traffic radar be excluded from those court proceedings. Contemporary commentators asked in amazement how a man as fair and sensible as Judge Nesbitt could ever have risen to his post!

As a local ruling, the decision affected only Florida. The case was never appealed. Had the state taken this decision up the judicial chain and had it been upheld, it would have become the law of the United States. Knowing this was true and that they had a poor case, local prosecutors simply took their lumps and retired.

As part of the his decision, Judge Nesbitt also pointed out several other curious truths. The judge admitted that defending against a speeding ticket was prohibitively expensive for most citizens. He also somewhat facetiously claimed that "the end of traffic court is not to serve revenue interests" and that proper training is vital for proper radar use.

It was about this time that a whole new industry blew over the United States. The first commercial radar detectors were big, klutzy affairs with a limited useful range. They appeared in about 1968. A few homebuilt models were built and tested in the mid-1960s, but distribution and need were limited. The technology involved in these early devices was extremely basic.

In 1973 the radar detector space race engendered by the double nickel really took off. First attempts at improving how radar detectors performed were mostly mechanical. These included adding cone antennas and lens-type signal concentrators. All this paraphernalia was blown off the market by the Escort Company in late 1973 when it came out with the first superheterodyne receivers. Temporarily "radar revenooers" were put to rout. Warnings from more than a mile away were not uncommon. Promises of being able to receive warnings from farther out than the radar could achieve a return were first fulfilled.

All top-of-the-line radar detectors today use some form of superheterodyne circuitry. Original superheat receivers leaked enough microwaves to trigger other near radar detectors. Users tooled down the highway, beeping each other in a manner that precluded anyone from free, unencumbered driving. Cops didn't have to patrol; radar detector units in private cars did their job for them. But, of course, revenues from tickets plummeted. As is true with all electronics technology, evolution soon leveled the playing field. Modern detectors will still sometimes trigger other detectors but only at relatively short ranges.

The industry reaction to these new, more foolproof, long-range detectors was the introduction of instant-on radar guns. This shift again threw the balance in favor of radar revenooers. Along with it, a caged-animal syndrome swept the land. This syndrome suggests that those who have never tasted freedom never miss it. Many drivers settled down to a life of government control at 55. They paid unfair, illicitly given tickets in the quickest, easiest possible fashion.

Yet a few freedom-loving men of action elected to fight on. Rumors continually surfaced regarding some type of countermeasure that either confused the mind of the cop's radar gun or caused it to yield up totally erroneous readings as predialed in the speeder's battle stars. Few people actually witnessed these units in operation, principally because they were absolutely illegal.

Reportedly, technology for these jamming devices came from electronics counterwarfare laboratories working on government projects. Rumor has it that they were developed by techies working on top-secret, black boxes for Uncle Sugar.

Men of action, interested in radar-jamming devices, will recall that car and driver magazines of one sort or another have run periodic articles on home construction of radar-jamming devices for private battle stars. These units work on the basic electronic assumption that one can jam radar with transmissions of the proper microwave frequency or with outright deceptive signals, as long as the power of the jammer exceeds that of the radar speed-gun return echo.

Solutions were expensive, technical, and uncertain in their application out on the street. But at last one author undertook both theoretical and practical research on the subject. Because detailed electronic results are difficult to summarize, those interested in jamming devices should both purchase a copy of Peter Desmond's *The Radar Jammer's*

Cook Book and secure the services of a competent electronics wonk.

Improvised radar-jamming devices have these characteristics:

1. They will work.
2. They are quite expensive.
3. They are very illegal.
4. Those who are not electronics techies will not be able to assemble, adjust, test, and deploy a workable jammer.

The first part you will need to make a radar jammer is a basic, commercial superheterodyne radar detector to turn the device off and on. You must take the very best model and modify it so that the warning alarm becomes a switch rather than an audible signal. This is the easiest part of the project. This switch takes the form of a female input jack hand-wired into the radar detector.

Next, you must use two pairs (4) of a device called a Gunn Oscillator. One pair is for the front of the vehicle and the other for the rear. These can be purchased from electronics supplies in either K or X band. You purchase them by specifying the frequency of output desired. They operate on a range from 6 to 10 volts direct current (DC). Users report good success in hiding these microwave generators in fog or driving lights mounted on the vehicle. It takes one of each on both the front and back to achieve acceptable protection.

The third component in an effective radar jammer package is a control unit. Because of legal considerations, no one outlet supplies all the necessary components. Finding one of these control units that will drive two pairs of Gunn Oscillators from 12-volt vehicle current is extremely difficult.

Surplus and new military remote units are out there for people who know what they are doing but are so pricey, even used, that there is no sense considering them.

For some strange reason now lost in the fog of war, Remote Systems, Inc., 12787 Nicollex Avenue S., Burnsville, Minnesota, produces perfect central control units. Ask for their EMC 5446 model. This unit will accept on/off signals from a modified radar detector and will drive the Gunn Oscillators at the correct power. The cost is about $600 each.

Men of action might think this procedure a reasonably simple do-it-yourself project for those with sufficient cash to complete it in a couple of spare weekends. The radar power generated by the Gunn Oscillators can be destructive to your eyes or gonads, and unless you wish to test via a tingling sensation in the aforementioned parts, an oscilloscope will be necessary. Oscilloscopes measure microwave output so that you can know if the jammer is actually jamming.

Jamming units actually made for the above-listed components have been tested by competent electronics people. They had access to traffic radars used by police. Their findings were that the unit worked most of the time, especially at ranges where police most often apprehend speeders. Glitches developed at great distances or at times when signal generators on the jammer's vehicle were pointed in the wrong direction or at curves or steep hills. Settings on the EMC 5446 control unit allow you to generate readings on the cop's reader of about 35, 45, 55, or 70 MPH and to black out his readings no matter how fast you are traveling. Complete scramble or blank appeared to be the most consistent setting in terms of outfoxing radar revenooers.

At about 1/8 mile, jammers worked a good percent of the time. Police radar readings were a blank. This is not uncommon when speed guns are used in high-traffic situations and will probably not cause any undue concern to cops deploying speed guns.

Radar-jamming units are practical and feasible in today's electronic market. Drivers who simply must get through quickly and unmolested and who have the cash to purchase parts for a jamming unit can do so. The only caveat is that someone who is skilled in electronics and possesses test equipment will probably be needed to hook the thing together and get it working properly on a vehicle.

Undoubtedly, many truckers will find these units to be vital to their business.

BIBLIOGRAPHY

Desmond, Peter. *The Radar Jammer's Cook Book.* Total Fiction Publishing, Ltd., U.S.A., 1992.

CHAPTER

Hiding

44

In 1947, a constitutional change was approved in Idaho that outlawed slot machines and all other gaming devices. Prior to this, they were openly deployed in numerous gambling dens in approving counties. Clement Crow was sitting in a small bar called the Ad Club, swilling cheap whiskey, when the owners of the establishment came in, picked up their one-armed bandits, and hauled them downstairs to the basement. Crow watched as a mason came in and neatly bricked up a wall, closing off the dreaded machines from the world.

Old bricks from the demolition of the livery were hauled downstairs and so professionally mortared that it was difficult to tell that the basement was now shorter by 5 feet. After aging a few months, it was completely impossible to tell that this was really a false wall hiding the valuable goods.

Court records can be used to substantiate the following scenario. In 1975, Clement Crow was still sitting at the Ad Club bar bending his elbow. The same people who bricked up the one-armed bandits were getting tired of him. By now old Clement was carrying quite a load. To make a long story short, they threw his sodden ass out in the street.

Clement picked himself up and as quickly as his unsteady condition allowed, walked to the sheriff's office. Unfortunately, this sheriff was in an especially nasty race for reelection.

Based on Crow's testimony, he busted down the Ad Club's basement wall and then, because the publicity was so good, busted the owners for harboring contraband. Eventually, after great profit for the attorneys, Clement was allowed back into the bar, the slots were sledged to death, and their owners got off with loss of their property, attorney fees, and little more.

The moral to this great American tale of the Wild West involves the fact that no matter how clever a person is with his hiding, there will always be someone just as clever with as much motive to find the object as the hiders have for it not to be found.

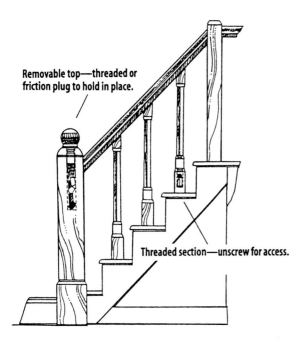

Removable top—threaded or friction plug to hold in place.

Threaded section—unscrew for access.

Small items such as drugs, jewels, or money can be hidden inside stairway posts. (Illustrations from *DEA Stash and Hideout Handbook*)

Anyone who has studied the art of hiding, read contemporary writers on the subject, and been subjected to a thorough government shakedown knows this as a basic fact of life.

An acquaintance of mine had his home completely trashed by the BATF. Before they got the warrant, the agents told him they were going to ruin his place unless he 'fessed up or ratted on someone on whom they could make a case.

Although the government kept its promise, virtually ruining the guy's home, he escaped legal harm. It was, however, by accident that he did so. The parts the government sought were taped to the bottom of his wastebasket. They trashed his place so completely that junk covered the potentially offending wastebasket.

Regardless of the circumstances, effective hiding techniques make clever use of hidden open space in one's building. This space should be covered from view or very difficult to get to. Those who are most clever about hiding are generally construction types who know a great deal about how buildings are put together and are painstakingly patient. The best hides are always the product of considerable concentration. Attention to tiny details when building the hide is invaluable.

As an example, who would have supposed that most wooden doors in a home are hollow, containing large amounts of usable space? Construction people know that it is easy to cut out a portion of the frame from a hollow door and make available a great deal of hidden space inside. You could make an access hole in the frame on the underside, stuff the core full of whatever, and then reglue the piece taken from the frame to complete the hide. Those who are truly paranoid should cut their access way into the door core from the bottom.

Finding these hides makes the government agents take the door off its hinges to look. On the other hand, it is less convenient to fill these stashes, and the hider must take care that the contents do not rattle when the door is opened. But they are quite secure when hiding small items.

Often relatively large amounts of space are available around doors, underneath the molding. Remove the molding and look around. Rifles and shotguns can be slipped between door frames and wall joists. When the molding is reinstalled, it will completely hide the weapons.

Floor joists present lots of hard work in trying to reach or see storage space. Generally, joists are spaced 16 inches apart and covered from above by plywood flooring and rugs or linoleum and from below by ceiling tiles. Professionals generally feel it is easier and less obvious to come down into this space from above when constructing a hide.

Peel back the rug or linoleum covering the intended hide spot. Carefully and cleanly cut out a square of plywood or particle-board flooring and subflooring. Remove a section reaching from halfway over a joist to halfway over to the next joist. Lift this up and there will be a space 16 inches wide and, depending on the building, a place up to 8 or 10 feet long, 6 to 12 inches deep.

Because ceilings below may not be very strong, it will be necessary to construct a sheet-steel or plywood box or hanging bracket affair to hold items placed in these hides. Fill up the hide. Place the solid chunks of flooring back over the open hole and roll the carpet back over the whole thing. A refrigerator or large sofa positioned over the top of the floor covering makes it less accessible to those searching for your hiding spots.

Some books on the subject of hiding suggest placing valuables in the backs of electrical outlet boxes or in false compartments in or under stairs. I suspect that federal agents have read these same books and will be quick to check out these relatively easy places.

Uncle Horace has a small sailing vessel with which he has crossed the Atlantic Ocean several times. On each trip, customs agents in Scotland and the United States went over his boat with a fine-toothed comb. It was not unusual for inspectors to take five or six hours examining Horace's relatively small boat. On one occasion in Scotland, one of the agents suggested that he repaint the inside of his boat, covering all the screws holding wall panels. He did, and now agents simply scan the paint to be sure no screws have been scarred from turning. Current inspections take 45 minutes or less.

Customs agents tell me that they can spot false bottoms in trunks or suitcases quite easily. Although these sound pretty sexy, false bottoms in drawers are also easily noticed by professional searchers. They quickly confirm their suspicions by the hollow sound made when thumped.

Large boxes of detergent or cake mix can be carefully unglued so that contraband can be hidden therein. But government agents are on to this scheme as well. Agents are trained to go directly to any powdery, messy materials and throw them around the room, creating an even greater mess.

If you have a large amount of canned goods in storage, surreptitiously opening one of these and replacing with hidden goods *might* work. Doing this properly is extremely difficult. Searching agents will spill the canned goods about and may hear the dull thunk when a stash can hits. Or they may notice its lightness. This, again, is a concept that is better in theory than practice.

Better stashes are those made by drilling up into table or desk legs an inch or two. These hollow cavities will hold a roll of bills or several rounds of ammunition without likely discovery.

Some hiders report outstanding results using a router to cut a cavity in a counter or table top. After filling the cavity with their goods, they replace the steel trim on the edge of the counter boards.

Members of the Italian resistance during World War II installed miscellaneous pieces of plumbing and sewage pipe in homes, hotels, and factories to look as through they were serving a valid purpose. Inside these fake plumbing pipes, they placed guns, explosives, and ammunition. Reportedly, these fairly easy-to-access hides were never found by the Nazis.

The trick here was to install very, very carefully so that the pipes really did look as though they served a valid purpose. They ran 4-inch cast-iron pipe from one end of a basement to another, stubbed into holes in the wall. After the holes, the pipe just ended. In many cases, these pipes were right out in plain sight. It took a set of building blueprints to determine that they were bogus, something the Nazis of that era did not have. Government searchers today may come prepared with a set of building plans.

The best hide I have ever been acquainted with was actually a hide for an indoor cache tube. Ever so carefully, we chiseled a hole in the concrete floor of an apartment complex. The hole was to accept a 6-inch posthole auger, with which fill down to 4 feet was removed. When we were finished, the hole just accepted a 6-inch floor drain cover. The hole in the ground just barely held a plastic 6-inch plastic cache tube.

We used sackcrete mortar mix to cement the floor drain cover in place. Because the hole we chipped was a bit ragged, it took about two hatfuls of mortar to close. While the mortar was still wet, we sprinkled a large amount of fine, black dust on it for coloring. After a couple of weeks, it was impossible to tell even by close examination that the floor had ever been redone. The drain went no place, and if someone tried to pour anything down it, he would assume it was plugged. Below, the 4-inch pipe held quite a load of valuables.

A business associate in Indonesia had a secret room in his large home. It was extremely well done by very talented craftsmen who worked for pennies per hour. He kept some pieces of art, jewelry, gold coins, and some videos in the room. But, alas, once someone was alerted what to look for or was aware of the fact that there could be a room, it seemed obvious that something was there. Internal dimensions just didn't work out. Someone interested in robbery would have been immediately suspicious. Pounding and bumping on the walls would have confirmed his suspicions.

Based on that experience alone, it seems unlikely that something as big as a secret room

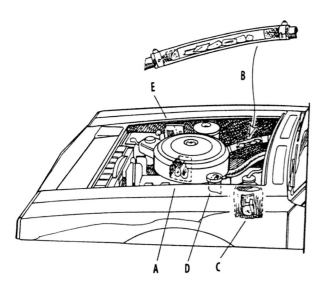

Under the automobile hood is a popular place to hide valuables or smuggled goods. Among the places to stash things: (A) in the air filter, B) in false heater hose, (C) in windshield washer fluid reservoir, (D) inside oil cap, and (E) in hollow voltage regulator.

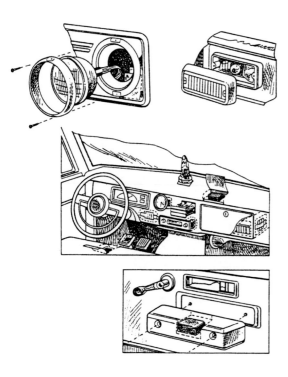

The automobile has other hiding places as well: behind headlights and taillights, behind the instrument panel and ornamental objects on the dashboard, and within arm rests.

would ever work, except perhaps in a castle, a large underground cave, or a home with scores of rooms.

People seem to be rather cavalier about hides in their automobiles—probably the same people who never have had their vehicle completely shaken down by customs agents at the border. Secret compartments glued to the inside back top of the trunk or welded to the vehicle frame simply don't work.

A friend living in Los Mochis, Mexico, had the only hide in a vehicle that I personally ever saw work. He took an old square air cleaner out of a Jeep Cherokee and had it cleanly and professionally mounted inside the engine compartment of his pickup truck. Hoses and electrical wires ran from the empty box in an official-looking manner.

It was a most professional job that looked very good. But the extraneous piece of equipment served no purpose except to carry the fellow's Ruger Standard Auto when he came across the border. Occasionally, he also brought some pea seed into California, providing a small additional economic incentive for the trip.

All around, people with hides in doors, under seats, and even in spare tires were getting nailed by the authorities. This guy went back and forth with great impunity, proving the value of his specific hide over and over.

To some extent, the minds of electronic metal detectors are clouded by the presence of building insulation. Good hides are sometimes made in places where one can access heavy overlapping layers of rockwool insulation. Cut out an internal cavity and place objects to be hidden in among the insulation. These places can provide some really excellent, hard-to-discover hides if you are careful about opening and closing them. Move the items in these hides in and out infrequently.

Heating and cooling ducts in some apartments can be used as successful hides. You can crawl way back into them, fastening hide boxes up into difficult places with metal screws or big magnets. These hides will be found by dedicated searchers, but not without their spending a great deal of energy.

The most powerful tools hiders have are their quick wits, in-depth knowledge of the structure in which they live, and time. They have to put a great deal of thought into their overall objectives. On the other hand, bad guys are not dumb either. They will bring great experience to their task of finding hides and will always do so if their political bosses instruct them to put their minds to the task.

BIBLIOGRAPHY

DEA Stash and Hideout Book. Boulder, CO: Paladin Press, 1988.

Connor, Michael. *How to Hide Anything.* Boulder, CO: Paladin Press, 1984.

Luger, Jack. *Big Book of Secret Hiding Places.* Port Townsend, WA: Loompanics Unlimited, 1987.

Robinson, Charles. *Secret Hiding Places.* Cornville, AZ: Desert Publications, 1981.

CHAPTER

Skip Tracing

45

Skip tracing is an exciting industry that has developed only during the last 50 years. Some of the people who work in this business make truly astounding incomes. Depending, of course, on an individual's ability to do this work well, in a creative, ambitious, effective sort of way, it is an ideal low-overhead, work-at-home endeavor for men of action who want large incomes as well as free time to pursue other activities.

In many regards, tracing people has become more difficult as those who do not wish to be found become more effective in their elusive ways. Yet modern desktop computers with more speed and power than last year's mainframes have dramatically leveled the playing field. Massive computer data banks make it possible to find out virtually everything about anybody. People who a few short years ago could hide behind a totally new ID can now be found relatively easily through ex-girlfriends, parents, children, purchase of hunting

license, membership in hobby groups, magazine subscriptions, and even through past employment records, all contained in massive data banks.

People all over the Western world, and the United States in particular, are attempting to drop out because of bad debts, bad marriages, court proceedings, legal determinations, mental illness, poverty, employment problems, or for other mostly government-related reasons. Finding these people for those they've skipped out on has become an excellent business for men whose quick, innovative minds make them extremely creative at solving problems. Income is based entirely on how much "smart labor" there is available to invest.

It takes little more than an orderly personality, telephone, file cabinet, a desk, chair, about $150 worth of reference books, and about $300 for the first month's phone bills to get started. A novice can use legwork rather than computers at the start, doing the research by mail, in person, and by phone, if he cannot initially afford a computer. Newcomers to the business have secured hundreds of customers by

This college student with only a telephone and a secondhand computer made more than $40,000 working as a skip tracer. (Photos by Ragnar Benson.)

circulating a simple, one-page letter to all the attorneys, banks, large retail stores, and automotive shops in their area.

Many missing people are easy to find because they do not know they are missing. When a person dies intestate (i.e., without leaving a will), the state is obligated to distribute remaining funds to the decedent's heirs. Often, these heirs are scattered across the land, without a clue that they ever had a rich aunt or uncle.

Finding these people earns a finder's fee that, in the correct circumstances, can be significant. Finders search probate court records in the county courthouse, looking for large estates for which no next of kin are listed. Working as a free agent, an aggressive skip tracer will try to locate members of a family that didn't even know they were members of that family or have completely forgotten about each other. Often, investigators also legally qualify nearest living next-of-kin as to their position in the blood line, based on their professional research.

Most people have some living blood relatives. A good investigator will find these people and then strike a deal for part of their inheritance. By doing their homework ahead, smart skip tracers do not start looking for hard-to-find relatives unless they know that inheritance is relatively large and that

they probably can find an heir.

Reliable estimates indicate that about one-third of all Americans have money in bank savings accounts or insurance accounts that they have completely forgotten about. These people are not skips nor are they hiding, they simply must be tracked down and told about the bank account they left at age 14 or whatever when they moved away.

A solid 2 percent of all corporate stockowners are estimated to be missing. In some cases this represents significant blocks of valuable stock. Skip tracers with good abilities can sometimes purchase lost account records from banks and insurance companies or even regular stock companies. Returns from these can be excellent, due in large part to the fact that the people to whom these funds are owed are not hiding, they are just ignorant.

Every state in the union has an unclaimed property division, usually in its revenue department at the state capital. Contact these departments about unclaimed property and see if some of the heirs can be found.

Locating natural birth parents has exploded into a lucrative industry in the United States. Countless thousands of adopted people are currently seeking long-lost parents. The only reason more do not look for lost relatives is because they don't know who can help them with their search. In many cases, 50 or more years have intervened, allowing the trail to grow very cold. Only those with excellent tracking skills have any hope of finding long-lost parents, sisters, brothers, or other family members.

Some work for the federal government is available to professional skip tracers. Housing and Urban Development (HUD)/Federal Housing Administration (FHA) has a private program in which funds collected in a kind of federal insurance program called an MIP are retained in an account in a mortgage holder's name. Commonly, the mortgage holders sold their homes, transferred their mortgages to new owners, and abandoned funds that were really theirs in an inactive account held by the government. Because the task of finding these people is monumental, the FHA has contracted this business out to private skip tracers.

Fees average about 30 percent of any funds in a missing person's account, or about $240 to $420 for each person located. Again, these people are misplaced, not hiding. Lists of the people owed government refunds are secured through HUD or, in some cases, private companies that provide more timely service.

One major additional opportunity for people who wish to make a living out of finding other people—other than deadbeats, rent cheats, lawsuit litigants, court witnesses, criminals under indictment, and those fleeing judgments—exists for the truly entrepreneurial at heart: judgment investing.

Judgment investing involves researching past court judgments that have been handed down in the local, small claims, and district courts, wherein judgments have been awarded that the beneficiary had no idea how to collect. Often the judge declares, "Yes, he owes you the money," but the plaintiff to whom it is owed already knows that but has no idea how to go about forcing payment. After a year or so, recipients of these judgments often forget about them, forsaking all hope of collection.

People engaged in this business go to their courthouse and browse through court records till they find judgments of sufficient age and dollar amounts that might be profitably worked.

Next they check boat, vehicle, and real estate registrations to see if any assets are listed in the name of the debtor. If assets are available, a judgment investor will try to purchase the judgment

from its current holder. Purchase prices are generally a few cents on the dollar. If the judgment is several years old and the principal has left town, holders are often most pleased to sell.

Some experts class auto repossession with skip tracing. It is skip tracing, since customarily the most difficult part of this business is locating the debtor and his unpaid-for vehicle. Banks and finance companies will pay to locate the guy and the vehicle, but the real cash comes when one picks up the vehicle itself and returns it to the finance company.

Modern banks and finance companies usually keep a record of the vehicle key code. If not them, then the original dealer will have it. People in the skip/repo business can go back to the bank and dealer to have new keys cut. This completely does away with the need to use sophisticated skills to break into and start targeted vehicles. It also creates a situation where the real skill in this entire enterprise involves finding the guy who took off, owing a bill on the vehicle. This is ideal work for skip tracers who do not want to learn how to pick car locks and pull and jump ignition switches.

Skip tracers may also work with modern-day bounty hunters, or they may also work as the guy who brings in the badass himself. Most really good skip tracers are more intellectual in nature, not given to going out with handcuffs and Mace in search of a rapist who has jumped bail. Bounty hunting is a very interesting, adrenaline-producing occupation often kept separate from skip tracing.

Obviously, skip tracing is central to all of these enterprises. It is the difficult part of this work for which admittedly not many men of action are suited.

Usually, someone becomes interested in skip tracing as a result of experience gained looking for a friend or relative on a personal basis. Some people turn finding a debtor who skipped while owing them a personal bill into a very enjoyable enterprise. Some people go to work in agencies who do this sort of work, gaining their experience in this fashion. Either by on-the-job training or by self-acquired skills, those who learn are always assured a fairly lucrative job.

Lists of sources of information as well as computer data banks relative to finding people are many. It is virtually impossible to summarize all the sources of information available. Those serious about this business will amass literally truckloads of reference books. In some cases, these volumes are too expensive for private ownership, but can be found and used in local libraries. Cross-reference books such as R.P. Polk, which list residences by street location (including occupation of the residents and telephone numbers with names), are excellent examples. These reference books start at $150 for small communities and can cost in the thousands for larger cities.

Locating a long-lost relative may include going back to a 1972 Polk's directory to learn the names of neighbors in the targeted individual's area. You may then look at a modern Polk to see if these neighbors are still living at their old locations. A new skip tracer is not likely to be able to afford to purchase directories, of which Polk's is only one example of many going back 20 or 30 years. You must use the public library.

Start a skip trace by amassing *all* the details possible about the sought-for individual. This data include kids' names and ages, spouse, occupation, hobbies, church groups, Social Security numbers if possible, bank preference, etc. No personal detail is insignificant in this business. You can, for instance, almost always find a person with children by noting where the kids' school records were transferred. If the target is a hunter and fisherman, he may be found by searching through state records of hunting and fishing licenses.

Next, check former neighbors, former landlords, former and current employers, relatives, and fellow employees. They can often be located from afar by using city directories that list names by street number and phone number.

Check phone books and information operators by using one method or another to inveigle street addresses. Instructions in one skip-tracing text explain how you can declare an emergency to an operator, asking that an urgent message be sent to the holder of an unlisted phone. When this number is dialed by the operator who won't give out the number, the dial tones are tape recorded, allowing you to use an electronic gizmo purchased at Radio Shack to decipher the number. Another telephone company number taken from these references allows you to call in to find out who really lives at that number and address.

Post offices have forwarding addresses on file. At times, you can talk local delivery people into revealing information by one pretext or another.

These can be UPS or postal employees. Several computer bulletin boards keep all forwarding addresses in the United States in current files. City records are a mine of information if the subject ever paid a parking ticket, used city water or sewer services, had public utilities, subscribed to cable TV, or even had garbage pickup. Leave no stone unturned. In addition to these records, you can check complete police records, building permits, and even something as common as dog permits. Many have names and addresses of relatives that would be of value.

In smaller cities, some local merchants or banks will have excellent information, and every neighborhood, big or small, has its local gossip, who will always have some information of value to the skip tracer, even if it is nothing more than whom a teenage daughter dated.

It is validly reported that the telephone is a skip tracer's greatest weapon. In most cases this is true. You can locate the neighborhood gossip from 2,000 miles away by using crisscross directories to get names of former neighbors. But, in many cases, it is actually quicker, cheaper, and easier to go there in person for information. Most skip tracers have great stories about tiny, seemingly insignificant facts they picked up inadvertently while talking to people only tangentially identified with the case.

A great many sources of information are available at the county courthouse. All are open to the public, or should be. The trick is knowing whom to ask for what. Try traffic records, court records—both civil and criminal—voter registration, marriage licenses, occupation licenses, real property tax registries, and boat and vehicle registrations. Courthouse records are extremely valuable places to look if you suspect that the skip has lived or has currently moved to that county. The skip might not register to vote, but will probably have a vehicle that is licensed and may have applied for public assistance or enrolled children in school.

At the state level, look for driver's license history, record of citations, corporate titles, corporate officers, professional registrations, record of state employment, involvement in the National Guard, and, as mentioned, hunting and fishing license history. Those who have assumed completely new identities have been located because they shot trap, came home to mom and dad on Mother's or

Father's Day, or liked to fly model airplanes.

If you know the skip's Social Security number (secured from credit bureau files or from driver's license information), some small bits of information are available from the Social Security Administration. This agency will forward a letter to "lost relatives, neighbors, or friends," but a reply is not assured. The IRS will also send out blind letters asking the recipient to reply when all that is known is a Social Security number.

Several military offices will, for a small fee, locate active or retired military personnel. Those who have been in the service only a few years and elect to drop out of sight probably cannot be traced through these offices, especially if the term of service ended several years ago. Nevertheless, if you suspect military service, the reference books have good addresses to write for information. A central office where civil service employees can be found is located in St. Louis.

Other government offices that keep records on citizens include the Federal Prison System, Interstate Commerce Commission, Office of Child Support Enforcement, Immigration and Naturalization Service, Office of Missing and Exploited Children, and the Customs Service.

Presently, there is a huge number of national computer data banks available to skip tracers. Some have every phone name and number in the United States on file. You can do state and national searches for surnames, Social Security searches, on-line crisscross searches, vehicle license searches, driver's license records searches, court records, and business searches, to name only a few. Depending on need, these records are available on a one-time basis at relatively reasonable cost, or you can subscribe to a continuing service. Some computer search companies will even locate a person's assets for those who wish to know about them.

Skip tracing, for those detail-oriented people who enjoy unraveling puzzles, is a very interesting and rewarding occupation. It can even become a way of life. Most observers see this as an industry with dramatic growth potential.

Hundreds, if not thousands, of additional sources of information not touched on in this summary are available to skip tracers. Some really excellent ones not mentioned may become the new professional's favorite sources.

However, this is not an easy business. It is imperative that you keep as many different cases as possible going at any one time. Rather than always going for the big brass ring, you should try for many smaller brass rings.

It is hoped that this bit of information will sufficiently stimulate readers' interest, so that they will go out and purchase the needed reference books and videotapes to make their enterprise successful. In some regards, this is a cookbook-type business. Still, it's that little extra bit of personal ingenuity that sets off really good skip tracers from the crowd.

BIBLIOGRAPHY

Erickson, R.G. *How to Find Missing Persons*. Port Townsend, WA: Loompanics Unlimited, 1982.

How Big Brother Investigates You. Boulder, CO: Paladin Press, 1992.

Investigating by Computer. San Mateo, CA: Video Intelligence, Inc., 1992.

Lapin, Lee. *How to Get Anything on Anybody*. Boulder, CO: Paladin Press, 1991.

McCann, John D. *Find 'Em Fast*. Boulder, CO: Paladin Press, 1984.

People Tracking. San Mateo, CA: Video Intelligence, Inc., 1991.

Thomas, Ralph D. *Finders Fee*. Austin, TX: Investigative Publications, Inc., 1991.

_____. *How to Find Anyone Anywhere*. Austin, TX: Thomas Investigative Publications, 1992.

CHAPTER

New ID

46

Top-quality skip tracers doubt that anyone in the United States could completely disappear without a trace. Most can cite case studies where someone went to a completely different place and changed his or her life-style but was still discovered. Times are changing in the United States, and with all the new information-driven technology it may now be impossible to disappear.

When Claude Dallas escaped from an Idaho joint, he had a great deal of sympathetic support and help from friends who assisted him in reaching a big city in far-off California. But, alas, Dallas had to work to stay alive, necessitating that he secure such items as a driver's license, union card, and Social Security card. He remained free only about 14 months in spite of some cosmetic surgery and some well-planned deep hiding. A simple check of those over the age of 30 who applied for Social Security cards would, by itself, have tipped off authorities.

Enforcement officials generally believe that it is improbable for most criminals to hide successfully under any circumstances. This is principally because the average criminal tends not to be particularly smart, and rather than lying low and working for a living, he usually goes out and commits another crime, bringing the law back into the picture.

Official pronouncements notwithstanding, the primary reasons people cannot assume a new ID successfully are generally social and not legal. Social creatures that we are, we find it difficult to completely cut ourselves off from children, parents, spouses, hobbies, social institutions, employment patterns, training and educational backgrounds, and the many other things with which we as humans become involved. A favorite trick, for instance, of those chasing after someone with an assumed new ID is to secure the telephone records of a surviving parent or girlfriend. Some investigators have even gotten their men by staking out relatives' homes at Christmas or on Mother's Day. Claude Dallas was apprehended because he phoned his parents.

If one is willing to completely, irrevocably give up an old pattern of life, forsaking absolutely everything he used to do, it may be possible to assume a new ID in the United States and to maintain that ID for many years. However, this presupposes that a person is not on the FBI's most-wanted list and that law enforcement people are not presently engaged in a full-court press tying to locate him! It also assumes one can stop subscribing to the *Wall Street Journal*, flying model airplanes, going to the ballet, practicing martial arts, bowling, talking to one's parents or siblings, attending the Mormon Church, or working as a cement mason. Even collecting fine wines and eating in Thai restaurants will be forbidden if these were previous passions.

Most people cannot be either so committed or so scared that they will do all of these things for very long. For those who wish to give it a try or simply know for academic purposes how to go about building a completely new ID, the following are the steps that must be taken. Please note that these suggestions are completely impossible if you do not have several thousand dollars in pocket money to establish a new ID or have spent considerable time and money securing a new ID way ahead of the actual need. Some but not all of these devices can be accomplished beforehand while you still have your old mailing addresses and telephone numbers.

Those who must flee totally unprepared in the middle of the night will find their funds quickly dissipated as they exist in small borderline motels that can be rented weekly by simply jotting down whatever on the registration.

Renting cheap apartments by the month rather than cheap motel rooms will require references and a previous address. These might be fashioned by picking someone with your new name out of a phone directory in another city and then hoping that the apartment owner is too lazy to check your background.

Skip-trace literature contains many computer trace services that will find certain names on a state-by-state basis. You must be careful about using the new name, especially if two pieces of supporting documentation are required.

References are a bit tougher to fake. Many landlords find that as a matter of self-defense they now must run extensive checks. You cannot tell friends back at the old digs about an intended new life or allow a landlord or anyone else to check back with them. People who have pulled off renting from a regular apartment complex where references are checked rent first from a little sleazebag motel where they befriend the owner. They then move into the new complex using their new name, listing the motel and its owner as both "prior residence" and as a reference. At times, this works, especially if you have put down a lot of cash on the new digs.

In an emergency, you could get around this problem (at least temporarily) by throwing in with a group of street people and allowing do-gooders to find shelter and support for you. This might allow you sufficient time to research a new name and get new references and a new ID program going. You also might lose your entire bundle of restart money at the hands of the kindly, gentle people of the street.

A new ID might conceivably pay rent six months ahead, claiming he never rented in the United States before and therefore has no references. Some landlords might accept this explanation, electing not to do any checking because rent is paid so far in advance. Some new IDs claim they told their landlords that all their identification was stolen coming into the country from their previous home and that all they have is cash from the insurance settlement. This might work with greedy or gullible landlords, but not with the cops.

Now, assuming either some good advance preparation or at least a 5-pound box of walking cash, three items of identification and a good, well-thought-through story are needed. These include, not necessarily in the order of ease or necessity, are a new birth certificate, a new Social Security card, and a new driver's license.

Also you will require a completely new persona that explains the fact that you are getting your first driver's license and Social Security card at age 40.

Rehearse this tale over and over again, expanding and elaborating so that every contingency is covered. My personal favorite when applying for a driver's license is to claim that I have been overseas and that I either gave up my old stateside license for the current Thai or Turkish one I have, that my papers were ripped off, or that all I retain is this old international driver's license. You could also claim that all you have left is an old baptism certificate. If you have a copy of another foreign (but non-European) country's driver's license, it is usually extremely easy to copy, with your new ID and, of course, an old picture.

One friend hired a careful Thai lady to hand letter, in Thai, a facsimile of her old Thai driver's license. It was done on old fiber paper, similar to the one she had in Thailand. He put in his new American name in the blanks as well as his new birth date and place of birth. Nothing else was intelligible. An old black-and-white photo cut from another picture was pasted in the proper place. A clerk in a medium-sized U.S. city took this and one other piece of ID and issued a new state license.

At this point, the new ID-er must have a residence address to which to forward the license unless an instant-issue state is being dealt with. There are more and more of these, negating the requirements that you rent an apartment or secure a mail drop first.

Some clerks will accept an international driver's license, which are extremely easy to fake, as anyone who has seen one will agree. Use a copying machine or a computer scanner to produce a blank form. One fellow claimed his papers were stolen overseas and that all that was left was his recently printed new ID business cards and his recently made up (fake) driver's license.

International driver's licenses are printed on light-gray cover-stock paper available at any full-service stationery shop. The license itself is a simple little affair with picture *stapled* in place.

Photocopy a white copy, whiting out the old name and address. Photocopy this onto the colored stock and then color in the official seal with red pencils. These seals are extremely simple. They can be done freehand or by taking 15 minutes to produce a cutout stencil.

Making up a bogus international driver's license is so easy that most people feel that the toughest part is getting an original from which to work. Originals are issued by the American Automobile Association (AAA) from its many regional offices throughout the United States. Usually, it can have the document ready in two to three hours. Two passport photos are required, which one must bring to the AAA office. Have a valid state driver's license in the name the international license will be issued to. This is not a problem because all that is needed is a format that will be copied using a new ID name.

Among the tools to work with when establishing a bogus ID are a passport, birth certificate, health certificate, and international driver's license. (Photo by Ragnar Benson.)

What do you use for a second piece of ID? Try a library card or something like a baptism certificate, business card, briefcase with your name or initials imprinted on it, check-cashing card, or anything else you may think of. Many of these can be produced with computer scanners and laser printers.

Some professional, knowledgeable ID mechanics suggest that making up a baptismal certificate is as good as any piece of new ID you can acquire. These can be used to secure driver's licenses, mail drops, apartment rentals, checking accounts, and other simple ID, such as check-cashing cards, supermarket cards, and—perhaps with the correct story—a new credit card.

Start by purchasing a blank baptismal certificate from a Catholic gift shop in any large city. Have a story ready about laminating a copy for a friend's child who is about to be baptized. Be sure that there are no copyright dates on the certificate and that correct writing instruments or typewriters are used. Pay attention to details.

Using an old typewriter or fountain pen, fill in the certificate. On the bottom, trace in two different witness' signatures taken from other documents such as canceled checks. Use a different-color ink for the priest's signature.

Some certificates have a place for a stamp. No official is likely to know now, 32 years later, whether the seals should be gold embossed or impressed the way notaries' seals are. Purchase a gold seal from a stationery store. Using a U.S. half-dollar or a foreign coin of the correct size, emboss the seal and affix it to the certificate.

Antique the document by lightly roughing it over with a fine piece of steel wool. Do a thorough job of pulling off all the new finish and print. That done, soak the document in a mixture of 1 cup of cold water and 2 teaspoons of instant coffee. Kill the coffee odor by subjecting the document to tobacco smoke for 10 minutes. Place the paper in an oven at 200°F for 6 to 8 minutes and the job is done. The final result is a document that looks and feels very old and frail, which, along with proper supporting documents and a good story, can even be used to secure a Social Security card.

Social Security people generally accept baptismal certificates in place of birth certificates. Modern Americans from much-divorced, relocated families have made this necessary. The harder problem will be convincing Social Security clerks why a man of 40 never had a card before.

It has worked to claim that one is a newly escaped member of a religious order of a type that does not believe in Social Security for biblical reasons. These people are around most rural communities in the United States. Modest amounts of research will uncover them. Affecting clothes, haircut, and speech might help a bit at the Social Security office. Be prepared to explain why you now want a card.

Some of these religious groups are old-order German Baptists, old-order Brethren, Mennonites, Amish, and many other kinds of Anabaptists. If the clerk is alert, she will recall that Anabaptists don't baptize infants, but you can claim you were baptized at age eight. However, most clerks won't know this. Another sometimes successful ploy is to claim that the Social Security card is needed for a 16 year old whose name appears on the baptismal records. Most of the time, a birth certificate is needed, but some clerks just let the matter slide.

It often helps immeasurably when dealing with petty functionaries to have cards, letterhead, embossed carry pouch, or whatever right out in plain view. You can lay these in front of a clerk, lending a great deal of weight to the contention that you are who you claim to be. Some of this stuff can be name tags made up to look official, with an impressive-looking imprimatur, employment badge, or even such innocuous items as store discount cards or local grocery check-cashing cards. Haphazardly, display these while searching for the baptismal

certificate. You might still bring your international driver's license, which has required photos.

Absolutely any ID made in the United States today can be faultlessly reproduced using computer scanners and laser printers. The equipment for this costs only about $3,000 at present, and the operation is not difficult. The only problem, as with passports and some official government IDs, is getting the necessary print stock on which to run the new ID. It is still *very* difficult to successfully fake a passport.

Once you have a bogus driver's license and a Social Security card with fictitious name and number, the dam is broken. Open bank accounts, secure charge cards, purchase vehicles on time, and get imprinted checks, dog license, hunting license, or whatever your heart desires. Just don't call mom from your new location!

Probably, the single most important item required for a new ID is a new birth certificate. This can either be a real one acquired using the identity of somebody about your age who died in infancy or a totally new birth certificate made with computer scanner and laser printer. Some users report good success with totally fabricated birth certificates when applying for a passport—which is the principal reason for acquiring a new birth certificate. Others have gotten into deep kimchee trying to pass bogus documents off at this level.

Although not as easily done now as it was a few years back when the concept first surfaced, it is still relatively simple to secure a genuine bogus birth certificate. States are currently trying to tie both death and birth certificates together so that a call for one will automatically bring up the other, if applicable. Success so far has been very limited. The principal current problem when in applying for a deceased person's birth certificate is that the document you receive may be stamped deceased. Generally, these stamps can be removed with ink or spot remover, if necessary.

Bogus but genuine (for that person) birth certificates are acquired by locating the name of a person of about your age and sex who died after 4 months but before 6 years of age. Look in newspaper archives of small- to medium-size cities in their obituary sections. If you pick a town too small, it won't have a hospital or paper or someone at the hospital may recall the incident. Most professionals recommend trying three or four names to see which one you strike on.

The problem here is that you must go to that city personally to root through the records. In many cases, newspapers have been sold, closed, or moved. Under these circumstances, inquire at the local library or state university library, which may have old microfilms of the newspapers.

The Mormon Church maintains excellent complete genealogical libraries that are open to the public. Check local phone listings for Church of Jesus Christ of Latter Day Saints and call and ask about genealogical archives that are maintained locally. Tell them you are just starting a search of your ancestors and family background. They will tell you where to go to look at their extensive microfilm library of deceased Americans. Pull out any set of names in a preferred state and start looking. Note down any who are listed as deceased infants.

Visit these archives when others are likely to be at work. Never show up on Sunday or Monday or in the evenings. Most people find three or four potential new identities in the first few minutes of looking.

Having found an individual of the correct sex and ethnic background, call the local hospital of that city and tell whomever you are speaking to that you are that individual and would like a certified copy of your birth certificate. Ask what fees and documents are required and what to send to expedite receiving a certified copy. If a glitch is going to develop, it will be obvious during this call. If problems surface, simply hang up and go on to another city and hospital. If all goes well with the conversation, send a letter of request along with the requested payment.

The hospital representative may ask for a notarized request. In this case, make one up that includes a bogus corporate seal lightly impressed on the document in place of the notary seal. Seals of various sorts are available at most stationery stores. On numerous occasions, official-looking stamps have been made by impressing half dollars or foreign coins into an "official" paper or seal. If this doesn't work, move on to the next deceased child and to a less cautious, less restrictive hospital.

Those who have used this plan recently claim it is still extremely effective. After you have acquired a new birth certificate, driver's license, and Social Security card, passports are extremely easy. Take the birth certificate along with several current passport-quality photos to the courthouse or post office where you fill out a form, take an oath, pay $55, and send the material off for processing.

With a new passport to add to the pile of documentation, you are home free, provided old habits and a big mouth do not get you back in trouble.

As a final gesture, have someone call the local newspaper at the place from which you disappeared, claiming that he or she is calling from a funeral home in Pocatello, Idaho, and that an obituary should be run on the old you, because you used to live there.

The problem here is that you must pay for obituaries, and this could leave a paper trail to you or a friend or relative of yours. Papers won't print without payment, but you may be able to express mail cash instead of paying by cashier's check or credit card.

As mentioned, this all works well in theory. Experts claim, however, that it won't really work. Sooner or later someone will show up who recognizes the old you. The hider may go back to racing stock cars, buying hunting licenses, or whatever he did before, and then alert skip tracers will have him. It is said in this industry that someone *always* knows where a person is.

At any rate, this is how the experts have done it.

BIBLIOGRAPHY

New ID in America. Boulder, CO: Paladin Press, 1985.

Reed, Barry. T*he Paper Trip, I & II.* Boulder, CO: Paladin Press, 1981 and 1984.

Yount, Johnny. *Vanish.* Boulder, CO: Paladin Press, 1986.

CHAPTER

Bar Fighting

47

Because sane, reasonable people do not generally get into bar fights, there is a real dearth of experts with actual experience who can provide valid instruction. It's the hen-and-egg syndrome: only macho nuts get into very many bar fights and who wants to take instruction from a nut?

Since very few smart people voluntarily get into bar fights, it is significant that the few who do agree on critical points. Peyton Quinn and Marc "Animal" MacYoung are two men who, between them, have survived dozens of brawls.

You just know that they arc giving us the real goods when you read their books. For instance, the first 17 pages of Quinn's *A Bouncer's Guide to Barroom Brawling* provide the following succinct advice about how to stay out of a bar fight: if you suspect a fight is imminent, get out of there!

"It is never worth the price you will have to pay to duke it out with a stranger. Those who get into bar fights *always* end up in jail, in court, in hospitals, and maybe in the graveyard. Not worth it to prove one long lost macho point," Quinn says. And he is the guy who is most likely to win a bar fight.

Absolutely the best way to win a brawl is to *not* get into it, both Quinn and MacYoung agree. This advice based on the concept that the best way to counter a blow is not to be there when it arrives.

Quinn has been in jail many times as a result of bar fights, enough that he is absolutely convinced that he does not want to go to prison. "Prisons are different than jails because they have libraries, basketball courts, and one stays longer," Quinn quips.

Even if you succeed in beating your antagonist—who no doubt deserved every blow—to a pink pulp, the boys in blue will show up with handcuffs and the guy's friends will show up in court. Civil suits for damages are common. The chances of surviving a bar fight physically, legally, and financially are zero.

The tallest of the three men at the counter was about 5'7". "We're the Bradleys, and we got the contract to keep the peace at the Tippecanoe Dance Hall," they said. Back in the 1960s, the Tippecanoe Dance Hall in Tippecanoe County, Indiana, was a jumpin' place. A minimum of 3,000 horny teenagers showed up Friday, Saturday, and Sunday nights to drink and dance. Up to this time, no one had ever been able to keep order.

Fights of various kinds were epidemic. Some caused thousands of dollars of property damage as well as great physical harm to participants. This was the age of consenting adults, but, even so, management and the Tippecanoe County sheriff agreed things had to change.

As it worked out, hiring Old Man Bradley and his two sons was a stroke of pure genius. They were small enough and young-looking enough that they blended in with the surging, milling crowd. Before they started, they bought every pair of handcuffs we had as well as our entire stock of CN/CS gas—which at the time was considerable.

Whenever anybody started in on any macho BS, or the Bradleys got wind of a feud brewing, two of them slipped up on either side of the badass. The third team member hosed him down thoroughly with a type of tear gas that caused the victim to retch on the floor. Fumes from his soaked shirt kept wafting up till the guy was so sick and weak he couldn't move. Close friends and acquaintances retreated in revulsion.

As soon as the belligerent was down, they handcuffed him and dragged him out of the bar while someone got a mop to clean up. All the bad guys were stacked up like speed bumps on the front lawn. Hard-core offenders who pulled knives or guns were turned over to the sheriff. Lesser belligerents were left to dry out on the lawn. Occasionally, some were still there the next morning.

Never a blow was struck by the Bradleys for the three years that they kept order at the dance hall. It was so tame that people actually started coming there just to dance and drink.

There are many points to learn from this account, the greatest being that experts don't get into bare-knuckle bar fights. So why do people get into bar fights when experts who have been there before agree that running is wise? Again, the experts agree.

Bar fights occur because macho people who are confident of themselves and their life-styles are not paying proper attention. Bullies tend to attack newcomers who seem self-satisfied and comfortable with situations that these insecure bullies believe should be perceived as threatening. If somebody is not obviously threatened, they are liable to lash out.

Remember the martial arts guru who said the best way to avoid a blow is not to be there when it arrives? It is wise to avoid places where fights might happen, rather than prove a point and get into one. Women's libbers who believe they have a right to go *wherever* they please *whenever* they please are especially guilty. They fail to realize that even tough, streetwise men avoid some joints.

Civilized people should not have to pay special attention to where they go or what they do, modern social theorists suggest. This is another bankrupt theory promulgated by liberated females who seem to think they should be able to go into tough biker bars unmolested because some men do. Some men go into these places and get the shit kicked out of them. They have the law on their side, but women may suffer even a worse fate in these joints.

How do you know if you are in a situation likely to degenerate into a fight? If, for some reason, you must remain in questionable circumstances, you must be extremely aware of everything going on around you. Saloon warriors are unable to set up a confrontation without telegraphing some very real clues.

Some experts refer to a potential troublemaker as a "hard eye." Those who accurately assess their personal potential for a barroom brawl continually scan the scene for hard eyes. After identifying active potentials, they begin monitoring body posture, facial expressions, and hand movements. "Always watch the hands," successful brawlers advise. There may be knives, sticks, guns, and even signs of tension and anguish indicating that mentally these fighters have got themselves into a corner that might be skillfully opened. The awareness skills of those who have survived a couple of barroom confrontations become very well developed.

Different experts have worked out various methods of trying to defuse tense situations. Some use humor; some just go over to the hard eye and BS with him a bit. Others play up to the guy's ego, allowing him to boil down slowly and calmly, the same way he boiled up. Huge amounts of self-confidence and alertness are required to make these ploys work.

Seasoned barroom bouncers report that many fights flare up over women. Some are actually instigated by women who want to see their men get tough. One expert says that when he is approached by a sodden brawler who wants to fight over his woman, he always apologizes and says she may be the most beautiful woman in the world but he doesn't know because he left his glasses back at the bar.

No matter how one does it, effective bar brawlers are alert to potential trouble and quick to think of some way to allow pressure to escape harmlessly. All agree that guys with these skills really win big in bar fights. On the other hand, male or female, one should never get in a fight for a friend. Their problems should always stay their own.

Movies notwithstanding, bar fights are always concluded in two to five seconds. As a general rule, the first punch, which is often a sucker punch calculated to blindside its victim, settles the matter. This is another reason experienced brawlers watch the other guy's hands. They cannot take the chance of falling victim to a quick sucker punch.

Experts advise that many signals will be sent by macho wackos before they attack, if you are but alert. When these signals come in, watch the hands, show no fear, and react calmly. One very experienced bar fighter, who has cracked dozens of heads, likes to look the hard eye in the eye and tell him, "I think I am going to be sick and puke all over everything." Another often-used device is to go berserk. Some of us can do this much better than others, but between the two, everyone can either play sick or play crazy. Whatever you do, don't take your eyes from the other guy's hands. If he is also watching your hands, this character may already have survived several bar fights. No permanent damage may have resulted, or the guy may be a pro acting like just another barfly.

Expert bouncers agree that there is little correlation between martial arts and bar fighting. Dojo workouts are generally stylized affairs, structured for pussycats, they say. Peyton Quinn says he has never had his martial arts robe on during the more than 50 bar fights in which he has engaged. Martial arts training helps, Quinn says, but setting up the stylized moves common to a dojo is not possible in a cluttered bar or even in a parking lot.

One favorite device Quinn used when working as a bouncer was to tell his tormentor, "Let's go outside and settle this." Once outside, he just smiled and said that this was all just bullshit, walked back inside, and locked the door.

If a potential ambush looks inevitable, immediately locate someone who is an employee of the joint. Even if it is only a doorman, bookkeeper, or bartender and not a bouncer, go over and point the hard eye out. Ask for help. Do *not* say something like, "That guy is giving me the evil eye," or "That guy is making a move on my woman, and if he continues, I will be forced to kill him."

A stupid macho declaration like that will identify you as a potential troublemaker or badass, and it will establish legal grounds for murder one should things escalate to that point. Small-town prosecutors particularly don't like troublemakers and will go to great lengths to be sure that they are made examples of.

Experts advise, however, that if it becomes apparent that you absolutely must fight, you should do so with great intensity and determination for the five seconds' duration.

Don't hesitate to land the first blow, but make it a really good one and then follow up instantly with additional blows. Once the guy starts down, save your hands and kick him vigorously. Don't let him get up and make trouble again. This is not a sporting contest; the object is survival with the least possible damage.

Mike Tyson once broke his fist in a bar fight. Use open hands to deliver blows; they are less likely to break that way. A good shot to the opponent's head usually decides the contest, but heads are tougher than hands. In this regard, a quick, hard forehand to an opponent's nose is often decisive.

No matter what level of martial arts training you have, never kick above the waist. Bar fights are usually dirty, messy close-in affairs. Fighters used to battling at a distance usually find themselves on the ground pummeled by a size 12, especially if prior training has been some form of martial arts that does its work from a distance.

Be forewarned that 99 percent of the first shots a belligerent will try will be either a right roundhouse to the head, a right upper cut, or a knee to the nuts. The last of these three is especially common, but even novices who have never been in a bar fight before are on guard for a crotch shot.

In this sequence from his excellent book, *Bouncer's Guide to Barroom Brawling,*
Peyton Quinn offers visual instruction on not contesting the opponent's power and
using economy of movement and continuous attack.

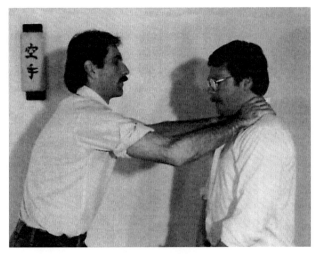

1. The attacker (left) closes the distance with the defender (right) with a front choke. The defender immediately senses the possibility of the knee strike to the groin and has already stepped back slightly. His hands drop, palms down to defend against the groin strike.

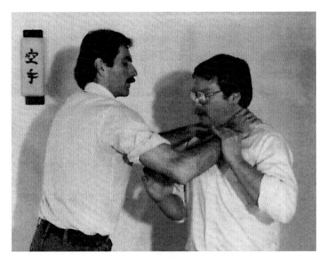

3. Notice that the opponent's power has not been contested at all to this point. This leaves the attacker's hands in their original position on the defender's throat, making them unavailable to block the elbow strike. Also, since the attacker still has his initial throat grip, he feels everything is still going according to plan and is thus totally unprepared for the elbow strike.

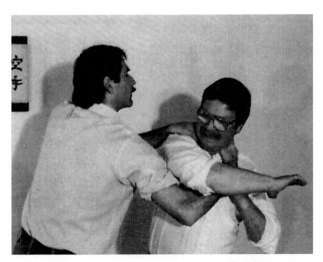

2. About a quarter of a second later, the defender captures the attacker's right wrist with his left hand. This is done only to hold the attacker's hand in place and for tactile feedback, not to try to remove it. With his hands on the attacker's body, the defender now can sense the hand movements and shifts of weight that precede other attacks. Notice that the defender's right hand has begun to move between the attacker's two arms. The defender twists his body with this motion, which chambers the forthcoming elbow strike.

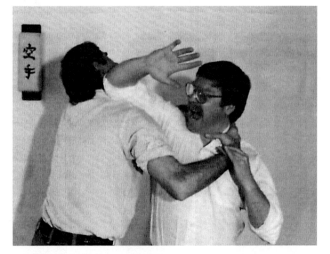

4. Bammo! The elbow strike connects. It carries the defender's entire body weight because of the essential hip rotation that chambered this blow, as seen in the previous two photos. Note that the defender maintains his hold on the opponent's right wrist. If the attacker breaks away or frees his hand for a blow, the defender knows immediately and can counter appropriately. A powerful blow like this elbow strike makes the attacker see the little purple points of light against the black background.

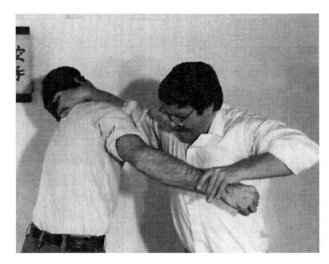

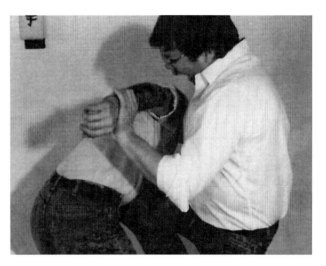

5. The instant after impact, the defender rotates his wrist to change his grip on the attacker's wrist as the elbow blow becomes a grab behind the neck. Note how the defender's right hand, already in motion from the elbow strike, was naturally set up for the grab behind the neck. This is an example of economy of movement. Observe the position of the defender's hands on the attacker's body; the leverage achieved on an already stunned opponent sets up the neck/wrist spinout.

7. The knee to midsection has further weakened and stunned the attacker. The impact has bounced the defender's hand off the attacker's neck. The hand comes back down and lands on the back of the attacker's head, sometimes gripping the hair. Note how the defender has rotated his body from the previous photo while maintaining his grip at the attacker's wrist. This prevents the attacker from regaining any balance, making recovery impossible as long as he is kept in motion. This is similar in concept to "running the mark"; here he is spinning the mark. The defender uses this leverage to drive the attacker's face into the rising knee.

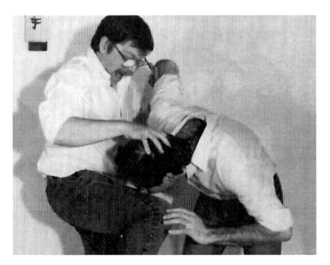

6. The defender forcefully drives the attacker's arm up as he pulls the head down. This is done in one quick, snapping motion that doubles over the attacker to receive the rising knee strike to the midsection (ideally, the solar plexus).

8. Once is not enough! The impact of the knee to the face has bounced the defender's hand up again. This time it comes down as a shuto to the neck. Note how the defender still maintains control and tactile feedback by retaining the attacker's right wrist. This entire sequence represents the concept of continuous attack.

No single sucker punch will be effective in even 40 percent of bar fights. It can only be said with certainty that blazing initial speed and the probability of a shot to the head will usually carry the day. Along with not foolishly waiting for an antagonist to take the first shot, bar fighters practice balanced twisting or dodging, evasive movements calculated to avoid or block sucker punches.

Often these are done in conjunction with a counterstroke. Mashing your right had into a guy's chin, as *his* initial blow passes harmlessly under your armpit, is an excellent example.

Twisting slightly to the right to allow a blow to pass and then hammering down hard on the other guy's nose and eyes is another excellent combination. These simple twist-around-and-strike measures take excellent advantage of the old street fighter's adage that suggests it is good not to be there when the other guy's blow arrives. If you are cool and calculated about it, these balanced dodges are not tough, especially if your opponent is carrying a load of cheap whiskey.

A shot to the nose can be followed up by a quick knee to the groin. But remember, no crotch shots on the initial comeout, and no kicks above the waist. Expend maximum energy. Do not allow the fight to last past a few seconds. The longer it lasts, the more likely you are to get hurt.

One expert, after clubbing his attacker down with a telephone, noted that it is wise to use whatever weapon is available. Bar fighting is not honorable or sporting.

Although you should always be alert so that it doesn't happen, grappling or double-teaming may lead to your being grabbed from behind. In this instance only, your response should be a bit canned. Immediately snap the head back sharply against the nose, ear, or eye of the grabber before he can get in tight and close. Drop down and either chop at his nuts or sharply grab a leg. This is also effective against a head lock.

Experienced bouncers can deal successfully with a large assembly of antagonists, all of whom are intent on beating your brains out. The trick here is to bloody one or two of the assembling attackers quickly and viciously before they get organized. If possible, quickly hit another one as well. As a result, no one will wish to step up and become the next victim.

Marc MacYoung summarized all this very succinctly when he noted that "self-defense isn't fighting; it is awareness. Everything else is just details."

But always recall that famous line in the song "The Gambler" with its admonishment to know when to walk away, know when to run! Successful fighters always claim that in 100 percent of the cases, it is best to walk away and, if that doesn't work, run!

BIBLIOGRAPHY

MacYoung, Marc "Animal." *Cheap Shots, Ambushes, and Other Lessons*. Boulder, CO: Paladin Press, 1989.

Quinn, Peyton. *A Bouncer's Guide to Barroom Brawling*. Boulder, CO: Paladin Press, 1990.

CHAPTER

Hostage Rescue Units

48

Djibouti, formerly a French colony in Africa, located on a tiny spit of sand on the Red Sea opposite Saudi Arabia, is not a particularly hospitable place even in the middle of winter. Djibouti is only a few degrees north latitude and seasons change little. Old master sergeants in the French army stationed there claimed their seasons were hot and wet, hot, very hot, and hotter than hot.

A little-known, not well-publicized drama began to unfold on Djibouti on the morning of February 3, 1976. In an attempt to beat the blistering heat, both for mechanical and personal reasons, an old Citroen bus coughed and wheezed its way along the low coastal highway before full light that fateful morning. Although not all the little school kids on the bus would survive the day, life, such as it was in this remote colonial African outpost, was fairly pleasant.

The 30 kids on the bus ranged in age from 8 to 17, with most at the younger end of the spectrum.

All were sons and daughters of French air force personnel stationed in Djibouti. French law and custom prevailed, and compared to Paris, serious crime was not a problem.

Yet everyone knows that things in the Third World are never as they outwardly seem. At that very moment, a small band of Somali raiders organized from one dominant northern clan had completed two nights and one day of slithering into position along this main coastal road. Nobody saw the raiders silently sneak in through the low-lying, pebbly, flat, clay terrain.

At the same time, two additional cooperating raiders slipped into a Somali border post a few miles distant.

Brandishing AK-47s and large knives, the bandits pounced on the bus in the gray predawn light. Once aboard, they cheerfully threatened to cut the driver's throat if he did anything less than exactly as they said.

Under orders from the four hostage-takers, the bus driver drove onto a flat spot in a large open area only a couple of hundred meters from the Somali border, where a small, brown, mud-and-stick building and a white pipe gate marked the border. Obviously, Somalis at the border were cooperating. Two terrorists waiting at the border joined the four on the bus.

At 8 a.m. the terrorists issued a proclamation claiming that unless certain political prisoners were released from jail, they would begin to slit the children's throats. Young girls in the group were at higher risk because Somalis considered female children to be of no value. No one questioned the fact that these extremely tough Somalis would carry out their threats.

Word of the kidnapping immediately reached France, where an elite unit of the *Groupement d'Intervention de la Gendarmerie Nationale* (GIGN) were alerted. Nine well-trained antiterrorist-unit men with full equipment were immediately flown to Djibouti. The flight took about four hours.

The terrorists had picked their parking spot fairly well. The nearest cover was a few large rocks about 200 meters distant. It was only under the greatest duress that the nine hostage rescue unit (HRU) men of GIGN crawled unseen across the blistering hot gravel to behind the rocks. Ambient temperatures were hitting 126°F at 2:00 p.m.

Because rushing the bus seemed impossible, the HRU captain elected to try to snipe out all the terrorists from 200 meters simultaneously. But the movement of the children in the bus precluded all nine French snipers from getting their men simultaneously bull's-eyed. The antiterrorists continued to wait in their hot ghillie suits and desert fatigues.

Occasionally, some of the terrorists walked to the Somali border post, where they were relieved on a rotating basis. The nerves of the French snipers were as tight as new Levis because of the baking heat and the need to keep their cross hairs on a terrorist's head.

Since it also seemed probable that the Somalis at the border post would come to the aid of the terrorists, arrangements were made with the 2nd Foreign Legion Parachute Regiment, some of whom had children on the bus, to engage the Somali army if necessary. Because of the flat, open terrain, these soldiers had to remain deployed some thousands of meters to the rear to avoid detection.

At 3:00 p.m., the terrorists agreed to allow some food on board for the kids. The food was laced with tranquilizers in hopes that the children would fall asleep and leave the windows clear for the snipers.

At approximately 4:00 p.m., the snipers had all of the terrorists covered at once. In perfect unison they fired, instantly dropping four terrorists on the bus. A fifth terrorist out on the ground tried to run but also had his head blown off!

As predicted, Somali border guards instantly returned fire. The HRU unit was in precarious position and pinned down, but the elite French soldiers did manage to hit 10 more of the extremely fierce Somali soldiers. While the Somalis discharged their weapons in the direction of the snipers, each sniper shot coolly at specific Somalis.

The GIGN unit would have lost had it not been for the timely arrival of the paratroopers who, with blood in their eyes, were already moving when the fire order was given to the snipers.

As soon as they could in the hail of bullets, three GIGN men ran up to the bus in an attempt to keep one terrorist from getting back to the children. The terrorist boarded the bus and summarily sliced the throat of one child but was shot down before he could continue.

This dramatic hostage-rescue action saved 29 kids, but the whole incident is virtually unknown outside France.

Men of action need to be aware of the tactics and training of HRUs worldwide. In this day of increased government intervention, one can never predict when they might be arbitrarily labeled a terrorist and shot on sight by trained snipers. Most countries with HRUs prohibit their use against citizens, but this has obviously not been helpful in the United States.

As a result of great international embarrassments at Munich, Entebbe, and the Depunt train hijacking, a surprising number of countries around the world have established elite HRUs. In some cases, it is surprising that countries with little terrorist history have perceived a need for HRUs. Most units are prohibited from harassing their fellow citizens, but one must expect that if something is done that the government really dislikes these elite soldiers will be deployed.

Probably the most highly trained, best-equipped group in the world is the British Special Air Service (SAS). The SAS was originally formed as a military raiding and intelligence-gathering unit, but it has been used increasingly in an antiterrorist role. The best marks for training, leadership, and equipment are usually given to the SAS. It is sometimes used against fellow citizens.

After the death of 11 Israeli Olympic athletes, Germany formed a special HRU. These 188 men of the *Grenzschutzgruppe* 9, or GSG-9, are only marginally less well trained, managed, equipped, and led than the SAS. They are assembled only as an antiterrorist group.

Israeli HRUs are also very good, ranking at the top of the world's antiterrorist groups. However, most knowledgeable people do not wish to classify the Israeli *Sayaret Matkal*, as it is named, as an antiterrorist unit. Frequently, these people have been called on for retaliatory or preemptive strikes and assassinations, which many people believe is terrorism itself. Also, this outfit has its roots in the early fight for liberation when terrorism and military action were poorly differentiated.

Probably because of lingering fears in the United States that an elite force used to combat terrorism would eventually be used against its own citizens by a despotic leader, its formation was done only reluctantly. But in November 1977, "Chargin' Charlie" Beckwith was given the task of forming a unit to carry out "deep penetration raids, intelligence-gathering, POW rescues, and other similar missions." Known in the United States as Delta Force, this group has remained mostly military in its training, mission, and composition.

Eventually, the FBI was also given the task of forming a special tactical group called the Hostage Response Team. These men spent a great deal of time, money, and effort training in hand-to-hand combat, assault, forced entry, high-tech surveillance, sniping, and countersniping. As predicted earlier, these elite units have been principally called on to pounce on politically incorrect individuals.

Fortunately, some of the FBI indiscretions have come home to haunt them in the form of bad publicity, including needless casualties within their own units. As a result, moral training and equipment are considered to be inferior to that of the SAS, GSG-9, and *Sayaret Matkal*.

The U.S. Delta Force, which has not been turned on private citizens, has nevertheless been hampered by a high level of infighting, political micromanagement, and indecision, as illustrated by its one major engagement, the hostage rescue attempt in Iran.

A surprising number of countries worldwide have decided that national pride dictates they have their own HRUs. It is a matter of grave concern when politicians find that they are not sovereign within their own boundaries, leading to some spirited contests to see who can have the best all-around HRU. One wag has even suggested that hostage rescue may become an Olympic sport.

In addition to the United States, United Kingdom, Germany, and Israel, which have already been discussed, other nations currently with HRUs include France, Holland, Italy (with two rival groups), Spain, Belgium, Sweden, Norway, Finland, Denmark, Portugal, Switzerland (which leaves oversight of its HRU function to local cantons), Ireland, Greece, Turkey, Australia (having one of the best but smallest HRUs), New Zealand, Canada, South Africa, Japan, Korea, Singapore, Hong Kong, Indonesia, the Philippines, Thailand, Pakistan, Brazil, Argentina, Venezuela, Ecuador, Chile, Oman, Tunisia, Morocco, Sudan, and Egypt.

The list includes many people and cultures that one would initially have never thought would need a HRU. Mastering the political will to put a credible HRU together must have been quite difficult in most of these countries. Trained HRUs are enormously expensive, for example, and if a unit is notoriously unsuccessful, political ramifications are severe.

As a general rule, most smaller nations' antiterrorist units are quite good. Some hardly have enough members to keep them both in training and on alert, but generally these forces are thought to be adequate.

Larger, wealthier countries have better units, but, as a rule, even the least of these smaller groups is better equipped, better trained, and better led that the average terrorist group. In a few Third World HRU situations, ongoing intelligence—vital during the unfolding of an incident—is lacking. The professional judgment of some team commanders may also be colored by cultural bravado. This is especially true in the case of Egypt's commandos, who managed to lose 57 hostages during an assault in Malta on a terrorist-held airliner.

In the former Eastern Bloc countries, antiterrorist duties were generally assigned to Spetsnaz troops. For soldiers (which these troops actually were), these units were quite good. Yet they were definitely not extremely highly trained, well-equipped specialists on par with those of other countries' special HRUs. They just did not have equipment, cohesion, leadership, and unit training necessary to be classed as an elite HRU.

The current extent and status of Spetsnaz in the Commonwealth of Independent States is unknown, but one must assume they are out there someplace. Most of these men did not have other jobs to which they could move.

The training emphasis for any HRU depends a great deal on the home environment of the nation for whom its members are deployed. Swedish and Norwegian antiterrorist units, for instance, spend a great deal of time in or on the water. They practice para-scuba, small-boat, water soldier, and water infiltration techniques. These Scandinavians often practice securing offshore oil rigs, and their equipment reflects the fact that it must remain functional in salt water.

SAS members are routinely deployed on field trips, traveling about Europe and learning how to work in various airports. They practice being luggage handlers, plane refuelers, airplane chandlers, and small-equipment operators. By so doing, they can be deployed as what appear to be regular service staff at airports experiencing a terrorist incident.

Israeli HRU members must, at a minimum, speak Hebrew, English, Arabic, and one other language fluently. Radio communications, electronic surveillance, demolitions, rappelling, small boats, infiltration, martial arts, and knife fighting are all stressed. An estimated half of Israeli training should be considered as on the job because it is done on neighboring countries' sovereign territory.

All the world's antiterrorist forces stress the use of electronic listening devices as a means of intelligence. As soon as possible, hidden miniature microphones, TV cameras, infrared imaging devices, night vision, camouflage, exotic photography, and many other devices are used to determine exactly who the terrorists are, their function in the incident, and where they remain generally during the siege. Electronics land navigation, high-speed driving, marksmanship, aircraft operation, tank operation, and other exotic military skills are continuously brought into play against terrorists.

Some units cross-train more than others, so that they are all good snipers, radio men, and demolitions experts. SAS people still learn Morse code. U.S. and British units rely on extremely skilled experts within their groups who have a natural talent and passion to pursue more difficult technical duties. Other members may be able to perform these functions well but not brilliantly, as some gifted members can.

Antiterrorist units are expected to train about 12 hours per day year in and year out. Many special night exercises are thrown in. It is a full-time job, with one completely trained unit always available for immediate deployment. Often, team members are rated pilots, tank jockeys, electricians, welders, and other less prosaic, but practical specialists.

Effective units anyplace in the world have their own choppers and armor available for instant deployment. It is neither wise nor desirable to have to rely on the other guy for anything that might be needed in a hurry to get the job done.

HRUs are extremely expensive for any country to maintain. Large numbers of expensive men are required for an effective, somewhat prepositioned force, and realistic training is expensive. Drop, cut, and burnout rates can be high for a number of reasons, and this necessitates that expensive replacements be continually recruited and retrained.

Equipment costs, especially electronics, are truly breathtaking. Night vision goggles, for instance, which every man has as just another piece of equipment, cost $7,500 each! Sniper rifles are $3,000 each, and this doesn't count helicopters, armored personnel carriers, and other big-ticket items.

Effective training requires construction of elaborate structures called "kill houses." These are set up so that various photos of potential assailants are projected on the house walls, along with realistic dummies used in common hostage situations. Teams of HRU men practice handling various scenarios to the point that out in real life they seldom face anything they haven't seen before. Other training scenarios include using mock-ups of places or, in a few cases, old, shot-up plane bodies kept for specific training purposes.

National pride in an HRU force is understandable. Iran, for instance, had a fairly effective HRU, which also served as an elite palace guard. Eventually, the shah used these people on many occasions to stomp his own fellow citizens. When power shifted, these soldiers were dealt with in a most severe manner. These are also the lessons of Nuremberg where the plea of "orders are orders" was held not to be a valid defense against common decency.

One can only hope and pray that these elite soldiers in our own society exercise restraint, compassion, and common sense when dealing with regular citizens. If not, we will continue to see our wives and children gunned down for little more than a perceived lack of political correctness.

BIBLIOGRAPHY

Geraghty, Tony. *This Is the SAS*. London: Arms & Armor Press, 1982.

Thompson, Leroy. *The Rescuers*. Boulder, CO: Paladin Press, 1986.

Action Careers

49

Of all the people around the world, Americans do not have to be stuck in dull, mundane, physically secure 9-to-5 jobs. Dozens of excellent, exciting opportunities exist for those who are demonstrated risk-takers and can motivate themselves in a self-employment context. They must also be somewhat innovative in their approach to life and its continual challenges, but exciting jobs await those who are.

Several of these especially rewarding occupations, such as stuntman, bounty hunter, and skip tracer, are covered in separate chapters. Many relatively minor action careers employ relatively few people in the U.S. but are still available to those who watch for them. Some, such as explosives handler or river-rafting guide, will never employ very many people. Many of these careers are relatively simple and require little education. They can be self-taught or undertaken independently by reasonably bright, motivated people.

A few such careers as missionary and Peace Corps volunteer are not action careers in and of themselves; they simply open the door to action-type opportunities.

Other such action careers as secret service agent, FBI agent, or spy really are long-term careers. They require a great deal of proper education as well as physical and mental conditioning to do the work.

In the case of Peace Corps volunteers, for instance, one is very much stuck in the mud—both figuratively and literally. But, as volunteers in Korea and Kenya told me, "We have great opportunities to buy valuable items cheaply and then inexpensively ship them to Europe or the U.S. at great profit." The Peace Corps is supposed to be a socialist organization where the word "profit" is never mentioned, but as a volunteer in Thailand confessed, he slipped over the border into Burma on several occasions, where he purchased valuable uncut gemstones that he had professionally cut in Bangkok for great profit.

Peace Corps people are, in most regards, little more than secular missionaries, peddling our government's latest line. Once on the field, workers are not monitored or supervised except in the most cursory fashion. Incredible as it may sound, a

FBI agent in training. (Photos by Ragnar Benson.)

fundamental aspect of Peace Corps work is that there are few to no job criteria or expectations. In several countries, it has been the official government position that a Peace Corps volunteer is someone with nothing to do.

Peace Corps training comprises a smattering of language, culture, local economics, and local living conditions orientation. In-country volunteers receive handsome per diem allowances, travel money, medical/dental insurance, subsidized shopping, and a relatively large readjustment allowance payable on completion of a two-year tour of duty.

Personnel requirements are up a bit from the Kennedy years, when intense visionary excitement swept many trained "generalists" into the organization. Today agriculture specialists, construction workers, medical workers, heavy equipment operators, computer technicians, electricians, and other such people are demanded.

What recruiters fail to tell new prospects is that the Peace Corps has been thrown out of 21 countries, generally for gross incompetence and for a general failure to produce tangible results.

The average age of those in the Peace Corps ratchets up and down, but it is said to be about 30 today. Adult dependents can legally go along. Professionals swear that the days of volunteering, being selected, receiving a bit of training, jumping on a plane, and then riding around till they find a place they like in that country are forever over. But Peace Corps volunteers have a maddening habit of showing up in nice places such as Chiang Mai, Thailand, and Baguio, the Philippines.

Work in this atmosphere would be deadly boring if one did not have a nimble, searching mind looking for other opportunities. These could include smuggling, gun running, manufacturing, police work, military training, raiding into adjoining

countries, and acting as a tour guide for visiting Americans. Officially many of these opportunities are much frowned upon, but anyone who has traveled in rural Third World countries knows of specific instances where they have occurred.

About 10,000 people volunteer annually for foreign travel with the Peace Corps. The number actually accepted fluctuates tremendously but has averaged about 4,000 annually of late. Call 1-800-424-8580 for current information and a printed packet that includes an application form.

Alert, intelligent entrepreneurs not bamboozled by government rhetoric find the Peace Corps to be a great springboard into something that is often very much an action career.

Work as a missionary also allows people to live in an inexpensive foreign country on relatively valuable U.S. dollars. Missionaries do a great deal of hunting, fishing, trading, and, in some cases, manufacturing. They meet and interact with interesting, powerful people, and a significant number hold very few Bible teaching sessions. In many places, they provide extension services, teaching people how to raise better crops, build roads, bridges, houses, and, at times, projects as large as community power-generating plants. One famous missionary formed a group of tough mercenary fighters who tracked down and neutralized terrorists. They even made raids into neighboring countries. In times past, missionaries often acted as paid informants in a country, but this function supposedly has fallen into disfavor.

Most difficult part of being a missionary involves learning a new language. Anyone who intends to maintain financial support back home had best learn at least enough of the local dialect to convince the home folks. If it is a common language (such as Spanish or French) it is best to learn well, lest someone at home decides to practice on you. If it's an obscure language such as Korean or Sichuan Chinese, the truth may remain buried.

Most missionary jobs do not require the knowledge of a theologian or Bible scholar. Some Bible studies must be organized, but Third World people must work long hours to survive and cannot sit in classes very many hours per week.

Medical and mechanical skills are probably in most demand, although you need not be an expert in most places to be out ahead of the locals in these fields. The ability to teach English is also in demand, and you could learn the native language while teaching English.

Two separate, but effective paths exist to break into foreign mission work: the first is more difficult at the start, but the second provides more long-term security.

Plan one entails mapping out a place of service in great detail. This business plan should indicate a proposed foreign location and outline specific work that will be undertaken. Research the people, needs, culture, working conditions, and the likelihood that rich Americans will be motivated by compassion for these indigenous peoples.

Having put what amounts to a business plan together to help the poor, starving Armenians—or whatever—you must get busy and sell it to private companies, wealthy individuals and philanthropist organizations, including, in some cases, churches and government organizations. Ask for monthly support to get to wherever and undertake the humanitarian effort outlined.

A second method of getting into foreign mission work involves spending time at a Bible college or seminary. Try to pick up a working knowledge of Biblical doctrine related to a targeted denomination. Industriously study the place in the world where you wish to work.

The next step is to begin making applications at various mission boards and organizations in your church. Under the auspices of their churches, aspiring missionary candidates travel around raising funds to go to "the field."

Pay is not great, but opportunities in hundreds of other business-type activities abound. All you need is to be alert for them. One missionary made a bundle organizing a truck delivery system through Indian country in northern Kenya. At first, he served only other missionaries, but soon the business expanded greatly.

If foreign travel is not your bag, there are great occupations right in the U.S. of A. that should keep your mind focused.

Providing security for various VIPs who need a bodyguard and are willing to pay for this service should furnish enough action for just about anyone. But remember that as a bodyguard it is your duty to get shot rather than the clients.

People currently hiring bodyguards include entertainers, athletes, businessmen, foreign

These bodyguards are protecting a politician overseas.

politicians and bureaucrats living in the U.S., foreign politicians who do not trust their own home uniformed services, and, increasingly, U.S. politicians and political/religious people. The pay varies depending on positions and experience, but averages about $250 per day.

Most clients want bodyguards who can blend into the woodwork and, while doing so, can provide some other quasi-worthwhile service such as scheduler, grounds keeper, or driver. In the case of name-brand entertainers, this may include being a semifriendly goon.

Bodyguards must be physically fit, possess a high degree of presence and not be prone to using violence or losing their temper. Some are very good divers, martial arts experts, and/or proficient with firearms and explosives. In all cases a bodyguard is considered to have failed if he does not exercise sufficient diligence to keep his man out of trouble. If shots are fired or a car is rammed, even to take out a bad guy, this is considered to be a failure under the above terms.

Ex-police, secret service, and military people seem to get into the bodyguard business as a result of their being available at the right time in the right place. A client's level of paranoia plays a great role in determining if one will be hired.

Most bodyguards start their careers helping friends in the business or working for an expanding company that offers bodyguard services. Men who are

Being a photojournalist often allows one to travel to exotic places and witness historic events.

good at the business and who develop a nose for staying out of trouble will soon find their client giving referrals to others needing similar services. Some companies hire professionals. These are consultants who oversee practical security needs, which are carried out by individuals in that company themselves.

Men who get into this business often find themselves doing a variety of assignments ranging from security consulting and private investigating to actual bodyguard functions.

Those who are good with a camera, but otherwise have little formal education, sometimes find excellent work as photojournalists. During times of war, this occupation can pay tremendous dividends if one does not also get shot in the process.

Photojournalists often start as free-lance sports photographers for local papers. If they do that well, they may start to sell news photos that they happen onto as a result of always carrying a camera.

The next jump is to offer larger regional papers photos of current news. This is done by listening to the police radio and then being first on the scene. After the photos are in the camera, call regional newspaper editors asking them if they are interested. If they are, process and print the photos and ship them to the editors.

If action photography seems to be your forte, there will soon be a photo or two originally purchased by local or regional papers that is picked up by the wire services. They will call and attempt to negotiate a price to run the photo.

Locals pay from $10 to $25 per photo. Wire services pay from $150 to $250. After publishing a

few wire photos, you can go big-time free-lance by approaching a wire service editor and telling him that you intend to go to Bosnia or some other hot spot as a stringer.

Find out where to send these photos locally so that they can be used by the wires. Personal expenses required to get into this business can be quite high, but for those willing to take chances, the payback can be pretty good. After a while, good photojournalists may even go on the staff of some large news organizations. This happens quickly when you are alone on station in some remote corner and it blows up. Again, fate or circumstance dictates fame and fortune.

Men who really enjoy working with explosives have sometimes put an excellent business together as explosives handlers. Local communities who do not have experience or funds necessary to bring in the really big-name guys from afar will sometimes hire local experts. In many cases, military demolitions experts from a close-by base and/or FBI experts will be called, but for routine handling of old dynamite and, perhaps, ancient, left-behind war souvenirs, there occasionally is a place for the expert explosives handler.

Some of these people who have developed large libraries and broad expertise also work as expert witnesses on explosives-related legal cases.

Pay for the explosives expert can be quite good, but next-to-nothing for several months between jobs. An expert who goes to an old farmstead to remove a quarter-case of old, old deteriorated dynamite from a chicken house might get $1,200 from the property owner for his expertise. These jobs generally come by courtesy of the sheriff's office after a new city-based owner calls in asking what to do about explosives he found on moving to the country. Expert witnesses in court usually get about $1,000 per day, plus expenses.

Explosives handlers usually start their business by running their own commercial explosives-handling service for farmers and contractors, quarry operators, and ranchers. They pass out business cards to local law enforcement people till, finally, they start getting jobs here and there, looking after errant explosives. People do not substitute bravado for common sense and knowledge of the field and remain in this business for long. In some cases the expert confirms that there is a really serious problem that calls for the guys from the military base.

As in all action careers, you must have the expertise and also be available when the opportunity comes along.

Work as a fire fighter is available to about every able-bodied male in virtually any community with a volunteer fire department. Many otherwise sedentary accounting or banking types really enjoy the rush of hearing a siren going off and knowing that they are obligated to drop everything, run out the door, and jump into their own emergency vehicle complete with flashing lights to take off for the fire.

Those who wish to add excitement and thankful accolades of fellow citizens to their lives need do little more than stop down at the local fire station and talk to the chief. In some places where the force is all professional, there are still sometimes openings in the auxiliary.

Volunteers will be sent to a great many schools to learn to fight various types of fires effectively and not get killed. You can work your way up through a great number of skill levels. Some progress through the organization to the point where they become fire inspectors, local chiefs, or other full-time professionals.

Included in the study program will be a great deal of hands-on training, driving big fire trucks, rigging horses, computing water pressure, and tearing up buildings so that exotic suppressants can be applied.

Initially, pay is all psychological except for the occasional communities that pay a token minimum wage. Some experienced volunteer fire fighters eventually take their skills out to private industry where they receive good pay as the corporate fire team manager.

Just about anyone can get a job as a volunteer fire fighter in about any small community, but some young men elect to go the route of full-time paid smoke jumper.

Smoke jumpers are highly trained, fairly well-paid professionals who are sent in twos and threes to control remote fires while they are still small. To some extent, helicopters have replaced parachutes, but the concept of a highly trained expert in superb physical condition still applies.

Smoke jumpers attend fire schools in McCall, Idaho; Redmond, Oregon; Missoula, Montana; and

A river guide and his clients set up for Wild Sheep Rapids on the Snake River in Hells Canyon, the deepest and narrowest gorge in North America.

Fairbanks, Alaska. Schools are run by the U.S. Bureau of Land Management (BLM). Those interested can contact their nearest Forest Service office or the BLM for current application requirements and school dates.

After completing three weeks of training, graduates live in small groups around the country, where they will continue physical training and practice on any small, local forest fires. They can be deployed almost instantly in any of the 50 states and Canada. Smoke jumpers are usually housed in small camps in mountainous, forested western states. It's a nomadic life that does not usually retain its appeal for many years. Yet it is an interesting and exciting subset of fire fighting open to younger people in excellent physical condition who are looking for adventure.

Kids raised in rural areas where hunting and fishing were common often become hunting and fishing guides. These are relaxed, modestly good-paying jobs for outgoing, friendly people who like being with people. A good general knowledge of the outdoors and any quarry are necessary, but not to the level that one might suppose.

Those working out on the land and water and who are taking people out almost daily soon acquire a sense of the game. They learn about the weather, how it affects game, and how migrations work, and

Being a hunting guide allows you to use your knowledge of the outdoors to make a living—at least during the season.

they generally gather information that someone who flies in for a week's visit thinks is almost magical.

Guides talk to other guides and generally share information regarding concentrations and techniques. In this day and age, people seldom expect to encounter large concentrations of fish and game.

In spite of occasional adrenalin rushes, guiding is not as strenuous or as exciting as many other action careers. It is, however, a very satisfying means of making a living. Often, factory workers use guiding as a second job that they undertake part-time. Probably the worst part of guiding involves knowing the country and how to field-dress and handle fish and game. Packing some big game species to the road can be tough. If you have a poor sense of direction, guiding is not a career choice for you.

Men who live in game areas, who enjoy getting out, and who have accumulated some equipment such as a boat and motor, four-wheel-drive vehicle, and other smaller gear, often start a guiding business because they are already out on the country. From time to time, they hear of friends and acquaintances who would like to go hunting or fishing. Some men with equipment let local resort and other commercial operators know they are available. In a few areas, the shortage of half-knowledgeable guides is so serious that resort owners use college boys to take people out.

Process servers and repo men are, in many regards, a natural outgrowth of being in the skip tracing business. Those who can do the job of finding people effectively, can then jump to the next, more profitable level and serve the actual papers or repo delinquent vehicles themselves.

Process-serving work comes from attorneys who have tried the sheriff and found that he is not a skip tracer. In most cases, people do not want legal papers delivered to them, making it more of a job than just driving to a people's residences and handing them papers. Proper legal procedures must be followed, as explained by attorneys with papers to serve.

Repo work comes from banks and finance companies with the odd private job occasionally thrown in (e.g., dad wants his Mercedes convertible that his daughter ran off with returned).

The real work is always finding the skips, but, unfortunately, this is not generally the part that pays well. If you can find the work, one repo or one legal papers service per week will keep body and soul together. Those who are good at it may do more than one project per day, and income can mount up.

Working the two latter professions includes association with some very un-nice, tough people. It can be psychologically rewarding, but dangerous— almost on a par with bounty hunting.

Many men find it possible to combine skip tracing, process serving, and repo work; this field is private investigation.

Most of our states now require that private investigators be licensed, with the exception of those states that permit a PI to work for a single law firm or business at any one time. But rules vary, and some states are so strict that the only way to go to work as a PI is by your working for another licensed firm first, or you can carefully manage your activities so that they do not violate any laws. Attorneys for whom you work will know the rules; or else check in one of the books available on PI work.

Private investigations can include anything from workers' compensation fraud to locating lost relatives to ferreting out the assets of debtors. Premarital investigations are said to be good business. Most PIs claim their work load is increasing as a result of the complicated, often-convoluted times in which we live. PIs are patient, thorough people who know how to dig out buried truth.

Most people who do private investigations will admit that, often, new assignments are a long time coming in. At the start of his business career a PI will spend long, lean weeks taking his card around to law offices, banks, and finance companies trying to drum up business. Then when business happens, he is often called on to be at two or three places at one. Private investigation work is almost always time sensitive in that you must do the work *now*, or it is of no value. It is also work that must be done on a one-on-one basis.

PI work can be accurately summarized as work where the one doing the greatest amount of innovative waiting and demonstrating the most thorough stick-to-it-iveness will prevail. In many cases PI work is deadly boring. People who do not like to do skip tracing and people watching, including keeping careful records, should not attempt this line of work.

PIs must be able to go to court as credible witnesses, know the rules of evidence and how it must legally be collected, and how the law regarding trespass and invasion of privacy apply. For this reason, PIs are often retired police or military who are used to rooting around till they find answers their clients require.

When assignments get thin, PIs need to look around for other work out there waiting to be picked up. Running shoplifting seminars or prevention campaigns for private merchants is a good example of related work that can be available. Knowledge of electronics and listening devices can lead to some not quite legal assignments. One PI went to work in a restaurant to try to discover how raw steaks were disappearing out the back door.

Generally, good PIs provide all the services their client attorneys request. But they must decide ahead if they will take cases if they fall outside those that are entirely legal.

"Gone fishing!" is what you can say every day if you're a fishing guide.

A file cabinet, orderly mind, good camera, video camera, tape recorder, phone, desk, reference library, cards, and stationery are all that is required to go into business unless state laws also require a license. Many PIs get their start working for other established PIs, law enforcement agencies, or the military. Many PIs operate out of a home office.

Action-oriented men who, for one reason or another, are on a dull college career path often ask if there isn't something besides bean counting, design, personnel management, or inventory control, and that has more pizazz and danger involved. There are jobs that require a college degree and are exciting and challenging, but they also require some sort of skill, such as lock picking, electronics, surveillance, or management.

Other examples of skills often demanded are a working knowledge of Spanish or French for the border patrol. An accounting or law degree is usually required by the FBI, but it is also impressed with language and computer skills. Special knowledge of paper manufacture, printing, computer hacking, and highly developed investigative skills are required for consideration by the Secret Service. However, all these government agencies are especially impressed with computer and language skills.

Those who wish detailed current information on employment with any of these agencies should call or write their local offices as listed in the phone book. Pay, especially after a few years, is adequate and field assignments are often made in long increments, allowing for some semblance of domestic tranquility.

Other than possibly the FBI and the BATF, these government agencies have not yet acquired a reputation for preying on average citizens, as is the case in most Third World nations. Men of action with proper training can, in good conscience, at least inquire about employment at these federal agencies.

Great numbers of other action careers await those who wish to go after them: race car driver, gun runner, rodeo cowboy, skydiving instructor, river-rafting guide, international courier, martial arts teacher, spy, test pilot, and many others.

Those wishing more information with specific, detailed instructions on how to enter these and other action careers should secure a copy of *Action Careers* from Paladin Press.

There are so many different alternative work choices in this book that men of action who are tired of their dull, 9-to-5 routines are bound to find one they like.

BIBLIOGRAPHY

Benson, Ragnar. *Action Careers*. Boulder, CO: Paladin Press, 1987.

CHAPTER

Stuntman

50

The adrenalin-producing, challenging, never-stuck-in-the-mud career of a movie stuntman is a natural for many men of action. Most adventurous men are already engaged in such physically demanding activities as hunting, shooting, rodeo riding, race car driving, mountain climbing, martial arts, hard-contact sports (e.g., football or basketball), and even seemingly mundane work like construction and fire fighting. Because men of action are so well situated to becoming stunt players, this action career is among the few considered separately.

Although any trend is subject to change, the current use of stuntmen in movies of all types is at an all-time high. Several recent magazine articles have wailed and moaned about the fact that directors are demanding too much. "People are being killed by being asked to perform feats that are much too dangerous," they complain, "in an attempt to satiate thrill-seeking movie-goers." It is true that, by historical standards, movie production budgets for stunt players are extremely high, but it is also true that even though some high-profile fatalities have occurred, performance of stunts is entirely voluntary—a contract between two consenting adults, if you please.

One can easily substantiate the dramatic increase in the use of stunt players by noting the credits that follow virtually any movie. Even "nonviolent" movies always list six or eight stunt players. James Bond epics are noted for their extremely daring, innovative, and often dangerous stunts. Stunt player credits for some Arnold Schwartzenegger and 007 movies will often number 30 or 50 or more! Because of the American infatuation with elaborate special effects and action-packed movies, it appears certain that ever more of these specialists will continue to be in demand. As with any very vigorous athletic activity, stunt playing is basically a young man's game. It is a high-turnover, high-demand occupation that has all of the elements that men of action desire.

The best estimates suggest that about 5,000 people currently make claim to being stunt players in the United States. Only an estimated 1,200 to 1,500 may actually make an acceptable, full-time living at this business, however.

Stuntmen work for about $365 per day as flat-rate extras. As stunts get hairier, a good stuntman who has agreed to do a difficult gig will negotiate what is known as a "bump." This is an extra payment above the basic day rate.

Negotiations for a bump are done with the movie stunt coordinator or director. If the movie has extensive stunts, it will require a stunt coordinator to handle the many aspects involved to get them performed to satisfaction. If only a punch or two is thrown and the worst fall is a routine one through a window or downstairs, the main director will handle the business. Both have an excellent idea of what various stunts should cost. Routine stunts like falling from four stories, rolling down stairs, or engaging in a barroom brawl generally do not command a bump.

At times, a group of stuntmen will band together to offer a contract price for all the stunts in a movie. By so doing, they all participate in the special skills and financial rewards of the scarce swordsman or high-altitude plungers in the group. They also agree internally on how the money is divided, saving movie managers that headache.

Aircraft stunting, explosives, and some firearms work are handled by specialists outside the stunting community who are hired for that specific purpose. Someone with these skills may find work in Hollywood, but not starting as a $365 per day extra.

Stunts can be both common and unique. There is a common repertoire of stunts that all must know, such as throwing a punch, being punched, falling off a roof, being kicked in the crotch, and performing high-speed vehicle rollovers. But in many regards, each major gig is unique to that movie.

Directors and writers have an idea as to how each of the stunts they have written into the story should look. Their first act of implementation is to talk the specific stunt over with the stunt players to determine both whether it can be done and at what cost. At times, an overly dangerous gig is modified a bit at the counsel of the stunt players to provide better odds for survival, better crowd appeal, and a better price.

Bumps run from $350 for a car rollover to perhaps $5,000 to jump out of an 18th-floor window. Top bumps occur when chances of survival uninjured are 50-50. These are the James Bond-type gigs that have never been done before and for which there is absolutely no chance of surviving a miscalculation. Bumps for these stunts have ranged up to $50,000.

As a result, the 10 best-paid Hollywood stunt players make about $250,000 a year. The next hundred pull down around $100,000. Average stunt players who remain fully employed make about $40,000 to $50,000 per year.

Stuntmen in many regards are in hurry-up-and-wait positions. They can never keep production crews waiting. Even a one-minute tardiness will probably result in dismissal. Few stunt players are ex-military, but it is often said that this hurry-up-and-wait Hollywood attitude is best learned in the military.

Short-course stunt schools are often run on an ad hoc basis by master stunters in Hollywood. These are more like seminars, but they only run a day or two and provide a great deal of information for a novice who has not had a chance to work with specialists. Unfortunately, almost all these short courses are offered only in Tinsel Town.

Outsiders are usually shocked to discover that spectacular, breathtaking stunts *always* start with pencil, paper, and calculator. Increasingly refined mathematical calculations are vital. Good stunt players are no dummies who took basketweaving rather than physics in school. These are top athletes who paid attention in math and physics class. Those who do stunts by guess and by gosh, just jumping out of planes when they feel the time is right, are too accident prone to find employment in modern Hollywood.

Despite their reputation for womanizing and heavy drinking and doping, most stunt players are very steady and reliable. Wild-assed renegades don't work long because no director can risk having a messy schedule-wrecking problem on his set.

Smart, athletic men who wish to become stunt players can do so by in three ways: 1) learning basic stunt moves, perfecting a specialty, and then joining a troupe; 2) knowing somebody who is making a movie, or 3) starting as a simple walk-on extra. An untrained novice with no contacts can only start by doing extra work. When you sign on as an extra, you should mention any special skills such as throwing punches, tumbling down stairs, or being shot off a building. You may be hired as an extra, a sort of director's insurance program allowing more flexibility during the shoot.

Those who are successful at getting into movies must do sufficient research to find out when movies are to be filmed in their area, whom to see for an audition as an extra, and what to do and say after reaching the correct person.

Because of the need for a fresh look, as well as the escalating costs in the city of glitz, more and more films are being made other places. Georgia, Texas, and Washington are three examples of states where a large number of films are currently being made. Every state has a film commission whose sole duty is to attract full-length movie productions. These commissions are located in the state capital. A quick call to information for the state film commission number and a follow-up call to the appropriate office will confirm if and when a major shoot is planned for one's area.

Depending on the movie, all sorts of parts are open. Westerns usually require a number of barflies and dance-hall girls, parts for which almost any woman could qualify. Someone may be needed to swim a river, follow a team of horses, or even cook on a campfire.

See the administrative director, the director, or the stunt coordinator as soon after the film crew gets into your area as possible. Prepare a *very short* pitch outlining your abilities, a printed business card, and a one-page pictorial of you in your regalia that can be left with various people.

Most experts advise that you do not need an agent to break into the movie business. Larger agencies won't have time for new people, and smaller ones tend to be disreputable. Most experts agree that the notion that an agent will find work for a stuntman is mostly illusory.

One extremely successful stuntman did extensive research, learned to do local community-requested theatrical-type stunts, and then organized a small group. His troupe worked on contract for Western restaurants, theme parks, dude ranches, flea markets, conventions, and even company picnics, doing staged holdups and shoot-outs. It advertised in the yellow pages under entertainment to secure some of its gigs, and when a movie came to a small town nearby, the director, anxious about finding talent in such a backwater, hired the troupe at once. It had references, experience, and a list of stunts its members could perform. This led to work in a series of movies.

Stuntmen are generally concerned about starting as extras, fearful that they may continue to be cast as extras without a real shot at the big money. Making the jump from a regularly hired extra to a stunt player probably will require a headshot, a professionally done four- or six-photo series printed in color on one page. These close-up photos must show the aspiring stunt player, bit actor, or whatever in his gear and in a position for which he is best suited. Traditionally, these portfolios cost about $600 to produce and duplicate.

When done by aspiring, talented amateur photographers, however, the cost often falls to $200 or less. Color photocopies further reduce the costs of these pictorial résumés that are handed out to potential employers.

At an audition, talk very little; be courteous, eager, and positive; emphasize your experience, not your inexperience; state that you *are* definitely available, because this is your profession; give them your headshots; know in detail your *complete* wardrobe size; don't hustle the part or autographs; and always carry two pieces of picture ID.

There are other, often complicated on-set protocols and rules that you must master after being hired. These include promptness, patience, silence on the set, listening carefully to the stunt or extras coordinator, taking care of your wardrobe, and refraining from fraternizing with the stars on the set. There are a huge number of additional unwritten rules too numerous to mention in this short introduction that you must pick up on the job by being quiet and being observant.

Extras work at most an hour or two per day. They must, however, be on instant call, often leading to an extremely boring week or two while the movie is being filmed.

Stunt men bring along their own personal pads and equipment. Larger, more costly equipment needed for specific gigs is rented for the shot by the production company. Being certain the ropes, bags, nets, and other equipment are adequate is the duty of the individual stunt player.

Every stunt is approached in a thoughtful, thorough, calculated manner. Even common gigs can cripple or kill if handled cavalierly. If the stunt is difficult, the stuntman will spend a long time discussing the shot with the stunt coordinator to be sure he understands exactly how the gig is to look, where the cameras will be located, and how he will come through it. They may specify special air bags, nets, or harness. In the case of car rollovers, they agree on tires, roll bars, transmissions, and vehicle type. All contracts are verbal, including any bumps for that gig.

In some cases the director may not like the way the stunt looked after completion. If it is a minor stunt, such as rolling a car, stunt players will agree to do it again. The cost of such props as vehicles keeps this from becoming abusive.

Stuntmen are covered by the movie company's medical insurance and their worker's comp insurance. Suits for injuries on the part of stuntmen are very rare. Production companies and directors are generally not held liable for stunts fully explained to a stunt professional. Those who do sue never work in Hollywood films again.

Contrary to widespread rumors, actors never, ever do their own stunts. Some actors might be able to do some stunts, but it is too risky. Movie production companies are always covered by insurance, should any of their principal talent be incapacitated and unable to continue the shooting schedule.

Directors who allow actors to do stunts are held negligent under the terms of most insurance policies if a featured actor is disabled. As a result, insurance companies will not pay for delays in production while everyone waits for the principal to recover. No director will assume these levels of risk. This guarantees that expendable stunt players will always be used. This is true even for relatively minor bits of action such as throwing a single punch.

In the past small men did stunts for women and children. They still may stand in for children, but women do their own stunts now.

It just takes a few lucky breaks and some hard work to get a routine down to break into this action career. Hundreds do it every year by starting in small communities where competition is not so severe.

Stuntmen seem to make their own breaks and are quickly to where they are working a hundred days a year, receiving significant bumps for many of these days. It's a risky business, but it is also rewarding.

BIBLIOGRAPHY

Benson, Ragnar. *Action Careers*. Boulder, CO: Paladin Press, 1987.

Bucklin, Jack. *Stuntman*. Boulder, CO: Paladin Press, 1992.

CHAPTER

Bounty Hunter

51

Professional bounty hunters much prefer to be called bail-bond enforcers. But knowledgeable men of action know this profession, by any name, to be in the Old West tradition of paying an agent to bring in a fleeing fugitive.

This is a tremendously exciting, dangerous, adrenaline-producing way to make a living, but one in which—unless circumstances align themselves perfectly—is not generally available to the average man. As far as I have been able to determine, no woman has ever made bounty hunting a full-time occupation. Some do work as skip tracers, but this is not where the big money is.

The duties of a bounty hunter include taking a specific fugitive into custody in a sane, legal manner and delivering him or her to a jail with little or no physical damage to either party. Pros validly point out that these fugitives are generally resigned to their fate. They are civil and criminal prisoners,

not prisoners of war taken in some sort of military engagement. Court cases in support of this philosophy are many. Those using excessive force to bring their subjects back to court for trial are likely to be the subject of civil action themselves.

Bounty hunters must be extremely glib, well-spoken people. They must have a plausible pretext for everything they do and for all of the information they seek. As one expert remarked, "This is a business of individuals who could talk their way into Iran dressed as a rabbi." This is somewhat of an exaggeration, but it is true that bounty hunters must think very well on their feet or, as another pro said, "they will get busted on the head."

Bounty hunters work on contract for bail-bondsmen who have put up bail for a person who has been arrested, jailed, and charged but is then released on the guarantee (or surety) of the bondsman.

Those being bailed, or their friends and relatives, must put up a significant amount of collateral with the bondsman. The amount depends on the bail set by the court, the seriousness of the crime, and the accused's past history. Bondsmen set their own fees on the basis of the amount of the bond they guarantee. Usually this is 10 percent of the total bond. Sufficient collateral must be given to the bondsman to cover his exposure, but his fee is usually covered in cash.

According to common-law precedent, bail-bondsmen are legal surety for the accused. Traditionally, in ancient England, surety providers could come only from members of a local family in good standing. Those providing surety absolutely guaranteed that the accused would be in court to face the judge on the appointed day. This old legal definition has been relaxed a bit to include professional, paid bondsmen in America.

If the accused does not show up for the court appointment on the proper day, the court will generally set a maximum time ranging from 120 to 180 days during which surety must produce the guy or the cash. If the accused is a total skip, the bondsman must come up with the full bond amount, which can range from a few thousand to millions in the case of some nefarious drug dealers. Depending on the circumstances, a bondsman may not have taken enough collateral, or the pledge may be something like a house, racehorse, or yacht that is hard to liquidate quickly for cash.

In some cases where a skip is likely, the bondsmen or the court may demand a cash bond in the full amount set by the court. Drug dealers are notorious for putting up huge bonds and then skipping safely back to Nigeria, Colombia, or wherever.

Forfeiture of bond, however, does not release the accused from the duty to eventually stand trial. If one jumps bail, he has paid to escape temporarily but has not paid for the crime. Police and FBI will go after high-profile political prisoners, but in lesser cases it is up to the bondsman to bring his guy back into court.

In some cases, large sums of money may be at issue. An accused not known as a badass who is arrested for car theft would probably be bonded out at about $5,000. For this, the bondsman would probably demand $1,500 in cash and $4,000 in collateral. Collateral would be such items as cars, guns, motorcycles, stocks, bonds, stereo equipment, or just about anything of real value. Often doting parents put up the deed to their houses to cover errant kids.

Bail-bond contracts contain clauses and stipulations that require the subject to abide by all court orders and appointments or be subject to immediate rearrest. Expenses to oversee the accused are also chargeable to the collateral. Good bondsmen keep track of those they have out on bail via parents, attorneys, and friends. A great deal of information is required on the form the accused fills out at the time of bail.

If it appears that the accused is even thinking about skipping, those putting up the collateral or the bondsman may order a rearrest as a precautionary measure. It is not unheard of for parents or friends to coldly reevaluate the extent of their exposure, deciding the next day that their guaranteeing bail was foolish. In such cases, providers of collateral may ask that the accused be rearrested and rebonded, releasing them from their collateral obligation.

Many bonding agents make their own arrests whatever the circumstances, becoming both bonding agent and bounty hunter. In many cases, female bonding agents find this work difficult, especially when some giant logger skips out on her. As bonding agents get older or busier or even more apprehensive regarding bad actors, they may hire professional bounty hunters, who agree for a slice of the pie to bring a guy in. As mentioned, expenses are charged against collateral. Bondsmen develop a knack of knowing who might skip, but it is by this device that parents who have raised a jerk sometimes lose the family home.

Bounty hunters who live in reasonably highly populated areas and who can line up several cases per week can make some pretty good bucks at this work—depending, of course, on whether their bodies hold up to the abuse. Bonding agents who might be hanging out for $5,000 on a contract will gladly pay $1,000 to have their skip deposited safely back in jail. Basically, the philosophy "jump bail and go back to jail" applies.

Bounty hunters must work and act professionally. They must portray businesslike toughness that will both enlist cops, intimidate any skip, and comfort a bondsman. This is often really difficult. Novices or wannabe bondsmen must recognize that getting into a fight a week with a skip won't hack it.

Effective bounty hunters almost always bring their charges in with an absolute minimum of blood and confusion. In this regard, a glib tongue and proper dress count for a lot.

Since most of this work is done in larger cities, bounty hunters carry pistols in an environment where necessary permits are difficult to obtain. Professionals believe that although they seldom use their sidearms, it is important to display one, to keep the other guy from using his.

Good bounty hunters are law-abiding citizens. They attempt to comply with all state and local ordinances in the completion of their jobs. Most call the local police or sheriff's officers who are in charge of fugitives after they have positively identified the skip but before an arrest is made. They tell the officers that they will be placing a bail-bond skip in custody and that they may or may not request backup support. The intent is to be timely, professional, and legal. The majority of police officers are happy to have someone else take care of one of their problems.

Usually when a bail-bond is forfeited, the court will issue what is called a bench warrant. This means that although you as the agent of the bondsman can arrest the accused, so can the local sheriff. Conflicts do not generally arise if the sheriff believes that the fugitive will be handled in a proper, timely, legal manner. This is another example where clothes and reputation can make the man more credible. This also becomes one less case an otherwise busy sheriff's department may have to handle.

Paperwork requirements are minimal. Secure a copy of the bail-bond contract from the bondsman, a certified copy of the bail, and an arrest authorization issued by the court. Some bounty hunters also carry a copy of the agreement they have with the bondsman. Members of the local sheriff's fugitive detail can provide copies of the bonding slip and a photo of the subject in many cases. This comprises all of the legal, technical documents needed to bring in a fugitive. Again, those who appear professional secure better, quicker, cooperation from law enforcement people both at home and at the skip's new location.

Most bounty hunters rely on verbal contracts with the bondsman, stipulating how much will be paid and which expenses are chargeable to the

A bounty hunter needs a good description of the fugitive he's seeking, plus flashlights, handcuffs, and weapons for self-defense. He also needs intelligence and maturity to know when to use them. (Photos from *The Bounty Hunter* by Bob Burton.)

project. Some professionals, however, feel more certain of being paid if they have it in writing. They are not in the business for yucks, and the fact that they won't work for a given bondsman in the future won't pay the rent now.

Professional bounty hunters claim that the average skip usually is not smart enough to secure a new ID. "They just seem to hang around the same old neighborhood," one expert said. Yet quick, inexpensive skip tracing is the core of a bounty hunter's business. "If he can't be found, he can't be brought in, and there's no profit to me," another experienced pro observed.

Skip tracing those who have missed their court date is not nearly as difficult as finding long-lost relatives, missing heirs, or some deadbeats. Bounty hunters generally have more information— including relatives, employers, spouses, and references—listed on the bonding contract and booking slip than they can use. Bondsmen are not virgins; they are experts at getting down a great deal of beneficial information of great value to use if the guy becomes a no-show.

Without retracing the chapter on skip tracing, it is probably sufficient to point out that bondsmen and bounty hunters ask first of friends and relatives who have supplied collateral for the guy. As much as they may like the skip, they will also not wish to

Bounty hunter Bob Burton pats down two jumpers for weapons while his partner Ralph Thorson keeps them from making threatening moves.

Burton handcuffs each man, snapping the cuffs on the left wrist first.

Into the car they go for a trip to the precinct, handcuffed and seat-belted into place.

One partner should keep an eye on the arrestees at all times.

lose their homes, cars, or gun collections because of what is probably a less than exemplary citizen.

Probably, the greatest problem for bondsmen and bounty hunters occurs when bondsmen take questionable collateral, and the accused is charged with a relatively minor crime and elects to run far, far away. Under these circumstances, a bounty hunter in Seattle may not be able to afford to travel to a small town in eastern North Carolina to take a guy into custody and then bring him back, even when reasonably sure that the fellow is there.

It seems hard to believe in this day and age, but successful bounty hunters often resort to using private wanted posters to locate skips who have disappeared into a high-population neighborhood. The posters includes a photo of the fugitive taken at arrest and supplied by the sheriff's office, the skip's

physical description, his last known address, the offense for which he is wanted, and the reward being offered. They personally circulate the posters around the neighborhood. Experts claim that a reward of $100 to $150 is usually sufficient to induce a waitress or paper boy to provide information. They also strongly emphasize that when dealing with informants you always pay reward and information money promptly and fairly and that you *never* allow the bad guy to know how he was found or in any way compromise the people who gave you information.

Bounty hunters view fugitives as rent money on the hoof. The trouble is that they have fled because they like the idea of being out footloose and fancy free, as opposed to being locked up. Although taking custody of the fugitive is dangerous, you cannot simply go in, break down the front door, and march the bastard out at the point of a shotgun.

First, when making an arrest, you must positively identify the skips you are after. This is not always easy. A fugitive may be living in a different place with different people, with a different job, and with or without the beard that was an identifying feature. Long, dreary hours of surveillance are often required to confirm that you have the correct person in site.

If a bounty hunter must sit in a car on surveillance in a small, residential neighborhood, it is wise to have a plausible story ready in case a neighbor calls the cops. Doing your homework beforehand and telling the local police what is going on pays big dividends at this point. Cops who already know what is happening won't drive up and spoil the surveillance, and they may even assist in case of problems. Experts point out that local police virtually never are a problem unless the peace is being disturbed.

When, for some reason, it is impossible to stake out a neighborhood successfully, try offering a neighbor $100 to call when the fugitive shows up. By doing so, you have hired a surreptitious crew to perform work that might otherwise have been impossible.

Once a skip has been positively identified, it is show time. Less than 5 percent of fugitives try to resist in any way, but taking custody is always initially hairy. Perhaps because they exude uncertainty, novice bounty hunters seem to get all of their career resistance during their first few weeks in business.

Keep control of the situation by sternly informing the fugitive that he is under arrest for failure to appear. If he argues, inform him that the police have a warrant for his arrest and that he will have to come with you. Order the fugitive to turn around and put his hands against the wall. Handcuff the guy and thoroughly him search for weapons. Besides the obvious danger a hidden weapon presents to you, it is very bad for a jailer to find a hidden weapon after the fugitive is delivered back to jail.

If the suspect runs, you cannot shoot. Always try to prevent this by maintaining the element of surprise. Lock the cuffs on him before he recovers. Professional bounty hunters are usually of intimidating size. Invariably they have a good-sized backup man to help.

Much litigated and tested rules and regulations pertaining to bounty hunting support the fact that you can legally enter the property of another at any time, using whatever force is necessary without additional process to bring in a fugitive. The process is likened to a sheriff rearresting an escaping prisoner. This authority extends only to the 50 states, not to foreign countries.

Prisoners are returned as quickly as possible to the court of jurisdiction from which they fled. Performing this return can involve a trip across town in your car, across the state by van, or by lengthy flights from the far corners of the nation. At the time the prisoner is turned over to jailers in the county of jurisdiction, the bounty hunter must also provide a certified copy of the bail bond.

After weeks of boring surveillance that was only successful when the two bounty hunters paid an informant $300, the pair was ready to collect their rent money. However, a party was in progress at the fugitive's crummy little cold-water walkup. Not wanting to create a big, perhaps uncontrollable, scene, the two men continued watching from their van till after 2 a.m., when everyone seemed to leave.

Silently, they walked up two flights of stairs to the fugitive's apartment door and quietly tried it, but it was locked. One of the men, a 6'3", 230-pounder, backed up a bit and then rammed it full speed, tearing the inner sill away from the door jam. Almost simultaneously, they hollered, "You're under arrest, you're under arrest!"

It appeared that no one was in the apartment. With their adrenaline high now fading, the two men started to search. They found their rent money hiding under the bed off which he had rolled before they turned on the apartment lights.

He was so excited that he had badly messed his pants. They had to let him put on a clean pair before slapping on the cuffs. All this while the hapless guy babbled on almost incoherently about not being bad, the charges being false, and that he would give the pair of bounty hunters $10,000 to let him go (the price of his bail bond).

Ironically, they hauled his weary ass down to the jail, but the bonding company from whom they were supposed to get $800 went bankrupt and never paid. It was, however, a fairly typical pickup, requiring lots of bravado, skill, and patience, but which returned the bounty hunters nothing.

It seems unlikely at this point that average men of action will find the necessary circumstances wherein they either encounter a friend in the business who needs a backup or a bail-bondsman who has a skip that he is willing to pay you to bring in.

Yet it is an interesting and exciting business that, if nothing else, is fun to be aware of.

BIBLIOGRAPHY

Benson, Ragnar. *Action Careers*. Boulder, CO: Paladin Press, 1987.

Burton, Bob. *Bail Enforcer*. Boulder, CO: Paladin Press, 1990.

_____. *Bounty Hunter*. Boulder, CO: Paladin Press, 1984.

CHAPTER

Martial Arts

52

Master gurus in the business claim that too much of what Westerners know about martial arts comes from the movies. Martial arts, they say, is a philosophy/lifestyle/art/religion that is not necessarily aggressive. Westerners have erroneously given martial arts that bad rap, they claim.

In the context of martial arts, a Western film's demonstrated ability to show supposed experts breaking boards, smashing cement blocks, punching through walls with their heads, and even flying surrealistically through the air in quasi-acrobatic maneuvers fills up theaters. Martial arts demonstrations emphasizing grace, beauty, and flow are usually boring to most U.S. audiences, whereas in Japan, similar exhibitions play to overflow crowds.

Americans would have remained bored were it not for Bruce Lee and Jean Claude van Damme, who supposedly took on whole squads of bad guys in carefully choreographed street fights. Americans,

it seems, love violence and cannot appreciate martial arts stripped of it.

Broadly speaking, Orientals engaged in martial arts divide martial arts into two distinct art forms: hard and soft. Westerners really enjoy hard martial arts such as karate and kung fu, with their fast, high kicks; violent, quick movements and throws; and strong emphasis on physical training.

On the other hand, Americans who have even seen tai-chi chuan often do not recognize it as a martial arts form at all. These delicate, almost dancelike, slow moves are thought to be nothing more than an early morning stretch that contributes to good health. Tai-chi is what old pensioners do in the park at 5:00 a.m., one American businessman told me as we sped through Hong Kong to an appointment. Tai-chi appears to be the ultimate soft martial art. The truth is much more obscure.

Even some Orientals who have practiced tai-chi for 35 years do not fully appreciate that their carefully studied moves are actually a 2,000-year-old facade for an ancient, prohibited martial art form called dim-mak, but is by far the deadliest martial art, if one is forced to confrontation. This, these gurus claim, is the reason dim-mak practice became tai-chi. It was forbidden but surfaced in a disguised form.

Dim-mak is the mastery of relatively soft blows delivered to vital acupuncture points. Proponents claim that it takes at least three lifetimes to learn dim-mak properly. Ironically, practitioners claim that it is both a deadly application leading to severe neurological shutdown *and* a powerful healing application. Westerners who have casually observed row upon row of old, gray men and women in the parks of Hong Kong and Bangkok practicing tai-chi are hard-pressed to detect either function.

Even casual observers are aware that martial arts proficiency is telegraphed via a colored belt worn by participants. The awarding of these belts is taken seriously. Real martial arts aficionados in the United States were not amused when the kid in *Karate Kid* asked the old Okinawan gardener what kind of belt he had and was told one from J.C. Penney.

Neophytes are given white belts to wear until their third month of continuous practice. Four white-belt grades, called kyus, are part of this transition. One is expected to practice three days per week at 1 1/2 hours per session to earn belts. Belts are awarded in roughly the following order: 5 months = yellow; 7 months = orange; 1 year = green; 1 1/2 years = blue; 2 years = brown. After that one earns the coveted black belt, but accumulations of training do not cease. Persistent workers earn a first-dan black belt at three years, working up to an incredible fifth dan at 35 years!

It is not unheard of for some especially motivated martial artists to work on two or even three different disciplines simultaneously! In this regard, use of martial arts as a religious way of life becomes abundantly clear.

Interest in and dedication to the martial arts will probably lead to its acceptance as an Olympic sport in the not-too-distant future. Most experts attribute pressure for its inclusion in the Olympic games to Western practitioners, most of whom consider it a sport. Orientals, in contrast, tend to consider it a religion, with no place in Olympic competition. Knowledgeable observers both Eastern and Western resist this move to the Olympics principally because it is the only hard-form martial art that will be featured,

moving the art further from its Oriental roots and more to a Western concept of sports competition.

Oriental practitioners view martial arts as a means of learning confidence and developing self-control. Martial arts is actually a means to *stop* fighting in direct opposition to the Western spin of how to *start* a fight and bring it to a successful conclusion for the instigator. In the eyes of practitioners, martial arts experts teach self-control and self-discipline, thus allowing one to "find an honorable path around most conflicts." This is the essence of Mr. Miagi's, life as exemplified in *Karate Kid*.

Martial arts is not synonymous with street fighting. Some trained martial artists who also engage in street or bar fights find that the alertness, balance, and conditioning derived from their training are helpful but definitely not decisive when they are engaged in a desperate, no-holds-barred, down-and-dirty brawl.

Martial arts students receive instruction and practice in an mat-covered gym called a dojo, while wearing an oriental robe, called a gi. Even in the hard-forms practice, sparring is very stylized. Desperate shots commonly encountered in the streets, such as eye gouges, knee stomps, and vicious shots to the kidneys or groin, are prohibited.

Contests in the dojo tend to be ritualistic, where one tries to score points with high, showy kicks to the head or stomach. Martial artists who graduate to the streets quickly find that one-shot, point-accumulating, fancy moves so popular in the dojo are often ignored by antagonists who view these encounters as combat rather than contests. Along the same lines, black belts dislike sparring with white belts because the latters' moves are unconventional and unexpected, sometimes leading to injury.

Modern Westerners applaud the move of martial arts away from the esoteric and toward street-practical. Traditional Oriental-trained experts, however, claim it is much more practical to exercise discipline and avoid conflict altogether.

It is important to note that in two stylized martial arts, high kicks and back kicks both earn extra points during sparring matches. Out on the street, experts who have been in numerous fights consider these tactics to be virtually suicidal.

Martial arts are linked to the Orient's three main religions: Buddhism, Taoism, and Confucianism.

What started as self-defense systems two centuries ago have evolved into a way of life in Asia.

Psychological studies have confirmed that the further one goes with his martial arts training, the *less* aggressive he is likely to be. Westerners are somewhat familiar with boxing as taught in almost every YMCA. Boxing gyms smell like sweat because people train hard and violently in these places. Dojos generally smell nice and fresh. If during the course of sparring at a dojo, there is blood, the contest stops immediately while healing measures are employed. Blood in a dojo is an obvious breach of technique. In contrast, a boxing match is seldom held where bleeding does not occur. Those objectively evaluating martial arts—either soft or hard form—need to keep these contrasts firmly in mind.

Of the 250,000 martial arts practitioners in the United States, only about 70 (or .03 percent) a year report any kind of serious injury. This is certainly less than any contact sport and some supposedly noncontact sports like basketball. Some say this low casualty rate is the result of martial arts being a sissy sport, when in fact it is the result of the practitioner's high physical conditioning and an Asian philosophy that eschews conflict.

More than a dozen systems of karate exist, but some of the differences are minor. As a general rule, Korean and Japanese styles differ in that Korean is hard form and Japanese is soft. Korean styles are less than a century old; certain Korean styles are so young that some of the founders are still alive. Chinese styles, from which Korean forms evolved, can be either soft or hard.

KOREAN MARTIAL ARTS

Taekwon do is the major Korean martial arts form. It is probably the most popular form of karate worldwide. It is a powerful discipline that emphasizes kicks rather than hand techniques. It involves a series of stepping, blocking, and kicking movements usually performed solo but in unison with dozens of similar trainees striking out at imaginary targets.

The single, powerful blows characterizing this martial art may be delivered with the arms or legs. Equally powerful blocks and a strong spirit, called kata, are also used. Taekwon do's strong emphasis on single, powerful strikes is said to lead to a

rigidness that places one at a disadvantage during a real street fight.

Tang soo do is another form of Korean karate that is a bit less rigid in its execution. Training methods and techniques are said to be more practical and adaptive than taekwon do. Enthusiasts who obtain most of their martial arts information from movies recognize that Chuck Norris is a tang soo do man. Tang soo do does place more emphasis on hand strikes, but high kicking is still a major part of this discipline.

Hapkido is the last Korean martial art form that men of action may encounter. This style is said to be more balanced and integrated that other Korean forms. Elements include throws, joint locks, hand techniques, and power kicking. Generally, this is said to be the most practical Korean form, if one actually is intent on fighting.

There are similarities between all Korean forms, but one has to realize that there are only a limited number of ways to kick, punch, or throw an opponent. It is the unique emphasis on technique, mix of technologies, flexibility, and training methods that sets each discipline apart.

JAPANESE MARTIAL ARTS

Japanese forms of karate are slightly less power oriented than Korean forms. However, many still do not quite qualify as soft-form martial arts. The atmosphere in most dojos teaching Japanese-style martial arts tends to be a bit less shrill and therefore more pleasant to less aggressive people; many women prefer the Japanese varieties.

Wado ryu is a recent style that began in 1939. It is characterized as a circular soft form with emphasis on smooth and flowing throws.

Three additional schools named *gojo ryu, isshin ryu*, and *shotokan* make up this general class of Japanese martial art. Other than shotokan (which is a power, hard-form style somewhat similar to taekwon do), these styles are very similar. Casual observers cannot tell them apart.

Japanese *judo* is primarily the discipline of throws. There is no punching or kicking in judo, but it is underestimated as an actual self-defense art by people unfamiliar with its form.

During execution, two people generally grapple with each other, jockeying to create an opening that

The foot stomp is a great distraction tool, as demonstrated here by Sammy Franco. This grappling-range tactic is known for breaking toes as well as causing excruciating pain for the recipient. This technique is performed by forcefully stomping on the opponent's toes with the heel of your shoe. (Photos from *Street Lethal* by Sammy Franco.)

will permit a decisive throw. Judo training is extremely tiring. Only those in good physical condition can endure more than a few minutes of the intense grappling needed to keep from being thrown on their asses.

Jujitsu is a more commonly accepted martial art form in the United States because it better fits American temperament. It is an aggressive form, combining the hip throws of judo with some of the strikes of karate. It favors heavy strikes over fancy high kicks.

Because both judo and jujitsu require a large amount of close-in grappling, they do have some street value. These forms are especially useful for short, stocky men who can make good use of hip throws.

Like judo, where attempts are made to throw an opponent without injury, *aikido* is also a fairly soft Japanese martial arts form. There is no punching or kicking in traditional aikido. Throws are the basic movements. Someone using properly executed akido movements can usurp an opponent's superior strength and use it against him. Obviously superior strength is never contested in aikido. The intent is never to destroy, but only to neutralize an attacker.

Aikido movements are flowing. They attempt to painfully move an opponent off balance and then keep him off balance till he is down. This Japanese form incorporates surgical-type nerve punching and pain-compliance techniques. Aikido, as a result, is often deployed by women as their martial arts form of choice.

CHINESE MARTIAL ARTS

There are a great number of Chinese systems having only extremely minor, often purely esoteric differences. Basically, they are all types of kung fu, a hard martial art.

Kung fu emphasizes punching and kicking techniques somewhat reminiscent of Korean taekwon do. About 2,000 years ago, kung fu did filter out of China into Korea. Therefore, similarities should not be surprising. Some styles of kung fu have devolved into something similar to tai-chi, but others have retained some powerful, deadly moves.

Kung fu suffers immensely from the fact that most old masters (those with 35 years of training) have not been allowed to leave China. In the United

States, kung fu can either be hard form or a sophisticated exercise. Instruction, it is said, is often marginal, but one must settle on which form to learn before undertaking training.

Bruce Lee, something of a legend in martial arts circles, developed a very recent discipline he called *jeet kune do*. It is an innovative, fast-paced style that borrows heavily and shamelessly from almost every other martial arts form. Basically, jeet kune do impresses people because it's extremely quick; it has application out on the street; and its innovator, Bruce Lee, is so venerated that it will often be encountered, or at least mentioned in martial arts literature.

FILIPINO MARTIAL ARTS

Isolated from the rest of Asia by water, the Philippines developed its own form of martial arts that only somewhat resembles the others. These are hard styles, called *arnis*, *escrima*, and *kali*. Again, actual differences among the three are minor.

Basically, Filipino martial arts are not really unarmed combat in the mainland Asia and Japanese sense of the word. Filipino styles make extensive use of sticks and knives.

Old Ferdinand Magellan was reportedly beaten to a pulp by a Filipino with a stout stick while the Portuguese explorer packed a giant Spanish steel sword. Another version suggests that Magellan stepped on a poisonous snail while wading ashore in the Philippines. But this snail account does little for the adrenaline levels of martial arts people.

Perhaps because it is an aggressive hard form and because of the use of "impure" weapons, Filipino martial arts are not widely taught in the United States. Those who have experienced this style claim it has street value, but until Chuck Norris or some other martial arts movie director does a film about Filipino disciplines, they will probably remain somewhat obscure.

• • •

In general, most busy Westerners are put off by the three years required to halfway master any of these disciplines. Yet there are those few adherents who enjoy discipline and the unique philosophical considerations of the various forms of martial arts.

In this t'ai chi ch'uan series, the posture known as a "single whip" can be used to strike no less than four dim-mak points on the body. Dim-mak was the original name for t'ai chi, which translates as death-point striking. It is considered the supreme ultimate boxing. Here, Erle Montaigue, one the world's foremost authorities on dim-mak, demonstrates. (Photos from *Dim-Mak: Death-Point Striking* by Erle Montaigue.)

This brief summary of various styles is not meant to favor any one form over another, only to summarize their various places in the culture as a whole.

If there is a broad appeal in martial arts philosophy, it is evidenced by worldwide interest in warfare/business applications of martial arts. Two international best-sellers—*The Art of War* by Sun-tzu and *The Book of Five Rings* by Miyamoto Musashi—graphically document this synergy. The fact that both books continue to be in demand in both the United States and Europe speaks volumes about the practical application of martial arts in the business world.

The following photographic sequences illustrate the use of martial arts tools for street self-defense.

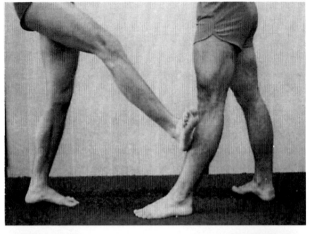 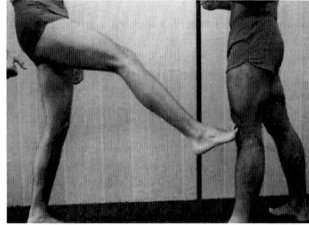

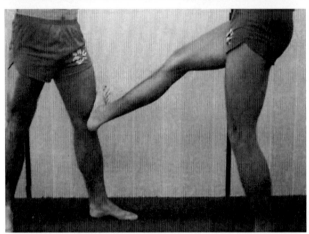 

Kicks are some of the most effective martial arts techniques for self-defense. Here martial artist Ted Gambordella demonstrates the front heel kick to the shin, front snap to the kneecap, front heel kick across the kneecap, and a front snap to the coccyx. (Photos from *The 100 Deadliest Karate Moves* by Ted Gambordella.)

BIBLIOGRAPHY

Christensen, Loren. *Anything Goes.* Boulder, CO: Paladin Press, 1990.

Franco, Sammy. *Killer Instinct.* Boulder, CO: Paladin Press, 1991.

_____. *Street Lethal.* Boulder, CO: Paladin Press, 1989.

_____. *When Seconds Count.* Boulder, CO: Paladin Press, 1994.

Gambordella, Dr. Ted. *Fight for Your Life.* Boulder, CO: Paladin Press, 1982.

_____. *The 100 Dirtiest Karate Moves.* Boulder, CO: Paladin Press, 1982.

MacYoung, Marc "Animal." *Fists, Wits, and a Wicked Right.* Boulder, CO: Paladin Press, 1991.

_____. *Pool Cues, Beer Bottles, and Baseball Bats.* Boulder, CO: Paladin Press, 1989.

_____ and Chris Pfouts. *Safe in the City.* Boulder, CO: Paladin Press, 1994.

_____. *Safe in the Street.* Boulder, CO: Paladin Press (video), 1994.

_____. *Violence, Blunders, Fractured Jaws.* Boulder, CO: Paladin Press, 1989.

Montaigue, Erle. *Dim-Mak.* Boulder, CO: Paladin Press, 1993.

Quinn, Peyton. *A Bouncer's Guide to Barroom Brawling.* Boulder, CO: Paladin Press, 1990.

"A Way to Stop the Spear." *The London Economist.* May 15, 1993: 11.

Wilson, Jim. *Commando Fighting Techniques.* Boulder, CO: Paladin Press, 1999.

CHAPTER

Credit Bureaus

53

Generally, men of action live such convoluted, wild lives that they seldom ask for or expect to be granted credit in any customary sense of the word. It's like they used to say about Richard Nixon, "Would you loan money to this man?" For most of us, the answer would be a resounding no. We loan to each other for reasons having nothing to do with traditional creditworthiness.

Many compatriots have the philosophy that "wealth is transitory" and that if one was supposed to hang onto money, the authorities would have put handles on it.

Living this sort of hand-to-mouth existence has some charm. Even at the current low-interest rates, one who pays cash, for instance, for a new $10,000 truck will save about $2,000 over the following five years, the most common term for which most new automobiles are now financed. And this is money that does not have to be earned and therefore render state, local, and national taxes.

People who do not purchase on credit can buy a lot more of everything because they avoid a kind of middleman. It's an involuntary avoidance to be sure, but the benefits are very real. Witness the Amish or the Old Order Brethren whose religion forbids financing purchases. They end up with huge, valuable estates, while bankers and finance companies in the region shrivel.

In that regard, men who choose to live the life of a soldier of fortune in the old classical sense are actually fortunate when the system strips their credit away. They end up with more money for guns, ammunition, sniper rifles, and explosives—all taken right out of the mouths of bankers.

Yet there are the occasional instances when you must apply for a credit card, purchase a new vehicle, or even rent an apartment, requiring a conventional credit check in the finest tradition of middle-class America. In this case, you must be willing to play the credit bureaus' game.

Men of action usually discover their credit is not so hot only when it is refused. It should not be, but

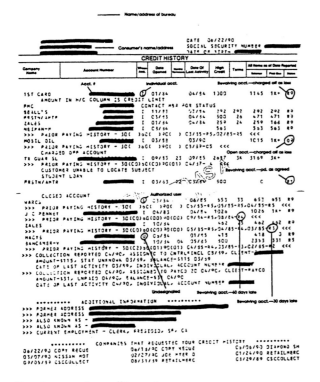

Sample copy of a credit report.

In the past seven to 10 years, all that has changed. Today few, if any, actual credit reports are confirmed by phone by local merchants. Only large companies with sophisticated computer networks are able to input records that are taken directly from large company computers.

Four computerized giants now control the industry. The fact that a person did not pay his bar bill or library fines will probably not make it into the record. Chances are virtually 100 percent that your local credit bureau will be an agent of one of the following:

1. TRW Credit Information Services
    595 City Parkway West
    Orange, CA 92667

2. CBI/Equifax
    Box 4091
    Atlanta, GA 30302

3. CSS
    624 East North Belt, Suite 400
    Houston, TX 77060

4. Trans Union Credit Information Co.
    444 N Michigan Avenue
    Chicago, IL 60611

To a great extent, these agencies and their many local offices are regional. Most are more heavily represented in specific areas. Changes are pretty good that there will not be two or more of these large companies in your area. If there are, refusal forms from the merchant will explain which agency's report was the basis of your refusal. Even so, it is wise to secure copies of your credit report from both agencies, if there are such, even though the cost doubles. Usually, but not always, the information is similar but check anyway.

Reading credit reports is not entirely intuitive. Other than the two to three weeks of time saved in picking up a report in person, you also have the advantage of being able to ask about terms and codes. Sit down in the credit bureau's office and read it till all the meanings are clear. Credit bureau personnel consider themselves librarians who keep records that they try to accurately report to their subscriber customers. They don't care personally that you have lousy credit.

often it's a blow to their pride. Who, for instance, among us wants a friend with good credit?

You could say that this refusal is much like closing the barn door after the horse has departed. But the analogy is not accurate, and, as we now know, refusal is not final.

Getting a credit problem resolved definitely requires that you know which problem to resolve. You must get a credit report in hand so that it is possible to determine who is passing the bad rap. After being refused credit because of a report from a credit bureau (a private agency that collects and catalogs credit information from banks, finance companies, and private businesses and sells it to lending institutions), you can secure a free copy of his credit information. Otherwise, securing a copy of your credit information from a credit bureau costs between $8 and $14.

Securing personal credit reports can be done by mail, but it is best done in person at the local credit bureau office. Almost every city of any size has a credit bureau, where dealing in person is far quicker than using the mail. Personal contacts in these circumstances are advantageous.

Until recently, compilation of credit information was handled by little mom-and-pop type operations.

Notice that reports from credit card companies, banks, and merchants are posted horizontally across the page. These list the dates accounts were opened, the maximum dollars of credit extended, terms of repayment, date of last activity, and current status. Current status is the toughest part of the report to decipher. Codes are based on an "R" scale, with R1 indicating that the person pays his bills before the postman can even deliver them and R9 signaling that the account is so delinquent it was turned over for collection.

Any other really bad stuff—such as adverse collection proceedings, legal actions (civil, not criminal), bankruptcies, etc.—are listed at the bottom of the report. These list companies to which collections were referred and the status of these collections—whether they were eventually paid in full, what arrangements have been made for small monthly payments, etc.

It is quite common for Americans to have largish phone and utility bills that, after changing addresses, they inadvertently do not pay because of some clerical screwup until they are contacted by a collection agency, or for them to have charges on their bills that a former spouse or acquaintance ran up. These adverse items remain on one's record for seven years.

Many men of action, especially if they are young, run into trouble when they don't have anything good or bad on their records.

Credit bureaus are also legally required to keep a list of companies that have requested credit information from them. Generally, all of this stuff is kept for seven years even if it is not adverse. Neophytes who look at their credit reports for the first time are often surprised to see the following:

1. Items they had completely forgotten about.
2. A lack of detailed personal data that they had expected.
3. Accounts that are not entirely accurate.

Some general confusion exists in our society regarding detailed credit reports that do list such subjective factors as personal character, work habits, type of job, integrity, marriage situation, family relationships, and other private data. In times past, these sorts of reports were sometimes compiled for insurance companies on individuals. However, more and more, they are falling into disrepute because of inherent errors, outside criticism, and citizen suspicion, as well as the fact that subscribers often quit the credit bureaus when they found the information to be erroneous, which it often was. In cases where insurance companies require personal information, they often secure it themselves rather than relying on an outside source.

As a result, do not be surprised at the lack of personal detail in your credit report. Chances are that, other than your current job, past job tenure, home address, past residence addresses, and marital status, there will be very little. Those who have judgments and suits recorded against them will find these listed, but they are already available to the public at the court house anyway.

At any rate, take the time to go through your report in minute detail to identify those items that are adverse and those that are laudable. Since most of the data is computer generated, right from the banks' or stores' computers, it does no good to argue or become bristly with the credit bureau lady.

In some cases, you can secure change at the credit bureau office by simply and nicely pointing out errors. It is also no trick to update your address from a crummy part of town to a new, better apartment or even a neutral post office box, if necessary. Credit bureau clerks are information nerds. Switching your place of employment and wife's name and salary are also easily done in person, verbally. Some credit bureaus request written confirmation of changes, but this is usually just to facilitate work flow.

Three fairly effective methods are available by which you can get adverse, default, or turned-in-for-collection information removed or modified. Contrary to popular rumor, not all of the techniques work, and none are particularly easy, principally because credit is such a critical matter in our society. Credit granters vigorously guard their right and ability to secure some kind of information on those they are considering loaning to.

Professional "credit mechanics" who usually charge hundreds of dollars for their services for what appears to be mundane, unimaginative information have recently become a plague for credit bureaus. These experts recommend that under terms and conditions of the Federal 1972 Fair Credit Reporting Act, individuals who have adverse items on their records can protest these items. Originally, this device was set up to allow people to have erroneous, inaccurate items removed from their records. Professional credit mechanics recommend that you simply protest every adverse report on the assumption that credit bureaus cannot verify every protested account as required by law. Accounts not reverified in 21 days must be dropped from your record.

The theory, in this instance, is that reporting banks and merchants will not have the time and inclination to reverify most protested accounts in the time allotted and that many of these adverse records will simply drop from the record by default. To some extent this works, but credit bureaus have reacted by often refusing to reverify. If and when this occurs, you can protest the credit bureau's lack of compliance with federal law and complain to the Federal Trade Commission. This often is effective, but recent reports indicate that if your protest has the earmarks of a credit mechanic, it will automatically be disallowed, sometimes even for honest mistakes on the part of the credit bureau. This is another reason to go to the office to talk face to face.

After refusal, you can hire an attorney and sue in district court, or even better, in your local small-claims court. In the case of district court, your attorney will map out the strategy to be deployed and papers to be filed. Dollar amounts that you can claim in small-claims court are less, but so are the paperwork and legal scheming. For a private citizen, winning in small-claims court requires great attention to detail and lots of preparatory work.

The clerk of a small-claims court is at the local county courthouse and can explain all the details involved in filing a complaint and serving papers on the credit bureau.

Another method involves going into the bank or local merchant and telling someone there that you wish to clean up your credit records and asking if there isn't some means by which a settlement can be negotiated. Most merchants have written off these old bills so that any payment is like free money to them. Promises of modest weekly payments of $5 or $10 may result in the merchant's informing the credit bureau that this account was handled satisfactorily. This routine works even though you may be paying on the bill for years. If just a few bad reports can be turned around on your record, the whole thing may look much better to a new lender.

Also, search through your own records and dealings to find any credit grantor with whom favorable business has been conducted and list it on the record. It will be obvious that credit bureaus do not contact many credit grantors in the local area. Water, gas, electricity, and phone bills that have been paid faithfully should be noted as people who can verify good credit. Take the names and addresses of these firms to the credit bureau. It will take a few weeks, but the bureau will verify the accounts independently and include this information in your record.

If you cannot negotiate with major creditors or find enough counterbalancing accounts that were paid on time, and do not wish to go to court, there is one other approach.

Federal law permits debtors with bad credit items on their records to insert into your file an explanation of 100 words or fewer of "why, when the factory closed, your kid got sick, and your clotheshorse ex-wife ran up accounts" you had to file for bankruptcy. This statement, if cleverly and emotionally compiled, might sway the resident loan officers at the bank. If that's your last recourse, it's all there is left to do.

Yet it seems probable that true men of action do not have credit problems. They move around too much and are either in the chips or out depending or what sort of assignment they conjure up for themselves.

Men of action are by nature self-reliant foragers. They know that if they must, they can go out in the fields and hunt and gather till the next big deal comes in.

Nevertheless, we need information on credit bureaus and their reports in our back pockets just in case. . . .

BIBLIOGRAPHY

French, Scott. Credit: *The Cutting Edge*. Boulder, CO: Paladin Press, 1988.

Hammond, Bob. *Credit Repair Rip-off*. Boulder, CO: Paladin Press, 1994.

_____. *Credit Secrets*. Boulder, CO: Paladin Press, 1991.

_____. *How to Beat the Credit Bureaus*. Boulder, CO: Paladin Press, 1990.

_____. *Life after Debt*. Boulder, CO: Paladin Press, 1992.

White, J. Arline. *Credit Mechanic*. Boulder, CO: Paladin Press, 1991.

CHAPTER
Trapping
54

For purposes of this chapter, trapping includes the use of steel spring-type traps, both leg-hold and killer types, and steel snares to harvest small game, generally for their pelts. Those who have used traps to any extent are well aware that the best, most concise expert in the world could not provide a person with sufficient information to become a good trapper in one short chapter. One book couldn't do it, as evidenced by the fact that most good trappers have dozens of books on trapping. Some of these guys don't read much, but they do have books on trapping.

Perhaps readers will learn enough in this short section to catch a critter or two, thus persuading them to get some personally administered training and some of the many books on the subject.

Trapping as a way of life and an occupation goes back to the first opening of North America. Early trader-trappers found eager buyers among Indian trappers who immediately saw the techno-logical advantage of the white man's metal snare wire. Compared to the Indians' traditional rawhide/fiber snares and rock deadfall traps, the white man's snares were miraculous. But, as is true in any actively growing industry, trapping technology did not hibernate.

About 1840, Sewell Newhouse, a resident of Oneida Castle, New York, invented a spring-activated leg-hold trap. The trap design itself was not particularly earthshaking, but his ability to use good spring steel and to temper these springs so that they remained alert and taut over long periods set them apart. Newhouse's traps were guaranteed not to shatter when tripped in extremely cold conditions. Initial orders were mostly from Oneida Indians who, at the time, lived in the area.

Newhouse's traps gained a great reputation for ruggedness and reliability. Business grew dramatically during the period we refer to as the opening of the West. His trap design changed hands a number of times and several competitors emerged. But the only real technological leap forward didn't come until the Conibear trap of the early 1960s.

A seasoned trapper and his catch. (Photos from *Survival Poaching* by Ragnar Benson.)

Most old duffers who have trapped off and on for years can easily recall when Conibear killer traps were invented by an obscure Canadian tinkerer about 30 years ago. At the time, Conibear killer traps were hailed as an eagerly awaited quantum leap in technology that had eluded the industry for about 100 years.

Conibear traps are simply described as collapsible rectangular steel frames activated by a type of leaf spring that snaps the frame shut as an animal passes through. Whereas leg-hold traps can pinch the fingers of careless users, Conibear traps are known to break wrists and arms.

Conibear traps are sold in four sizes: a 110 is about 5 1/2 inches square and has one spring to power it; a 120 is the same size but has two springs; a 220 is 7 1/2 inches square and used for larger, heavier-bodied critters such as big coons and possums; a 330 will kill any game animal in North America in which the trapper can induce it to put its head. As of this writing, a local trapper reports catching and killing a young 150-pound bear and a large cougar in a 330 Conibear.

These are dangerous traps that will immediately kill any dog, large beaver, or river otter, among others. In some states it is illegal to set a 330 out on dry land.

A government trapper working for the state of Oregon used 330s for coyotes (although most trappers have trouble inducing coyotes to place their heads in one), foxes, badgers, beaver, feral dogs, and porcupines. By some strange combination of poor planning and bad luck, this professional trapper got his arm into a 330. It broke it nicely just above the elbow. One-handed, the hapless fellow could not remove the "infernal machine." As a result, he walked back to his pickup trick, which he then drove about 25 miles, in great pain, to the nearest clinic. In the process he found it necessary to crash through three gates maintained by local ranchers to keep their livestock separated. These ranchers were not pleased with the poor fellow's work that day. At the clinic, the trapper had to coach the technicians on how to remove the trap.

Tales of this sort followed the early use of Conibears. Some older trappers swore they would never use Conibears, but most trappers eventually found that when properly deployed, they were quite effective. Today, most trappers agree that Conibears have earned a useful place in the trapper's kit when used in combination with snares and leg holds.

One must also appreciate the fact that old-fashioned wire snares also have a place in a man of action's inventory. Some very smart critters that are virtually impossible to take with Conibear or leg-hold traps are relatively easy to take with snares. Coyotes, foxes, bobcats, and even wolves (to a limited extent) are good examples. Snares remain more functional in bad weather than steel traps of either kind, are extremely cheap, can be made at home, are easy to hide from both critters and trap thieves, and are ideal when used in large numbers to saturate an area.

As a general rule, leg-hold traps are used around baits on deer, snares are used on infrequently traveled game trails to collect more wary critters that push through the brush with their heads held up from the ground, and Conibears are used in water runs on beaver dams and in places where instantly killing the critter is desirable. Skunks dispatched in a Conibear, for instance, are much nicer to handle. They still stink, but at least they are not trying to shoot the trapper from the trap. Little animals such as skunks, muskrats, and mink are tough to take in snares.

The first advice I had when starting my career as a trapper at the age of 9 came from an old, old veteran at this business.

"Sonny, set your trap along the creek in a place where the animals run," he said.

I studied the situation extremely carefully, finally concluding that one worn place was definitely an animal run. It was. Grandpa's pigs trampled the trap flat crossing the creek!

It took several years, but eventually I learned that trappers must become skilled practical naturalists who learn where animals are likely to travel at any given time of the year.

It is incredibly tough to teach a novice trapper, even in person, how to observe places where animals swim, walk, dig, crawl, or eat. People either develop a sense for these observations out in nature or they do not. Many trappers admit that they learned most about their quarry watching a fox in a meadow catching mice, a muskrat cutting cattails for dinner, or a mink patrolling a creek bed.

Some knowledgeable trappers recommend spending a few hours with a seasoned trapper listening to him talk about what he sees and how he would set for it. Most young trappers get their start in this fashion. They then begin the process of patiently poking around the forests and swamps on their own till they can see what is going on. It takes a number of years to acquire enough background to be halfway competent, but there really are no shortcuts. Unfortunately, the supply of veteran trappers has dwindled because low fur prices made following this line of work unrewarding. Finding professional help outside of books is a very real problem for the novice.

Set Conibear traps in little, low feed areas in swamps, in front of dens, and in trails frequented by animals that more or less hug the ground when they walk. Weasels are abundant, but they are so small they often slither right through a Conibear or a snare. Muskrats are creatures of habit that are easily taken in Conibears. Mink, skunks, coons, cats, squirrels, and beaver will all stick their heads in Conibear traps without thinking. River otters virtually cannot be caught without using Conibears.

Most trappers find that snares are much better for getting coyotes, wolves, and foxes than are Conibears. Bobcats and exotics such as marten and fishers can be taken in either type trap quite successfully.

Use a couple of strands of number 16 or 18 wire to hang an appropriate-size Conibear in a muskrat run or the entrance to a domed cattail house. Use large Conibears held up by two sticks poked in the mud to guard a beaver dam spillway or canal to a feed area. In other cases, it may work to place the trap at trail's end right at a feed area. Some carnivores, such as mink, weasels, badgers, or skunks, can be enticed into a hole guarded by a Conibear baited with a piece of fish, bird, or deer. Cornfields near creeks or rivers will be decimated by coons and possums running in to get at the new corn. Set either leg holds or Conibears in trails leading from the water's edge.

Foot-hold traps run in size from 0 (used for common barn rats and weasels) to number 4 (used to hold coyotes, wolves, big badgers, and bobcats). As a kid, I used number 5s and 6s for bear, but these traps haven't been made for years and are so valuable as antiques that no one would risk putting one out in the woods.

Novice trappers generally spend too much time worrying about which trap to use for which animal. I have caught 120-pound critters in very small traps and lost 35-pounders in large traps before my anchoring techniques were fully thought through. As a general working rule: the higher the trap's model number, the bigger the beast they will hold. This is not entirely valid; I have caught bears in number 4 traps designed for coyotes and badger by fastening the trap to a drag log rather than staking it solid. By using a heavy log drag, the animal could not get a dead pull necessary to get out of the trap. It struggled along, tearing up brush and leaves and producing an easy-to-follow trail. Although many muskrat and mink trappers stake their leg holds solid, I find it best to wire the trap chain to a floating stick drag, allowing the animal to pull out 50 or so feet, where the weight

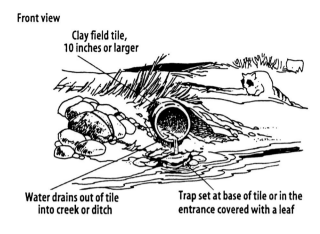

Front view

Clay field tile,
10 inches or larger

Water drains out of tile
into creek or ditch

Trap set at base of tile or in the
entrance covered with a leaf

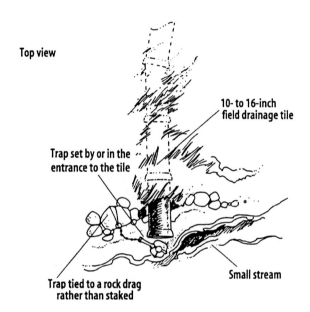

Top view

10- to 16-inch
field drainage tile

Trap set by or in the
entrance to the tile

Small stream

Trap tied to a rock drag
rather than staked

Tile trap.

of the trap either drowns it, or it finds a bit of brush cover to sit and hide.

Betty Lou Teasdale grew up in Central Africa, where she and her younger brother often set out leopard traps around native goat kraals. Bait was usually a partly eaten goat carcass. One day they caught a great, nice tom, but they had left their gun at home. While the younger brother ran for Mom and her .22 rifle, Betty Lou occupied her time teasing the fiery, yellow-eyed critter with a stick. After mom had shot it, they discovered much to their shock that the critter was held by only one toe! The trap, however, had been fastened to a semimovable log drag.

My first muskrat was in a trap in front of our old clay-field drainage system tile. The sign indicated that several of the aquatic creatures called the pipe home. As I walked up, there was a rat in one of my traps held securely with a long 2 x 2 stake in the mud. Just as I readied to shoot, it pulled out of the trap and scurried to safety in the pipe. We were very poor in those days. The loss of a $1.50 skin weighed heavily. Today, I seldom stake traps.

Foot-hold traps are found with a bewildering variety of different springs used to power the jaws. Most common are the long springs. As the name implies, a long U-shaped spring protrudes from the trap. When size numbers reach 2, physical size not only increases, but each trap also has two springs. Long-spring traps are cheaper and more durable but definitely tougher to hide successfully. Few animals will knowingly walk right into an exposed trap. Leg-hold traps must be hidden so the critter can neither see, smell, nor feel the trap before it's on him.

Other spring configurations include jump traps having a single large spring under the trap jaws. Depending on whom one talks to, these traps either jump up higher on the critter's leg or throw the leg out of the jaws as it goes off. Jumps are easier to hide because they are much more compact.

Coil-spring traps are energized by coil springs, as the name suggests. They are also compact but seem to weaken rapidly, especially when left set in water.

Leg holds must be hidden in the exact places where animals place their feet. The trapper must be careful when covering the trap that dirt does not run in under the pan, precluding easy operation.

Most trappers use leg holds around bait, but this is, at best, an imperfect science. At this writing, I have two well-hidden number 3 jump traps next to an old winter-kill deer carcass lying up on the mountain. There are also several snares out 50 feet from the bait along some trails. But, in spite of the fact that dozens of coyotes range through the area, none has been hungry enough to come to the bait. Probably, the birds will have the carcass picked clean before any coyotes come for what seems like a free meal.

Snare and Conibear traps seldom freeze or snow in. Leg-hold traps are continually freezing in spite of use of salts and liquid antifreeze.

Many trappers make their own snares out of 3/32-inch steel aircraft cable. They use small 1-inch-

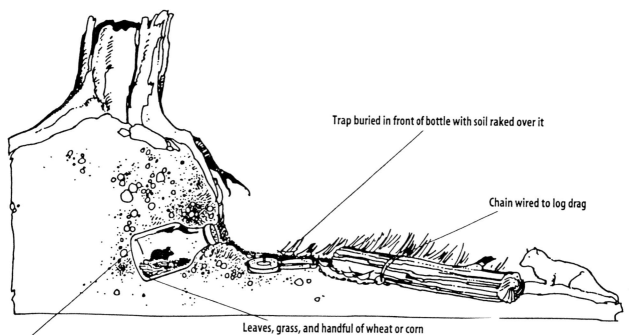

Trap buried in front of bottle with soil raked over it

Chain wired to log drag

Leaves, grass, and handful of wheat or corn

Mouse in bottle buried in a dry area beneath an old stump

Live-mouse trap.

long L-locks to keep the snare from opening again once it is pulled about an animal. Other trappers purchase all of their snares ready-made for about $2 each. Home manufacture costs about $.40 each for all the components.

A snare is hung by a thin support wire from a convenient bush or tree in a game path. If there are no trees, drive in a stake made from a convenient weathered branch. Tie the snare up about 8 inches high at the bottom with a 9-inch loop. Coyotes and bobcats do not mind running their heads into a steel noose. They apparently think they are just pushing through brush. Coyotes will fight the snare till they tighten the lock sufficiently to choke themselves to death. In the process, you will consume a snare per critter. Usually the snare will be too kinked to use a second time.

In the deep, dark recesses of their private thoughts, most experienced trappers will admit that there is no bait or scent that will reliably call all critters into their traps all of the time. Even the very best scents and most natural baits call only hungry animals relatively short distances. Coyotes, bobcats, and foxes are walking past my deer-carcass bait because this year mice are easy to catch. Good trappers get the critters they do because they

develop their powers of observation, allowing them to see where animals have run, dug for food, or gone to a den, and set their traps there.

Friends who trap trade different game sets that they find to be especially good producers. The following is a short list of simple sets that have proved themselves through the years. They are extremely simple and, thus, are excellent for neophytes. They are dependent on your being willing to use either snares, leg holds, or Conibears, as circumstances dictate.

Tear a medium-size hole in a beaver den and place a 330 Conibear in the breach. If they are bank beaver—without house or den—look for the place where they come out to eat on trees and brush. You may get an otter in a den set but probably not in a beaver's feeding area.

Early and late in the season, muskrats cannot hardly resist coming over to look at a piece of apple placed on the trigger of a 110 Conibear set at water's edge. In the middle of the winter, they won't move enough to make any bait work.

Use inexpensive snares in large quantities set in game trails wherever one sees sign of a coyote, fox, or bobcat. Try to chose heavily used trails, but you can make up for quality with quantity.

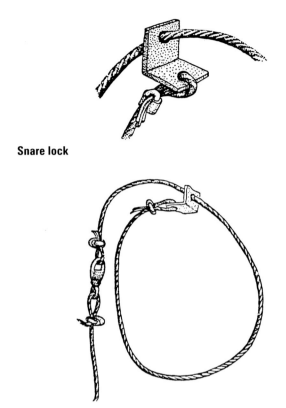

Snare lock

Bear snare with L-lock

Place old 2 x 12 boards 10 feet long or more at an angle against a chicken house, old barn, the back of the garage, or whatever. Any skunk, coon, or possum that comes around will scoot under these boards to stay out of sight. Set either a leg hold or Conibear back about a foot into the tunnel. Farm and domestic animals won't get into these traps even though they are placed relatively out in the open. There is no need for bait.

Dirt-hole sets simulate places where dog-like animals have buried food (e.g., holes in the lawn where a dog hides a bone). Dirt-hole sets mimic these circumstances out in the wild. It is an all-purpose set that will take anything that comes to bait.

Pick places where coyote tracks indicate that they are traveling regularly. Carefully, scentlessly scrape out a small hole about a foot deep. (Extra dirt from the hole is placed on a piece of clean canvas on which the trapper kneels while making the set.) A leg-hold trap is carefully buried in the mound of dirt pulled out of the bury hole. Bait buried down in the dirt hole is usually a small piece of wild rabbit skin or guts, pheasant feathers, or similar material. These sets improve considerably with age.

Coyotes, foxes, skunks, mink, badgers, coons, possums, bobcats, and weasels all can be caught in dirt-hole sets. Trappers dislike catching more common, less valuable critters in dirt-hole sets because the sets are so time consuming to make up properly.

Dirt-hole sets are basic to any land trapper's repertoire, but two improvements help dramatically. Catch a live mouse and place it with a handful of grain and dried grass in a quart mason jar sealed with a perforated lid, allowing the mouse to live and give off a smell.

A second trick is to use a snare rather than a leg-hold trap. Place a simple 3/32-inch-wire snare opened to about 9 inches over the bait hole of a dirt-hole set. Secure the snare to a drag log of about 12 pounds for coyotes. It won't catch mink, skunks, or coons, but coyotes that scratch in the hole after bait will end up with a locked snare on at least one paw. At times, they end up caught by both front feet. Once the loop starts to tighten, the coyote's natural reaction is to pull tighter, cinching the thin wire down even harder. Even very shy, trap-wary coyotes do not seem to mind placing their feet in a snare loop.

I do not have to trap for an income any longer and, given the current state of the economy, most likely could not make ends meet doing so. Probably, the greatest utility for trappers today involves controlling thousands of animals such as coons and skunks that have proliferated across the land in the absence of any other controls. These critters are decimating duck and game birds while frightening citizens with their high incidence of rabies. Trapping also provides edibles in times of need.

Thousand of books have been written on the subject of trapping. Some of the older editions are very entertaining. One never does learn all or even a significant portion of all there is to know about trapping. If you like animals and enjoy nature, you will enjoy the challenge of maintaining a harvest program of the small game animals in the area.

BIBLIOGRAPHY

Benson, Ragnar. *Ragnar's Ten Best Traps*. Boulder, CO: Paladin Press, 1985.

Harding, A.R. S*teel Traps*. Columbus, OH: A.R. Harding Publishing Co., 1935.

Martin, Dale. *Into the Primitive*. Boulder, CO: Paladin Press, 1989.

CHAPTER
Survival Skills
55

For the purposes of this volume, survival is staying alive no matter what the circumstances—even after everybody else has given up and gone to their reward. Survival referenced here is definitely not the yuppie sports activity popular in the 1980s where participants hiked into deep mountains and forests in search of hidden meanings.

Right now, people are being called on to survive in cities, in their urban homes, and on the streets of America. Real survival is so much down-and-dirty, difficult, despicable work that those who have genuinely been exposed seldom participate again voluntarily. Survival is also an extremely complex endeavor. No two people will ever use identical plans, even in very similar circumstances. The only thing that it always similar is the overall philosophy.

You must always remember that survival preparation is a journey, not a destination. Those who are going to survive are constantly making preparations. There is always one more skill to learn

or one more technology to study. Those who have been making survival preparations for years sometimes discourage newcomers, who see an incredible amount of work ahead.

A fellow survivalist, for instance, recently bulldozed in a nice, deep, two-acre pond, completing his requirements for water and some food in a survival context. To me, that action seemed to be the culmination of years of work undertaken to improve his rural retreat. My first inclination was that he now had everything pretty well squared away. But at this writing, this fellow has started in on yet another fairly expensive project to run all of his retreat's considerable refrigeration from solar panels. There is no telling what he will do after figuring that business out.

Apparently, the Nez Perce Indians of northern Idaho and the Pacific Northwest were some of the world's first true survivors—at least in a well-thought-through, philosophical sense. Most of our continent's native people huddled around a meager little campfire in the winter, slowly dying of hunger and exposure,

Domestic ducks are a fine choice for survivalists. They require little care; will eat foliage no other animal will touch; seldom get sick; and provide eggs, fat, meat, feathers, and down. (Photo from *Live Off the Land in the City and Country* by Ragnar Benson.)

which explains why, in part, only an estimated 2 to 3 million Indians were on hand when the Pilgrims landed. Nez Perce Indians were not in the category of those who periodically died of exposure. Famines happened to other tribes, not the Nez Perce. All else being equal, Nez Perce lived longer, allowing them to accumulate more complex skills.

When Lewis and Clark became the first white men to see the Nez Perce in 1804, the two explorers were almost dead of starvation. "We were in real need of a friend," they wrote in their journals, "and the Nez Perce helped us greatly." For six months, the Nez Perce had known that the whites were on their way. Although they had never seen a white man, Nez Perce hunters and soldiers already had firearms. It isn't known exactly what the Indians told Lewis and Clark because no one in their party spoke fluent Nez Perce. But it appears that old Twisted Hair said something to the effect that "you didn't plan very good, white boy."

The Nez Perce tribe avoided starving in winter because they were planners, fully understood basic survival rules of thermodynamics (something the yuppies never got right), and had developed the basic survival rule of threes.

The principle of thermodynamics, an inviolate truth, dictates that you can never expend more energy (calories if you wish) securing food than are earned in the basic hunting and gathering exercise by which these foods are collected. This also extends to gathering wood for heat, water to drink, or whatever. The rule explains why people cannot live on wild berries or nuts in the woods, and why those who engage in sport hunting techniques during the time of survival will quickly find themselves wasted away, their strength dissipated, and probably dead.

The rule of threes is a bit tougher to articulate but no less vital. It emphasizes that in truly desperate survival situations men absolutely require only three things to stay alive: food, water, and shelter. In some circumstances, shelter can include a structure or proper clothing. Usually it involves both. This list is obviously short, but every item is essential. Lack of one leads inevitably to death.

Witch doctors of various cultures often try to throw in a fourth item they call self-actualization. This is taken to mean that if humans do not have a bit of refinement or culture—such as books, songs, dance, and art—they will wither and die. Even in very desperate circumstances, such as the interior of Africa, revolutionary Iran, or Lebanon, survival is always a temporary estate. Reading books might be nice, but when will true survivors have time to read? Self-actualization is probably not absolutely essential. Readers must decide for themselves.

The rule of threes has a second part. Those who wish to survive must plan to have three separate and distinct sources for the food, water, and shelter they must have to live. This is the rule of threes, originating with the Nez Perce Indians.

For example, as a source of food for the winter, the Nez Perce had fresh salmon and steelhead from the rivers; dried fish, which had been preserved against the time when there was none or the runs might fail; and domesticated horses and cattle, which they grazed on the hills. Some other tribes considered eating cattle to be vile and the life of a stockman an abomination. In winter, their stock sought shelter in the lower valleys with the families of Indians. When droughts came, they moved up into the mountains where more rain fell.

Wild foods from the forests and plains comprised yet another, fourth, source of nourishment. Some of these products were handled like gardens. Many Indians absolutely refused to tend gardens. In summer the Nez Perce dug and dried bag after bag full of camas roots. They also snared deer, elk, and wild sheep.

Obviously, if even two sources of food failed, they had others to fall back on. These do not include using the many quail, grouse, ducks, rabbits, and even bear that lived in the region.

The Nez Perce were the only Indians that learned to selectively breed their stock before the Anglos arrived to their lands in force. Some East African tribes keep large herds of cattle, but they are allowed to breed promiscuously and are seldom slaughtered for food. Africans consider cattle a tangible sign of wealth in a bank from which one seldom, if ever, makes a withdrawal. As a result, these cattle cycle up in numbers, destroy their range, and then die wastefully in the drought and from sweeping epidemics.

Although some traditional tribes in North America would not eat some foods under any circumstances, Nez Perce ate whatever it took to stay alive. They were masters at survival planning.

During the winter, it became extremely cold and bitter with really deep snow on some of the high Nez Perce country. They had little semipermanent villages scattered around in good hunting, fishing, and grazing areas, but they were perfectly happy to move into deep, sheltered valleys where they set up skin teepees. Their water came from rainfall, snow, rivers, lakes, and springs.

Modern survivors don't need to copy the Nez Perce, except in concept, because we have a far greater breadth of skills and knowledge. However, their basic philosophy is both valid and vital. Dangers to the Nez Perce were almost entirely natural.

Modern survivalists have gone through the nuclear phase, the yuppie phase, and the economic-crash phase. We now know with absolute certainty that all major survival scenarios in recent history have been caused by despotic governments. Survival situations for all of us will be caused by government. Those who realize this truth can better plan for it.

At this writing, members of the Branch Davidians just stood trial because they attempted to keep their own government from killing them. The signs in the United States are ominous. Homeowners in California lost their homes because the government prohibited firebreaks around their homes when it was asserted that a native rat might be adversely affected.

In retrospect, this government war on its citizens should be no surprise. Stalin had two and perhaps three individual KGB directors who each

Deer can be a main source of meat for survivalists.

oversaw the execution of more of his own citizens than the total number Adolph Hitler killed in Germany. Mao ordered an estimated 25 million fellow Chinese killed. Virtually every one of the 47 sub-Saharan nations has engaged in genocide against its own people. The abeyance in this by the United States to date is only temporary.

The lesson is clear: if our survival is threatened, it is almost certainly going to be from our own government. We can deploy the rule of threes, implemented on the basis of basic physical laws, but we must be aware that our survival plans are never complete.

Food needs can be accommodated by trapping wild game, collecting semiwild edibles (if you recall the law of survival thermodynamics), cultivating a garden (including fruit trees), raising domestic animals, and storing a few basic foods such as dried peas, lentils, and rice. No locally available food item, including dog, cat, rat, muskrat, and even pigeon, can be outside the range of what a survivor will consume.

Gardening is an extremely valuable survival skill. The garden, however, should be disguised by random planting. Straight rows are a sure sign of civilization.

Just a few of the tools that survivalists may find handy when trying to live off the land.

Because most food is available seasonally, you will have to learn to store food items. Domestic and wild animals can be left alive till the time of need. Yet cyclic breeding seasons and migrations can cause periods of want if you are not careful. Gardens in North America are extremely seasonal. All domestic animals are left alive till one runs out of food, explaining why flocks of chickens ran round every pioneer cabin.

Various means of preserving food include drying, canning, freezing, and storing fresh in a root cellar. Many survivors actually plan to use freezers because preparation by this method is very quick and easy. Fish, which can easily be trapped out of local rivers and ponds in great numbers, can be frozen, dried, or canned (in the last instance, can bones and all; bones are a good source of calcium). Under some circumstances, drying can be time consuming and energy intense.

Canning fruits and vegetables in reusable glass jars is relatively quick and easy, but you must stockpile a few supplies as well as learning how to carry out this process. Our grandmothers all knew how to can, but we are not our grandmothers.

Home gardens will easily pay for themselves while the survivor learns. Every locality raises things slightly differently than others. The only way to find out how is to jump in and practice with a working garden. You can only hope that vegetables that do well in your area are those that are good to eat.

True survivors who view their situation as imminently threatening will have to find a somewhat remote place in the country to which they can retreat when necessary. As many of the simple survival criteria as possible should be met at that place of retreat. Perhaps it will be with an uncle or nephew, grandparent or whatever, but history demonstrates that it is much tougher to survive in the city than in the country. You may purchase a few acres in the country on which to place a small house, travel trailer, tent, or a plastic tarp. Or you may have to live in a dugout in the ground, in a barn, in a boat, or in an old bus.

Clothes are part of one's shelter package and should be assembled for utility and durability rather than to satisfy some preconceived notion or fashion.

Shelter requirements also include the need for energy. Energy is used to produce, preserve, and prepare food supplies, as well as for pumping water and keeping warm. The rule of threes applies to energy the same as food, water, or shelter. Survivors can prepare by using a wide range of methods, including storing 55-gallon barrels of diesel, stockpiling wood, installing solar panels, harnessing wind and water power, using steam or diesel-powered generators, and taking advantage of other natural energy supplies. Survivors in Wyoming and Kentucky, for instance, may find small seams of high-grade coal on their property that can be exploited in case of an emergency.

Water could be supplied by any combination of three of the following: a well, spring, creek, pond, lake, or distilled saltwater operation. You could also catch rainwater in barrels or filter swamp water. It is usually not energy efficient to melt ice or snow, but collecting rainwater is an excellent alternate plan for water.

One excellent (and usually free) source of fuel for the shelter is cutting your own fire wood.

Power for the generator can be considered part of the survival shelter requirement.

One requirement for survivalists is a weapon with which to hunt and protect the family and farm. At the bottom is an AR-15 in .223 caliber that belongs to the author's wife. Above it is the author's FN assault rifle in .308 caliber.

You must keep contingencies in mind learned from the experiences of other survivors. Bacterial purity of drinking water falls dramatically in times of crisis, for instance. At this writing, a liter of clean drinking water in Baghdad sells for the same price as a liter of gasoline. Forewarned, the solution is simple. Knowledgeable, prepared survivors keep chemicals and filters available to purify water.

As mentioned, survival is a journey, not a destination. Some people come through these hard times without seeming effort. Survival is difficult, often disgusting, dirty, dawn-to-dusk work. Crisis living will not be similar to presurvival conditions. Survivors quickly learn that a benefit of artificial lights is to allow them to labor on into the night, putting up food.

Requirements for survival are not many. Anyone can think his way through most of them.

Finally, you must keep up hope. Human governments are extremely temporal. They quickly pass from the scene. Survival, contrary to what you may think while doing so, is not forever. Really tough conditions will pass. You must keep your head down and hopes up and not become a target for despots temporarily in control. Remember that those who have planned ahead can emerge to start life anew.

BIBLIOGRAPHY

Benson, Ragnar. *Live Off the Land in the City and Country.* Boulder, CO: Paladin Press, 1982.

_____. *Survival Poaching.* Boulder, CO: Paladin Press, 1980.

CHAPTER

Defending Your Retreat

56

In many regards, defending your retreat is the culmination of most of the skills and techniques covered in this volume. Men of action learn and practice these various skills because they are interesting and exciting and because, as a practical matter, possession of these techniques allows us to lead the free and independent lives we ardently desire. Like the man said, it wasn't always fun, but it was always interesting. Defending your retreat is the serious part of all of this.

When my book *The Survival Retreat* came out in June 1983, one of the paramount problems facing retreaters, as I pointed out, was defining who *exactly* is the enemy. Without a clear understanding of whom we face, we cannot defend ourselves or our property. Our enemies determine how we prepare our defenses. Saddam got it wrong and lost a lot of people. He knew whom to defend against but prepared using methods valid 50 years ago. Branch Davidians also got it wrong and went down in flames.

At the time of *Survival Retreat*, I speculated that we might possibly have to defend against foreign invaders, hungry marauding neighbors, roving leaderless gangs of mutinous soldiers, anarchist citizens, or our own totalitarian government. History has clearly supported the truth that the common citizen's greatest, most pervasive enemy would always be organized government.

George Washington pointed out almost 200 years ago that "government is not reason or logic, it is the exercise of raw force. Government is either a wonderful servant or a fearful master." Recent events have substantiated that the United States is not an exception to history and that good old George knew what he was talking about.

In many regards, finally coming to this conclusion makes the entire process of retreat defense a bit easier. We now know with certainty whom we must defend against. Prospects for those who look realistically are not bright. In Laos, Cambodia, Vietnam, and Afghanistan, extensive government use of gas and chemicals has been

Underground houses like the one on top can be very useful as shelters, but they aren't much fun to live in. The house on the bottom is camouflaged from three sides, gives good earthen protection, and yet allows good light and ventilation. (Photos from *The Survival Retreat* by Ragnar Benson.)

documented. And in those countries, governments killed their own citizens with materials forbidden by international convention. It was another loathsome chemical agent, not poison gas, we are told, that the FBI used in Waco. And we were so naive as to believe that our own government's "police action" against citizens might be different.

Contemporary military strategists suggest that the best way to neutralize enemies is to fix them in place and then destroy them piecemeal. This is, of course, what will happen to those whose retreats are discovered and which subsequently become government targets. Nevertheless, experts who have studied these matters point out that the alternatives are even worse. The Battle of Kursk, fought as a defensive action by the Russians and as an offensive one by the Germans in World War II, was the single turning point that cost the war for the Germans.

In a survival situation, history teaches that you must never become a refugee. Voluntarily abandoning your position to wander is suicidal. At best, refugees are at the beck, call, and whim of petty bureaucrats for absolutely everything from food, water, and health care to reading material. At worst, people who offend the bureaucracy will be hunted down individually and taken out by ruthless governments if they are also refugees.

The rule is to stay at the retreat as long as possible where modest levels of self-defense, food, water, and shelter can be maintained.

A second rule regarding retreat defense is equally simple: it is a serious mistake to let anyone know about the retreat and or the designated area that will be maintained as a refuge. This includes not ever talking about the retreat, its supplies, its plans, or intended defenses, and not inviting strangers into the retreat. World War II admonitions that loose lips sink ships certainly apply to retreats.

Efforts to camouflage and hide the retreat must be clever and thorough. If a retreat is discovered, the government can always bring in more and heavier firepower than private citizens can accumulate. In a pitched battle, retreaters cannot realistically defend against main battle tanks. Assuming that your group took out a tank with well-placed, high-explosive mines, government officials could be expected to bring in additional tanks or use rockets, bombs, or cannon to retaliate.

Advice that you should never become a refugee and that you violate basic military tactics by becoming fixed in place when manning a retreat seems contradictory. It is not. Those who carefully plan their retreats and keep their existence a close secret are not really fixed in place. If they are discovered and surrounded by government authorities, they have, in fact, fixed their enemies in place. Then, if the retreat location is compromised and surrounded (fixed), you can—by clever use of terrain and movement—actually end up fixing the enemy in place. FBI snipers were not, for instance, out killing women and children in other places during Waco.

This is not much help to individual victims whose retreat has been surrounded and who may, like defenders of the Warsaw ghetto, be slowly ground down. But as Aleksandr Solzhenitsyn wrote about his fellow Russians, "If we had individually

Blowing up a bridge leading to your retreat may not stop all foot traffic in your direction, but it certainly will limit the number of vehicles that can reach you.

Being near a good source of fuel is an absolute must if your retreat is in cold country. Without wood or coal for heating and cooking, the danger of freezing is imminent.

used whatever means at our disposal, even if it were pitchforks and scythes, Stalin would never have been able to kill 25 million of us."

Retreaters who pick their terrain carefully have a definite advantage over those who are also fixed in place encircling them. Those who really know the country might be able to slip out unseen to execute some costly (in terms of men, materiel, and psychology) raids on the enemy. Escape and survival are, of course, paramount in any credible retreat-defense scenario. But producing any casualties among the enemy, especially if it is the second or third incident, could be politically and socially devastating to that enemy.

Retreaters who are serious about their business must start looking for the best retreat site they can find as soon as possible. Starting yesterday is probably a bit late. Look for basic survival requirements of food, water, and shelter to be sure that they can be provided by the retreat's location. Defenders must learn the country perfectly so that they can never be absolutely cut off by outside aggressors. Those who know their country and realize the nature of the forces they face can plan escape-and-evasion routes and positions from which

to snipe and observe the enemy. Mines can be set out to protect approaches to the retreat.

It is pure speculation, but think of the consternation the Davidians would have created had they been able to snipe into the backs of their attackers.

Homemade explosives can easily be set that would blow the tread from even a modern Abrams tank. But this is, at best, a temporary solution. It is better to pick locations that preclude the use of heavy equipment.

Those whose retreats are cut off by government forces should expect that very quickly they will be bugged to the extent that every conversation is heard and recorded and most of their internal movements will be recorded on videotape. Waco demonstrated that, in a bunker situation, there is very little that can be done to defend against sophisticated electronic devices available to the government. Defenders may have to whisper in each other's ears or write out lengthy notes.

Government electronics people, for instance, had both Randy Weaver and the Waco church completely wired using powerful hidden microphones within days of the start of the standoff.

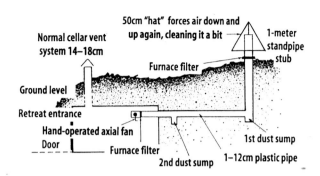

Normal cellar vent system 14–18cm

50cm "hat" forces air down and up again, cleaning it a bit

1-meter standpipe stub

Furnace filter

Ground level

Retreat entrance

Hand-operated axial fan

Door

Furnace filter

1st dust sump

2nd dust sump

1–12cm plastic pipe

Drawing air into a root cellar retreat through a ventilation system creates a positive air pressure that tends to keep dust from seeping in. Natural warm-air ventilation may be sufficient for the retreat if there are few people and filters are not placed in the line.

Agents boasted that nothing said or done within the retreat escaped official scrutiny.

As a result, it is extremely difficult to handle another vital element of retreat defense. You can maintain a better defense if communications to the outside world are maintained. Communications, in this case, might be telephone, private land line, radio, cellular phone, a reader board, or even rockets carrying messages to the media, which is intentionally cut off from the victim. Koresh erred seriously in not having some sort of line open to the outside world.

He did have telephones the first few days before the government appropriated his lines, but they were deployed foolishly and wastefully trying to proselytize outsiders. Had Koresh made some trendy claim that government agents had abused some of his women followers or arrested and beat children, leading to an outbreak of shooting, he might have garnered more sympathetic outside press. Koresh's political harangues to the press did absolutely no good.

Had he simply and calmly stated over and over that there were no illegal guns in the compound and that they were arbitrarily attacked because of their religious beliefs, they would have built additional credibility as well as some sympathy. Later, if Koresh had had some sort of open line to the outside, he could have rebutted charges of plural marriage, child abuse, drug use, and people being held against their will. Authorities floated all those accusations because they knew full well they could not be discredited.

Maintaining outside communications would not have been easy. They might have had to resort to Morse code delivered by light flashes, carrier pigeons (when deployed quickly), or even loudspeakers.

In some regards, retreaters in a big city might have had an easier time of it than rural retreaters. Food and water will be more difficult, but shelter—especially from heavy equipment—might be easier. At a minimum, retreaters could get to their retreat in the city where moving to the country may be next to impossible.

Gradual perimeter reduction is a common tactic of government forces. They will shrink the defense perimeter till they are actually nibbling on the walls of the retreat itself. If explosives are available, heavy armor can be stalled, and easily made antipersonnel mines might make authorities reluctant to risk casualties. Most incident commanders seem to know down deep in their hearts that they are about to engage in what is really a immoral exercise and may refuse to put their own people or the defenders at risk. Currently this seems true in the United States, but this may change.

It has been suggested that had Koresh either appealed personally to fellow Americans or tried to capture and redeploy one of the APCs, things might have turned out differently. This requires a great leap of faith, but speculation is nevertheless interesting.

Solidly built buildings on a narrow neck of land surrounded by deep swamps or high in a rocky crag can be protected more easily and for longer periods. Approaches to them are easily mined. Most people, however, will have to make do with more common retreats such as dug-in root cellars, basement shelters, or high-rise shelters as were used in bombed-out sections of Beirut. These almost indestructible shelters in Beirut got their strength from the fact that several feet of rubble from burned and bombed-out stories above fell into a heap, protecting the lower stories from mortar, rocket, and artillery fire. Streets and alleys were sufficiently cluttered and crowded so that armor and heavy equipment could not usually be brought up.

However, those who hid in these places had to sneak out through the rubble daily to find food and water, all of which had to be purchased. In a strange sense, they did a shift on the battle line and then went home at night, much like workers in a factory.

Retreaters have successfully lived in or under road tunnels, bridges, subway tunnels, public building basements, old grain silos, unused coal bins, potato cellars, and old fuel tanks, as well as many other unlikely places. In such cases, the fact that these were odd retreats and that their occupants kept a low profile made them effective.

Retreaters must know how they intend to get to their destination when the flag goes up. This is important enough for employment of the rule of threes. As discussed in the last chapter, the rule of threes says that if it's critical that one's pants stay up, the wearer should use a belt, suspenders, and shirttail buttons (i.e., have three separate and unrelated sources to achieve any objective or need, be it water, food, or transportation to the shelter).

My first contact with this concept applied to leaving a place of great danger for one of relative safety. This was not really getting to a retreat, but many similar principles apply.

Bill Munchkin was working for the U.S. government in Saigon about the time North Vietnam launched attacks against remaining government forces in 1975. Bill said it didn't take a genius to read the handwriting on the wall. Retreating and surviving for Bill involved successfully getting out of Vietnam. He had, he told me, three separate plans for getting out when things turned to worms.

Bill was an excellent pilot who could, if necessary, fly a requisitioned Lear or 727 out. He was also prepared to bribe a fishing boat captain to take him to Thailand. If both those failed, he planned to drive a truck carrying three 55-gallon barrels of fuel up Highway 9 through Laos into Thailand. As it worked out, when Saigon fell, Munchkin simply took a taxi to the airport and boarded a commercial flight to Hong Kong.

Similar rules apply when doing any international work in dicey, backwater areas. People must know exactly where they are and have three alternate but workable plans to get out if things turn sour.

Knowing when to head to the retreat is sometimes a more pervasive problem than setting up the retreat. Many true accounts tell of retreaters who left for their retreat two years too early, forgoing additional opportunities to strengthen and supply the retreat, or of people who had excellent retreats set up but never made them in time. Great numbers

Each person in the retreat should be trained to do the jobs he or she is well suited for. Some people are not psychologically able to handle a gun.

of Russians during the 1917 revolution fell into this latter trap. Jews in the early 1930s in Germany, Austria, and Poland were similar victims. Minions of the deposed shah of Iran also suffered grievously when the shah left before they did or could.

Retreaters must have some sort of trip wire that signals a quick, immediate withdrawal to the retreat is now in order. Munchkin left when the North Vietnamese were 50 miles north of Saigon. There are no hard-and-fast rules regarding when, exactly, to hole up—especially during these times of arbitrary government rule. Most experts claim that retreaters who are not alert to their political and social surroundings and who allow greed to overpower good sense are most likely *not* to make it to their retreats in a timely manner.

At this point, you have to believe that little more needs to be written regarding specific weapons and explosives needed at a retreat. Each retreater will have to study his own situation thoroughly to know exactly how to deploy in the most efficient, effective fashion. Sufficient supplies must be available at the retreat to do the intended work.

Defending a retreat is psychologically tough. Usually retreats are garrisoned by family members, including women and children. You cannot realistically expect to run quasi-military operations using family members. It just doesn't work to expect to send sons and daughters out on patrol when casualties are likely.

Yet the presence of family members does strengthen retreaters' resolve once blood is spilled. The example of the Warsaw ghetto is an excellent one. Once the Jewish families knew positively that they were all dead anyway, they exacted an extremely high toll from German troops who went in believing they were engaged in a simple mop-up operation. As it worked out, German casualties were huge. The operation took more than five months when the politicians said it would be five days at most.

The lessons to be learned are as follows:

1. In a tough fight at the retreat, the government wins only if defenders give up.
2. It is the government itself that will end up fixed in place and slowly destroyed.
3. Everyone in the retreat must know how to deploy all of the weapons and explosives at their disposal. There can be specialists but no key people. Everyone should have a clear idea how the retreat is to be defended and at what point they are in a full-court press.

In summary, plans to retreat are simplified by the knowledge that our government will be the aggressor, and that it is stupid to look at history and believe it could not happen here. You must carefully and meticulously plan the retreat far in advance with a sharp eye toward mitigating the advantage of heavy weapons a government will likely deploy. Rural retreats have the advantage of self-generating food, water, and energy. City retreats are practical and possible under the assumption that the best place to hide a tree is in the forest.

You must realize that government forces will always assume that a retreat is fortified and that they will attempt to isolate retreaters as much as is possible. You can turn this "fixing in place" on its ear by maintaining some communication with the outside world and by creating unacceptable casualties among the forces of evil. This is, of course, extremely difficult because enemy forces will deploy sophisticated electronic devices, as well as a great many psychological ones, in an attempt to confound retreaters.

If it comes to a fight, retreaters must realize that they are already dead if their retreat has been discovered and made a target. Perhaps if they resist with great vigor they may escape alive. History teaches that virtually no one has ever come to a retreater's rescue.

But as Winston Churchill said in one of his better speeches, "Never give up. No, I say, never give up."

BIBLIOGRAPHY

Benson, Ragnar. *The Survival Retreat*. Boulder, CO: Paladin Press, 1993.

CHAPTER

Eating Cheap

57

ourteen years after he married, Ronald Metzger finally spent $50 on meat for his family. That is $50 total, not $50 a year or—as is often the case—$50 per week. Metzger is not a vegetarian. His family consumes meat at virtually every meal. He is a basic farmer with an eighth-grade education who lives the simple, old-fashioned life of a food scrounger. Therefore, he spends very little for daily needs, but other than claiming "I don't spend much," he doesn't know what his monthly or yearly food bills total. Some estimate not more than $15 per week.

Metzger's peculiar religion precludes him from turning up his nose at anything prepared in a sanitary manner or at consuming any special foods, as he calls them. In our eyes this would mean consuming much of a variety. What the Metzger family eats is good, but it's also very boring. On the plus side, they don't eat as much as some other people because it's the same thing day after day.

In addition to how to save money, this chapter and this entire book are about self-reliance. Those who can make an exciting life for themselves without relying on indulgences from the government have a tremendous advantage over the rest of the world. Securing inexpensive, nutritious food is a major daily consideration for everyone, whether they acknowledge it or not.

Those who scrounge their food for little or nothing have an immediate advantage. They can afford to wait for good opportunities while staying out of a system that could destroy them. Being willing to pay cash for food demands earning enough to pay the government almost 50 percent in taxes. Workers are then subjected to additional senseless and onerous regulations by those who have taken their money in the form of taxes. People like Metzger are better off staying out of the system in many ways not immediately obvious to those who haven't taken the time to think about it. Metzger doesn't deal with the EPA, NEA, IRS, BATF, SSA, FHA, or the local planning and zoning commission.

Eating cheap is a philosophical commitment.

Numbers of similar-minded people, reckoned on the basis of heads per square mile, inhabit India and China. Both peoples have similar ruinous to brutally fascist governments holding them down. But whereas famine and pestilence are still endemic in India, the Chinese people have managed to find a way to feed themselves reasonably well.

As in the example of farmer Metzger above, we personally might grow weary of Chinese fare day after day, and perhaps an average Chinese diet would not contain sufficient calories with which to maintain a vigorous work schedule. But, more important—all things being fairly equal, which they pretty much are—Chinese eat relatively well while Indians continue to experience periodic famine and plagues reminiscent of diebacks among overpopulated species further down the food chain, such as lemmings.

Those who contrast these two cultures quickly discover why Indians starve and Chinese thrive. Chinese will eat virtually anything as long as it is prepared in a clean, neat fashion. At the same time, Indians have hundreds if not thousands of petty religious taboos that relegate them to the status of starving beggars. Chinese (more specifically, Cantonese) eat bird nests, shark fins, frog skins, duck feet, insects, weed seeds, and sea slugs—all the while convincing themselves that these items are culinary delicacies.

Half the Indians don't eat pork or many shellfish or reptiles, the other half won't eat beef, and a great percentage won't eat meat in any form. Most of India lies within a temperate zone, allowing production of two or more crops per year on the same piece of ground. But an estimated one-fifth of the grain produced in India each year is gobbled up by hungry rats. Chinese people, in stark contrast, busy themselves hunting down rats to cook for dinner. Rice rat is a great delicacy in China.

Shrimp abound off the coast of Somalia, but the people there will neither fish for nor eat them because they believe shrimp are really locusts that have blown out to sea, and these Muslims won't eat insects. The point to all of this is that successful, cheap eaters must set aside a great deal of cultural baggage.

All of us have heard rumors about the sudden disappearance of feral cats and dogs in some U.S. communities after a family of Vietnamese or other Asians has moved in. Perhaps some of these tales are true, but even if they are not, it is heartening to hear that a commodity previously wasted might have been put to productive use.

This is not to say that cheap eaters must go around eating moldering road kill or promiscuously digging through Dumpsters. One must remember that a principal reason for eating is to stay healthy. Recreational eating should, in the eyes of a cheap eater, be relegated to a distant second place. "We should eat to live," goes the old saw, "and not live to eat."

Our old friend, Ron Metzger, does scrounge up roadkill deer, which has eventually come to comprise a significant part of the family's meat. But he doesn't take anything that is bad. When he hears about the deer too late, or investigation indicates that nothing is salvageable, he does not eat it just because it was free.

One time a farmer gave Metzger 120 live 3-year-old stewing hens. They were so tough they had to be cooked six hours before they could be eaten. Metzger and his family jumped at this opportunity, butchering and freezing all of the hens in two days.

Nobody else wanted the old hens, but again food desirability is completely in the eye of the beholder. Some young African bush warriors, complete with hair plastered in place with cow shit, threw up on the ground when I ate a fresh fried egg in front of them. "But bwana," they pleaded, "do you know where that egg came from?"

A great deal of edible, nutritious food ends up in Dumpsters because of foolish, overstrict sensitivities or rules on sanitation. A friend discovered dozens of unopened but crinkled boxes of corn flakes thrown in the Dumpster by supermarket personnel after a fork lift had accidentally brushed a pallet loaded with the stuff.

Supermarkets and restaurants throw out literally tons of clean, edible fruits, vegetables, and meats, often for the flimsiest of reasons. Employees would use it, but store policy generally prohibits them from taking it home. Supermarket managers claim they can't place damaged packages on sale because of liability laws, selling it to employees would encourage additional damage and might also lead to shoplifting. But scrounging through supermarket Dumpsters on a regular schedule is only one of many

Harvest season is short for most grains, and much usable food is left in the fields. Farmers will often let foragers in after the harvest is done.

Wild prickly pear cactus leaves are nutritious and mostly free for the taking. (Photos by Ragnar Benson.)

ways in which regular citizens such as Metzger feed their entire families on a couple of dollars per week.

So how do died-in-the-wool, effective, cheap eaters do it? It is a philosophical commitment that makes them alert to all opportunities around them and the initiative to seize these opportunities when they appear. Also, cheap eaters tend to go down the food chain a bit further. They purchase or scrounge closer to the producer and packer. They never allow foolish pride to spoil their scam.

In Metzger's case, he was at it so long that friends, neighbors, and even some government authorities habitually called him whenever there was an opportunity. Being a farm laborer, he could drop everything to respond immediately if a deer was hit on the road. He also had a regular route he traveled looking for any opportunities. One of these was checking behind local grain elevators to see if there were any piles of spilled peas, beans, wheat, or corn he could sweep up. He quickly discovered which days food was likely to be thrown into Dumpsters behind supermarkets and restaurants.

Metzger also looked for wild edibles. He knew that during the pioneer days of this land that his great grandfather and other forebears lived almost entirely from the wild products of the land. Those who study the issue closely realize that we still live off the land. But the process is more hidden, mechanical, automatic, and cultured. For cheap eaters, this requires going out into the forests to scrounge wild edibles that no one else thinks about. Some, like our Vietnamese friends,

consider these to be the many cats and dogs running wild.

Whether deer, squirrels, rabbits, coons, possums, or even common rats, these animals cannot be collected by using sports hunting techniques. Trapping is the only time-efficient method for them.

Everyone is the United States lives near at least one of two truly outstanding sources of wild vegetables: cattails or acorns. Just one-half acre of wild cattails, for instance, will feed a large family wonderfully. In the spring, young root sprouts can be collected and boiled much like asparagus. During the summer, pollen can be collected and used much like wheat flour. Green cattail flowers can be collected and boiled, similarly to sweet corn. In the dark of winter, cattail roots can be gathered and eaten whole or made into a kind of flour.

Acorns from mighty oaks are another extremely common edible. These must be gathered immediately after they drop in the fall, the hulls broken off, and the meat separated. Crush the meats and then soak them in fresh water. Acorns contain varying amounts of toxic but extremely soluble tannic acid that must be removed before they can be eaten safely. Cakes baked from crushed or ground, thoroughly washed acorn meats are tasty and nutritious.

Cheap eaters soon learn to deal with both farmers who raise food and processors who add shelf life to unprocessed agricultural products. There is a different angle to talking to each one successfully. Easiest are processors who think in terms of wholesale sales but also throw away tens of thousands of pounds of products during their average production cycles. Depending on the packer, raw agricultural products are dumped because the material is slightly off grade, size, or even color, not because they have lost their nutritional value.

Learn what foods are raised and processed in your area and what time of year are they are harvested. The harvest season for most edibles is very short.

During the short time the harvest is underway, incredible bulk buys can be made both of waste products, processed products, and perfectly good raw products straight from the farm.

Techniques vary, but generally effective food scroungers have good success showing up at packing plants during harvest, asking a fork-lift driver or other available employee if they can purchase cull product. Friendliness and nice, clean but modest dress convey the proper impression at this point. There will be tons of reasonable-quality products that they are paying someone to haul away. The trick is to talk the employees or manager into allowing you to high-grade out a couple of tubs of edibles. For many reasons, management cannot allow people to run around the plant scrounging cucumbers, carrots, asparagus, or whatever. If possible, check with a trucker hauling the stuff to a feedlot, or if one of the employees says, "Yes, it's over there," thank him profusely and get in and out very quickly. Don't be a pest. Dress, act, and talk like one of the people at the packing shed. Those who look like counterculture types who make their living begging won't get far. Those who look clean and neat but down on their luck are often given the keys to the city.

Farmers are somewhat similar in outlook. They see hundreds of tons of their products wasted in the fields every year. This sort of waste troubles them greatly, but they are extremely reluctant to allow scroungers in to glean these perfectly good products. Contrary to popular opinion, farmers are generally fearful of nonfarm visitors. They fear that visitors might trample or steal the crops, hurt themselves, corrupt their children, disapprove of their politically incorrect life-style, bring other uninvited friends, or be a pest during an especially hectic harvest season when everything must go like clockwork. Farmers use fertilizers and pesticides that they believe city people will never understand.

At one time, I intervened with a very charitable farmer who owned an apple orchard. High winds had knocked large numbers of apples on the ground, which could not be salvaged and sold. At first, this farmer refused to allow a genuinely dirt-poor family to pick up the apples.

"They would probably just steal the good ones and complain about the weed killers I spray to keep the place clear," he said.

Later, after meeting the young couple, he let them get all the apples they needed.

Successful scrounging requires careful observation of crops locally grown by farmers. Determine which month the crops will be harvested. Knowing which crops will be harvested is important because food scroungers must preserve the stuff themselves. In the case of fresh corn, peaches, potatoes, apples, green beans, fresh peas, and others produce, there is a great deal of work to be done to freeze or can them. We refer to raw products here, not TV dinners.

Decide if and how you can home process these edibles, as well as the harvest time. Well before harvest, approach a local farmer or two about allowing you to glean in their fields. Dress like they do, but don't make it an affectation. Mention that funds are short—not that you are poor. Farmers are often very poor themselves, forced by the economics of their business to finance new, reliable trucks, tractors, and combines, thereby draining their available cash but making them appear rich. Leave your "Save the Whales" bumper stickers at home and, especially in the Midwest, do not use profanity when speaking with farmers. Always offer to pay a bit for the privilege of gleaning the surplus harvest or of collecting small potatoes or whatever. Farmers will seldom take the few dollars offered, but they like to be asked.

Approximately 12 percent by weight of potatoes fall through the sorting sieve back onto the ground because they are too small. Tomatoes are harvested two or three times. Any remaining are left to rot. Fresh green peas and beans are destruct-harvested (i.e, any that survive the process are left for the birds). Huge quantities of edibles can be gleaned if you can find a cooperating farmer.

Today, there are not nearly as many livestock producers as there were as recently as 20 years ago. Many folks with farm backgrounds recall purchasing older, worn-out laying hens, runt pigs, or bum lambs. These situations still occur, but there are fewer livestock producers who have sizable numbers of such animals, and, because of automation, they have less time to deal with them. Livestock producers do have tremendous numbers of runty, poor, crippled critters around that they are often pleased to see someone else have. Often, these animals are summarily sent to livestock auctions where they go for a pittance. A 90-pound runt pig, for instance, might bring $5 on a night when a regular pig brings $110.

You must identify livestock farmers in the area and then stop by to chat a bit about the weather, low crop prices, and the grandkids. After a bit, inquire if some aged layers or runty pigs or calves might be available. Start with modest questions, always offering to pay. Most cheap eaters report that after they build a relationship, so much good, edible livestock comes their way they can scarcely keep up with the butchering.

Livestock is a lot like field crops. Producers won't always have everything around. One farmer may have six runts in July but nothing for the balance of the year. Other than learning how to butcher and provide human energy, all of this stuff is virtually free.

A notorious cheap eater who helped with this chapter reports that just this spring a pond owner gave him 52 live ducks that he wanted removed, absolutely free. Another guy last year had a dozen live rabbits and yet another gave up five grown goats for $5. And these instances weren't even from livestock producers disposing of culls.

In the process of implementing a cheap-eating program, don't overlook the basic role of eating more of simple, cheap foods. In this regard, dried peas, beans, and lentils purchased in bulk in a local store, if they cannot be gleaned, are an excellent plan. Two pounds per day at a cost of about $.25 per pound retail easily sustains a life at modest labor. By augmenting it with only modest amounts of greens and scrounged meat, you have an excellent but bland diet.

Dried peas, beans, and lentils have the added advantages of having a long shelf life and being light and portable. During the westward expansion of country, pony soldiers carried them as basic rations. Ronald Metzger, our earlier example of a consummate food scrounger, secures permission during harvests to rake up quantities of peas and lentils accidentally spilled in the field. After cleaning and sorting them, he has great quantities of excellent food. Half a day's work often yields enough cheap edibles for his family for a year.

Besides securing wild fish, game, and vegetables/nuts (such as cattails and acorns), gleaning farmers' fields, purchasing unwanted livestock, buying or scrounging from packers, and collecting food thrown out by others, most successful cheap eaters also cultivate a garden. Even a relatively tiny plot of ground will return hundreds of dollars worth of edibles.

Gardening is not particularly easy, but virtually everyone anyplace in the United States can produce something to eat from the soil if they take time to learn local techniques and conditions, weather patterns, and fruits and vegetables that do well in their locale.

By raising products not scroungeable from local farmers and packers, cheap eaters diversify their menus. Until fairly recent times, virtually every family had a garden. Space and sunshine requirements can be minimal. Some folks raise just tomatoes and lettuce in window boxes. Others surreptitiously plant beans amongst the shrubbery in front of their homes or in the berm around the parkway.

It is difficult to overemphasize the role of even a simple little garden in creating more self-reliance. Soldiers in Thailand, Korea, Kenya, Burma, the Philippines, and Turkey, to name a just a few places, all plant gardens. Then, if their rations or wages do not arrive on a timely basis, they don't have to resort to begging or selling their weapons to maintain life.

Eating cheap requires hard work, great resourcefulness, and extensive planning. Those who have previously suffered privations are more likely to be effective scroungers in the present. Some people, like the Metzgers, find beating the system using these methods to be enjoyable recreation as an end in itself.

BIBLIOGRAPHY

Benson, Ragnar. *Eating Cheap*. Boulder, CO: Paladin Press, 1982.

CHAPTER

Homemade Booze

58

Strange things happen while sitting in an old, beat-up red pickup truck waiting for the hounds to push a wild boar over Wildcat Gap. Especially if your talkative companion is a full-fledged, honest-to-God, redneck, son-of-a-gun, "Dixie"-whistling, Southern moonshiner.

"Haven't touched a drop in over 20 years," old Dick, the self-acclaimed but now-reformed 'shiner told me. But, if I was going to have one, it would definitely be some home brew and not the junk they sell in the store.

"We don't make 'shine no more," Dick continued, "cause makin' 'shine is a powerful bunch of work, they sell it in every store, and they quit makin' half-gallon glass mason jars. Can't hardly find anythin' to put it in," he intoned with all seriousness.

I bit my tongue rather than ask what kind of a party one could go to requiring more than two full quarts of 190-proof booze. Instead, I listened intently as a very sincere, very bright, dedicated man representing a dying culture unraveled his fascinating tale.

Good, clean, high-grade booze is not technically difficult to make in the United States. Right now, not much is produced. But you can expect that as taxes on legal booze continue their upward spiral, it will again be profitable to whomp up the occasional batch of moonshine.

Under the old regime, according to Dick, it was really lots of physical work to produce a batch of hooch. Stills had to be located a minimum of 2 1/2 miles from any road. Cord after cord of wood had to be cut. "We packed sugar and corn in bags into the still and finished booze in half-gallon jars out," he said.

"I remember carrying six 10-pound bags of sugar at a time up over those steep hills. The wood had to be dry so it didn't smoke, and all of that was lots of work, it was!"

Stills are often located in idyllic, remote settings like this.

Having just run over the hills after old Luke and Reb, our eager hounds, I could appreciate the gravity of Dick's comment about all that work. This didn't even count the labor required to raise field corn needed to provide a malt base for the booze. Following the old mule around the field is, in and of itself, back-breaking work. Modern hooch makers do not necessarily have to raise their own corn, but they must secure a supply of starch from some source.

It is possible to use potatoes, but a spud's starch content is relatively low; they don't grow well in the hills of Tennessee, Kentucky, and North Carolina; and—most important—my moonshine-makin' friend only knew the recipe for corn whiskey.

Four-times-refined corn whiskey, made with sparkling, clean equipment and pure spring water throughout the process is not too bad, provided it is cut back to less explosive 90 proof (45 percent) before consumption. The trick here, besides fanatical cleanliness, is to use as much stainless steel, plastic, and copper equipment as possible. Stay far away from aluminum pots and ladles, lead-soldered copper-pipe connections, and any water containing chlorine.

Depending a great deal on how much product you wish to produce and how quickly, a still plus ancillary products will cost about $250. Cost of ingredients is almost nil. The still itself can be used many times over, spreading costs dramatically. Yet the longer it takes to whomp up a batch and the more one produces, the greater the risk. For this reason, moonshiners often use larger equipment than one would initially seem necessary.

Two separate, fairly distinct components characterize the booze-making process. There are mixing and fermenting the mash and distilling the alcohol.

Start the mash process by securing a very clean, well-lit room with either a scrubbed-down cement or wooden floor. A few makers use plastic, but most hillbillies think wood is best. Assuming a 260-gallon total mash load, take 3 bushels (180 pounds) of corn, wash it down thoroughly in pure spring water, and spread it out one kernel deep on the well-cleaned floor. Dried corn should be weighed *before* it is washed.

Allow the grain to lie in the warm room completely protected from mice and vermin for about 10 days until most of the kernels have swelled and sprouted. The place will smell like a brewery. Ambient temperature must be maintained at about 80°F during the sprouting process. Grain sprouting can generally be done any time, except during the winter, provided there is a source of auxiliary heat to keep temperatures reasonably constant. Dry climates require that you spray a fine mist of water on the grain, keeping it damp.

Sprouting can be done on a spare bedroom floor, garage, shop, or barn floor, or even in the attic. Some people use newfangled plastic tarps to cover the floor, but most old 'shine makers like plain old wood or concrete.

Suspicious ridge runners claimed that one had to drive to Nashville, Knoxville, or Louisville to purchase sugar. "Don't want to make those federal guys nervous," Dick said. But this would be a long drive for some of us. Any large grocery store that sells bigger sacks of sugar would be acceptable. Perhaps in 'shine country, store owners keep track of sugar sales, but it is doubtful if they do elsewhere. Since you will transport your sugar mostly by vehicle and your sis won't need the material for a dress, you can use either paper or cloth sugar bags. Again, assuming a 260-gallon batch of mash, purchase about 150 pounds of granulated sugar.

Also purchase ten 26-gallon plastic garbage pails with tight lids. Whiskey mash must ferment in airtight containers, but this is relative. Pressure from the CO_2 gas generated by the mash will blow oxygen away that if present would kill the yeast.

Resorting to anything fancier than press-on lids is not necessary, provided these are fairly secure.

Ten 26-gallon garbage pails will produce about 25 gallons of refined, uncut booze if all 160 pounds of sprouted corn and 150 pounds of granulated sugar are used.

Hooch makers will also require a small, wooden boat paddle with which to stir the mash. Everything in the mash so far is just feed. The active ingredient is 10 pints of Fleischmann's dry yeast, needed to provide the little growies to start turning sugar and corn into booze. One must also purchase enough Calgon water softener (sodium carbonate) to throw three-quarters of a cup in each mash barrel. Calgon is a type of water conditioner that allows the yeast to be more efficient.

Fill each container about one-third full of pure water, throw in 18 pounds of sprouted corn (assuming you will make mash in ten 26-gallon garbage pails), 15 pounds of sugar, 1 pint of dry yeast, and 2/3 cup of Calgon. Stir up the mixture briefly. It should start to foam. As soon as it settles down again, finish filling with water.

Before setting the mash back to ferment, you must add enough water to bring the contents of each barrel up to the top. Use good, clear spring water again, but be cautious. Spring water tends to flow at about 58°F. Water this cold will cripple or even kill the yeast fungi. Experienced 'shine makers either let the water warm in large tubs or slowly draw it through a long hose set out in the warm sun. Snap the lid on each bucket and then sit back for 10 days and wait for the yeast to do its work.

Fermentation works best in temperatures ranging from 84 to 86°F and should never fall below 70°F. For this reason, most hooch is made in warmer climates. Experienced 'shine makers sometimes use a carefully monitored hot water or electric heating coil to heat the mash. Internal bubbling will slow, thus requiring more than 10 days to cure if the mash cools to 70°F. Experienced 'shine makers know their temperatures intuitively. Amateurs should use long-stem glass thermometers slipped through a small hole bored in the lid for the purpose of monitoring mash fermentation.

Do not disturb after the lids are in place. Usually, leaks around the lid allow CO2 to escape, but if pressures build against the lids, drill a very small relief hole.

Mash working to plan will soon smell pretty ripe. Secretions from the yeast that are growing and multiplying are the alcohol we are anticipating. Unless temperature swings during fermentation slow the process, it will take about 10 to 14 days for the alcohol generated to kill the yeasts. When the bubbling stops, the mix is ready to distill out the alcohol.

At this point, you must put together some equipment that is a bit spendy. Purchase four stainless-steel, 5-gallon pressure cookers, and two large electric hot plates. Pressure cookers of this size are tough to find in stainless, but a few specialty stores can order them. Aluminum pressure cookers can be used, but most moonshiners claim they leave a slight taste in the booze.

Also purchase three additional long-glass, lab-grade thermometers. These read temperatures in centigrade as opposed to Fahrenheit. All following temperatures are in centigrade.

Have a good machine shop cut the bottoms out of two of the pressure cookers and the tops off of the other two. Heli-arc the two pieces together, creating two 10-gallon pressure cookers. This part of the project is expensive, but if not undertaken, the process of distilling the booze from the mash will take so long you will either lose interest or get caught in midproject. All of this is a very smelly business. It was not for nothing that Southern crackers made their hooch on windy ridge tops. If done in town, you will end up either sharing with the neighbors or in the slammer.

Remove both safety valves and pressure gauges from the pressure-cooker lids. If there is no large rubber O-ring in the pressure gauge hole, purchase one of the correct size. It must hold the thermometer in the lid securely without leaking. Stick the thermometer down through the hole into the lid far enough so it won't touch the counter when the lid is removed.

Into the former pressure relief hole, thread a copper fitting that will accept 3/8-inch flexible copper tubing. Run this tube up about 4 inches and then down in shallow coils for about 8 feet. These spiral coils must be run through a water jacket, bucket, stock tank, or the spring itself. Cooling these coils takes large quantities of water. Adjust the flow so that cold water coming in from the bottom pushes hot water out the top of the cooling tank.

Rig up a small rack that holds the closed jugs, bottles, and pails set to catch the distilled booze as it comes off the distillate tube.

Do not disturb the settled mash barrels. Carefully fill the pressure cookers with mash ladled off the top four-fifths of the plastic mash barrels. Secure the distillate tube and thermometer in place and fasten on the pressure lid. Place the cooker on an electric heat pad. Instead of cutting firewood, you will cook the mash the steady, easy way with electric heat.

Watch the top thermometer. Never allow the temperature of the cooker to go above 96°C. Monitor the cooling coil very closely. If it starts to sputter or blow, turn the heat down. It takes some practice, but 'shine makers often run two pressure cookers at once, doubling their output. You want to get rid of the mash as quickly as possible.

The flow of alcohol out of the cooling coil will slow and stop about the time the cooker temperature starts to zoom upward. This is a sign that the alcohol is all boiled off. Carefully set the cooker aside and allow it to cool. Premature opening before pressures have equalized can result in a horrible mess. Keep cooling and refilling till the mash is all reduced to first-run alcohol, amounting to about 50 gallons of very raw hooch.

"It's good hog and b'ar bait," my friend said. Dump the cooked mash and the dregs from the bottom of the barrel someplace where it will either be consumed by cattle, hogs, or bears, or in some out-of-the-way forest location where errant breezes will carry off telltale odors.

Good booze must be refined three additional times to purify it. The first run takes longer and, in some regards, is a bit more difficult to handle. Thorough cleaning between batches is time consuming. Runs two through four go relatively quickly. But, one must be continually alert so as not to burn or overcook the alcohol.

Maximum temperature the second time is 94°C, as read on the cooker's thermometer. Rises in temperature will occur very quickly as the alcohol is boiled out, leaving a bit of scum, water, contaminants, and miscellaneous gunk. Again dump the residue in the safest manner possible and clean the coolers thoroughly.

Dump the second-run distillate into the cookers and run it through a third time. Third-run temperature should not exceed 84°C. Again, monitor it very closely.

The final fourth-run booze is much like fine vodka. It is absolutely sparkling clean and has no taste or smell. The maximum temperature for the fourth run is 82°C. This is pure 190-proof, uncut booze. You should have about 25 gallons of the stuff. Two-hundred-proof booze is not possible outside a laboratory, but this 95-percent stuff is still far too potent for practical use. "Anyone who consumes much more than a single mouthful will become too relaxed for service," my friend says.

Use either distilled water purchased from a druggist or grocery or especially tasty spring water to cut the finished product back to about 90-proof.

Depending on how you cooked the mash, 260 gallons should now equal about 23 to 25 gallons of uncut booze or about 115 fifths of 190-proof moonshine. When they are diluted with water, you should have at least *50 gallons* of good booze. This should be enough for private use for a long, long time. Perhaps my old 'shine artist buddy had a point about the half-gallon Mason jars.

Obviously, no one is going to use this much booze very quickly. Storing it presents few problems, provided you use clean glass jars that are airtight. Even 90-proof booze has a strong affinity for smoke, moisture, odors, and dust that will contaminate it. Many 'shine artists store their booze as 190 proof, cutting it shortly before putting it into service.

Our hounds never did scare up a hog or a bear in Wildcat Gulch. We all did, however, have a crackin' good time talking with and about a vanishing breed of individualist whose great knowledge may irretrievably pass into history.

Perhaps, having read this short analysis, a man of action or two will feel a moral obligation to keep the tradition alive. Obviously, we cannot allow this great body of information to pass. Who will tell our grandchildren about moonshine?

But as old Dick the moonshiner said, "Always cut dry wood, so's the smoke from the cooker doesn't give you away. And don't get greedy and sell very much of the booze, especially to damn Yankee strangers. Remember, there is Yankees and there is damn Yankees."

The cost of homemade booze is about $8 a gallon for the first batch, amortizing all the equipment on that one first batch. After that, all you have to pay for is the ingredients, and that brings the price down to about $4 per gallon. If the government keeps raising taxes on booze, look for small batch operators to again proliferate.

BIBLIOGRAPHY

"Dick the Ridge Runner," interview by author, Robbinsville, NC, November, 1993.

Krohn, James C. *The Good Booze Recipe and Cookbook*. Boulder, CO: Paladin Press, 1988.

CHAPTER

Survival Poaching

59

North American Indians developed and perfected almost all survival game-gathering techniques that are now referred to as poaching. Native Americans intuitively knew that sports hunting techniques, as advocated by white men, generally consumed more calories than were earned back in meat.

However, Native Americans tended to look in horror on those who killed strictly for sport. There was no practical sense to this, they said. There was also no harm, claimed Native Americans who knew about the renewability of wildlife. But they could also never predict the extent to which technologically superior whitemen would fill the land.

Native Americans, with their year-round gathering techniques—including digging young from their dens, destroying nesting birds, and trapping pregnant females so they could eat their fetuses—were no more noble conservationists than early white hunters. However these considerations are purely speculative as it is firmly established that a survivalist is not a sports hunter, and even very good sports hunters cannot survive. Survivors must use ancient Native American methods that are now illegal.

Even dedicated sports hunters find the subject of survival poaching interesting. Until people are in desperate circumstances, they must generally adopt management concepts recommended by sports hunters, or they will end up with little or no wild game on which to base their outdoor activities. These interesting Native American game-gathering techniques would have depleted the game and ultimately led to the Native Americans' demise if there had not been so very few of them or if they had had general access to modern technology. After the introduction, for instance, of steel snare wire and steel traps, white fur traders often had problems convincing Indian trappers to make their catches when the skins were prime and the animals likely mature rather than trapping year round.

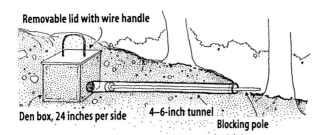

Removable lid with wire handle

Den box, 24 inches per side   4–6-inch tunnel

Blocking pole

Den trap like those used by Native Americans. (Unless otherwise noted, illustrations taken from *Survival Poaching* by Ragnar Benson.)

In a survival context, the first place you should look for food is in the local lakes, streams, rivers, and ponds. Old Mother Nature is more generous with wild edibles produced in water. Additionally, many of these water critters are customarily overlooked by people who can't see them. Some of these include carp, bullheads, turtles, suckers, snakes, crayfish, and—of course—frogs.

Many bodies of water are filled with millions of tiny stunted fish that can be the basis of good meals if one can only get them efficiently in large enough quantities. Obviously, hook-and-line sports methods won't work for 2-inch bluegills. An intermediate method called a trotline might work. This is a well-known technique in the southern United States that is virtually unknown in the eastern, northern, and western regions.

Trotlines are single, heavy, long lines on which a great number of 18-inch leader lines with hooks and sinkers are attached. These are stretched across rivers and ponds and baited with rugged, long-lasting bait, such as chunks of pork liver or fresh fish. Hooks are generally smaller than commonly used and the rigs are left unattended for days at a time.

Fish traps are used to collect large numbers of fish almost everywhere in the world. Giant ocean models differ little from creek and pond traps other than in size and entrance mechanisms. Basically, fish traps are 16-inch circular devices made from heavy chicken wire: the wire size determines the size of fish that can be held. You can even use 1/4-inch welded wire to catch minnows and small crayfish.

A wire end is fastened in one place and a long, narrow cone in the other. Bait can be anything thrown in the trap, but, generally, experienced users prefer a can of dog food punched through several times. Fish swim into the funnel to the back of the trap, but cannot find their way back through the little hole to the outside once they are inside.

Stream and lake harvesters also use small generators to produce an electrical shock, agricultural chemicals containing 200 percent or more rotenone, and explosives to bring fish to the surface in quantity. Probably, fish traps are best because you can sort for size both when constructing and checking the trap. By so doing, only those fish really needed are taken. Other mass methods of capture require cleaning and processing large quantities of fish at any given time. Once fish are in a trap, they stay in good shape till the owner needs a meal.

After aquatic critters, birds are probably the next-best source of food. They have the advantage of flying off to the neighbors for food and water. These birds range anywhere from wild turkeys to sparrows, all of which can liven up a pot. Little birds like sparrows must be trapped, but, at times, turkeys, pheasants, and duck-sized birds can be profitably shot if you know where they are and you are reasonably certain of ground-sluicing several with one shot.

All birds from ducks to meadowlarks can be taken by baiting a small fish hook with a grain of corn or wheat. Use light monofilament fishline. If the birds are feeding in the area, they will pick up the grain, hooking themselves in the crop. This is an effective method if you can locate feeding areas. Just to go out in a wooded area or pasture field and throw out a line is never productive.

Birds always look up when caught. They won't duck down under a barrier to escape. Most birds such as ducks and pheasants won't even pull their heads back down through an open hole once they have stuck it up through.

Native American bird gatherers constructed small, square, pen-like structures made of split logs and branches. These blocky little traps had enough cracks and openings so that the birds could see light above, but could not slip through the walls or ceiling to freedom. To use this, dig four 5-inch-deep trenches in the soil, running from outside in, under the trap.

Game birds used to scratching around on the ground for corn or wheat will follow bait placed in the trenches up into the trap. Throw some grass and leaves in the trap to partly obscure it. Once in the trap, birds try to escape upwards. Looking back in the trench doesn't occur to them.

These bird traps can be made out of virtually any scrap lumber or wire. Wire is ideal because the birds will poke their heads through it and not withdraw. Usually, the system works best if the area is baited prior to setting the traps, establishing a feeding area.

Pigeons and sparrows can be blinded with a light on their roost or caught in V-top wire flight traps during the day. Bait the trap with a pan of finely ground flour, catching the first few, which then become bait for others.

The V-opening into the trap should be just wide enough for the bird in flight to drop through into the trap, but not wide enough to allow escape with the its wings extended. These are costly and obvious traps, but they do corral lots of edibles, if placed in areas where clouds of sparrows, blackbirds, and pigeons are accustomed to feeding.

A piece of 1- to 2-inch mesh chicken wire can be stretched parallel to the ground between heavy stakes. The wire should be between 4 and 6 inches off the surface. Any bird feeding under this wire will stick its head up through the mesh, never being able to draw it down again to escape. The size of bird targeted determines the mesh size and distance off the ground. Using barley for bait, with 2-inch mesh set 10 inches high, I have even caught wild turkeys.

These kinds of traps work very well when placed near duck feeding areas in a marsh. Ducks feed under the mesh set about 4 inches above the water level and also do not think to pull their heads down, once through the mesh. These traps are a bit more difficult to set than their basic simplicity would suggest, but they are efficient, inexpensive, discreet game getters.

Traps that hold animals alive and well, catching at the same time more than one critter, are few and far between in the real world. Yet something of this nature would be extremely valuable for the survivor. An old Native American trick involves burying a lookalike den in the ground in which animals take up residence. When needed, they can be caught and taken out. It is the only candidate for such a device that I know of and—according to users—should be kept a military secret.

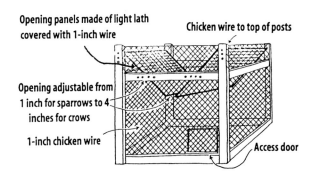

Flight traps are used to capture birds.

Construct a solid-wood box about 24 inches square. Use the best grade of lumber available because the box will be underground for a number of years. These traps will continue to produce as long as they do not deteriorate. Place a good lid on the box that overlaps the sides and that can be pulled straight up to examine the interior of the den.

Cut a 4-inch-diameter hole in one side of the box. Bury the den box at least 6 inches under the ground with a buried 4-inch pipe running to the hole in the den box. Surface this den entrance pipe at least 16 feet away from the box.

After a year or two in the ground, every den-type animal in the area will use the box to stay overnight in when they are in the area. Place a long pole with an appropriate-size disk fastened to the end near the trap. Use this push-in to confine any critters in the trap to the nest box. These traps catch rabbits several at a time, foxes, coons, possums, skunks, squirrels, mink, muskrats, and even the occasional pheasant. Placement determines which you will catch.

Trappers usually check these traps once every two weeks during the time they need something to eat. At other times of the year, they simply ignore the trap. Critters using these facilities will simply run in and out, taking care of their own needs. Set near creeks and swamps, these traps attract large numbers of muskrats that, when killed and bled, are very good eating.

As kids we made good money catching and selling snapping turtles to those who liked to eat them. Today turtles of any kind are an often-overlooked food source. In many places, turtles occur in great numbers. Lines baited with a great

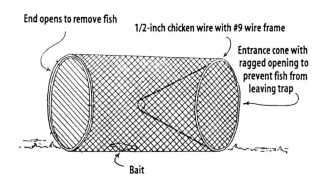

End opens to remove fish

1/2-inch chicken wire with #9 wire frame

Entrance cone with ragged opening to prevent fish from leaving trap

Bait

Chicken-wire fish trap.

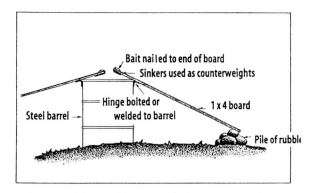

Bait nailed to end of board

Sinkers used as counterweights

Hinge bolted or welded to barrel

Steel barrel

1 x 4 board

Pile of rubble

Barrel trap used for rats (floating variation may be used for muskrats and turtles). (Illustrations on this page taken from *Live Off the Land in the City or Country* by Ragnar Benson.)

gob of gristly old meat will catch turtles. Use strong lines, tied to number 18 wire, which in turn is fastened to a very sharp hook. Little mud turtles won't sever conventional fish line, but snappers definitely will. Turtles are also caught in funnel-type fish traps if the entrance is sufficiently large.

Barrel traps are universally useful for everything from barn rats to turtles to muskrats. Use heavy rocks or old iron to sink a clean 55-gallon barrel with its open top about 4 inches from the surface of the water, marsh, or ground in some cases. Using very small hinges, fasten light 1 x 4 boards about 4 feet long out from the top edge of the barrel. Weight the short end of the board extending over the open barrel so that any critter that crawls up the gangplank to a bit of bait unbalances the board down into the trap, dumping itself inside. Use small lead wheel weights as balance adjusters. Proper function is dependent on the board's being as balanced as possible. These

traps catch many animals at once and are relatively easy to maintain.

One of the principal sources of food for Native Americans across the continent was the white-tailed deer. They could not sport hunt them, but the deer—as well as any other large game—could easily be snared.

Use regular 3/32-inch aircraft cable, wire, or whatever else is available to make a loop. One expert commonly uses telephone lines conveniently located all over the county as material for his deer, bear, and elk snares. Construct with an L-shaped, anti-backslip lock as shown in the chapter on trapping.

Deer and, to some extent, elk are very much creatures of habit that basically stay in one area until harassed away or the weather changes, pushing them out. You must learn their trails to and from feeding, bedding, and watering areas for the time of year you intend to snare them. During deep snow, deer restrict their travel so much that deep trails are cut through the snow.

Neck snares for deer are set about 2 feet off the ground in frequently used trails. Loops are about 12 to 16 inches in diameter. Some people put stops in the loop so that the deer only collar themselves rather than choking to death in their fright.

Do not set a snare solidly tied to a tree or spring pole. This will almost always choke the deer to death, producing a carcass that is not that nice to handle or eat. It is best to secure the snare wire to a 12- to 16-pound green limb drag 3 inches in diameter and 5 feet long.

Once the deer is in the snare, it will pull off through the brush, dragging the branch along. As the snare gets tighter it will struggle until it's out of breath and then just hunker down. Only a modest amount of skill is required to follow deer and drag, and the meat is usually in much better condition. Simply walk up and silently cut the critter's throat.

Large game—including moose, elk, and even bear—can, at times, be caught in leg snares. Use standard 3/32 cable 6 feet long with a drag, but set the snare relatively flat in a trail frequented by these critters.

Loops are put out at a 15-degree angle with the top end held up with light wire and the bottom resting on the ground. The size of the loop is about 14 inches. The idea is to get the critter to place its foot in the snare, dragging it along till it slips tight. Leg- or foot-caught snared critters get pretty well chewed up. Anyone who sees the carcass will know exactly how the critter was got.

Place logs or stones in the path, steering the critter into stepping into the wire. Animals are not usually wary of snares, since it is a simple case of mechanically steering them in the way they should go. Big elk and moose-size beasts are tough to snare around the neck, although it is sometimes done. Be certain there are no horses in the area, unless you wish to eat them: they are extremely easy to foul in a wire, cutting them up horribly. Owners get very upset when this happens.

A favorite but long-deceased uncle of mine often snared bears in bait sets. He used wild honey and old buttermilk as bait. Uncle waited till a bear was working the set pretty heavily before putting out his snares. Smaller 3/32 cable is okay for bears, but you must use a drag that is slightly heavier than that used on deer, or about 25 to 40 pounds. Then expect to follow the drag for at least a quarter of a mile. Uncle employed the services of a small dog to track the bear once it got into a snare. The few I saw caught tore down some standing poplar, they were so upset. He shot them with a .22 single-shot pistol.

In a survival context, do not overlook trapping and consuming some of the many feral dogs and cats roaming our country. Trappers working even what are considered remote locations report that they often have to clear out as many as four or five dogs per square mile along with dozens of house cats. Cities that have fallen into anarchy, such as Beirut, Madrid, and Washington, D.C., always seem to have a pack of semiwild dogs running about. These can be shot for food, if local conditions permit, or they can be snared silently. Domestic dogs and cats are extremely easy to snare. The real trick is doing so without those around knowing what is going on.

Try baiting dogs, cats, or any urban critter into a hidden area inside a garage, behind a hedge, or under a porch. Another trick is to place a snare on a drag allowing the animal to pull off down the street. Feral dogs and cats seldom go crazy in a snare, as is always true with coyotes and fox. You can usually walk down the street with snare in hand, retrieving the critter as if it were on a leash.

Several national papers report that wild animals—including coons, possums, squirrels, rabbits, and animals as large as deer—are proliferating in suburbia. These critters constitute a wonderful food source, both now and in an emergency context. Suburban animals have multiplied principally because animal rightists have joined with nonhunters and accumulated enough political muscle to restrict the harvest or totally prevent it from being made.

With semidomestic animals, where the challenge is to keep their taking a complete secret, mechanically trapping them can be quite difficult. Think of shooting them at night with a silencer-equipped rifle or of snaring them. More difficult techniques are available, but snaring is so easy that there is no reason to try them. Perhaps in an emergency situation, attitudes might change, but, right now, you must plan to trap these deer by the most silent, unobtrusive method possible.

There are two lessons to be learned from this chapter:

1. Plan in a survival context to take wild game wherever possible.
2. Be constantly on the alert for opportunities and then to deploy methods that work silently, unobtrusively, and effectively to harvest large numbers of critters at a time in traps requiring little work and attention.

Those who feel they could profitably use a complete, detailed analysis of survival poaching techniques should get the book, *Survival Poaching* published by Paladin Press. There is no other book in print remotely like it.

BIBLIOGRAPHY

Benson, Ragnar. *Survival Poaching*. Boulder, CO: Paladin Press, 1980.

CHAPTER

Revenge

60

George Hayduke is, without a doubt, the mother of all creative revengers. Because he is so good at this business, one can only wonder what Hayduke must be like to live next door to or work with. No one, it would seem, has as many different classes of people on which to ardently, expertly seek revenge.

Retribution and revenge are personal matters, carried out personally by extremely clever, creative people who find that, in our complex society, they have no other alternative but to take matters into their own hands—or minds—or whatever. Some of these wonderfully funny ideas won't work, or they are so complex they can't work. The fun in this case is probably just imagining that these revenge techniques are falling on one's victim.

One of Hayduke's collaborators must have been smelling nerve gas when he suggested the airline caper summarized on page 14 of *Make My Day*. With a supposedly straight face, we are told to find a generic airlines employee uniform, snap on some sort of credible clip-on badge, carry an official clipboard, and stride merrily into the bowels of an airport terminal. It would be fun, we are told, to pull up to a baggage carousel and start to throw other people's luggage off the belt into a huge pile.

We can validly ask, "Why bother?" But, more important, we should ask where to get the airport uniform we are so cavalierly told to wear. A great many really fine revenge techniques start with the supposition that we can acquire uniforms, official seals, identification tags, corporate stationery, a senator's Social Security number, or whatever. Locating these required items under a few unique circumstances might be possible—but come on, George—give us a break! Most are practically impossible.

What we desperately require are real-life, valid, workable concepts that real people can actually pull off. Putting Superglue in a mark's Preparation H tube might actually work, but dropping frozen, spoiled turkeys on an animal rightist from a light aircraft seems—well—a bit weird!

Probably, the best revenge I ever witnessed falls in the category of unique to totally unrepeatable. A small group of us worked as laborers on a farm. We were just common folks who sweated and grunted a lot for our daily bread. One of the guys managed to meet and marry a very sophisticated city girl who had little use for our life-style. Had it not been for our companion, she would not have had one thing in common with us or to say to us.

This woman was one of those super-good-looking ones who never had to learn to get along with people except on her terms. She never lost an opportunity to let us know, either. Her job at the university in town allowed her to dress and smell sweetly, in sharp contrast to us poor country hicks.

But that was before the hog had a heart attack. While loading our hogs for market, one big fat barrow laid down and started quivering. One of the group whipped out his knife and cut its throat, saving the meat from total loss.

Because it was a very hot day, we were forced to immediately gut it. Hogs are usually scalded, but we simply cut off its head, skinned it, and cooled it out with a hose. This was not the proper way, but it was all we could do under the circumstances.

Here we had a perfectly good hog's head with long pink snout sticking up in the air from its flat-on-the-ground position. Beady, yellow eyes gazed off into the clouds, adding to the effect.

It is lost in history who came up with the concept, but we took the hog's head down to the lady's trailer house, putting it to good use and extracting our ounce of revenge for being put down for eight long months. The head fit into the toilet bowl perfectly. It's soft nose stuck up about an inch above the seat. In the dark of the john it was not immediately recognizable.

We pretty much forgot about the stunt till 4:45 p.m., when she was due home from work. We collected in the shop to watch without telling her husband. Soon her car was on the road and into the trailer house parking spot. As we supposed, she came home and went right into the john before starting dinner.

An absolutely blood-curdling scream soon shook the mobile home. We thought she might have genuinely hurt herself from panic. But that was all. We never heard another peep from her or her husband nor did we ever see that hog's head again.

Apparently, she was a bit tougher than we gave her credit for.

Anyway, the moral to this absolutely true, verifiable tale is that revenge is clever, opportunistic, and probably not widely replicable. It is also extremely funny. That is obviously why good old Hayduke enjoys putting out his revenge series and why his readers are so faithful.

One could conceivably find a situation wherein a cranky, obnoxious, ne'er-do-well neighbor left his sprinkler hose lying in the front yard, as Hayduke suggests. Letting it run in his window well or filling up his garbage can, which is set on angle against the front door, is easily possible. In response to the doorbell, a properly balanced load might indeed spill ruinously down inside the house. According to Hayduke, some revengers have even gotten two cans to spill simultaneously into an entranceway and down the stairs of a split level.

Mr. Zombie, an ex-garbageman, suggests pouring a gallon of diesel fuel onto a crabby neighbor's garbage and torching it. Zombie is probably correct when he speculates that the crab will be busy for several days dealing with that mess. In many cases, collection companies will refuse to take the resulting muck and, of course, the city EPA-Gestapo will be right there bitching.

One of my brothers got on a binge a few years back of scooping up every roadkill he happened upon and stuffing it into the next rural mailbox he came to. It was unclear if he was upset with roadkills, farmers, rural mailboxes, or the fact that he had to drive to work every day. In retrospect, this was neither creative nor positive revenge. It wasn't clever or well-thought-through, nor did it target any real bad actors. It probably wasn't even very funny.

But some broad-based, universally applicable revenge techniques are worthwhile. Any of us who have been around awhile have been ripped, poked, and plundered by our smiling bankers. It isn't easy, but one can rent a safe deposit box anonymously or in another name at targeted banks. If one is on a budget, purchase or scrounge an old-fashioned, 8-day wind-up clock with an extra loud ticking mechanism. Lock this in the box and in a few days the bank will be calling around trying to figure out what's going on. Eventually, they will have the lock pulled so they can look.

Another, more expensive but more effective device involves placing a tape player from an old telephone answering machine, or any tape player that will endlessly repeat itself, connected to a timer purchased at Radio Shack, in the lock box.

Record a message that basically says, "Help, help! This bank is holding me prisoner in this little, bitty cell. Please. Get me out of here!" Use ultralong-play lithium batteries to power the player longer.

Another revenger claims he rented a safe deposit box in the name of a man on whom he wished to bring down retribution. Most banks know almost all of their customers by sight. Renting in another name, without ID even at a branch where the mark is unknown is sometimes more difficult than renting anonymously or with a totally fictitious ID.

A teller at a local bank said that someone once left a transistor radio playing in one box. The bank got in a person with a stethoscope to figure out exactly which box it was. After identifying the station, the bank simply tagged the renter's file and left everything alone. Eventually, the radio played down, and the fellow came in for a talk.

Dr. Paul Wilson, an avid admirer of Hayduke, suggests playing on people's fears. Once when he was working his way through school as a logger, he encountered some yuppies camped on private land in the mountains. At evening campfire he joined them, regaling them with stories about great numbers of snakes he encountered in the area. Before he left for the night he put a small stick at the bottom of each camper's sleeping bag.

Next morning they all reported that on sliding a bare leg onto the stick they were paralyzed with fear. But the tree huggers did not move on. The next night he secreted poison ivy in their bags. Most people are allergic to poison ivy, and some people are very allergic to it. Wilson had, as is common to woods workers, acquired something of an immunity to it. His new-found acquaintances quickly found better trees—closer to a doctor and hopefully on their own property—to hug the very next day.

Many no-longer-amorous females reported to Hayduke that they had successfully placed poison ivy in floral arrangements sent to former friends. This is somewhat sophomoric revenge, but a technique reminiscent of our youth. During that time, no poison ivy ever went to waste, and few survived who were genuinely allergic.

The Bills did not allow their neighbor's frequent, noisy, late-night, hot tub parties annoy them. They simply crept through the bushes and placed three large boxes of Cream of Wheat in the tub. Delicious odors from the cooking cereal blanketed the neighborhood. It was several weeks and several hundred dollars before the noisy neighbors got that straightened out.

According to Hayduke, a vast number of neighborhood problems that could not be resolved face-to-face in an impersonal manner are created when irresponsible people allow their pets to run about promiscuously. Suggested remedies include pouring diesel fuel on the animal, especially its private parts. It will run home howling and, when let in, stink up the owner's house. After it has time to lick itself clean, it will barf all over the floor.

Lisa in Little Rock says that she has remedied problems with amorous cats and dogs coming around. She simply catches and neuters the males, sending them on their way. This is not a difficult procedure, she says, after spending an afternoon as a volunteer in the community neuter/spay clinic.

Another revenger uses a basting tool to pump liquid soap or cod liver oil down the throat of stray dogs that are sent home to do odd jobs around the owner's house.

Using a doctor's prescription form that he scanned into his computer, Neil Nixon was able to create some authentic-looking letterhead on his laser printer. He sent a letter to a mark, getting revenge on both the doctor and the mark, who were members of a fascist environmental committee.

Nixon's phony letter done in the name of the doctor asked the mark if she would accept $250 to allow study, photography, and eventual publication of her rare, unfortunate, ugly skin condition. This took work and planning, but the doctor and the mark were at each other's throats like hungry wolverines.

Many jerks, we are told, are foolishly proud of their vehicles. Effective revengers watch for their chance to do petty, annoying, somewhat expensive damage to their mark's vehicles. Most effective, if the vehicle is open and you have access to a live chicken, is to throw it inside the mark's vehicle. Left for one hour, the smell can never be completely removed. Left for a day, the vehicle cannot be driven about in winter. But, realistically, most people today don't have a clue about where to get a live chicken.

Next in order of vehicle nastiness involves tying a double strand of 50-pound monofilament fishline to another near car's bumper, a tree, sign, or parking meter. Fasten the line securely to the mark's plastic grill. When leaving, he will jerk out an expensive and very obvious portion of his vehicle. Pride will preclude his not fixing it.

With this third device, we leave readers with the task of reading all of Hayduke's many volumes themselves or of searching their own imaginations for their own techniques. Those who perfect good revenge techniques should contact Hayduke, not me. I am not really into this stuff.

Gasoline engines can be absolutely, irrevocably destroyed by placing about five common mothballs in the gas tank. They dissolve, causing the engine to burn so dirty that it seizes in a relatively few miles. Unless dissolved in water and mixed with alcohol, sugar does not work at all, but mothballs are easy and effective.

Yet it is, perhaps, a sad commentary on our society that we are forced to seek redress for grievances by revenge methods rather than working the situation out in an open manner. However, it is an observable fact that there are an increasing number of folks around who have little regard for others' feelings or for their own persons, property, and privacy.

Revenge should be rationed and used sparingly and, above all, cleverly. Using a meat cleaver approach says as much about the one employing the techniques as it does about the mark.

BIBLIOGRAPHY

Hayduke, George. *Make My Day*. Boulder, CO: Paladin Press, 1987.

_____. *Sweet Revenge*. Boulder, CO: Paladin Press, 1989.

_____. *Up Yours*. Boulder, CO: Paladin Press, 1982.

Conclusion

Most of the topics covered in this volume include information that the government would rather you didn't have. At the current rate of official action, serious proposals may soon be floated that require a federal license to teach martial arts and to register experts.

Yet this is a hypocritical position at best. Detailed information pertaining to explosives, to cite just one example, is easily available on a number of computer bulletin boards and in official government publications devoted to explaining how improvised explosives can be made.

When the government's role was limited (not so very long ago), the government seemed to have few secrets, and it did not seem necessary for the average citizen to know these few secrets. Now, when the government has become an intrusive monster, one can only wonder why its minions wish to do so much in a corner. It seems strange that, on one hand, we are told that we shouldn't know about certain subjects, and on the other many official publications explain them in detail.

Not being a martial arts person, I was surprised to discover that virtually all disciplines trace their origin to government intervention that precluded average citizens from defending themselves. Why is it, one is forced to ask, that all governments degenerate into a faceless force trying to make citizens dependent on it? In that regard, what logic drives government officials to deny the legal use of pepper-gas spray to individuals in places such as New York City and California?

In all cases, I used as wide a range of topics for this book as was practically possible. Those who feel that important skills were omitted should write to me in care of Paladin recommending specific additional subjects.

Because space is limited and I tried to cover as many different subjects as possible, many categories may have been summarized and condensed past the reader's liking. In cases where an interest in a specific subject has been sparked, please refer to the original texts from which the material was taken. All are listed at the end of each chapter.

Some very complex subjects and skills are virtually impossible to summarize. Trapping, both for critters and men, is a good example. I have been at this business for more than 50 years and still know only a fraction of what is out there.

If they find the subject intriguing, readers must attempt to build a good library on the subject and obtain as much personal training as possible. Again, citing a real-life example, it seems impossible to me for an uninformed person to become proficient with explosives without killing himself, *unless* he had an expert instructor who personally walked him through the process.

As is always true, it has been personally fun and informative to put this volume together for faithful Paladin readers. In many cases, I did not realize that I myself needed information in certain areas until I studied it. No doubt, this will prove true with first-time readers who never realized that they might benefit from a subject as narrow as "Eating Cheap," for instance.

As the man said, "These are perilous times." I hope that this book will remove some of the peril.